Frontiers of Screen History

Frontiers of Screen History
Imagining European Borders in Cinema, 1945-2010

Edited by Raita Merivirta, Kimmo Ahonen, Heta Mulari, Rami Mähkä

intellect Bristol, UK / Chicago, USA

First published in the UK in 2013 by
Intellect, The Mill, Parnall Road, Fishponds, Bristol, BS16 3JG, UK

First published in the USA in 2013 by
Intellect, The University of Chicago Press, 1427 E. 60th Street,
Chicago, IL 60637, USA

A catalogue record for this book is available from the
British Library.

Cover image: Film still from Aki Kaurismäki's *Le Havre* (2011).
Photograph by Marja-Leena Hukkanen
Cover designer: Ellen Thomas
Copy-editor: MPS Technologies
Production manager: Bethan Ball
Typesetting: Planman Technologies

Part of the Studies on Popular Culture series
Series editors: Bruce Johnson and Hannu Salmi
   (International Institute for Popular Culture, Finland)
Series ISSN: 2041-6725
Electronic ISSN: 2042-8227

ISBN 978-1-84150-732-3

Printed and bound by Hobbs, UK

Contents

Borders Crossed, Borders Within

Post-Colonial Borders and Cultural Frontiers

Acknowledgements

This book would not have been completed without significant input from many people. It is the first volume of the series *Studies on Popular Culture* by Intellect Books (Bristol, UK) and the International Institute for Popular Culture, IIPC (Turku, Finland). The idea for this volume was conceived in the research project *Cinematic Cartographies of European History, 1945–2000*. The project (2009–2013) is funded by the Academy of Finland, and is led by Professor Hannu Salmi (Cultural History, University of Turku). The editors would like to thank the aforementioned institutions and people for their kind support and the Academy of Finland for the funding we have received. We are most grateful to the scholars who reviewed the individual chapters and the book manuscript for generously sharing their time and expertise. We would also like to express our gratitude to Damon Tringham and Ellen Valle for helping us with the language and style. Thanks are also due to Professor Tom Conley for his thoughtful foreword to the book, to the staff, especially Bethan Ball, at Intellect, for all the help we received during the production of the book and, finally, to the authors of this volume for their enthusiasm and contributions.

Foreword

In epigraph to this collection of thirteen powerfully argued and elegantly limned essays the team of editors cites Lauri Törhönen's *Raja 1918/The Border* (2007), Richard Holm's *Gränsen/ Beyond the Border* (2011) and other films to capture the spirit of a project addressing how matters of religious and national identity, migration, transnationalism, and cultural and psychic frontiers mark eleven nations in the European ambit. Vigorously written, each chapter is a piece in a kaleidoscope showing that what informs cinema and national conflict in one area can be refracted through others. Seen thus, as if each were a prism, the essays cut into issues that we can now grasp in renewed consideration of what over two decades ago Fredric Jameson called *a geopolitical aesthetic*. We now know that it belongs, perhaps better than any other medium, to cinema. The films considered in *Frontiers of Screen History* are all situated in the post-World War II era, many in the dust still settling after the crumbling of the Berlin Wall and in the acrid smoke of our memories of 9/11. In one way or another, each of the essays bears geopolitical resonance. How and why is what the paragraphs to follow will seek to examine through film theory.

In his *Geopolitical Aesthetic* (1992) Fredric Jameson studied geopolitics through the expanding production and distribution of cinema on a global scale. In his view the seventh art had become a visibly major player in shaping a massively collective imagination and thus for the ends of capital a perniciously valuable tool. Jameson showed how film, the medium embodying ideology as Louis Althusser had understood it over twenty years earlier, had to figure in the dialectics of cognitive mapping. In an initial sense cognitive mapping could be construed synonymous with psychogeography, the relation that an individual holds and continually renegotiates with the spaces and places in which he or she lives.[1] It entails the invention of a sense of being, the coordinates of which can be fancied as the rhumb lines of overlaid mental maps whose borders and vectors the individual retraces in accord with what is near and far and both past and present. It can be said to be born of intuitions that we find (and in finding also losing) ourselves in an inalterable totality whose frontiers, if frontiers there are, are well beyond our ken. For practical ends cognitive mapping attends to shifts and turns of identity a person experiences in the vagaries of everyday life. The cartographer of cognition, who can be anyone whosoever, accounts for his or her imaginary affiliation with collective bodies, with mental landscapes, and with inherited or imposed ideas of cultural appurtenance. It is especially vital for the cartographer to relocate his or her positionings in relation to these affiliations. Shifting (or in Jameson's idiolect, transcoding) them according to situation – say, within a field whose borders move swiftly as the sheaths of light of the aurora borealis in the arctic sky – we shape our psychogeographies in view of a Totality (upper-case in Jameson's lexicon) or a *Tout ouvert*, an open Whole (the term, also in upper-case, belonging to Gilles Deleuze) that is the world at large. In this way the cognitive mappings taken up in *Frontiers*, whether in national or transnational contexts, are geopolitical. The circumstances in which they are found are, as each article demonstrates, pre-determined or moulded by the broader histories in informing the spaces and places in which they live. At times, as in the Parisian *banlieue*, they are isolated or ghettoized; at others, say, in an architectural firm in East Berlin, political inertia smothers creativity; at others still, when gender and religion are at stake, they mark the plight of Irish women of Catholic background during the Troubles in Northern Ireland; or they may be Swedish females who, transgressing the roles assigned to them in inherited roles dictated by traditional divisions of labour, open new subjective itineraries in the global sphere.

The cognitive mappings that the essays study through cinema respond, whether obliquely or directly, to a European geopolitical heritage. Its origins are found in Herodotus, for whom power and space are functions of each other, and notably along geographical and existential borders. As a modern founder of the concept, Friedrich Ratzel felt compelled to teach geography to Prussian students in order to persuade a growing population that, because of its resemblance to other states to the west, their territory ought to be annexed to Germany in the hope of building a new nation in the aftermath of the Napoleonic invasions. Entailing demography, economy and politics, Ratzel's notion of human geography led to the formulation of 'laws' drawing strict lines of demarcation to apportion people and their *habitus* to given topographies. Based on Darwin, his laws concerning 'vital space' later served the rationale for those shaping the policies of the Third Reich and, as a consequence, bore on the new mapping of Europe on the heels of World War II – felt in the essays in this volume that examine the Iron Curtain and the Berlin Wall – when a different sense of geopolitical geography began to take hold. Technological progress witnessed in the development of aerial transport and environmental control caused inherited borders to dissolve and, with their dissolution, the former mentalities that affiliated given peoples with their places of origin. Frontiers defined by rivers, chains of mountains or coastlines gave way to an irrefragable 'international institutionalization of frontiers', a situation in which geopolitics began to designate 'the rivalries of powers on territories [...] that are not abstract spaces, maps or platitudes without "rough edges", surfaces divided between "centers" and "peripheries" of men-producers as economists believe' but, rather, areas defined by the drawing of frontiers resulting from relations of force (Lacoste 2010: 33–35).[2] Movement within and across spaces defined by language and religion is driven by international economic pressures: which is what, from a given geopolitical angle, each of the thirteen essays in this volume take up in detail.

Cinema is the privileged geopolitical medium because it is at once topographical and geographical, and no less at once local and global. The authors study films that may be confined to specific strata of populations who forge new existential territories within or across national borders – among others, in Finland or Sweden or between Turkey and Germany – or generally in milieus that tend not to accept them.[3] The essays address what film historian Thomas Elsaesser eloquently calls *double occupancy*. They broach, too, the ways these and other groups, marginalized within the spaces they occupy, invent new and different modes of life that often go unperceived among the host countries. They constitute what Michel de Certeau had called alternate *arts de faire* or ways of doing in the sphere of everyday life (2010). The films taken up are either symptoms of social conflict that circulate within and across defining borders or else prompt the spectator to account for what they are *not* doing or camouflaging – as noted in some Cold War films crafting the 'Red Menace' for American audiences or even when a gifted Spanish director, engaged in a rewriting of the Spanish history of Oceanic Conquest for the ends of the international commemoration of the Quincentennial of 1492, edulcorates facts or leaves aside not only the effects of the Columbian 'discoveries' but also the re-taking of Grenada that resulted in the expulsion of Moorish culture from continental Europe. As one author has shown in relating Etienne Balibar's reflections to the project of this volume, when seen together the films and the essays that study them deal with the paradox of the singularities of European spaces. All of them remain riddled with inherited ideas about geographical and ideological borders, and too, issues at once utopian and pragmatic, that concern European unification in a global context. Such, the essays imply, may be the matrix of the majority of European filmmaking since 1945 (Balibar 2004).

In this volume films are shown either addressing the geopolitics of locales or, to the contrary, they are seen skittering away from them. In both instances the spectator has the task of sorting through the relations they establish between their politics and their aesthetics. What makes cinema so effective is indeed the visual and aural immediacy we witness of the relations. It is a fact that when a film promotes a politics its aesthetics tend to become a function of propaganda whereas, if it seeks to veer away from its politics for what might be an art for art's sake, its contradictions, brought forward in the dialectic every spectator establishes in the viewing of a film, become glaringly clear.[4] Hence the essays prove what Jacques Rancière has made of the political aesthetics of cinema attending to borders and shifting territorial zones:

There is no politics of cinema. There are singular figures according to which filmmakers are employed to conjoin the meanings of the word 'politics' by which a fiction in general can be qualified and a cinematographic fiction in particular: politics as what a film addresses – the history of a movement or of a conflict, informing a public of a situation of suffering or injustice, and *politics as the strategy belonging to an artistic way of doing things*: a manner of accelerating or decelerating time, confining or broadening space, synchronizing or disrupting view and action, linking or unlinking what is before and what is after and what is inside or outside. We are tempted to say: the relation between a matter of justice and a practice of justness. (2011: 111, emphasis added)

Each of the essays that follow seeks a *justness* in what it studies, either in the film itself (such as in psychogeographies of London alternate to what mainline culture had imposed as a dashing new Britishness of the 1960s), or in what the mediated success or downright failure of a project the film itself makes clear (such as the architects redesigning areas of east Berlin, or in the gripping images of Northern Irish prisoners on hunger strike during conflict with British expeditionary forces). The authors all inquire of the *justice* of the films in terms such that the imposition of the force of law or of political decisions that rehearse or re-create issues of power and space at the root of geopolitics. We see in the films critical approaches that open readers and viewers onto what Rancière calls 'tragic irresolution' where the promise of a dialectical cinema shifts less towards synthesis than open-endedness, where there results, in his words, 'a new distribution of words and gestures, times and spaces' as well as a 'fixed point in order to evaluate the manner by which these filmmakers have sought (to address) the fractures of history, the upheaval of trajectories among territories, injustices and new conflicts' (Rancière 2011: 126).

In other words, the spectator is asked to reconsider inherited lines of demarcation – national, gendered, cultural, linguistic, economic – and to redraw them with an aesthetic justness that does justice to the critical relation we hold with space, place, action and execution in our experience of film. The editors and authors of *Frontiers of Screen History* accomplish just that. They bring forward the geopolitical issues at the basis both of films of world-wide distribution, known to many, and others, shot within confining conditions or in highly local places, remain unknown within prevailing canons. And they do so with stunning success.

Tom Conley
Harvard University

Tom Conley is a member of the Departments of Visual and Environmental Studies and Romance Languages at Harvard University, and recent fellow at the Radcliffe Center for Advanced Research where he is finishing a project on legacies of auteur theory. Tom Conley has recently authored the books *Cartographic Cinema* (2007) and *An Errant Eye: Topography and Poetry in Early Modern France* (2011). Some of his translations pertaining to theory, philosophy and cinema include Marc Augé, *Casablanca: Movies and Memory* (2008), Gilles Deleuze, *The Fold* (1993), Michel de Certeau, *The Writing of History* (1988) and *The Capture of Speech* (1997). With T. Jefferson Kline he is editing the Wiley-Blackwell *Companion to the Cinema of Jean-Luc Godard*.

References

Althusser, L. (1992), *The Geopolitical Aesthetic: Cinema and Space in the World System*, Bloomington: Indiana University Press.
Augé, M. (2009), *Casablanca: Movies and Memory*, Minneapolis: University of Minnesota Press.

———— (2011), *Une double vie,* Paris: Editions Payot.

Balibar, E. (2004), *We, the People of Europe? Reflections on Transnational Citizenship*, Princeton: Princeton University Press.

Conerly, M. (2006), *Psychogeography*, Harpcaden: Pocket Essentials.

De Certeau, M. (1990), *L'Invention du quotidien, 1: Arts de faire,* (ed.) Luce Giard, Paris: Gallimard; (in English as *The Practice of Everyday Life*, translated by Steven Rendall [1984], Berkeley: University of California Press).

Guattari, F. (1993), *Cartographies schizoanalytiques*, Paris: Galilée.

Jameson, F. (1992), *The Geopolitical Aesthetic: Cinema and Space in the World System*, Bloomington: Indiana University Press.

Jameson, F. (2009), *Valences of the Dialectic,* London: Verso.

Lacoste, Y. (2010), *La Géopolitique et le géographe*, Paris: Choiseul, pp. 35–37.

———— (1988), 'Le Rivage des Syrtes, un roman géopolitique', *Hérodote* 41, pp. 13–15.

Rancière, J. (2011), 'Conversation autour d'un feu: Straub et quelques autres', *Les Écarts du cinema*, Paris: La Fabrique editions, pp. 111, 126.

Stain, H. E. and Niederland, W. E. (eds) (1989), *Readings in Psychogeography,* Norman: University of Oklahoma Press.

Notes

1   As a tributary field it studies the vagaries of mental mapping and how it pertains to subjectivity. Early points of reference include Martin Conerly, *Psychogeography* (2006) and Howard E. Stain and William E. Niederland (eds) (1989). Further work in that direction would of course include the psychogenesis. In *La Relation d'inconnu* and other clinical studies in psychoanalysis Guy Rosolato noted that practically all communication functions in accordance with 'signifiers of demarcation', that is deictic markers that indicate positionality when a subject is engaged in his or her environment and in cognition of experience within it. Two recent works that attest to the confluence of cinema, autobiography mental mapping are Marc Augé's *Casablanca: Movies and Memory* (2009) and his recent (and yet untranslated) *Une double vie* (2011).

2   Elsewhere Lacoste defines a geopolitical aesthetic through a reading of Julien Gracq, in what he calls the novelist's taste 'for border zones,' for frontier zones, 'this tropism of edges that takes careful note of the military organization of a territory' where 'different levels of power operate in the "spatial mechanism" of an apparatus of state' (1988).

3   Existential territory is a term that Guattari (1993) coined that shares much with de Certeau's concept of invention.

4   Dialectic is used here in consonance with Jameson's *Valences of the Dialectic* (2009, especially 67–68). The monumental study book-ends his *Geopolitical Aesthetic*.

Introduction

Encounters with Borders

– Attention, border.
– Police. Shoo, shoo. [*The trucker hides Elias behind a curtain in the truck cabin.*]
– Maybe he has papers.
– Doesn't look like that. Perhaps you picked up a terrorist.
– Rubbish. Terrorists travel by planes or trains and have papers. He's starving.

This dialogue takes place between two German truck drivers making their way to Hamburg somewhere in Central Europe in Costa-Gavras's *Eden is West* (2009). The truckers have picked up the protagonist of the film, an illegal immigrant named Elias (Riccardo Scamarcio) – or Alias, as he is sometimes ironically called – on his way from the Aegean Sea to Paris. Elias's last name, nationality and native language are never disclosed; he represents one of the thousands of illegal immigrants trying to cross borders into Europe without papers. Elias has some French but otherwise relies on miming and sign language as he travels through Europe and to the imagined Eden of Paris. On the way, he encounters a number of obstacles familiar to illegal immigrants with no papers: he suffers from cold and hunger; he is robbed, sexually exploited and used as cheap labour; he is pursued by the police and his trust is betrayed. Yet, even though the 'official' Europe does not welcome him, he is helped by 'ordinary' men and women in various European countries. *Eden is West* is a highly topical film taking part in the contemporary debate in Europe about illegal immigrants and powerfully illustrating the plight of those who try to cross the heavily protected borders into Europe.

Illegal immigration, especially from Africa and the Middle East, and the adversities (illegal) immigrants face in Europe have been recurrent themes in recent European films. In *Dirty Pretty Things* (Stephen Frears, 2002), Okwe (Chiwetel Ejiofor), an illegal Nigerian immigrant working in a London hotel, is ironically threatened with the police by the director of the hotel after Okwe has found a human heart in one of the bathrooms. In this film, a London city hotel becomes a transnational meeting place of immigrant workers and a scene of illegal immigration and crime. As the medically trained protagonist Okwe soon finds out, the hotel is a centre for prostitution and for harvesting organs for illegal trade – in exchange for the organ, the donor is given a passport and a new European identity. This can also be understood as an allegory: in order to adopt a new identity, one has to give away something of oneself. The hotel and the surrounding Western London become a dystopian urban space and a centre for negotiations about new European and diasporic identities and the selectively inclusive and exclusive European borders.

The main protagonist of Philippe Lioret's *Welcome* (2009) is a young Iraqi refugee, Bilal (Firat Ayverdi), who has trekked thousands of kilometres from Kurdistan to Calais. He attempts to make a living in the community of struggling illegal immigrants and asylum seekers and to find a way to travel across the Channel to England to live with his girlfriend and her family. The Channel becomes a concrete border not only between two nation states, but also between two separate lives and identities. Crossing the border becomes a matter of life and death for Bilal, as his only remaining option is to try to swim across the Channel. In the same vein, Aki Kaurismäki approaches Europe's problem with refugees and illegal immigrants with warm humanism and sentimental, bittersweet humour in *Le Havre* (2011). The film depicts the attempts of a young West African boy Idrissa (Blondin Miguel) to sneak from the small French port city to London to reunite with his mother. French border guards hunt the 11-year-old Idrissa, who finds shelter in the bohemian community of Le Havre. Despite its fairy-tale approach, *Le Havre* has a socially-conscious mission as Kaurismäki criticizes Europe's policy of border closing which treats refugees like dangerous criminals. Yosefa Loshitzky broaches this recurrent theme of contemporary European film and discusses the concept of 'fortress Europe'[1] in present-day Europe in *Screening Strangers: Migration and Diaspora in Contemporary European Cinema* (2010). Loshitzky (2010: 1–6) argues that Europe inclusively continues to erect racial, ethnic, political and religious boundaries.

After the Cold War, Europe has been increasingly defined by migration across national boundaries. Perhaps unsurprisingly then, there have been public discussions and debates regarding asylum seekers as well as legal and illegal immigration in several European countries, such as the United Kingdom, Sweden, Germany and France. For example, in October 2010, German Chancellor Angela Merkel stated that the attempt in Germany to create a multicultural society had 'failed utterly'. Merkel urged immigrants to integrate more fully into the German society. Similarly, British Prime Minister David Cameron announced in his famous speech in February 2011 the failure of multiculturalism in the United Kingdom and demanded that immigrants embrace a British identity, instead of staying outside the majority culture. Filmmakers have explored and challenged these types of demands for 'new' European and diasporic identities, and studied the changing borders of Europe during the past decades.

Eden is West, Dirty Pretty Things, Welcome and *Le Havre* are illustrative examples of recent European cinema having a growing interest in the themes of European borders, immigration, inclusion and exclusion. Influential scholars such as Hamid Naficy have developed theories of migrant and diasporic cinema and how cinema has functioned as a political tool and a means of visualizing immigrant identities and counter-stories for people living in exile (Naficy 2001: 6–15; see also Berghahn and Sternberg 2010: 3–4). A number of recent films have explored the diasporic experience from multiple viewpoints and challenged the concept of 'national' as a privileged dimension of identity-formation (Higbee and Lim 2010: 11). Therefore, it is important to consider how cinema strengthens prevailing national and cultural spaces, and simultaneously takes part in negotiating, undermining and further imagining their borders. Cinema not only depicts and represents various borders and frontiers but actively constructs and deconstructs them. Paradoxically, borders that divide also unite and produce cultural exchange.

This book examines the various meanings of borders and frontiers in European cinema after World War II, and addresses ongoing European debates regarding nationalism, transnationalism, migration and multiculturalism. However, while immigration and multiculturalism are treated as important and topical themes in this book, this volume approaches 'frontier' and 'border' as multidimensional and multidisciplinary concepts and offers a variety of national and cultural perspectives on and historical analyses of borders in films made in and about Europe between 1945 and 2010. The chapters examine borders and frontiers, as well as spaces within and outside those borders and frontiers, from geographical, spatial, national, social and cultural perspectives. Europe has seen dramatic developments during those decades, from the end of the World War II and the Cold War period, to the collapse of the Soviet Bloc and the subsequent redrawing of the borders. While the key frontier of Europe was between the East and the West up to the late 1980s, not only have both official as well as cultural borders changed since then, but also events such as the traumatic disintegration of Yugoslavia or immigration to and within Europe have created new (and modified older) borders. More recently, during the early 2000s, the changing borders of the European Union have been a topic of a constant debate as well as anxiety and distress. Consequently, borders of more distant pasts have been re-examined, also in films.

The Finnish-Russian film *Raja 1918/The Border* (Lauri Törhönen, 2007) acknowledges the often problematic and even arbitrary nature of a state border. Set in the aftermath of the Finnish Civil War of 1918, and on the border between Finland and Russia just months after Finland had declared herself independent of Russia, the film highlights the difference between state affairs and the everyday life of common people. The latter are trying to cope with the austerity brought upon them by the events – Russia, too, has suffered greatly from its own civil war succeeding the communist revolution. For the people living on both sides of the border, generations-old economic and social connections become difficult, and in some cases impossible, to maintain. Matters are worsened by political and militant organizations which are trying to exploit the natural flow of people and goods in the region. The film depicts a situation in which a border divides people against their wishes. The tragic result of such a division is the loss of natural cultural connections and, in time, the creation of juxtapositions between people.

A more recent Swedish film *Gränsen/Beyond the Border* (Richard Holm, 2011) approaches the idea of borders from more ambiguous viewpoints. The film, set in 1941, tells the story of Swedish soldiers guarding a backwoods border line between Sweden and German-occupied Norway. Trusting the woods and the night to provide him with cover, one of the soldiers decides to cross the border without permission. He is captured by the Germans, and his comrades decide to attempt his rescue. What ensues is an adventure into film history, as the film refers to story elements and imagery from many classic World War II films. The Nazis are predictably sadistic, and are even possibly planning to invade Sweden: conveniently, the operation plan is found by the Swedes in the wreck of a crashed plane. The film appears to cross the border between history and fiction, as it depicts a conflict between the official Swedish policy of remaining neutral and many (we have to assume the squad represents a larger social group) of her people, who not only detest but are actively fighting Nazi Germany.

Beyond the Border depicts borders in a straightforward and simplified fashion. As a medium, however, cinema has contributed to mental redrawing of borders in various ways, and it offers paths for spatial imagination. Tom Conley (2007: 1–3) argues that films have an implicit relation with cartography. Conley has compared the cinematic images to maps: both can be approached as images that 'locate and pattern the imagination of its spectators'. Films use maps as a narrative device, but more importantly, they are maps in themselves: they often seek to colonize our imagination by invisible storytelling techniques and articulation of space. The idea of a (national) border is crucial for the cartography of European cinema, and it has been explored in several scholars' works during the last ten years. For example, Sandra Barriales-Bouche and Marjorie Attignol Salvodon (2007: 5–9) argue that the interconnections between geographical, historical and cultural boundaries as well as local, regional, national and global borders have become increasingly important in contemporary European cinema. European films self-consciously question the borders of Europe and show Europe as a space that needs to be redefined.

In the same vein, Luisa Rivi (2007: 2–6) understands cinema as a privileged site for debate on European borders, especially due to cinema's important role in commercial and transnational cultural production. Through international cooperation in the production strategies and transnational film themes, national cinematic borders have become more flexible (see also Nestingen and Elkington 2005). Consequently, rethinking nation states and national borders and identities has become a recurring theme in film narratives. However, as Mike Wayne argues, despite the fact that European nation states and identities are often understood through constant change and crises, mythic understandings about national identities have deep roots in our cultural apprehensions. According to Wayne, this can clearly be seen in recent British cinema, where conservative images of Britishness prevail (Wayne 2002: 139). As we see, through cinematic storytelling and framing techniques, cinema maps new European borders and provides imagery for the changing identities and frontiers.

Conceptualizing frontiers and borders

'This is the West, sir. When the legend becomes fact, print the legend.' This famous quote from John Ford's *The Man Who Shot Liberty Valance* (1962) captures the image of the American frontier as mythic tale, where the line between fact and fiction is blurred and confused. As Richard Slotkin (1995: 4, 10–14) has demonstrated, the idea of frontier has had, and continues to have, a special meaning in American popular and political culture. The myth of the 'Wild West' was created by sensationalist writers and dime novels and finally established by Westerns. It has become a historical cliché, which is still constantly used as legitimization for 'necessary' violence and interventions in American foreign policy.

The clash between savagery and civilization is one of the essential features of the frontier myth, according to which the white man's conquest of Native Americans was a prerequisite for the advancement of civilized culture. Somewhat ironically, the new nation was eager to condemn the same mentality as imperialism in relation to earlier European colonization of the world.

As a film genre, Westerns created a visual image of the frontier myth, and the idea of frontier in films is thus generally associated with the American West. The creator of the television series *Star Trek* (1966–69), Gene Roddenberry, envisioned his science fiction as a kind of futuristic space age version of *Wagon Train*, a popular Western television series (1957–65) and moved the frontier to space. The legendary opening narration of the *Star Trek* saga begins with 'Space, the final frontier'. It is easy to understand such a claim in an era in which there were fewer and fewer places on Earth yet to be explored. However, the longer the series ran, the more there were episodes dealing with the past: Native Americans, the 'Wild West', ancient Rome, Nazi Germany, 1930s' Chicago and so on. The concept of 'frontier' was, accordingly, understood in a broader cultural and political sense. Similarly, in film analysis the uses of the concept of 'frontier' are not restricted to the Western film genre or its derivatives, such as 'space Westerns', but 'frontier' can be applied to the analysis of any film genre.

According to the *Oxford English Dictionary*, a 'frontier' is '[t]he part of a country which fronts or faces another country; the marches; the border or extremity conterminous with that of another' and in the United States '[t]hat part of a country which forms the border of its settled or inhabited regions: as (before the settlement of the Pacific coast), the western frontier of the United States' (Cent. Dict.).' Border, on the other hand, is defined in the *Oxford English Dictionary* as (1) '[a] side, edge, brink, or margin; a limit, or boundary; the part of anything lying along its boundary or outline', (2a) '[t]he district lying along the edge of a country or territory, a frontier; *pl.* the marches, the border districts', (b) '[t]he boundary line which separates one country from another, the frontier line', (c) '[w]ith various prepositions, e.g. *within, in, out of*, and in other connections, *borders* is equivalent to "territories, dominions, limits"'. The *Oxford Dictionary of English* tells us that the noun 'frontier' is 'a line or border separating two countries', also 'the extreme limit of settled land beyond which lies wilderness, especially in reference to the western United States before Pacific settlement' and ' the extreme limit of understanding or achievement in a particular area'.[2] The latter dictionary defines 'border' as 'a line separating two countries, administrative divisions, or other areas', 'the edge or boundary of something, or the part near it'.[3] For example, Klusáková and Ellis note in their discussion of frontiers as a concept in European history that 'frontiers of their very nature are regions where two or three cultures, languages, and societies collide and interact with each other' (2006: 1).

In her famous study, Gloria Anzaldúa (1999/1987) 'maps' the cultural space of the Texan-Mexican borderlands ('la frontera'). Her theoretical premise is universal: 'In fact, the Borderlands are physically present wherever two or more cultures edge each other, where people of different races occupy the same territory, where under, lower, middle and upper classes touch, where the space between two individuals shrinks with intimacy'

(Anzaldúa 1999: 19). She emphasizes the psychological, sexual and spiritual border*lands*, as if to claim a (geographical) space is needed to chart differentiating and coexisting cultures and mentalities. Perhaps it is true, especially if we break the space down to the level of individuals, as Anzaldúa does. As we have seen, films have explored national and political borders, but they have also attempted to identify, challenge and imagine frontiers of another kind: social, ethnic, religious borderlines, which are equally important and historically constructed. One example of the sometimes paradoxical nature of borders is gender: calling attention to gender and gendered patterns of, for example, political structures or cinematic representations, is a key way of pursuing gender equality. However, this might also highlight the differences between genders and gender identities.

In this book, we see 'frontier' as a concept that stirs one's imagination. Frontier is, arguably, wider and more vague as a concept than is 'border'. With frontier, there is an implication of relative vastness and something uncharted, even uncertain. In turn, border appears to be if not fixed, at least under negotiation, and at some level at least, drawn. It may be argued that border implies exclusiveness, whilst a frontier is a demarcation zone, a cultural no-man's-land not strictly defined by borders. One such frontier exists between fields such as history and film studies: in a scholarly study of film and history, where does one end and the other begin? The division should not be understood as a border of competing academic fields, but a fertile frontier for scholars. Peter C. Rollins has used the very metaphor of frontier in relation to academic acknowledgement of the power of the media today, calling special attention to the study of history and film (Rollins 2007: 1–9). Jim Collins (1993) also explores the frontier in his article on developments in film genres in the late 1980s and early 1990s. Using Westerns (fittingly) as his case in point, Collins argues that genre films can be divided into two groups. One eclectically combines elements of various genres, the other pursues cinematic purity. The first-mentioned group of films embraces irony, whilst the latter body of works excludes it. What the two approaches share is the engagement with the past, especially that of the film genres. Without questioning Collins' division, we must also consider, theoretically at least, the reception of films among cinemagoers. Each spectator interprets a film in a unique way, and this constitutes a frontier around the border of Collins's 'typology'. Irony, for example, is located in the 'eye of the beholder'.

The scope of this volume covers a major part of the film medium's history, and it also explores films depicting history before the invention of film. History is here understood as the past, as well as accounts of the past. Some of the films examined here are set in the present, whilst others are 'historical' films, as in set in the past. All of them are seen in their historical contexts. Many of the films examined here were, without doubt, produced not as 'documenting' a moment in time but as stories about the lives of (usually fictional) characters. Yet, for a scholar, films offer invaluable sources on social and cultural events and phenomena. They do not necessarily record history but depict and represent it, often influencing contemporaries' – and scholars' – understanding of the past events and sometimes even inventing them. A pioneering historian to study film, Marc Ferro (1977), writes about intersecting points between cinema and history, in which film works as a source and as an agent of history. Ferro's examples include scientific usage (i.e. documentation) of film and his most famous case, propaganda in fiction film. Yet films also contain elements which the makers most likely never intended to include. How can we tell the difference and whether it matters? This problem hints at an understanding of a frontier in scholarly study of film: the problem of contextualization. A film does not have a predefined or given context, rather the individual researcher always constructs a context within the borders of academic enquiry.

In the last ten years, a number of books have been published on European cinema, and some on border-crossing and migration in cinema.[4] However, this is the first book to explore comprehensively the topics of 'frontier' and 'border' in the cinematic history of Europe. It deals with topics and themes pertaining to film history, film studies, cultural studies and cultural history. In addition, it touches the fields of geography, political history and gender studies. The book investigates filmmaking historically as a form of active defining, constructing and challenging of various European borders and frontiers. This historical emphasis distinguishes the book from other works that focus on cinema and borders.

Challenging national borders and cultural frontiers

The volume begins with a section dealing with one of the most important and (in)famous borders in modern history, the Iron Curtain. In the aftermath of World War II, large areas of the world were separated by ideological and political rifts, which in many places led to economic and, in time, cultural divisions between regions and people earlier closely connected with each other. The most dramatic new border, in Berlin physically a wall, was, of course, set up in Germany. The country became two states, with two 'new' nations engaged both in coming to terms with history and attempting to cope with the present and the future. The section features four chapters, three of which analyse German cinema from a number of viewpoints and in several contexts. **Hannu Salmi** analyses Wim Wenders' *Die Himmel über Berlin/Wings of Desire*, the 1987 film set in the Cold War era West Berlin. Salmi understands cinema as a (re-)framing process: films do not only depict reality, they actively construct our understanding of lived and experienced environments. He argues that Berlin was undergoing historical change both in reality and cinema, which becomes clear by analysing the key themes of the Wenders' film on the time-space continuum.

Jacqui Miller analyses Rainer Werner Fassbinder's 1970 film *Der Amerikanische Soldat/ The American Soldier* and asks, 'What is wrong with a cowboy in Hamburg?', and the answer, at least in retrospect, is 'nothing'. Miller contextualizes Fassbinder's film in the tradition of post-war German cinema, from the 'rubble films' through the decades up to the 1980s, mapping the complex and sometimes paradoxical relationship Germany has with American culture. At the same time, Germans have been forced to come to terms with their own past. The result of this combination has been a cultural dialogue which has always been active. **Marco Bohr**'s chapter on Peter Kahane's film *Die Architekten/The Architects* (1990) likewise deals with cinema as a source, a document and an agent of history. The film was made when

East Germany was collapsing, and this became not only a key spiritual element for the film, but Kahane used the medium of feature film to criticize the Socialist system, a trait sometimes forgotten in relation to DEFA, the East German film company. As is often the case, artists working in a totalitarian state will find ways to voice their discontent at the system, and Bohr's analysis shows this was true in the case of the Kahane film.

The final article examines the world divided by the Iron Curtain from an alternative viewpoint. **Kimmo Ahonen** argues that American B-movies of the 1950s were not only obsessed with finding communist agents in the United States, but were offering solutions to a pressing problem of the era, that of 'winning the Cold War'. He has chosen two films for close reading, *Guilty of Treason* (Felix E. Feist, 1950) and *Red Planet Mars* (Harry Horner, 1952), and shows how imaginary Cold War battlegrounds were set up both in Europe and in space. In addition to the predictable democracy, the films also offer the Christian religion as means of winning over the suppressed people of the communist bloc. Ahonen also demonstrates how the filmmakers referred to actual East European events as inspiration and used American newspapers as a medium in propagating their ideas to the public. This serves as another reminder of this volume's key argument: as a cultural and social medium, cinema should not be understood as a passive 'reflector' but a polyphonic form of art and entertainment which actively participates in topical, as well as historical, debates.

The volume continues with a section that focuses on alternative borders and frontiers. Borders are with us in our everyday life, and films have not only reflected the prevailing borders, but also created, reinforced and questioned them. Films thus reveal the interplay between dominant and oppositional ideologies. European cinema has dealt with the borders between different social classes in many ways, from the social codes of the French upper class in Jean Renoir's *Le Règle de Jeu/The Rules of the Game* (1939) to Aki Kaurismäki's criticism of the EU migration policy in *Le Havre* (2011). Kaurismäki, whom the American film critic Andrew O'Hehir (2011) recently called the 'last major Marxist left in European cinema', has dealt with the question of class divides throughout his 30-year career as director.

Kaurismäki, who has been vocal in his opposition to the political process of Europeanization, is often regarded as a distinctively Finnish film director, although his films cannot be attached to a singular national identity. His films are examples of border crossings: they are both national and international; they combine the features of American B-budget crime movies with those of French new wave films; they owe homage to Robert Bresson as well as to Yasujirô Ozu. **Sanna Peden** emphasizes the transnational aspects of Kaurismäki's films in her chapter 'Crossing over: On Becoming European in Aki Kaurismäki's Cinema'. She takes a look at the metaphorical borders in the films of Kaurismäki, such as those between the past and present and East and West. Peden's expansion of terminological and theoretical work on Kaurismäki and European identity provides a substantial contribution to the corpus of Kaurismäki studies. By examining *I Hired a Contract Killer* (1990) and *Pidä huivista kiinni Tatjana/Take Care of Your Scarf, Tatjana* (1993) Peden argues that the negotiation of spatial, temporal and emotional boundaries in the films reveals the emergence of a new, 'doubly occupied' European reality. These films can be interpreted as implicit commentaries in which the idea of post-Cold War Europe is questioned and redefined.

Films have identified social and ethnic borders within nations and communities. One can find several depictions of 'slum-dwellers' in many American films dealing with urban crime, but questions of ethnicity, oppression and violence in an urban environment have been increasingly present in European films as well during the last few decades. Slavoj Žižek has emphasized the 'territorial character' of the slums within state frontiers. Slums are 'white spots' in the official map of the state territory, where the state has partly withdrawn its control (Žižek 2009: 426). In 'The Cité's Architectural, Linguistic and Cinematic Frontiers in L'Esquive', **Jehanne-Marie Gavarini** discusses the cinematic representations of *banlieues*, which are liminal and complex border areas located on the edge of French cities. The poor and segregated French suburbs are home to immigrants – many of them from the former French colonies – and their children.

Gavarini analyses how *L'Esquive* (Abdellatif Kechiche, 2004), participates in the continuum of *banlieue* representation in French cinema. The film's teenage protagonists are shaped by the design and geographic location of their neighbourhood as much as by their multicultural experiences in the *banlieue*. The visual obstructions that teenagers encounter stand for the physical and symbolic borders that separate the *banlieues* from French mainstream and affluent society. Gavarini discusses the use of visual and spoken languages as markers of this divide: the teenagers' use of slang and slurs in conjunction with their constant display of violent emotions is symptomatic of their marginalization and exclusion.

The representations of the (partly invisible) boundaries within the city are also the focal point in **Kari Kallioniemi**'s chapter 'Looking for Alternative London: *The London Nobody Knows* and the Pop-Geographical Borders of the City'. The City of London has been used both as a filming location and as a film setting, and it is often depicted either as an exciting and fashionable place or a city darkened by its past and invisible borders. The television film *The London Nobody Knows* (Norman Cohen, 1967), narrated by James Mason, challenged the 1960s 'Swinging London' dreamscape by depicting an alternative view of the celebrated city; London is seen through its hidden places, borders, localities and buildings. Cohen's cult-documentary has also influenced more recent films and alternative documentaries seeking the visible and invisible borders of London. Kallioniemi asks how Swinging London and its representative films are connected to the idea of the other side of London, dealt with in *The London Nobody Knows*.

The third section of the book focuses on films made after the turn of the millennium and is concerned with highly topical themes: migration, transnational journeys, hybrid identities and the family in recent European cinema. The three chapters of this section examine the internal as well as external borders of nations in Greek, Turkish-German and Swedish films. The family continues to be central in identity formation in twenty-first-century Europe and often represents roots, tradition or even the nation. All the three chapters of this section demonstrate that crossing geographical, cultural and social borders – and constructing a hybrid identity – often means negotiations with one's family.

Jessica Gallagher's chapter 'Between Hamburg and Istanbul: Mobility, Borders and Identity in the Films of Fatih Akin' explores transnational journeys between the heartlands and the border of Europe in recent Turkish-German cinema. Gallagher discusses the framing of national and cultural borders in Fatih Akin's films and the role borders play in highlighting some of the struggles that members of the Turkish diaspora in Germany face today. She points out that the notions of identity and hybridity are central to recent Turkish-German cinema; both *Gegen die Wand/Head-On* (2004) and *Auf der anderen Seite/The Edge of Heaven* (2007) present the negotiation of national and cultural identities, intercultural and intergenerational relationships and the search for somewhere to belong. Gallagher's analysis of border spaces and crossings in Akin's films through the framework of Hamid Naficy's 'accented cinema' shows that the German-Turkish characters' increased mobility and transnational journeys between Germany and Turkey do not represent greater liberation for them but in fact continue to demonstrate the limitations of a hybrid Turkish-German identity and existence. Displacement, homelessness and struggle with the negotiation of hybrid cultural identities are always present.

Heta Mulari's chapter on 'Transnational Heroines: Swedish Youth Film and Immigrant Girlhood' looks at images of immigrant girls in Swedish youth films at the turn of the millennium and explores the possibilities of understanding cinematic images of immigrant girls transnationally. Mulari focuses on *Vingar av glas* and *Bäst i Sverige/We Can Be Heroes!* (Ulf Malmros, 2002), but also refers to other films that deal with immigrant youth and girlhood, such as *Jalla! Jalla!* (Josef Fares, 2000) and *Bend It Like Beckham* (Gurinder Chadha, 2000), discussing the cinematic immigrant girl as a symbol of social and cultural change and anxiety. The films comment on the contemporary debate over immigrant youth, particularly immigrant girls and girlhood, and challenge and reimagine the relationship between national debates over youth and transnational cinematic images of girlhood in the context of youth film production. Rather than examining these films as 'immigrant films', Mulari analyses their representations of immigrant girls in the context of youth film production, both in Sweden and internationally, bringing a new perspective to youth and teen film research.

In her chapter 'Family as Internal Border in *Dogtooth*' **Ipek A. Celik** argues that the 'gated' family in Greek filmmaker Yorgos Lanthimos's *Dogtooth* is a commentary on the social problems that have emerged from the migratory confrontations in post-Cold War Greece and Europe. Celik suggests that although *Dogtooth* does not explicitly deal with migration and population movements in Greece, the film is nevertheless preoccupied with these themes; the story of the film's family can be read as an allegory of internal borders in and of Greece, and in extension those in and of Europe. Building on Etienne Balibar's theorization of 'internal borders' constructed within a Europe anxious about its multicultural present, she argues that the enclosed and incestuous family in *Dogtooth* represents the protected zone of the 'inside' and functions as a trope for the increasing anxiousness to protect the internal borders of Europe. Celik reads *Dogtooth* as a film that explores the impossible experiment of protecting a community through the multiplication of borders around it.

In the fourth section of the volume, three scholars explore how films construct and interpret intra-national and international conflicts as well as the borders and frontiers of the post-colonial European nations. Themes addressed in this section include gendered conflicts and embodied boundaries in Northern Ireland, the renegotiation of Spain as a post-colonial cultural bridgehead between Spain and Latin America and the historical, political and geographical borders of the British Empire. In all chapters, cinema is understood as a framing practice that imagines and challenges existing national borders and rewrites historical borders inside and between nation-states. In addition, the focus of this section is on genre and how storytelling practices and narrative choices become important in cinematic explorations of the post-colonial nations.

While films imagine and challenge geographical and national borders, they draw gendered and embodied boundaries as well. Since the late 1980s, there has been a growing interest in the representations of femininity and masculinity on screen. Cinema has frequently portrayed political and nationalist struggles as highly gendered: nationalist movements are usually masculinized projects where women are understood in the role of the silent mother or as the symbolic bearers of the nation. This section begins with **Raita Merivirta**'s chapter 'Gendered Conflicts in Northern Ireland: Motherhood, the Male Body and Borders in *Some Mother's Son* and *Hunger*', where she explores the gendered nature of political and national borders as well as the role of women, especially the Irish mother, and the suffering male body in the Troubles films. The focus of this chapter is on how two different films, Terry George's mainstream melodrama *Some Mother's Son* (1996) and Steve McQueen's art film *Hunger* (2008), constructed an understanding of the Republican protest and the hunger strikes as highly gendered.

Historical film can be understood as a power-related means of remembering and forgetting historical events and thus constructing understandings of national history. In the chapter 'Heartlands and Borderlands: *El Dorado* and the Post-Franco Spanish Cinema as a Bridgehead between Europe and Latin America', **Petteri Halin** explores the Spanish historical film *El Dorado* in the context of post-Franco Spanish cinema that negotiated the Spanish colonial history and the (post)colonial relationship between Europe and Latin America. The year 1992 marked the five-hundredth anniversary of Christopher Colombus's maiden voyage to the Western hemisphere. During the late 1980s and early 1990s, worldwide commemoration practices were visible in public debates, political decision-making and academic studies, as well as popular culture. As Halin argues, in these commemoration practices, the past was used as a commodity to form an understanding of a new democratic and international Spain. Further, through these debates the role of Spain as a bridgehead between Europe and Latin America was emphasized. Halin situates *El Dorado* in these commemoration practices and analyses historical film as a means of selectively rewriting history by remembering and forgetting.

Finally, in 'Subverted and Transgressed Borders: The Empire in British Comedy and Horror Films', **Rami Mähkä** explores, firstly, the transgression of borders in the audiovisual genres of horror and comedy. In this chapter, he argues that the borders between horror and comedy genres should be rethought and analysed in relation to each other. Secondly, through extensive research material on British horror and comedy films and television from the 1960s to the 80s, Mähkä looks at how horror and comedy films have de-constructed and re-constructed various political and historical borders of the British Empire. These audiovisual genres have, in their own distinctive ways, frequently addressed the theme of the loss of the Empire and how it has affected British identities after the Second World War. Mähkä explores the representations of the Empire and the similarities between comedy and horror through the concepts of the grotesque, transgression, subversion and the uncanny.

***

20th Century Fox's studio mogul Darryl F. Zanuck wrote in 1945 of American films as not only selling American products to the European market, but the 'American way of life' as well (Neve 1992: 91). Hollywood films tend to conceal their ideology through techniques of invisible storytelling, and they thus have an emotional appeal that, as David Bordwell (1985: 3) has suggested, 'transcends class and nation'. The classical Hollywood mode of storytelling has almost become the universal language of cinema. It is based on the idea of integration; films should solve ideological contradictions and appeal to different audiences, whichever religious or ethnic group they represent. Accordingly, mainstream fiction films, both American and European films, strive to smooth over the political and cultural contradictions within the nation. They not only depict, define and reaffirm borders but simultaneously break down the barriers of class, race and nation. Ultimately, borders are meant to be crossed, frontiers mapped.

References

Anzaldúa, G. (1999), *Borderlands/La Frontera: The New Mestiza*, San Francisco: Aunt Lute. First published 1987.

Barriales-Bouche, S. and Attignol Salvodon, M. (2007), 'Introduction', in S. Barriales-Bouche and M. Attignol Salvodon (eds), *Zoom In Zoom Out: Politics in Contemporary European Cinema*, Cambridge: Cambridge Scholars Publishing, pp. 5–14.

Berghahn, D. and Sternberg, C. (2010), 'Introduction', in D. Berghahn and C. Sternberg, (eds), *European Cinema in Motion: Migrant and Diasporic Film in Contemporary Europe*, London: Palgrave Macmillan, pp. 1–11.

Bordwell, D. (1985), 'The Classical Hollywood Style, 1917–60', in D. Bordwell, J. Staiger and K. Thompson, *The Classical Hollywood Cinema: Film Style & Mode of Production to 1960*, London, Melbourne and Henley: Routledge & Kegan Paul.

Brown, W., Iordanova, D. and Torchin, L. (2010), *Moving People, Moving Images: Cinema and Trafficking in the New Europe*, St Andrews: St Andrews Film Studies.

Collins, J. (1993), 'Genericity in the 90s: Eclectic Irony and the New Sincerity', in J. Collins, H. Radner and A. P. Collins (eds), *Film Theory Goes to the Movies*, New York: Routledge.

Conley, T. (2007), *Cartographic Cinema*, Minneapolis: The University of Minnesota Press.

Elkington, T. G. and Nestingen, A. (2005), 'Introduction: Transnational Nordic Cinema', in A. Nestingen and T. G. Elkington (eds), *Transnational Cinema in a Global North: Nordic Cinema in Transition*, Detroit: Wayne State University Press, pp. 1–30.

Elsaesser, T. (2003), *European Cinema: Face to Face with Hollywood*, Amsterdam: Amsterdam University Press.

Ferro, M. (1988), *Cinema and History* (trans. N. Greene), Detroit: Wayne State University Press. First published 1977.

Galt, R. (2006), *The New European Cinema: Redrawing the Map*, New York: Columbia University Press.

Halle, R. (2008), *German Film after Germany: Toward a Transnational Aesthetic*, Champaign: University of Illinois Press.

Higbee, W. and Lim, S. (2010), 'Concepts of Transnational Cinema: Towards a Critical Transnationalism in Film Studies', *Transnational Cinemas* 1:1, pp. 7–21.

Klusáková, L. and Ellis, S. T. (2006), 'Terms and Concepts: "Frontier" and "Identity" in Academic and Popular Usage', in L. Klusáková and S. T. Ellis (eds), *Frontiers and Identities: Exploring the Research Area*, Pisa: Pisa University Press, pp. 1–15.

Loshitzky, Y. (2010), *Screening Strangers: Migration and Diaspora in Contemporary European Cinema*, Bloomington and Indianapolis: Indiana University Press.

Naficy, H. (2001), *An Accented Cinema: Exilic and Diasporic Filmmaking*, Princeton: Princeton University Press.

Nestingen, A. and Elkington, T. (2005), *Transnational Cinema in a Global North: Nordic Cinema in Transition*, Detroit: Wayne State University Press.

Neve, B. (1992), *Film and Politics in America: A Social Tradition*, London and New York: Routledge.

O'Hehir, A. (2011), '"Le Havre": A Strange and Delightful Immigration Comedy', *Salon* 21 Oct, http://www.salon.com/2011/10/21/le_havre_a_strange_and_delightful_immigration_comedy. Accessed 25 March 2012.

Rivi, L. (2007), *European Cinema after 1989: Cultural Identity and Transnational Production*, New York: Palgrave Macmillan.

Rollins, P. C. (2007), 'Introduction: Film and History: Our Media Environment as a New Frontier', in R. Francaviligia and J. Rodnitzky (eds), *Lights, Camera, History: Portraying the Past in Film*, Arlington: Texas A&M University Press.

Scharf, I. (2008), *Nation and Identity in the New German Cinema: Homeless at Home*, New York: Routledge.

Slotkin, R. (1995), *Gunfighter Nation: The Myth of the Frontier in Twentieth-Century America*, New York: HarperPerennial. First published 1992.

Wayne, M. (2002), *Politics in Contemporary European Cinema: Histories, Borders, Diasporas*. Bristol: Intellect Ltd.

Žižek, S. (2009), *In Defense of Lost Causes*, London and New York: Verso.

Notes

1 The term 'fortress Europe' (Festung Europa) was originally used in the World War II Nazi propaganda to refer to the occupied continent.

2 'frontier *noun*' in A. Stevenson (ed.), *Oxford Dictionary of English*, Oxford University Press, 2010. *Oxford Reference Online*. Oxford University Press. http://www.oxfordreference.com/views/ENTRY.html?subview=Main&entry=t140.e0318490. Accessed 9 March 2012.

3 'border *noun*' in A. Stevenson (ed.), *Oxford Dictionary of English*, Oxford University Press, 2010. *Oxford Reference Online*. Oxford University Press. http://www.oxfordreference.com/views/ENTRY.html?subview=Main&entry=t140.e0093650. Accessed 9 March 2012.

4 For example, Galt (2006); Nestingen and Elkington (2005); Scharf (2008); Halle (2008); Elsaesser (2003); Brown, Iordanova and Torchin (2010).

Chapter 1

Imagining West Berlin: Spatiality and History in Wim Wenders' *Wings of Desire*, 1987

Hannu Salmi
University of Turku

Warum bin ich hier und warum nicht dort?
Wann begann die Zeit und wo endet der Raum?

—Peter Handke

'Today, the endangered frontier of freedom runs through divided Berlin. We want it to remain a frontier of peace.' These famous words by President John F. Kennedy were spoken on 25 July 1961, at the time of the Berlin crisis, in his radio and television report for an American audience (Mur 2004: 7; Brager 2004: 68; Schwarz 2004: 188). At the end of World War II, Berlin had been a battleground, and soon after the war it became the scene of another kind of battle: the Cold War. Five weeks before Kennedy's speech, First Secretary of the Socialist Unity Party and GDR State Council chairman Walter Ulbricht had stated that 'no one has the intention of erecting a wall!' (Gedmin 1992: 25). Two months later, however, the building of the Berliner Mauer had started. The year 1961 marked the drawing of a physical barrier between East and West; in the end, the 155km-long Wall enclosed the city of West Berlin, separating it completely from East Berlin – and from East Germany.

The emerging ideological gap of the Cold War was etched into the material world by the Wall, but it was to a large extent also a construct in the realm of the imagination. The divided city of Berlin was frequently used as a film location, beginning already in the late 1940s, but it can be argued that the most influential cinematic depiction of the city of the Wall was that directed at the very end of the Cold War era by Wim Wenders. This film was *Der Himmel über Berlin* (1987), known in English as *Wings of Desire*.

Wings of Desire can be interpreted as a film about the dividedness of Berlin, in which the Wall itself plays a crucial role. It is also of interest because Berlin changed radically once again after its filming; just a few years later, the Wall, which had had such a strong presence in *Wings of Desire*, was dismantled and torn down. Wim Wenders' cinematic homage to Berlin also serves as an access point to how borders and spatiality were imagined in Cold War Europe. It is noteworthy that the reception of the film was intertwined with political changes at the turn of the 1980s and 1990s. It was filmed in Berlin in 1986 and premiered at the Cannes Film Festival in May 1987. The West German premiere was on 29 October 1987. In many European countries it was released in 1988, the same year in which Mikhail Gorbachev introduced the concept of 'glasnost' in the Soviet Union. The Berlin Wall began to collapse on 9 November 1989. In Germany, *Wings of Desire* was re-released in July 1993 and was also circulated in the eastern parts of the reunited country.

In this chapter, I explore the ways in which *Wings of Desire* portrays the German metropolis and its topography: how it imagines the city space and draws maps of its own, and how this imagination relates to the notion(s) of history. In moving about in space, within the borders of West Berlin, the film describes the routes and sites of the city. My argument is that it refers to maps and itineraries that recalled pre-war – and pre-Wall – Berlin in the memories of its inhabitants. Here it is important to recognize that (deferring to Gilles Deleuze and Félix Guattari), maps are always superimposed upon one another: old maps are not replaced by new ones but are rather stratified over each other. In his *Cartographic Cinema*, Tom Conley has argued that cinema works like a map: both are forms of locational machinery. A film creates boundaries, transgresses borders, navigates in space, excludes some places by portraying others and shows places to identify with. The film, like a map, tells spectators where they are situated, directs their actions and shapes their understanding of where they are – and, simultaneously, who they are (Conley 2007: 1–22). It is important to see film not only as a narrative form of expression but also as a performative one. Films imagine and construct our visual – and aural – understanding of the environment. In this chapter, I analyse the transformations of Berlin city space on the screen from the perspective of one particular focal point offered by *Wings of Desire*. The following discussion emphasizes five aspects, all of which contribute to the ways in which the film intermingles spatiality and history: Berlin places and the idea of the 'angel of history', ruins and wasteland, maps and itineraries and, finally, the Wall. It is essential to note that Wenders' film did not merely reflect political changes: it participated in creating the dividedness of Berlin and in connecting the city's sites, maps and itineraries with memories of the past.

Cinema of place and angels of history

Wings of Desire is a film in which time and space are inextricably bound together. It can be characterized as an instance of cinema of place, and in that sense does not diverge from Wim Wenders' previous productions. Think, for example, of such films as *Alice in den Städten/Alice in the Cities* (1974), *Paris, Texas* (1984) or *Tokyo-Ga* (1985). Furthermore, one can argue that in Wenders' films the problem of spatiality is connected with the way the films have been made: the director is well known for his inclination not to use a tightly planned shooting script. Thus the outcome is enriched by ideas arising on location, inspired by places and by the overall circumstances of the shooting. When a film is not dominated by a temporally ordered, straightforward plot, spatial performativity comes to the fore perhaps more than temporally organized narrativity. An important background factor in *Wings of Desire* was also the fact that Wim Wenders, having been away from his home town and from Germany for a long time, wanted to make a film specifically about Berlin – and in Berlin. In the early 1980s he had had a painful experience in Hollywood in trying to work with the big studios on *Hammett* (1982), in a completely different production system. As Roger F. Cook (1997: 163–64) has pointed out, Wenders' time in the United States strengthened his views on the importance of improvisation and inspiration.

Right from the start, *Wings of Desire* makes it clear where the film is actually situated. In the beginning, the angel Damiel (Bruno Ganz) stands at the top of an important landmark, the Kaiser-Wilhelm-Gedächtniskirche (Kaiser Wilhelm Memorial Church).

Figures 1.1 and 1.2: First images of *Wings of Desire*.

This church has become a symbol of the traumatic history of Berlin: it was built at the end of the nineteenth century, but was severely damaged by bombing in 1943. After the war the city was about to demolish the ruins, but the people of Berlin sought to defend their memories of the past. This was especially important because the war had wiped out almost everything; there was not much left to preserve in the built environment. Finally only the main tower remained standing, and it is no coincidence that this tower in particular is a suitable place for the angel to watch over the actions of the citizens. Later in the film, the angels guard the golden ornament at the top of the Siegessäule. This victory column was a monument to the *Reichsgründung*, the unification of Germany in 1871, and at the same time a reference to the unity that was lost because of the war.

These two monuments, the Kaiser-Wilhelm-Gedächtniskirche and the Siegessäule, were essential components in the skyline of West Berlin. In fact Wenders had actually planned to use a third symbolic place, the Brandenburger Tor, as a gathering place of the angels, but this was replaced by a modern piece of architecture, the Staatsbibliothek (Lindström 2010: 44). Little wonder that Wenders used this location in his sequel to *Wings of Desire, In weiter Ferne, so nah!/Faraway, So Close!*, released in 1993. Obviously, the Kaiser-Wilhelm-Gedächtniskirche and the Siegessäule referred to the glorious past, to a time when Berlin was the capital of Germany. These monuments had become important points of identification for the people of the city; in particular the Kaiser-Wilhelm-Gedächtniskirche alluded to the *Eigensinn*, the obstinacy or persistence of the people, the insistence on preserving a connection with the past. Still, there were other points of identification in the city space, the Wall itself being the most important factor in directing everyday experience and reframing memories of Berlin. While the Gedächtniskirche and the Siegessäule refer to a Grand Narrative, a *longe durée*, the Wall seems to stop time, to bind people to the earth, to fragments rather than to narratives.

An important clue to understanding *Wings of Desire* was given by Wim Wenders himself. In 1991, four years after the release of the film, Wenders described the background of the project:

> The genesis of the idea of having angels in my Berlin story is very hard to account for in retrospect. It was suggested by many sources at once. First and foremost, Rilke's *Duino Elegies*. Paul Klee's paintings too. Walter Benjamin's *Angel of History*. There was a song by The Cure that mentioned 'fallen angels', and I heard another song on the car radio that had the line 'talk to an angel' in it. One day, in the middle of Berlin, I suddenly became aware of that gleaming figure, 'the Angel of Peace', metamorphosed from being a warlike victory angel into a pacifist. There was an idea of four allied pilots shot down over Berlin, an idea of juxtaposing and superimposing today's Berlin and the capital of the Reich, 'double images' in time and space. (Wenders 1991: 77)

As the quote reveals, by referring to Walter Benjamin's famous *Theses on the Philosophy of History* Wenders has himself exerted considerable influence over the interpretation of his work and has offered us a theoretical clue. Since the early 1990s, Walter Benjamin has been repeatedly connected with *Wings of Desire* (see Casarino 1990: 167–81; Cook 1997: 163–90; Perry 1998: 4–5). It is difficult to define when exactly the Benjaminian approach became intertwined with the film, but in an 1988 interview Wenders does not mention these origins: 'I was not all that conscious of it in the preparation, but as soon as we started shooting it became obvious how vast the possibilities of innovation were because of the invention of the guardian angel and the point of view it implied' (Paneth 1988: 5). The Benjaminian connection was certainly not noticed by the critic of the *New York Times*, Janet Maslin, who asked: 'Men have envisioned angels in many forms, but who besides Wim Wenders has seen them as sad, sympathetic, long-haired men in overcoats, gliding through a beautiful black-and-white Berlin on the lookout for human suffering?' (Maslin 1988).

In his later reminiscences, Wenders also mentions Paul Klee's painting *Angelus Novus*. Klee's image was in fact an inspiration for Benjamin as well, who wrote in his ninth thesis on history:

A Klee painting named 'Angelus Novus' shows an angel looking as though he is about to move away from something he is fixedly contemplating. His eyes are staring, his mouth is open, his wings are spread. This is how one pictures the angel of history. His face is turned toward the past. Where we perceive a chain of events, he sees one single catastrophe which keeps piling wreckage upon wreckage and hurls it in front of his feet. The angel would like to stay, awaken the dead, and make whole what has been smashed. But a storm is blowing from Paradise; it has got caught in his wings with such violence that the angel can no longer close them. This storm irresistibly propels him into the future to which his back is turned, while the pile of debris before him grows skyward. This storm is what we call progress. (Benjamin 1992: 257)

Benjamin's thesis is one of the most widely cited interpretations of modernity. Many scholars have seen the similarity between Benjamin's contemplative angels and Wenders' 'long-haired men in overcoats' (Casarino 1990; Perry 1998; Raskin 1999). There is certainly a melancholy view of history right from the start, when the audience sees Damiel standing at the top of the Gedächtniskirche and looking down. On the other hand, the storm is not 'blowing from Paradise' and the angels of history are not being propelled 'into the future'. While Benjamin's angels 'would like to stay', Wenders' angels have to stay among the inhabitants, making observations and recording history. It can be argued, perhaps, that the wind of modernity has already blown and has brought history to a standstill. It is also intriguing that in 1991 Wenders referred to the idea of 'pilots shot down over Berlin', as though these pilots remained in the city as guardian angels, angels of peace. In the 1988 interview, before the fall of the Wall, Wenders emphasized the message of peace:

I knew, before I even knew the story, that it was going to take place in Berlin and the city of Berlin carries the idea of peace very powerfully. It needs it more than other cities and also the desire for it is stronger than in other cities. Just as the freedom of the city is limited and its sense of freedom is more intense and almost unlimited. It is an extremely tolerant city. The peace movement in Germany started in Berlin and that's no coincidence. (Paneth 1988: 4)

In the pre-Wall interpretation, the angels of history are first and foremost angels of peace. Instead of Walter Benjamin, Wenders' words allude to John F. Kennedy's notion of the 'frontier of peace'. Berlin was the dividing line between East and West, and questions of freedom and peace were therefore of paramount importance. It is interesting to see, however, how the idea of peace is simultaneously undermined by the ruptures of history, which again, almost as though in parentheses, emphasise Benjaminian visions of history in *Wings of Desire*.

City of ruins and wasteland

In the opening scene, Damiel is standing at the top of the ruined church. The point of departure is to describe angels 'über Berlin', angels who can follow the lives of the people and listen to their worries and concerns but are at the same time helpless and unable to become involved with them. Roger F. Cook (1997: 164) has crystallized this setting: 'angels living in Berlin preserve the memory and even presence of Germany's history, while helping the inhabitants bear the burden of their nation's past'. This opening can be regarded as symptomatic in the sense that it also carries a reference to the history of Berlin as a history of ruins; after the war, the city was a true *Trümmerstadt*. This is also emphasized repeatedly later in the film, using documentary footage from World War II. These inserts portray the city in its sad appearance in 1945: mere heaps of stone and collapsed buildings. During the Cold War people were expected to concentrate on reconstruction, but traumatic memories intermingled with each other, including huge material destruction, war crimes and their treatment after the war and the construction of guilt. The ruined city was soon also echoed on the silver screen, when several films were made in the midst of the misery. If the ruins had somehow vanished from personal memory, they would have been renewed by the cinema again and again.

Already the first fiction film made in the GDR, *Die Mörder sind unter uns/Murderers among Us* (Wolfgang Staudte, 1945), opened with images of destruction. When the main protagonists appear on the screen, they are plunged brutally into the harsh reality of the present day. The Holocaust survivor and photographer Susanne Wallner (Hildegard Knef) returns to Berlin, only to find that her apartment is occupied by the alcoholic Hans Mertens (Ernst Wilhelm Borchert), a military surgeon who cannot escape his traumatic memories of the war. The surrounding ruins of Berlin become almost a symbol of their disturbed minds; everything has been shattered to pieces. In so doing, as Anton Kaes has pointed out, the film draws on the expressionist style of the Weimar cinema as well as features of post-war Italian neorealism (Kaes 1989: 12).

Figures 1.3 and 1.4: Above and Below.

According to Aristotle, it is important to distinguish between two kinds of memory. The active act of remembering is *mneme*: it refers to the conscious need to remember past things. *Anamnesis*, however, refers to unbidden memories, something that comes suddenly to the surface. In Emmanuel Levinas' terms, the former refers to the fullness of time, the latter to ruptures in time (Bernard-Donals 2009: 5, 18, cf. Samuel 1996: vii). In *Murderers among Us* Berlin is a landscape of unavoidable *anamnesis*. To draw on Raphael Samuel's famous work (1996): Berlin becomes a theatre of memory, but a theatre that is in pieces, a chaos. Interestingly, at the same time that people are struggling with memories they cannot escape, they have lost their history, their cultural heritage.

The ruined city of Berlin was soon shown on screens all over the world, and the city was not a signifier merely of the German trauma. It can even be argued that the ruins themselves had a cinematographic appeal to filmmakers, and audiences too were interested in seeing the effect of the war on the city that had been the heart of National Socialism and ultimately a decisive battleground. Roberto Rossellini made his *Germania anno zero/Germany, Year Zero* in 1948; that same year, Billy Wilder also came to Berlin to shoot *A Foreign Affair*, with Marlene Dietrich, Jean Arthur and John Lund. For many, World War II meant the collapse of European civilization. Antoine de Saint-Exupéry (1942: 20), for example, captured much of this atmosphere in his wartime novel *Pilote de guerre/Flight to Arras* (1942). While flying his mission, the pilot writes: 'There is no god here. There is no face to love. There is no France, no Europe, no civilization. There are particles, detritus, nothing more.' After the war Berlin looked like detritus, with piles of disintegrated wreckage; these are still visible in Wenders' *Wings of Desire*.

Wings of Desire depicts Berlin as it was in 1987, or during at least the shooting in 1986. The film unfolds mainly in the present tense, and documentary footage from the past is used in a very economical way. The film begins with black-and-white images of contemporary West Berlin. In addition to monuments, it shows street scenes, wasteland, open spaces near the Wall, private homes, clubs and hot-dog stands – places that dominate the ordinary lives of Berliners. As a counter-image to these, as a product of modernization, the spectator is led to the bright, spacious Staatsbibliothek, with its map room and other facilities, where the angels Damiel and Cassiel (Otto Sander) gather to observe the citizens. They seem to feel comfortable in the peaceful atmosphere of the library, this place where old books are preserved. Memories of the past, and the shocking, tragic history of the city of ruins, emerge as sudden flashes: they are like expressions of *anamnesis*, unbidden images that memory, wanting to forget, simply cannot banish. These shots reveal not only ruins, but people struggling to create a better life.

Wings of Desire employs both black-and-white and colour film. The first hour is almost entirely in black and white, and in this context the wartime footage in colour looks striking. The past seems to be strongly present. Black-and-white historical footage is also shown; finally, when Damiel has turned into a human being, the film bursts into colour. It may be argued that it is simply because of the vivid colours that the opening images of *Trümmerstadt* have such a powerful impact on the spectator. In an interview with Richard

Raskin (1999: 9–10), Wim Wenders explained that the colours of the documentary footage were actually unintentional. The filmmakers had two kinds of material at their disposal. On the one hand there was Soviet footage, on black-and-white 35mm film, very clearly 'directed' material even though it looked 'documentary'. It is known that the Soviet troops marched in several times so as to make it look better on film. On the other hand there was American footage, shot on 16mm colour film. This filming was more or less random, but because it was shot on colour stock it looked more 'cinematic'. Wenders decided that there was no point in removing the colours. Raskin's point is nevertheless important: the black-and-white world of the angels in *Wings of Desire* is contrasted to the human world, which is in colour. The harrowing images of war are thus in accord with the overall style of the film.

There is another scene in *Wings of Desire* where colour is used to emphasize the interface between fiction and reality. The American actor Peter Falk arrives in Berlin to make a film, located in National Socialist Germany. In the middle of the shooting, a female extra remembers how 'it really was', and documentary footage is used, again in colour, to show Berlin women toiling amidst the ruined buildings. In this scene fiction works to revive remembrance, but it is only a moment of unbidden *anamnesis*; soon history turns back into oblivion.

This sequence also brings to mind Walter Benjamin's notion of history. Benjamin (1992: 255) wrote in his fifth thesis on history that 'the past can be seized only as an image which flashes up at the instant when it can be recognized and is never seen again'. In the next thesis,

Figure 1.5: Documentary colour footage.

he argues that if one's purpose is to articulate the past historically, this should not take place in the spirit of Leopold von Ranke, trying to express how 'it really was' (Steinberg 1996: 1–2). The articulation of the past should aim at seizing a memory 'as it flashes up'. Wenders has clearly given expression to these flashes, or moments of *anamnesis*, by switching between black-and-white and colour images and by using flashbacks that connect the present day, the *Jetztzeit*, with the past.

Maps lost and refound

One of the most interesting characters in *Wings of Desire* is the old poet Homer, who is introduced in the first scene in the Staatsbibliothek. He is exhausted and has already lost much of his powers. The actor in this role is the screen veteran Curt Bois (1901–91), who had been acting on screen since childhood. After the National Socialists' rise to power in 1933 he moved to Hollywood and played minor parts in numerous productions, including that of a pickpocket in *Casablanca* (1942). In his later years Bois also played leading roles, such as Johannes Puntila in Alberto Cavalcanti's comedy *Herr Puntila und sein Knecht Matti/Herr Puntila and His Servant* (1960). At the time of shooting for *Wings of Desire* Bois was 86 years old and was well suited to represent a character who carries the heritage of the past with him.

Homer is the carrier of tradition, saying: 'I'm an old man with a broken voice, but the tale still rises from the depths, and the mouth, slightly opened, repeats it as clearly, as powerfully. A liturgy for which no one needs to be initiated to the meaning of words and sentences.' He goes on to lament, however, that today nobody seems to remember the storyteller: earlier people used to 'sit in a circle' but now they 'sit apart'. In the Staatsbibliothek, Homer opens a history book and looks at images from the past: 'My heroes are no longer the warriors and kings but the things of peace, one equal to the other.' But in the same breath he observes that nobody seems to tell stories of peace: 'Must I give up now?' Finally, he concludes: 'If I do give up then mankind will lose its storyteller.' Although the past unfolds in the form of memories of the ruined city, it seems evident that in the everyday life of the Berlin people historical stories remain on the margin. Homer is presented as the only conscious rememberer of the past, the maintainer of *mneme*. This can be interpreted as a reference to the German history trauma, the difficulty of talking about the past, even in the 1980s, although the most troubled decades had already passed (Kansteiner 2006: 3–6).

In Wenders' interpretation, the Berlin people live in the present-day, like a child, without knowing 'that it was a child'. The verses by Peter Handke are continued later, when Damiel's voice is heard saying: 'How can it be that I, who I am, didn't exist before I came to be, and that, someday, I, who I am, will no longer be who I am?' (Handke 2010: 8). These words refer to an identity problem, perhaps even to the fragility of life, asking what will ultimately survive or be able to continue over the course of time. What finally constitutes what we are? For Homer, understanding is closely linked with place, the surroundings where the individual lives, and with the continuity to which he has adjusted through his own actions and deeds. But in Berlin this connection has been broken.

Wings of Desire presents a cinematic interpretation of Richard Wagner's famous line in *Parsifal*: 'Zum Raum wird hier die Zeit', here time becomes space. In the scene where the angel Cassiel accompanies Homer, who is wandering near the Berlin Wall and looking for the Potsdamer Platz, the search for the temporal continuum modulates into spatial disorientation and loss. Homer tries desperately to find a place that has been important in his life but that no longer exists. Memory is not the only means of continuum for Homer; he seems to have a particular map in his mind that helps him to navigate in space.

Potsdamer Platz, near the Tiergarten, had been the centre of entertainment and business life in Berlin. Homer remembers the Potsdamer Platz as 'a lively place, tramways, horse-drawn carriages – and two cars, mine and that of the chocolate shop' – until, one day, everything had changed. Suddenly the place was full of flags and people were no longer friendly. According to Homer, the atmosphere of Potsdamer Platz had apparently been destroyed already before the war, but complete destruction came with World War II. After the bombing there was nothing left; the very heart of the city had disappeared. By the war the Potsdamer Platz became invisible, and the border between East and West Berlin was later cut exactly through the precinct; it remained unconstructed – except for the Wall, which was built in 1961. David Caldwell and Paul W. Rea (1991: 48) note interestingly that although Homer is presented as the poet of memory, the bearer of past experience, he does

Figure 1.6: Homer's search for Potsdamer Platz.

not seem to remember the turbulence that destroyed everything. It is as though the years 1933–45 had been erased from his mind. Why would he still be searching for the Potsdamer Platz if he knew and recalled it had been razed by war? Homer's character expresses the oblivion of the post-war era: he clearly has a map in his mind, a map of the past, but not one including the black holes of history. On the other hand, Homer's character embodies intense efforts to connect historical memory particularly with the time prior to 1933, the beginning of Nazi domination.

Later in the film Homer makes explicit reference to lost maps when he comments on how old roads, paths and traces have been forgotten:

> Only the Roman roads still lead somewhere, only the oldest traces lead anywhere. Where is the top of the pass here? Even the plains, like Berlin, have its hidden passes. And it's only there that my country, the country of the tale, begins. Why doesn't everyone see from childhood the passes, doors and crevices on the ground and above in the sky. If everyone saw them, there would be history without murder or war.

Homer's words seem to underline Wenders' original idea of peace. As long as 'the freedom of the city is limited', all 'passes' and 'doors' cannot be used or even seen. Instead of peace, the result has been catastrophe. Homer walks in the middle of an empty wasteland and concludes: 'I will not give up as long as I haven't found the Potsdamer Platz.' He has a map that no longer matches up with physical reality, and in an almost Deleuzean manner has constructed other maps superimposed upon it. Arguably, Homer's *mneme* has restored the lost map or has let it show dimly through the more recent layers. The same space means different places. For those Berlin people who no longer can recall the Potsdamer Platz, this same place looks like the border between East and West Berlin, a no-man's-land, even an emptiness that has been occluded by the Cold War.

Itineraries of city space

The narrative of *Wings of Desire* foregrounds angels who make observations about Berlin people and their concerns, but who are unable to participate in the real, bodily world. Even though the main characters are angels, the film is literally grounded, with the characters moving around mainly on foot. In an interview Wenders described *Wings of Desire* as a road movie, but vertical not horizontal. According to Assenka Oksiloff (1996: 32), 'its most dramatic sweeps are downward, tracing the perimeters of the city marked by the Wall, and inward, penetrating the complex identities that have formed within its boundaries'. Evidently, *Wings of Desire* builds on being above and below. The film starts with a hand writing down Peter Handke's verses. The next image shows the cloudy, grey sky above. Then an eye pops wide open, and Berlin people are shot from above, from an 'angel perspective'. Damiel is standing at the top of the Kaiser-Wilhelm-Gedächtniskirche, looking down sadly, and the children in the street seem to notice him. After these first shots the point of view ascends 'upward' and 'above': in an airplane, on the Siegessäule and on a trapeze. After the strong vertical tendency of the beginning, however, the film settles on earth, at the level of its inhabitants; the angels listen to people's thoughts, and Damiel blends into human life. It may furthermore be argued that the vertical gaze from above and the horizontal gaze navigating in space do not exclude but simply complement each other. In his *Cartographic Cinema*, Tom Conley (2007: 23–39) has analysed 'Icarian cinema', especially René Clair's *Paris qui dort/Paris Asleep* (1925), which starts with aerial shots over Paris. The first images map Paris and reveal its topography without people, almost like a sheet fallen from the hand of a cartographer. *Wings of Desire* too opens with an aerial shot, with topographical triangulation; but the map is living, in motion. After this, the film returns to earth and starts to move about in space.

Berlin in *Wings of Desire* consists in particular of walking routes, perhaps precisely of those lost paths that Homer wants to reach. The film, on the other hand, also has clearly fixed points, including historic monuments such as the Kaiser-Wilhelm-Gedächtniskirche and the Siegessäule, and modern constructions such as the Staatsbibliothek and the silent, untouched Wall. Liminal spaces between stability and mobility are the circus and the numerous hot-dog stands seen on the streets. The French circus company, named the Circus Alekan as a homage to the cinematographer Henri Alekan, stays in Berlin, and Damiel is enamoured of the beautiful trapeze artist Marion (Solveig Dommartin). It is in the circus that the black-and-white image suddenly bursts into colour for the first time, when Marion

Figure 1.7: Marion at the circus.

performs her magical tricks in the air. Marion becomes the object of Damiel's desire for life. Damiel gives up his wings, and perhaps receives a new kind of 'wings of desire'. At the end of the film the circus continues on its journey, but love and hope for the future remain.

As already noted, after the cartographic opening shots *Wings of Desire* remains to a large extent on the ground. This is particularly prominent at the end, when Damiel relinquishes his angelic identity and becomes a human being. He awakens by the Wall, sees his hand bleeding and understands his new humanness. The environment is deliberately depicted in such a way as to make the coordinates of the place observable. Damiel is in the Waldemarstrasse; from there he starts strolling ahead, undoubtedly without exactly knowing where to go. The spectator then observes the Glogauer Strasse and the Oranienstrasse, and Damiel's steps lead him through Kreuzberg, a part of the city that was known in the 1980s as an area with many artists. At Goebenstrasse 6, Damiel stops in front of a second-hand shop to buy some clothes; he now seems to be in Schöneberg, further away from the Wall, in streets that are 'walkable' for him. Locations can be identified later as well. Although the cinema has the power to create imaginary places and to connect unexpected spaces, Wim Wenders has purposefully constructed a walking route that has its equivalent in the West Berlin of 1987. Damiel walks almost ten kilometres, from the Wall to the Schöneberg. Simultaneously he looks for Marion, encounters and enters a rock club, and participates in a Nick Cave gig, probably like many of those travellers who knew West Berlin in the 1980s as a centre for alternative culture. In the course of this itinerary,

Figure 1.8: The wall at Waldemarstrasse.

Figure 1.9: At Goebenstrasse 6.

Wenders has documented a city that vanished soon after the demolition of the Wall. As the architect Fritz Neumeyer (1990: 51) put it, only a few years after the release of the film: 'In *Wings of Desire*, Wenders has memorialized this mythically laden, damaged city with its own poetics of space just in time, before the reconstruction and beautification of the city claims all space.'

Damiel's itinerary is his march towards humanity, a result of his transformation and a kind of reverse Via Dolorosa, ending with a sense of freedom. At the same time that the Berlin Wall is still standing firmly in place, Damiel breaks the invisible wall that has prevented him from participating in human life – now he is a Berliner and strolls the streets through the city. If Homer has lost his map, Damiel does not have one either, since everything is new for him. In retrospect it can be argued that his map has in fact been recorded on film, as an itinerary that a few years later would have looked quite different.

The Wall and the fragmented history

Following its release, *Wings of Desire* provoked vigorous discussion: film critics and cultural theorists of the late 1980s and early 1990s often characterized it as a postmodern work. *Wings of Desire* describes a fragmentary world, where grand narratives are no longer valid. Especially at the beginning of the film the world resembles a compilation of singular, individual perspectives. Brigitte Peucker (1996: 132) has described its image of the city: 'For Wenders, Berlin is the sum of its subjectivities, and each man is indeed an island linked, however, by a network comparable to the roads connecting monuments and public places.' The film foregrounds the human experience, but beyond each subjectivity there is an emptiness and a distance that have to be overcome.

The motif of distance and difference is encapsulated in the Wall. Berlin was above all the city of the Wall, and one could only imagine about the world beyond the stone barrier. There are references to the Wall that splits the city throughout *Wings of Desire*. As Peter Handke's poem puts it:

> Why am I me, and why not you?
> Why am I here, and why not there?
> When did time begin, and where does space end?

(Handke 2010: 8)[1]

Without doubt people living on the western side of the Wall frequently asked themselves: Why am I here, in a city surrounded by East Germany, and not 'over there', on the other side of the Iron Curtain? The post-war division of Germany had split families apart, and the border was thus closely linked with identities and personal histories. At the beginning, simultaneously with Handke's words on the soundtrack, the camera pans and shows the city on the other side of the border. There had of course been other cinematic treatments of this dividedness – for example Reinhold Hauff's *Der Mann auf der Mauer/The Man on the Wall* (1982), where the division into East and West Berlin is described in a tragicomical manner; but *Wings of Desire* gives a more philosophical treatment of the subject.

In *Wings of Desire*, Damiel and Cassiel watch the everyday life of Berlin people and compare notes; their role, however, as Cassiel comments, is to remain at a distance, almost as though behind the wall: 'Do no more than look. Assemble, testify, preserve. Remain spirit. Keep your distance. Keep your word.'[2] The life of the angels was at a 'distance', there was an irremovable obstacle between them and the ordinary people. At the same time, however, the angels represent continuity, history and memory. They are not bound by the borderlines of the physical world and can, if they so wish, go everywhere, even through the Wall. This is exemplified in the scene where Damiel and Cassiel surprisingly pass through the Wall to the other side, and the spectator sees street scenes from East Berlin. Angels can also move about freely in the guarded border zones, simply because they are invisible to humans.

When Damiel finally becomes human, he steps into a world where transgressing the Wall is impossible. After Damiel has awakened in the Waldemarstrasse the film turns completely into colour, and the colourful graffiti on the Wall seem to be particularly foregrounded by the director. Damiel's walk, towards the heart of West Berlin life, begins. Once he is human, he has to recognize the reality of the political border that permeates the city. *Wings of Desire* seems to emphasize that Damiel's future now lies in the human world, in its actuality, its *Jetztzeit*, rather than in utopian visions. While *Wings of Desire* has later been seen in terms

Figure 1.10: Cassiel at Siegessäule.

of what actually happened a few years later, and interpreters have been eager to find signs of the forthcoming destruction of the Wall, the immaterial trespassing of the angels across the border can hardly be construed as such a sign. The film refers to memories of the pre-Wall era, embodied in the character of Homer. It moves between past and present, and does not actually say anything about the future. It is evident, however, that the political transformation of 1989 also changed the way *Wings of Desire* has been interpreted. Wenders himself connected his work with the destruction of the Berlin Wall, as shown by the fact that he made a sequel to *Wings of Desire*, titled *Faraway, So Close!* (1993), describing the period after 1989. Now the angels, Cassiel (Otto Sander) and Raphaella (Nastassia Kinski) have settled at the top of the Branderburger Tor to observe the tensions of the newly unified city; but the borderline between angels and humans is still there.

While in the reality of the year 1987 the grip of the Cold War was already losing strength, it would be anachronistic to interpret *Wings of Desire* as a prefiguration of things to come. Again, the idea of the wall is central. In emphasizing that the film is a 'vertical road movie', Wim Wenders was implying that there was not much space in West Berlin in 1987 for a horizontal road movie – but in the end there is a great deal of horizontal movement in the film, on foot. It is clear that the consciousness of the presence of the wall is significant in *Wings of Desire*. The idea of the wall, or the border, has numerous ramifications in the film. The wall surrounds angels who cannot interact with humans, and it frames very concretely the city space that prevents Homer from walking in the places where the Potsdamer Platz used to be located. It may be argued that even the ability of the angels to walk through the Wall points to its opposite: the inability of humans to transgress the political border. There are references to other forms of trespass in the film, to borders that are – and have been – trespassable. Right from the start the Berlin people are portrayed as a multicultural community, and the quick sketches of everyday life at the beginning of the film include, for example, a Turkish family. In 1987, despite its closed, isolated position, Berlin was open to immigrants. Cultural boundaries were breaking down at the same time that the border between east and west, Kennedy's 'frontier of freedom', pervaded the city as an insurmountable obstacle. The presence of the Wall, and the restraints it alludes to, seems once again to foster its opposite, the openness of the city. The American actor Peter Falk arrives in Berlin by plane, almost as though suggesting that an 'air bridge' or airlift has always been important for Berlin. By these means, through its mixture of openness and introversion, Wim Wenders' *Wings of Desire* has crucially influenced the ways borders in 1980s Europe have since been imagined. The ideological conflict was still definitely there, but the change had already begun.

Wings of Desire raises the idea of the wall to a philosophical level by emphasizing the specificity of the border. These borders can be deciphered from all the details of the urban space. The driver states:

Are there still borders? More than ever! Each street has its own borderline. Between each plot, there's a strip of no-man's-land disguised as a hedge or a ditch. Whoever dares, will fall into booby traps or be hit by laser rays. The trout are really torpedoes. Every home owner, or even every tenant nails his name plate on the door, like a coat of arms and studies the morning paper as if he were a world leader.

According to the same driver, the Germans are in fact divided into numerous fragments:

Germany has crumbled into as many small states as there are individuals. And these small states are mobile. Everyone carries his own state with him, and demands a toll when another wants to enter. A fly caught in amber, or a leather bottle. So much for the border. But one can only enter each state with a password. The German soul of today can only be conquered and governed by one who arrives at each small state with the password. Fortunately, no one is currently in a position to do this. So … everyone migrates, and waves his one-man-state flag in all earthly directions. Their children already shake their rattles and drag their filth around them in circles.

This somewhat extravagant statement can be interpreted to mean that the gaze is directed less at the gap between the eastern and western blocs and more at West Germany and its fragmentary and distinctive character. This in fact recalls nineteenth-century discourse on Germany, before the *Reichsgründung* in 1871. Friedrich Nietzsche, for example, saw Germany as an 'atomistic chaos', full of egotistic aspirations (Salmi 1999: 38). In a sense, *Wings of Desire* presents the same thesis. It also underlines that it was particularly this atomistic heterogeneity that was the weakness that enabled totalitarian rule to emerge, and that despite all individual boundaries led to the German *Sonderweg*.

Conclusion

In *Wings of Desire*, the Berlin Wall seems to be everywhere. Ultimately this wall becomes a symbolic barrier: between Germans, and perhaps between human beings in general, there is a wall that everyone carries within themselves. There are borders that are never transgressed. This abstract meaning becomes obvious in Damiel's experience: 'I've been outside long enough. Absent long enough. Long enough out of the world. Let me enter the history of the world.' But then again one can ask if this is also a reference to Berlin itself, to the city that in the aftermath of World War II had been abruptly banished from history. The city surrounded by the Wall could not be the same metropolis and signifier that it had been in the 1920s. The Wall embodied the limits of this possibility.

Wings of Desire was an exceptional rendering of borders, sites and itineraries in 1980s cinema. Its reception history remains to be studied in detail, but it seems to be intertwined with the political changes of the early 1990s. In the aftermath of the Cold War, the American economist Francis Fukuyama (1992) gained worldwide publicity with his controversial claim that the end of the struggle between ideologies would mean the end of history. What Wenders is arguing, already before the dissolution of the ideological divide, is that there are always several overlapping borderlines, tensions and struggles: history may be forgotten, it may come back as variety of *anamnesis*, as Benjaminian flashes, or it may be submerged into oblivion – but it can never end. There seem to be several different notions of history overlapping in *Wings of Desire*: there is a consciousness of the national past, the Grand Narrative, represented by the Gedächtniskirche and the Siegessäule, there are unbidden memories that come to the fore, unavoidably, as remembrances of the trauma; but the film also offers an ahistorical interpretation as a counterforce to these, the idea of Germany as an assemblage of discrete, separate interests which ultimately contributed to the catastrophes of the twentieth century. Still, there is a passion for history in *Wings of Desire*. If the fall of the Berlin Wall signified for Fukuyama the end of history, *Wings of Desire* speaks strongly in favour of history as something to return to.

References

Benjamin, W. (1992), *Illuminations* (ed. H. Arendt, trans. H. Zohn), London: Fontana/ HarperCollins.

Bernard-Donals, M. F. (2009), *Forgetful Memory: Representation and Remembrance in the Wake of the Holocaust*, Albany: State University of New York Press.

Brady, M. and Leal, J. (2011), *Wim Wenders and Peter Handke: Collaboration, Adaptation, Recomposition*, Internationale Forschungen zur Allgemeinen und Vergleichenden Literaturwissenschaft, New York: Editions Rodopi.

Brager, B.L. (2004), *The Iron Curtain: The Cold War in Europe*, New York: Chelsea House Publishers.

Caldwell, D. and Rea, P.W. (1991), 'Handke's and Wenders's Wings of Desire: Transcending Postmodernism', *The German Quarterly* 64:1, pp. 46–54.

Casarino, C. (1990), 'Fragments on "Wings of Desire" (Or, Fragmentary Representation as Historical Necessity)', *Social Text*, 24, pp. 167–81.

Conley, T. (1997), *Cartographic Cinema*, Minneapolis: University of Minnesota Press.

Cook, R.F. (1997), 'Angels, Fiction, and History in Berlin: Wings of Desire', in R. F. Cook and G. Gemunden (eds), *The Cinema of Wim Wenders: Image, Narrative, and the Postmodern Condition*, Detroit, MI: Wayne State University Press, pp. 163–90.

Fukuyama, F. (1992), *The End of History and the Last Man*, New York: Free Press.

Gedmin, J. (1992), *The Hidden Hand: Gorbachev and the Collapse of East Germany*, Washington DC: The AEI Press.

Handke, P. (2010), Song of Childhood, *Wings of Desire: A Film by Wim Wenders*. Booklet. Blu-ray Disc AXM608, London: Axiom Films, p. 8.

Kaes, A. (1989), *From Hitler to Heimat: The Return of History as Film*, Cambridge, MA.: Harvard University Press.

Kansteiner, W. (2006), *In Pursuit of German Memory: History, Television, and Politics after Auschwitz*, Athens, OH: Ohio University Press.

Lindström, M. (2010), *Tarina kaipauksen kaupungista. Kylmän sodan Berliinin mielikuvat elokuvassa Berliinin taivaan alla 1987*, MA thesis, Turku: University of Turku, Department of Cultural History.

Maslin, J. (1988), 'The Rage of Angels', *New York Times,* 29 April.

Mur, C. (2004), *The Berlin Wall: An Issue in History*, San Diego, CA: Greenhaven Press.

Neumeyer, F. (1990), 'OMA's Berlin: The Polemic Island and the City', *Assemblage*, 11, pp. 36–53.

Oksiloff, A. (1996), 'Eden is Burning: Wim Wenders' Techniques of Synaesthesia', *The German Quarterly*, 69: 1, pp. 32–47.

Paneth, I. (1988), 'Wim and His Wings', *The Film Quarterly*, 42: 1, pp. 2–8.

Perry, N. (1998), *Hyperreality and Global Culture*, London: Routledge.

Peucker, B. (1996), 'Wim Wenders' Berlin: Images and the Real', in B. Becker-Cantarino (ed.), *Berlin in Focus: Cultural Transformations in Germany*, Westport, CT: Greenwood Press, pp. 125–38.

Raskin, R. (1999), '"It's Images You Can Trust Less and Less." An Interview with Wim Wenders on *Wings of Desire*', *p.o.v. A Danish Journal of Film Studies*, 8, pp. 5–20.

Saint-Exupéry, A. de (1942), *Flight to Arras* (trans. L. Galantière), New York: Harcourt Brace & Company.

Salmi, H. (1999), *Imagined Germany: Richard Wagner's National Utopia*, New York: Peter Lang.

Samuel, R. (1996), *Theatres of Memory: Past and Present in Contemporary Culture*, London: Verso.

Schwarz, U. (2004), *John F. Kennedy, 1917–1963*, Vacaville, CA: Bounty Books.

Steinberg, M.P. (ed.) (1996), *Walter Benjamin and the Demands of History*, Ithaca, NY: Cornell University Press.

Wenders, W. (1991), 'An Attempted Description of an Indescribable Film: From the first treatment for *Wings of Desire*', in W. Wender, *The Logic of Images: Essays and Conversations* (trans. M. Hoffman), London: Faber & Faber, pp. 73–83.

Notes

1   Warum bin ich ich und warum nicht du?
    Warum bin ich hier und warum nicht dort?
    Wann begann die Zeit und wo endet der Raum?
2   In German: 'Nichts weiter tun als anschauen, sammeln, bezeugen, beglaubigen, wahren. Geist bleiben. Im Abstand bleiben. Im Wort bleiben.'

Chapter 2

'What's Wrong with a Cowboy in Hamburg?': New German Cinema and the German-American Cultural Frontier

Jacqui Miller
Liverpool Hope University

It all began in Germany'. With those words, answering the question 'Are you a real American?' Richard/Ricky Murphy (Karl Scheydt), the eponymous American soldier of Rainer Werner Fassbinder's 1970 film, *Der Amerikanische Soldat/The American Soldier* sums up the essential themes of this chapter. Germany's distant and recent histories have meant that it is a country of shifting borders and consequently of fragmentary and ephemeral identity. The geographical borders have been in flux across historical eras, even as recently as reunification in 1990. This spatial flux has given rise to a yet more complex psychological and cultural shifting. To complete Ricky's answer: 'Once upon a time there was a little boy. He flew over the great pond'. Ricky is referring to his literal journey to America after World War II, but Germany also embraced American culture during this period. Just as Ricky returned to the Germany for which he professes fondness, so too, Germany's cultural relationship with America has been complex. Following the war, West Germany forged the Economic Miracle through funding provided by America's Marshall Plan. The psychological price it might have been said to pay was the *Tätergeneration*'s (perpetrator generation) silence about the past and the *Nachgeborenen*'s (those born after the event) anger at their failure to take the post-war opportunity to admit to and atone for complicity in the Nazi era; the cultural price being the *Tätergeneration*'s immersion in the palliation of American commodification and the *Nachgeborenen*'s rejection of this apparent cultural colonialism. This position is summed up by Cousins: 'A generation gap had opened up between German baby boomers and their parents who had either voted for Adolf Hitler or had endured him. An economic boom in West Germany began to numb the guilt felt by the country over the atrocities of the Holocaust' (Cousins 2004: 352–53).

Although the perspective offered by Cousins is usually taken as given, in contrast to most works on New German Cinema and its relationship with America, this chapter demonstrates a more complex interplay between post-war Germany, American culture and the representation both of that era and the present day in New German Cinema. The chapter will begin by setting a historical context for New German Cinema considering the post-war *Trümmerfilme* (rubble film), *Die Mörder sind unter uns/The Murderers are among Us* (Wolfgang Staudte, 1946) with regard to its establishment of themes that would subsequently resonate, particularly the shifting of borders and the reconstitution of Germany, followed by the Heimat (homeland) films of the 1950s, arguing that the latter at least sub-textually demonstrate an awareness of the post-Nazi trauma. This will be followed by a close critical analysis of five films from early New German Cinema, *Liebe ist kälter als der Tod/Love is Colder than Death* (Fassbinder, 1969), *The American Soldier*, *Katzelmacher* (Fassbinder, 1969), *Im Lief der Zeit/Kings of the Road* (Wim Wenders, 1976) and *Der Amerikanische Freund/The American Friend* (Wenders, 1977). It will be shown that, although there may be some expected critiques of the *Tätergeneration* and ambivalence towards American culture, it is erroneous to see post-war Germany as entirely complicit in a culture of denial, and the *Nachgeborenen* have found much to criticize in their own generation. Moreover, although American culture is certainly a source of fascination, it has not simply been imposed upon or injected into German mores, but, through layers of exchange has provided a site to work through the past and arrive at a genuinely German sensibility. Accordingly, for Wenders, Dennis Hopper's cowboy has a global frontier; both America and Hamburg.

Die Mörder sind unter uns: Post-war amnesia and aspiration

Immediately following the war Germany found itself in a state of literal disintegration. In political terms this was expressed by its partitioning into four Allied zones: French, American, British and Soviet, until the 1949 division into the Soviet Eastern German Democratic Republic and the Western Federal Republic of Germany. Although this particular national border shifting was unique to Germany, it shared a micro-level decomposition with many countries; the bomb sites which represented a loss of place throughout their cities. The first post-war films made in Germany used these settings for *Trümmerfilme* beginning with *Die Mörder sind unter uns*. The term *Trümmerfilme* is obviously specific to Germany, but films set amongst ruined buildings and bombsites were made across the globe. What is particularly Germanic is the look and tone of its *Trümmerfilme*. What might be termed British rubble films such as *Hue and Cry* (Charles Crichton, 1947) and *The Magnet* (Charles Frend, 1950) are brightly lit and optimistic, seeing the bomb-sites as places of liminality where class, ethnic and gender conventions may break down, and, dominated as they are by children, who seem to swarm out of, and almost grow from these sites, they seem to be places of regeneration and new possibilities. In contrast, *Die Mörder sind unter uns* draws heavily on past German film style in its expressionistic use of canted angles and low-key lighting, but also sets an agenda revisited from a range of perspectives by subsequent German cinema (see Figure 2.1).

The film concerns the immediate post-war relationship between a concentration camp survivor (although her reason for being there is not articulated), Susanne (Hildegard Knef) and an alcoholic doctor, Hans (Ernst Wilhelm Borschert). We learn that Hans drinks to blot out memories of being ordered to kill women and children by his commanding officer, Brückner (Arno Paulson). Discovering that Brückner is now thriving in the post-war economy, Hans almost shoots him in retribution for his war crimes but is prevented by Susanne who says 'We cannot pass sentence' and who makes Hans realize that instead

Figure 2.1: This image from the opening scene of *Die Mörder sind unter uns* shows the bleak Germanic style of the German 'rubble film' with its sharply canted angle, as well as the ruined buildings signifying a decomposed border, or frontier. The abandoned helmet in the foreground foreshadows Brückner's part in the 'Economic Miracle'.

'We must press charges. Demand atonement on behalf of millions of innocent murder victims'.

Although made in the Soviet occupied zone (Allan 1999: 1), *Die Mörder sind unter uns* is an appropriate starting point because it prefigures West German themes that this article examines in relation to Fassbinder and Wenders, most particularly the alleged 'amnesia' demonstrated in the post-war era by the *Tätergeneration* – Germans who were adult during the war years. Certainly it is coy about the Holocaust; we know Susanne has been in a concentration camp, but we do not learn why, and her glowing beauty and lack of traumatic memory seems to preclude extreme suffering. A newspaper headline proclaims '2 million were gassed: Report from Auschwitz' but this is not directly discussed at any point in the film, although Susanne's closing reference to 'millions of innocent victims' may be an oblique comment. As to Brückner's orders to kill 'women and children', although this is the cause of Hans' turmoil, it diffuses German war crimes into the kinds of atrocities routinely practiced throughout military history, and certainly perpetrated by both sides in World War II. Moreover, *Die*

Mörder sind unter uns prefigures several strands in the 1950s Heimat films beloved of the *Tätergeneration* which would again be addressed, particularly by Fassbinder, in films such as *Katzelmacher* (1969). Early in the film, Susanne is told that it is easy to forget the past if you have something to aim for. She becomes fixated by work and transforms the previously desolate apartment she shares with Hans into the paradigm of a bourgeois home. Brückner's business, turning military helmets into saucepans, is almost a parodic prophecy of the domestic Economic Miracle, the miracle, it could be argued, only made possible through the war's occurrence (see Figure 2.1). Certainly Brückner has a messianic gleam, at Christmas telling his employees they are 'working hard to build the Germany we all love'. However, although *Die Mörder sind unter uns* presents these aims as unequivocal aspirations, they are presented more ambiguously by the Heimat films, and are made ironic by Fassbinder.

Hints are also made in *Die Mörder sind unter uns* to encroaching American culture; Brückner laughs that his eldest son has recently been caught smoking an American cigarette, however it is less amusing to reflect that such cigarettes were the most frequently used commodity of barter between G. I.s and German prostitutes. Amongst film scholars from Thomas Elsaessar's comment on 'the hegemony of Hollywood over Europe' (Elsaessar 1976: 1) onwards, it has become a given that the course of West German film from the 1940s until the early 1960s was a product of American economic and cultural policy; an apparent desire to 're-educate' the German psyche away from Nazism thinly veiling the imperative to continue Hollywood's economic as much as ideological dominance (Gomery and Pafort-Overduin 2011: 303). In fact, it was apparent early in America's involvement in World War II that the Office of War Information wished to avoid inflammatory anti-German propaganda (Koppes and Black 1987: 108). Films such as the comedy-gangster *All Through the Night* (Vincent Sherman, 1941) made a clear distinction between Nazis (in this instance, Peter Lorre as Pepi) and 'good' Germans (the baker, Mr Miller played by Ludwig Stossel) – a phrase which now has such resonance it gave the name to a World War II-set neo-noir, *The Good German* (Steven Soderbergh, 2006) – and some films made during the war, such as *The Moon is Down* (Irving Pichel, 1943) went so far as to suggest that not all Nazis were inherently bad, but that they had become swept up in an evil credo. Partly such films wished to avoid antagonizing the domestic market; German-Americans were a significant element of the population, but there was also a longer-term strategy which recognized, even during the war, that America was likely to regard Germany as a post-war economic partner and so used cinema as an advance form of rehabilitation. Thus, while as early as 1944, *Meet Me in St Louis* (Vincente Minnelli), through lyrics such as 'Next year all our troubles will be out of sight' implied that the war would soon be over, and through its glossy *mise-en-scène* and rapturous depiction of the 1904 World's Fair posited a vision of American technology and consumerism that would define the 'American Century', it is unsurprising that the United States sought to replicate, through the device of cinema, this fusion of economic and ideological domination in Germany; its success would fuel the *Nachgeborenen's* anger against the *Tätergeneration*.

Heimat reconsidered: undercurrents in the 'cottage industry'

The structure of the immediate post-World War II German film industry was the result of a set of circumstances made up of geography, economics and ideology and again highlights the flux of Germany's 'borders' in each regard. Germany's position on the cusp of the Soviet bloc meant it was vulnerable territorially, a vulnerability that might be best protected not by occupying forces but dogma. This was captured by US secretary of State James F. Byrnes' 1947 statement: 'What we have to do now is not to make the world safe for democracy, but to make it safe for the United States' (Elsaesser 1976: 2). Economics played its part through the organization of the film sector. Decartelisation legislation effectively prevented the re-emergence of a centralized German film industry. Though supportive of rebuilding cinemas which became German-owned, distributors were mainly dependent upon American funding and most crucially it was very difficult for independent production companies to secure the funds needed for consolidation. Coupled with the flood of Hollywood films entering Germany, the home industry did not attempt to compete on the world screen and became what Elsaesser has described as 'a Bavarian cottage industry' (Elsaesser 1976: 3).

This 'cottage industry' produced the Heimat films of the 1950s. As Elsaesser's words imply, it has been axiomatic to regard Heimat product as at best, bland, at worst, risible, consisting of 'gynaecologists getting their patients pregnant, neo-imperialist "Sissi" films dreaming of Viennese pastry and Hapsburg glories, the Bavarian mountain musicals, the beer-mug and lederhosen comedies' (Elsaesser 1976: 3) and this judgement is not helped by the fact that Heimat was originally a vehicle for Third Reich cinema as 'the most convenient form for offering a romanticized, but completely depoliticized, view of country and nation' (Hake 2002: 76). Anton Kaes argues 'Nothing was more insidious to the young [New German Cinema] directors than the archetypal German genre, the provincial Heimat film with its unbroken tradition from the 1930s to the early 1960s' (Kaes 1996: 617). However, subsequent re-evaluation of Heimat has found that the oeuvre, in its various forms, in fact engaged in debate with key post war anxieties, which challenges the whole issue of the *Tätergeneration's* 'amnesia'. Rachel Palfreyman recognizes that 'critical and [...] iconoclastic filmmakers [...] consciously seek usable German traditions' in their work, citing specifically Fassbinder's engagement with Douglas Sirk's melodramas. Although Palfreyman goes on to note that post-2000 German filmmakers are making 'myriad efforts to modify, subvert or participate in the Heimat genre' (Palfreyman 2010: 147), I would argue that scrutiny of Heimat reveals its prefiguration of many of the themes addressed by the earlier work of Fassbinder and Wenders. Heimat issues and their subsequent exploration include the figure of the stranger in a community in *Katzelmacher*, the insertion of an Afro-German child into a bourgeois family in *Rio das Mortes* (Fassbinder, 1970) and generational conflict in *Kings of the Road*.

Heimat is seen to be particularly tainted by its association with the 'Economic Miracle', the term given to the 1950s project which again fused finance, from the American Marshall Plan, with ideology, the conservative pragmatism of Chancellor Konrad Adenauer, to produce *Wohlstandsgesellschaft* (the affluent society), stereotypically marked by repressive bourgeois practices as a means of obfuscating an uncomfortable past. Nonetheless, 1950s cinema, whilst appearing to medicate its audience with the delights of consumerism in sub-genres such as travelogues and musicals, made veiled censure through its relentless stress on 'an aggressive desire for self-advancement that not only revealed its petty-bourgeois or working-class origins but also acknowledged the relationship between sex, money and power' especially in the spheres of petty crime (Hake 2002: 107). These themes would reappear again and again for Fassbinder and Wenders.

A New German Cinema: the *Nachgeborenen* confront the *Tätergeneration*?

Heimat and the other German genres of the 1950s were highly prolific and attracted significant domestic audiences. However, their outwardly conservative perspective and lack of overseas appeal, coupled with the restrictive organization in the film industry outlined above meant that, whatever their influence on subsequent filmmakers and retrospective interest for cultural historians, during the 1950s, Germany, probably without exception, failed to produce any trailblazing films that marked at least part of the production of countries such as France, Italy, England and the United States. Exacerbated by a decline in cinema audiences shared by Western countries experiencing a television boom, the early 1960s saw a climacteric: at the Oberhausen Film Festival, 1962, twenty-six writers and filmmakers demanded a *junger deutscher film* (young German cinema) insisting:

> The collapse of the commercial German film industry finally removes the economic basis for a mode of filmmaking whose attitude and practices we reject. With it, the new film has a chance to come to life. […] This new cinema needs new forms of freedom: from the conventions and habits of the established industry, from intervention by commercial partners, and finally freedom from the tutelage of other vested interests. We have specific plans for the artistic, formal and economic realisation of this new German cinema. We are collectively prepared to take the economic risks. The old cinema is dead. We believe in the new. (Cook 1996: 659)

In the short term, this stage of the *junger deutscher film* produced few films of merit but the influence of the Oberhausen manifesto, quoted above, caused the state liberalization of grants for film production. This was the last piece in the triptych described at the time by Elsaesser as 'a triangle made up of the German film industry, the hegemony of Hollywood over Europe, and the media policy of the Federal German government. The latter especially has thrown up contradictions of which today's film-makers are the ambiguous beneficiaries' (Elsaesser 1976: 1). This confluence of circumstances facilitated the renaissance of German film art in the New German Cinema, occurring a decade or so after such movements had swept Britain, France and Italy, but almost in parallel with the New Hollywood in America. Comprising numerous directors, which, unusually, featured several women, the New German

Cinema was not homogenous or unified. Its geographical production split between Berlin and Munich, funding competition created an arena in which it was 'every man for himself' (Elsaesser 1976: 1), and it was perhaps inevitable within a group of talented artists working from the late 1960s to the early 1980s that there would be a diversity of approaches, indeed as a movement it too can be said to have shifting ideological and stylistic borders. The two directors singled out in this chapter have quite different places in the New German Cinema arising from their places in its history, and quite simply from themselves. Fassbinder is seen as its prolific, autodidact 'enfant terrible' whose death from a drug overdose in 1982 at the age of 37 having directed 40 films, many of which he wrote and acted in, as well as his numerous credits for theatre and television writing, acting and direction, marked the movement's final close. Wenders began his directorial career slightly later than Fassbinder, and, of course, has had a long and continuing career, of which the New German Cinema was only its first phase. Overall, it can be argued that his films reflect his highly educated (although dropping out of university, he began programmes both in medicine and philosophy) intellectual outlook.

Nonetheless, the New German Cinema was and is a recognizable movement and all involved were, as Elsaesser again describes, 'products of the historical and (film) political conjunction that both frustrates their work and makes it possible' (Elsaesser 1976: 1). The historical context has since been extensively theorized. Added to the tension between the *Tätergeneration* and the *Nachgeborenen*, Jörn Rüsen and Friedrich Jaeger have identified generational responses to World War II, including those of adult sensibility in 1945 (silence and negation) and 1968 (critical moral distance from the 1945 generation, compounded by identification with the victims of National Socialism) (see Palfreyman 2010: 146–48). Their time of birth would assign all the New German Cinema directors places in the *Nachgeborenen* and 1968 generation, and it has been taken for granted amongst film scholarship that this fuels their cinematic perspective:

> The generation of young filmmakers represented by *das neue Kino* grew up in an Americanized economically prospering Germany; they were only dimly aware of the Nazi past. Cultural historians have pointed out that since the collapse of the "Thousand-Year Reich", the German people have suffered from a kind of collective amnesia about the "brown years" of Nazi rule, 1933–45. The shock and humiliation of defeat, the appalling devastation of the material environment, the partitioning of the country, and the collective guilt for the most terrible acts of barbarism and genocide ever committed – all conspire to rob Germany of its cultural identity by robbing it of its past. (Cook 1996: 661)

Certainly these issues, Americanization and German cultural identity and historicity, are key, both directors having complex relationships with the two countries that seem to define their shifting cultural border, and it is important to recognize that this relationship was in flux throughout their careers. Paul Grainge, Mark Jancovich and Sharon Monteith say of Wenders: '[He] has frequently attacked the supposed colonization of the German mind by

Hollywood, both in his films and in print, but his films have remained fascinated with American popular culture and draw heavily on it' (Grainge, Jancovich and Monteith 2007: 410). Juliane Lorenz, who worked with Fassbinder at the end of his life, sums up his opus as 'the expression of an era, between 1966 and 1982, in a country which was then another Germany and which no longer exists' (Lorenz 1997: x). Fassbinder – perhaps because of his early death – did not have the American, or at least German-American, career of Wenders. However, he was certainly not only fascinated by American culture, but also found the definitions of success and America to be synonymous. Robert Katz recounts time Fassbinder spent in New York a few weeks before he died. A stranger walked up and thanked him for his films, which he loved. Apparently the director 'puffed up with joy' having achieved what Katz believed Fassbinder saw as his ultimate accolade: 'You are famous. America knows your name' (Katz and Berling 1987: 10). Indeed, just as Fassbinder referenced the work of Hollywood directors such as Douglas Sirk, his own work would influence future generations in Hollywood, such as the Coen Brothers' homage to the end scene of *Fox and His Friends* (Fassbinder, 1975) in *Miller's Crossing* (Joel Cohen, 1990) (Lewis 2002: 114). Conversely, as Fassbinder's position as a leading young director of increasingly international influence became secure, he felt an increasing self-onus to engage with his own place in German film history by focusing directly on that history. Saying 'As a German I can only make German films' (Shattuc 1995: 74) his later work included the 'FGR trilogy': *Die Ehe der Maria Braun/The Marriage of Maria Braun* (1979), *Lola* (1981) and *Die Sehnsucht der Veronika Voss/Veronika Voss* (1982) as well as *Lili Marleen* (1980) 'in which he rewrote the postwar years' (Hake 2002: 157). This transcultural slippage was summed up by Fassbinder's comment that 'he wanted to be "a German Hollywood director"' (Shattuc 1995: 74), an observation that will now be explored through three of his early films.

Love is Colder than Death: A New German Franco-American neo-noir

Love is Colder than Death is Fassbinder's first full-length feature film, a contemporary Munich-set urban gangster *ménage à trois* between petty crook, Franz (Fassbinder), his prostitute girlfriend, Johanna (Hanna Schygulla) and Bruno (Ulli Lommel) who might or might not be employed to betray Bruno to the 'syndicate' he has resisted. It is dedicated to three film directors, Claude Chabrol, Eric Rohmer and Jean-Marie Straub, the first two being leading figures within, the third associated with, the French *nouvelle vague*. From the outset, this signals the film, which is Fassbinder's most complex in terms of transculturated representations, and his relationship with those images. It both homages classical Hollywood and plays with contemporary Franco-American cinematic exchange but in so doing uses these as a conduit through which to critique modern Germany.

The opening dedication surely presumes some reverence for French filmmakers who had been Fassbinder's predecessors and whose contemporary he had become. This seems to be borne out by *Love is Colder than Death*'s cinematographer, Dietrich Lohman, talking about that phase of their collaboration: '"Nouvelle Vague" was very popular in those days, the so-called film noir, black-and-white and very evocative. We often tried to imitate the style, particularly in the early days, with *Love is Colder than Death, Gods of the Plague,* and *The American Soldier*' (Lorenz 1997: 84). However, in an interview specifically discussing *Love is Colder than Death*, while giving some praise to the New Wave, Fassbinder nonetheless damns with faint praise, saying of Jean-Luc Godard's films: 'I like them all, even *Two or Three Things I Know about Her*' (Fassbinder, Töteberg and Lensing 1992: 7) and also distances *Love is Colder than Death* from the French directors: 'If I'd made a film that was narrated conventionally all the way through, it would have negated itself, and then it would have been like a film by Chabrol, at best. If I'd done it differently, without the crime plot, simply using alienation technique, that would have had the same result; it might have turned out like a Goddard film' (Fassbinder, Töteberg and Lensing 1992: 5).

It is difficult to deny *Love is Colder than Death*'s *nouvelle vague* influences. Paul Cooke cites its 'echoes' of *A bout de souffle/Breathless* (Jean-Luc Godard, 1960) (Cooke 2007: 166), but I would argue it has much closer links to *Le Samouraï* (Jean-Pierre Melville, 1967). It is conjectural whether Fassbinder was familiar with Melville's work before he made *Love is Colder than Death*, but, as Joachim von Mengershausen said in the interview cited above, "Lommel [...] seems a bit, and not just a bit, like Delon in *Le Samourai*", a line of questioning the director ignored' (Fassbinder, Töteberg and Lensing 1992: 5). Certainly Bruno's costume of trench coat and Homburg closely replicates *Le Samourai*'s Jef Costello (Alain Delon), but that might just be a function of both characters' relationship with American noir gangsters. More telling is their shared relationship – almost 'friendship' – with costume; before going on a 'hit', Jef ritualistically strokes his hat brim as a form of comfort, and when Bruno's hat is taken off by a prostitute he quickly replaces it, acting as if a chink has been made in his self-assumed armour. Even more uncanny if it is mere coincidence, one of the cars Bruno and Franz steal is a black Citroën DS21, the car Jef steals on the way to his fatal hit, and which is one of the icons of his legendary 'cool'. However, the cultural triangulation continues. With regard to this film Fassbinder is more willing to acknowledge his debt to Hollywood than to French directors, citing a commonality with *White Heat* (Raoul Walsh, 1949) (Fassbinder, Töteberg and Lensing 1992: 5). In fact, *Love is Colder than Death* closely parallels a film made in the same year as *Le Samouraï* and which ushered in America's own 'New Wave' or New Hollywood, *Bonnie and Clyde* (Arthur Penn). Certainly, Lommel resembles Delon as Jef, but he is also strikingly similar to Warren Beatty's Clyde, while Johanna's blonde beauty echoes Bonnie's (Fay Dunaway). As can be seen in Figure 2.2, like the shifting mosaic of cultural influences and borders, characterizations and roles are slippery between the two films; in terms of looks, it is Franz who has C.W. Moss (Michael J. Pollard), Bonnie and Clyde's sidekick's 'homely' demeanour, but it is Bruno, not C.W. who is the outsider within the trio, and Johanna who takes C.W.'s act of tipping off the authorities. Aspects of the iconography function as an almost parodic homage to *Bonnie and Clyde* including a girl on a train temptingly sharing an apple with Bruno; although it was a pear eaten by Bonnie and Clyde moments before their deaths (arguably, in both instances the fruit serve as ironic Biblical references of betrayal). Further aspects of intertextual reference can be found in the *ménage à trois* which, through the display of what Fassbinder has described as Lommel's 'incredible beauty' (Fassbinder, Töteberg and Lensing 1992: 7) (echoing also the beauty of Beatty and Delon), foregrounds the homoeroticism somewhat buried by Penn and Beatty, the fetishization of weaponry and the confusion over parking spaces before the fatal shoot out.

Despite this evident Franco-American influence, as Hake argues, Fassbinder has 'moved beyond the formal allusions to Hollywood to reconstruct a specifically German mise-en-scène of violence' (Hake 2002: 155). In contrast to Melville or Godard's love letters to Paris or the lyrical nostalgia of Penn's 1930s Texas, Fassbinder's Munich is relentlessly drab, enervating and authentic, and there are hints that give the film a specifically German cultural context that weaves through and refreshes the Franco-American clichés. When asked by Bruno what she is thinking about, the girl on the train confounds his presumption that it is sex, by replying 'the revolution'. This implicit reference to the activities of Andreas Baader, a sometime member of Fassbinder's early Munich Action Theatre audience, is continued through the setting of two key scenes. In preparation for their spate of weapon-buying, murder and armed robbery, Bruno, Franz and Johanna steal sunglasses (the sunglasses and weapons detailed in the Figure 2.1) from a department store, and later, Johanna and Bruno pilfer and purchase in a supermarket. These scenes could be read simply as Franco-Hollywood homages. The stolen sunglasses reference the Ray-Bans that were one of Melville's own style

Figure 2.2: Franz, Bruno and Johanna or Bonnie, Clyde and C.W. Moss fetishizing Franco-American icons: Raybans and guns. (*Love is Colder than Death*, 1969).

classics, while the fact that the trio cannot seem to commit a crime without first assuming them signals this prop's overdetermination within American crime cinema's iconography. The supermarket is yet another exported cathedral of American consumerism, nuanced culturally by the sunglassed meeting between Walter Neff (Fred MacMurray) and Phyllis Dietrichson (Barbara Stanwyck) in the classic noir *Double Indemnity* (Billy Wilder, 1944). However, as Peer Raben, the composer of many Fassbinder scores, recalls, 'the Baader people [...] had a slogan: "Burn down the department stores" – to give comfortable Germany a taste of Vietnam' (Katz and Berling 1987: 34) and in 1968 Baader did indeed detonate two home-made bombs in Frankfurt department stores; Fassbinder discomforts smug Franco-American cultural chic with Germanic 'revolution'.

This Germanic flavour runs through the dramatic form of *Love is Colder than Death*. Cooke has argued that in the early days of the New German Cinema Hollywood is used 'not only as a parodic vehicle to critique the influence of this very culture on Germany, but also as the only available means of questioning German society itself' (Cooke 2007: 166). In contrast, Palfreyman, citing specifically Fassbinder's fascination with Sirk's melodramas, recognizes that this group of filmmakers deliberately engaged with 'usable German traditions' (Palfreyman 2010: 147). Although it is Fassbinder's later female-centric work, for example the FGR trilogy, that is most associated with Sirk's influence, elements are apparent from *Love is Colder than Death* onwards. Johanna's first words articulate the petite-bourgeois aspirations Hanna Schygulla will repeat through a string of roles: 'We ought to find an apartment where we can stay, have a child and some peace'. The score is used for particular melodramatic effect; when Joanna cleans the flat, 'muzak' emphasizes the artifice of their domesticity while the string quartet that plays against the supermarket scene adds parodic reverence to this critique of consumption.

Katzelmacher: The *Nachgeborenen* considers its own mistakes

These themes re-emerge in Fassbinder's next film, which looks at the contemporary German suburban youth milieu to address recurrent issues from the past, and I would argue, reverse the stereotype that New German Cinema exclusively condemned the parent generation whilst exonerating its own. *Katzelmacher* is a Bavarian slang term which has no precise English equivalent. Variously translated as 'cock-artist' or 'cat screwer' (in the sense of producing indiscriminate litters of children), it is essentially used to describe a sexually potent Mediterranean foreigner. The *Katzelmacher* in question is Jorgos (Fassbinder), whose arrival accelerates tensions apparent amongst a group hanging out in an anodyne neighbourhood. Melodrama persists; Marie's (Hanna Schygulla) opening words, closely echoing Susanne in *Die Mörder sind unter uns*, are: 'The important thing is to get on in life' while a recurrent 'chorus' scene features shifting pairs of usually female characters, who promenade between apartment blocks against a Schubert soundtrack, making idealized romantic conversation that the audience knows reverses the truth about their brutal relationships. However, rather than Sirkian melodrama, another Germanic form predominates. If Heimat films examined post-war 'key anxieties' such as 'guilt and perpetration, the integration of refugees and expellees, the high number of illegitimate babies born and rape' (Palfreyman 2010: 149), *Katzelmacher* is the paradigm of a reinterpreted example of Heimat, the only detail missing being an ending which restored peaceful accord.

The young couples in *Katzelmacher* are relentlessly aspirational but their respectability is a thin veneer covering prostitution (hetero- and homosexual), domestic violence, criminality and gossip. Indeed, this aspiration almost comically reveals capitalism's underside. Plans for robbery are justified because 'the main thing is to lead a better life than we do now'. Franz (Harry Baer) pays Rosy (Elga Sorbas) for sex; rather than admitting this is the only way she will agree, he boasts to his friends 'I can afford it because I work and I have enough money' although he has beseeched her to act 'as if it's love'. It is one of these schemes for economic betterment that triggers the main narrative; Jorgos is a 'guest worker', the euphemistic term for the immigrant labourers upon whom the Economic Miracle depended, renting a room from neighbourhood girl, Elisabeth (Irm Hermann). From the outset the group has used the language of prejudice saying of Rosy's casual prostitution 'It ought to be reported. A person like that shouldn't be free to mix with us' but Jorgos' arrival sends this into overdrive. Having very little German, he is oblivious to the comments 'Look at him. A foreigner. My God, what a stupid expression'. Recalling the work of an émigré director from Nazi Germany, Fritz Lang's *Fury* (1936), in which townsfolk in the American deep South take for granted the guilt of a newly-arrived Northerner when a young girl is kidnapped, gossip flares about Jorgos, from a false accusation of rape, to his politics: 'He's a Communist and it ought to be forbidden. He dares to come here and he's one of them. Something must be done'. That 'something' is a beating (see Figure 2.3) by all the neighbourhood men justified because: 'Revenge is only right and proper'. 'It wasn't nice here anymore'. 'Only we belong here'. Elizabeth's response to her boyfriend's participation is illuminating: 'You didn't have to take part. That wasn't necessary. If you hadn't done anything to help, ok. But taking part'!

Other than an Elvis record cover on a wall, and Rosy singing and dancing to an English-language pop song, *Katzelmacher* makes almost no American cultural references and is set entirely within the German context, including a tavern with checkered tablecloths, copious beer-drinking and traditional German artwork on its walls. Elsaesser notes '*Katzelmacher* must seem quaint to a European public, but a German audience will recognize the sardonic (albeit lovingly recalled) memories of the "*Heimatfilm*"' (Elsaesser 1976: 3). The dialogue from the group quoted above shows Fassbinder's general employment of Heimat's theme of the outsider being used to explore Nazi persecution, while the specific reference to failing to help being excusable might seem a clear admonishment of the amnesia of the *Tätergeneration* by the *Nachgeborenen*. However, this film has no representatives of the *Tätergeneration*; all the cast are young, and the subject-matter is an issue actually taking place within the Germany of 1969. It may have parallels with Nazi Germany, but in this instance, the *Nachgeborenen*, not their parents, and not post-war American influence, is culpable.

Figure 2.3: 'It is better to make new mistakes than to perpetuate old ones to the point of unconsciousness': the men administer a beating to a 'guest worker' the Nachgeborenen perpetrating the crimes of the *Tätergeneration* in their own era (*Katzelmacher*, 1969).

Through the film's opening quotation 'It is better to make new mistakes than to perpetuate old ones to the point of unconsciousness' (Yaak Karsunke), applied in Figure 2.2 to Jorgos' beating, Fassbinder is recognizing that his generation's Germany cannot always hide behind a culture of victimization as the heirs of the Nazi era and must not only recognize its past, but account for its present. This theme continues in *The American Soldier*. Again, echoes of crimes from National Socialism, almost camply signalled by a cop's leather uniform and cap are seen; one of Ricky's hits is a gay gypsy, herded with his peers not into a concentration camp, but its modern day equivalent, Gypsy colony no. 1.

The (German-) *American Soldier*

The American Soldier recasts German-American relations and their cultural and geographical borders through its literal charting of Ricky's journeys to and from the two countries as well as a series of reversed representations of classical Hollywood. It employs a variety of film styles, most obviously detailed homage to Hollywood gangster films. The frame composition of the cops, playing cards as they await Ricky's arrival to undertake a series of contract hits, evokes pulp noirs such as *The Killing* (Stanley Kubrick, 1956), but another heist noir is referenced more clearly. Doc (Hark Bohm) is not only a near physical double for *The Asphalt Jungle's* (John Huston, 1950) German Doc Erwin Reidenschneider (Sam Jaffe), but, salivating over pornographic pictures, shares his fatal obsession with young girls; the fact that Fassbinder's Doc is a cop not a gangster blurs not only the boundaries between the law and criminality, but also between the culpability of America for economically and culturally colonizing post-war Germany and Germany for failing to take responsibility for itself. Like *Love is Colder than Death*'s Bruno, Ricky wears a noir gangster costume, in this instance a white suit and homburg. This costuming is not only reflective of noir as a genre but also one of its iconic stars, Humphrey Bogart, and through the cross-referencing of Bogart, aspects of the plot follow but also reverse the Hollywood World War II film, *Casablanca* (Michael Curtiz, 1942). Ricky assumes Bogart's costume as well as his character's name. Fleeing Paris as the Germans invaded, Rick Blaine (Bogart) was supposed to meet Ilsa (Ingrid Bergman) at the railway station but she failed to show. Ricky too has a date at the station, to leave for Japan, another post-war American-occupied nation, whose interaction with American popular culture would later be explored by Wenders in *Tokyo-Ga* (1985) (Prager 2007:10), with Rosa (Elga Sorbas), but this time he breaks the date by killing her. Ilsa's betrayal was to have already been married, Rosa's is to be a cop, and although she truly loves him, Ricky cannot take the chance of her 'ratting'.

In *The American Soldier* Fassbinder's German-American cinephilia further explores the melodrama threaded through *Katzelmacher*. A chambermaid (Margarethe von Trotta) recounts a story that presages the plot of *Ali: Fear Eats the Soul* (1974), Fassbinder's interpretation of *All that Heaven Allows* (1955), a film made in and critiquing America by the master of melodrama, Douglas Sirk, who worked in the German film industry until 1937. In fact, Ricky's mother's life in an ornately furnished rural house, incarcerated with her strange younger son, matches the empty bourgeois life of *Heaven*'s Cary (Jane Wyman), while the lyrics to the haunting, dirge-like soundtrack song, cowritten by Fassbinder: 'so much tenderness/so much loneliness' sum up the characters' emotional isolation. Drives through the countryside evoke Heimat images, mirrored thematically in the complex generational relationships between Ricky, his mother and brother, as well as the returning figure (Ricky) disrupting a community. Although it would not be foregrounded until his mid-70s 'historical' films, Fassbinder is already utilizing another German filmic tradition, the Weimar style; the Lola Montez bar was first seen in *Götter der Pest/Gods of the Plague* (1969) and recurs here as an underworld cabaret.

The question asked of Ricky in Figure 2.4, 'Are you a real American' goes to the heart of the fluxing German-American border as the fusion of American and German culture seems personified by Ricky. Born in Germany, he seems to have grown up there (he is recognized by a neighbour on a return visit) and has spent enough time as an adult to have the cabaret chanteuse (Ingrid Caven) for an ex-lover. It is implied that he went to America with his father following his parents' divorce; he retains the name Murphy while his remarried mother is now Frau von Rezzori. Ricky's father was presumably a G.I., or a post-war industrialist; in either case he profited from the spoils of war and Ricky himself has returned on 'business', a business that is implicitly no more criminal than his father's. So although Rosa might be seen to be 'brainwashed' by Americana as she reads a

Figure 2.4: 'Are you a real American'? Ricky's journeys from Germany to America and back again epitomizes the shifting frontier (*The American Soldier*, 1970).

Batman comic, it is only 'natural' that Ricky will order ketchup with his steak. But if Ricky is both German and American, he represents the fraught relationship and lack of clear distinction between the two, but also contemporary German resistance to a nation and culture that has held it in thrall. Ricky is a Vietnam veteran. When asked by old friend Franz (Fassbinder) about Vietnam, he says it was 'loud', a term that could be a euphemism for America itself. Told by Franz that 'nothing happened here' Ricky replies 'I'm rather fond of old Germany just the same'. Ricky says he is not a 'real American'; he has German origins. Moreover, whatever Germany's current problems, and Fassbinder does not elide these, it has been at peace militarily since 1945, whereas throughout Indo-China and especially in Vietnam, America had continued the taste for war and colonization developed during World War II.

Kings of the Road: 'Everything must change'

While Ricky oscillated between Germany and America, Wim Wenders' cinema mainly centres on the road movie; whether moving between continents as in *Alice in den Städten/ Alice in the Cities* (1973) or within a country as in *Falsche Bewegung/The Wrong Move* (1974) or *Paris, Texas* (1984) his characters meander, the formless settings matching their own quest for identity. In *Kings of the Road* this projection of psychology onto geography is heightened as the location is the East/West German border, an arbitrary division, imposed by politics, not nature. It follows the aftermath of a chance meeting between Bruno (Rüdiger Vogler) who traverses the West German border towns restoring old cinema equipment, and Robert (Hanns Zischler), a paediatrician who has recently separated from his wife, as the two young men ride cross-country in Bruno's van. Like all Wenders' films, it makes philosophical exploration of the modern human condition, but is also specific to West Germany as both men seek to move forward through a resolution of their past. His marriage breakdown has put Robert's life in flux, but it seems Bruno has been rootless since childhood. When Robert tries to probe his background, Bruno says his truck is registered in Munich, but he evades revealing anything of himself. Asked how he copes on his own, he replies 'I get by. Better and better' although Robert admits 'I can't [cope alone].

This trajectory appears to be a classic working through of the *Nachgeborenen*'s confrontation of the *Tätergeneration*'s sins. The pre-credits sequence features a discussion about the closing of market-town theatres between Bruno and an elderly cinema owner who used to play live music for silent films. At first, this might seem like a lament for the loss of traditional crafts and independent businesses, but the musician goes on to complain that because of his National Socialist past, he was prevented from running a cinema for years following 1951, 'because of the Third Reich and so on' and for a whole year he had to sue to retain cinema ownership. Wenders is engaging directly with the 'lost' post-war years of German cinematic independence, but culpability is not given to America; the musician displays classic 'amnesia' and denial as he seems unsure even of his political party's name: 'SPD you know. I mean NSPDAD or whatever its name was' (see Figure 2.5). But Bruno and Robert eventually realize that anger is pointless. Robert visits his father, who, like Bruno is continuing to practice traditional craft, through his hand printing of a local newspaper, now reduced from a daily to a thrice-weekly edition, in a world that is leaving them behind, but his grievance against his father is universal rather than specific to a German past. His father was a verbose bully who dominated his wife. Having deliberately stayed away for years, Robert confronts his father and finds resolution through repairing the printing press and leaving an edition headlined 'How does one respect a woman'. Bruno now begins to open up about himself a little more. He reveals that his own father was killed during the war and agrees to go to back to the Rhineland where he grew up with his mother. Following a visit to a house where he might have lived as a child, Bruno cries, finally making emotional contact with his self. Although earlier he refused to engage with history, saying 'I am my story' he now admits that he is glad they visited the Rhine. 'For the first time I see myself as somebody who's gone through a certain time and that time is my history. That feeling is quite comfortable'. This experience may be specific to Bruno but as a metaphor, the *Nachgeborenen*, representing Germany today, can move on from denial and guilt. This is emphasized in a blackly comedic moment when Bruno lights a cigarette from the flame of a candle in the shape of a bust of Hitler; 'the old man' is now ridiculous.

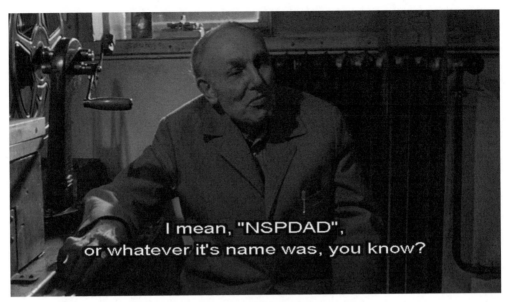

Figure 2.5: The *Tätergeneration* 'forgets' National Socialism? (*Kings of the Road*, 1976).

Within *Kings of the Road* intrusions of American culture are quite low key. The landscape is punctuated with Pepsi, Coca-Cola and Fanta advertisements and the men sing along to songs such as '*King of the Road*'. The real confrontation comes when their van reaches the literal border and they go into an abandoned American military checkpoint. The graffiti ranges from pop cultural colonialism: 'rock 'n' roll is here to stay', to military imperialism: 'let's get this place G.I'd', to America's own parallels with National Socialism: 'Ku Klux Klan'. Playing with the checkpoint's original telephone, Robert spots the latter scrawl and says he should have asked the operator for 'Lynchburg, Tennessee'. The point is that the men are not in thrall to America; they can criticize it. When Bruno complains that sometimes American songs run through his head uncontrollably without his paying attention to the lyrics, Robert famously quips 'The Yanks have colonized our subconscious'. However, it is not that simple. The soundtrack features American-sounding songs, but some of these were written for the film by German musicians, and another, '*Just like Eddie*', is a tribute to Eddie Cochran, but was sung by Heinz, who grew up in England but was born in wartime Germany. Clearly, Germany has had its own impact on transatlantic culture, and it *does* have a fixed geographical border; arbitrary, redrawn or not, the men run up against it. They recognize the past is done with and as young Germans they are responsible for their own futures, incidentally signalled by the proliferation of children – in a way recalling the British rubble films – seen throughout the film. Richard leaves Bruno a note on his windscreen: 'Everything must change'. His response: 'I'll do my best'.

The American Friend: there is nothing wrong with a cowboy in Hamburg

The American Friend moves further from a presumption of American cultural domination. Instead, it has as its essence the interplay between American and German cultures, its eclectic bricolage fusing the two to arrive at a global rather than nationalistic sensibility. Wenders filmed the novel, *Ripley's Game* (Patricia Highsmith, 1974) in 1977, its title and, to some extent, its year of release significantly revisioning the Euro-American relations originally portrayed by its literary source. Rather than a Francophilic, ex-patriot American living outside Paris, Tom Ripley (Dennis Hopper) commutes between New York and his house (surely not the *home* that is the novel's Belle Ombre), a decayed Hamburg villa, akin to the palatial, corrupt mansions of classical American film noirs such as *The Big Sleep* (Howard Hawks, 1946) and *Gilda* (Charles Vidor, 1946). The casting is also significant. Wenders used a range of European and American directors as character actors, most notably Nicholas Ray, who is associated particularly with the iconographic picture of American youth, *Rebel without a Cause* (1955) as well as film noirs, and Sam Fuller best known for challenging pulp-noirs such as *Shock Corridor* (1963) and *The Naked Kiss* (1964), but the intertwining of American and European exchange is heightened by the inclusion also of Daniel Schmidt (Swiss), Jean Eustache (French) and Peter Lilienthal (German). In relation to Highsmith's character, the casting of Dennis Hopper as Ripley is outrageous. It is impossible for a seasoned film spectator not to see all Hopper's roles filtered through the defining part as countercultural rebel, Billy in *Easy Rider* (Dennis Hopper, 1969); in other words, as ineluctably associated with the late 1960s American counterculture. A further Americanist overdetermination is added by the memory that the young Hopper had a supporting role in *Rebel without a Cause*. These anti-establishment notions of Hopper serve Wenders well; the myriad layers of this film through their *reversals* of the novel's prescriptions show that Europe has not been a passive vessel for the encroachment of American culture.

In the novel, Ripley sets up an English-born picture-framer, Jonathan Trevanny, who lives near him in France, where the bulk of the narrative takes place, to kill two Mafiosi, first on Hamburg's rail station and second on-board a train from Munich to Paris, for his occasional partner in crime, Reeves Minot. *The American Friend* keeps the essence of the plot – Ripley sets up Jonathan (Bruno Ganz) to kill, but nationality and place give the sense of being thrown into a pot, mixed about and recast. The main setting moves from France to Hamburg, and the killings take place on the Paris Metro and a train travelling out of Paris. Trevanny is now the Swiss Jonathan Zimmermann, and instead of Mafioso he is to kill American pornographers, flooding the German market; the gang boss, played by Sam Fuller, is known only as *Der Amerikaner/The American*.

Wenders has produced an exceptionally painterly film, especially in relation to Americana; as he has said, it has the 'look' of an Edward Hopper picture (DVD notes). Ripley's house has a bar replete with a pool table, illuminated by a sickly green glow from an overhead Canada Dry promotional light. He takes Polaroids of himself, and both recalling *Easy Rider* and anticipating Wenders' future film, *Paris, Texas*, he wears a Stetson and denims (see Figure 2.6) leading to his query: 'What's wrong with a cowboy in Hamburg'? This implied reference to a classic Western is significant for this chapter; every Western cowboy was pushing back the frontier, and Ripley's frontier is no longer merely within America but shifts between Germany and America; it is also worth noting that *Easy Rider* was a 'reverse Western', Billy (Hopper) and Wyatt (Peter Fonda) travelling from West to East. Ripley enters the film in a yellow cab, the street's *mise-en-scène* again redolent of the Western setting of *High Noon* (Fred Zinnemann, 1952), which, in a film layered with ironic reversals, gives contested meaning to Jonathan *Zimmemann*. These visuals are matched by the soundtrack of American and American-influenced English rock, as well as the casting of American folk musician, David Blue, and Ripley's self-recordings, in which he repeats President Franklin Delano Roosevelt's most famous words: 'You have nothing to fear but fear itself'.

In contrast both to what has been described as *The American Friend*'s American 'hyper-referentiality' (Fay and Nieland 2010: 142) and *The Talented Mr Ripley*'s reverence for Europe, European old-world culture is almost entirely missing, the only cultural product is the German pornography being displaced by its American version. We see classical Parisian sights: the Eiffel Tower, the Seine and its bridges, but they have the texture of tourist attractions rather than French authenticity, and other sights are ironic: the American hospital and the original Statue of Liberty. The film was produced in 1976, the year of the American bicentennial; Wenders is pointing out that America's world position was originally underpinned by French support.

Figure 2.6: 'What's wrong with a cowboy in Hamburg'? Dennis Hopper as Ripley in denims and Stetson evokes classical Westerns and the neo-Western, *Easy Rider*. This cowboy has a new, global frontier (*The American Friend*, 1977).

Unlike Highsmith's Ripley, Wenders' character no longer shuns America; he commutes between Hamburg and New York. The traditions of European craftsmanship seen in *Kings of the Road* are still glimpsed in Jonathan's picture-framing, but as Ripley says of himself, he does not make *anything*, 'I make money and I travel a lot'. He tells Jonathan he is bringing The Beatles back to Hamburg, implying American cultural largesse in re-exploiting a British band who modelled their music on American rock 'n' roll influences, honed their talents in Hamburg bars and found iconic status as American imports, most notably at Shea stadium. Wenders' intention, even in a time before full globalization, was to present a picture of 'one place' in which everywhere looks the same (DVD commentary). This is partly achieved by the omnipresent Americana, but also by his method of cutting, which refuses the spectator sure knowledge of characters' whereabouts. So much time is spent rootlessly in settings that defy borders; planes and trains, in hotel rooms. Is Ripley in New York or Hamburg? Sometimes it is almost impossible to tell.

Nonetheless, the principal setting is unequivocally Hamburg. Describing the process of adaptation, Wenders said: 'The story [in the novel] is set in France and Germany: the main character lived outside Paris and commits his murders in Hamburg. In the film we changed that around, and that turned out to be a much more significant change than I naively thought' (DVD notes). Wenders does not fully explain why the change is significant, but I would argue his film makes explicit the post-World War II American exploitation of the 'losing' nations, now Germany rather than the Italy which is implicitly referenced in the novel (Highsmith, 1955) and film (Anthony Minghella, 1999), *The Talented Mr Ripley*. Certainly Wenders was aware of the political nature of his cinema:

> Every film is political. Most political of all are those that pretend not to be: 'entertainment movies'. They are the most political films there are because they dismiss the possibility of change. In every frame they tell you everything's fine the way it is. They are a continual advertisement for things as they are. I think the American Friend is different. Yes, it's entertainment and it's exciting. But it doesn't confirm the status quo (DVD notes).

The 1970s political commentary is glimpsed in the Baader-Meinhof graffiti, and in challenging the 'status quo', the casting of Hopper becomes more significant, and again recalls the frontier motif of the Western via *Easy Rider* when recalling the notes Wenders made after viewing *Easy Rider* in 1969. Describing it as 'a political film', he begins by quoting Peter Fonda: 'Easy Rider is a southern term for a whore's old man, not a pimp but the dude who lives with a chick. Because he's got the easy ride. Well, that's what's happened with America, man. Liberty's become a whore and we're all taking an easy ride' (Wenders 1986: 26). This harmony of outlook between young American and German cultural filmmakers takes further *King's of the Road*'s plea for things to change. *The American Friend*'s setting, in a part of Hamburg that was being demolished and redeveloped evokes the bomb sites and *Trümmerfilme* of post-war Germany. But there is now a sense that Germany is rebuilding an authentic identity.

Conclusion

This article has explored post-World War II Germany's 'frontier' with particular reference to its relationship with the United States. It took as its starting point two widely-held premises. Firstly, that post-war Germany demonstrated a practice of amnesia towards its recent National Socialist past, effected in economic terms by American Marshall Plan funding and its subsequent Economic Miracle and affluent society, and culturally by a revelling in American consumer goods and popular cultural forms, particularly music and Hollywood cinema. Secondly, that the *Nachgeborenen*, represented in New German Cinema, took the long-deferred opportunity to confront the *Tätergeneration*'s complicity of silence and embracement of American commodity culture, through their films. The article's thesis has been that this is at best a partial aspect of a more complex process. Although the archetypal *Trümmerfilme*, *Die Mörder sind unter uns* hints at the appeal of American commodities for future generations and posits a Germany rebuilt by industry and material comfort, despite American control of the post-war German film industry, the predominating Heimat films troubled their conformist surface by an inclusion of recurrent themes which referenced National Socialism and its subsequent legacy. In this light, Heimat served as an influence on New German Cinema directors such as Fassbinder who was able, through, for example, *Katzelmacher*, to openly condemn the abuses at which Heimat could only hint. This brings to the fore the question of the *Tätergeneration*'s denials of the past as a cause of anger to the *Nachgeborenen*. Certainly denials are seen, most notably by the elderly cinema-owner in *Kings of the Road*, and generational conflict is depicted in that film between Robert and his father. But, as we have seen in *Katzelmacher*, the young generation is also capable of failing to learn from the past, and in *Kings of the Road*, Bruno has practiced denial in relation to his own experience of World War II; clearly the point is that anger is futile and that the *Nachgeborenen* must themselves fully acknowledge German history to achieve independence. By the mid-1970s, Germany had long since achieved economic independence from America. *Love is Colder than Death*'s mosaic of Franco-American references given a German refraction, and *The American Soldier*'s Hollywood reversals, as well as Fassbinder's recurrent allusions to German cinematic forms, and Wenders' subtle threading in *Kings of the Road* of cultural moments presumed to be American but with a German origin, show that American cultural colonialism had never been a clear-cut imposition. *The American Friend* in some ways serves as a literal and metaphorical post-modern *Trümmerfilme*, its Western motifs mirroring a recent interpretation that sees *Die Mörder sind unter uns* as following Hollywood Western conventions (Shandley 2011: 25–46). Hamburg is being rebuilt, and the globalized world has a new frontier which sees nothing wrong with a cowboy in Hamburg.

References

Allan, S. (1999), 'DEFA: An Historical Overview', in S. Allan and J. Sandford (eds), *DEFA: East German Cinema, 1946–1992*, New York: Berghahn Books, pp. 1–21.

Cook, D. A. (1996), *A History of Narrative Film*, 3rd edn, New York: Norton. First published 1981.

Cooke, P. (2007), 'German Neo-Noir', in A. Spicer (ed.), *European Film Noir*, Manchester: Manchester University Press, pp. 164–83.

Cousins, M. (2004), *The Story of Film*, London: Pavilion Books.

Elsaessar, T. (1976), 'The Postwar German Cinema', in T. Rayns (ed.), *Fassbinder*, London: British Film Institute, pp. 1–16.

Fassbinder, R. W., Töteberg, M. (ed.) and Lensing, L. A. (ed.) (1992), *The Anarchy of the Imagination: Interviews, Essays, Notes*, Baltimore and London: The Johns Hopkins University Press.

Fay, J. and Nieland, J. (2010), *Film Noir: Hard-Boiled Modernity and the Cultures of Globalization*, London and New York: Routledge.

Gomery, D. and Pafort-Overduin, C. (2011), *Movie History*, 2nd edn, London: Routledge.

Grainge, P., Jancovich, M. and Monteith, S. (2007), *Film Histories*, Edinburgh: Edinburgh University Press.

Hake, S. (2002), *German National Cinema*, London: Routledge.

Highsmith, P. (1955), *The Talented Mr Ripley*, New York: Coward-Mccann.

—— (1974), *Ripley's Game*, New York: Random House.

Kaes, A. (1996), 'The New German Cinema', in G. Nowell-Smith (ed.), *The Oxford History of World Cinema*, Oxford: Oxford University Press, pp. 614–27.

Katz, R. and Berling, P. (1987), *Love is Colder than Death: The Life and Times of Rainer Werner Fassbinder*, London: Paladin.

Koppes, C. R. and Black, G. D. (1987), *Hollywood Goes to War: How Politics, Profits and Propaganda Shaped World War II Movies*, New York: I. B. Tauris.

Lewis, J. (2002), 'The Coen Brothers', in Y. Tasker (ed.), *Fifty Contemporary Filmmakers*, London: Routledge, pp. 108–18.

Lorenz, J. (ed.) (1997), *Chaos as Usual: Conversations about Rainer Werner Fassbinder*, New York: Applause.

Palfreyman, R. (2010), 'Links and Chains: Trauma between the Generations in the Heimat Mode,' in P. Cooke and M. Silberman (eds), *Screening War: Perspectives on German Suffering*, Rochester, NY: Camden House, pp. 145–64.

Prager, B. (2007), *The Cinema of Werner Herzog: Aesthetic Ecstasy and the Truth*, London: Wallflower Press.

Shandley, R. R. (2011), *Rubble Films: German Cinema in the Shadow of the Third Reich*, Philadelphia: Temple University Press.

Shattuc, J. (1995), *Television, Tabloids and Tears: Fassbinder and Popular Culture*, Minneapolis and London: University of Minnesota Press.

Wenders, W. (1986), *Emotion Pictures: Reflections on the Cinema*, London and Boston: Faber and Faber.

Chapter 3

The Collapse of Ideologies in Peter Kahane's *The Architects*

Marco Bohr
Loughborough University

This chapter analyses the East German film *Die Architekten/The Architects* (Peter Kahane, 1990) in relation to the collapse of socialist ideology, the fall of the Berlin Wall and the opening of borders between East and West Germany.[1] Produced by the public-owned film studio in East Germany, Deutsche Film-Aktiengesellschaft, better known as DEFA, and filmed while the border between East and West Germany was steadily eroding, *The Architects* represents a unique cultural product precisely situated within the dramatic geopolitical shifts occurring at the end of the Cold War. This chapter seeks to uncover how the complex and sometimes contradictory power dynamics within a collapsing state ideology affected the production of the film, and, in turn, how these dynamics also became the subject of the film itself.

The central plot of the film focuses on the planning of a cultural centre in a large housing estate on the outskirts of East Berlin by a team of idealistic architects. At the beginning of the planning process, the architects are full of visionary proposals for a more fulfilled and sustainable lifestyle in the usually dreary and grey mass housing estates in the suburbs of East Berlin. Yet as the planning process unravels, more and more ideas are cut back or changed in accordance with demands from various government officials. When the final plans of the cultural centre have finally been accepted, they bear little resemblance with the initial drafts brought forward by the team of architects who have, one after the other, abandoned the project with disdain.

The chapter pays particular attention to the way the film is funded by DEFA, the funding body for films in East Germany, which has tended to align itself with the ideological agenda of the Socialist Unity Party, the SED.[2] The director of *The Architects* Peter Kahane thus had to carefully navigate the explicit and less explicit rules superimposed on DEFA by the Party. Yet as research has shown, throughout its history DEFA also defied the restrictions of the government by producing, at times, films that can be read as a critique against an overbearing and rigid socialist system (see for example Berghahn 2005). The chapter situates *The Architects* into a historical and theoretical context of DEFA films that represented an often-camouflaged form of critique against the regime of the German Democratic Republic (GDR). This chapter argues that through the use of metaphors and allegories *The Architects* lays bare the suppression of individuality and creativity, the dominance of state institutions and the culture of surveillance in the GDR.

The filming for *The Architects* began in October 1989, just as the border between East and West Germany began to dissipate. The chapter establishes that far from merely depicting a collapse of ideological and geographic borders *The Architects* in itself was a constituent of this collapse in its own right. In other words, I argue that the film is in itself a force in the dismantling of a dominant ideology. Lastly, considering that *The Architects* was granted full financial support from DEFA in 1988, the film is not only critical towards the socialist state, this chapter demonstrates that the support of the film itself signifies the collapse of an ideology even in cultural institutions considered loyal to the regime.

A critique of party politics

The film follows Daniel Brenner (played by Kurt Naumann), an architect nearing his forties who realizes that in the unyielding system of East German bureaucracy he is unable to fulfil his professional goals. Despite completing his studies with top marks, Daniel's talent is wasted in designing mind-numbing projects such as bus stations or electric power substations. Then, one day Daniel's former professor and mentor presents his aspiring yet also disillusioned student with a big opportunity: Daniel is to design a cultural centre in a large housing estate in Berlin-Marzahn on the outskirts of East Berlin. Fully aware of the overbearing bureaucracy and the political difficulties that such a project entails, Daniel accepts the offer only under one condition: that he can pick his own team of architects.

The first task of contacting his former colleagues and classmates already represents a major hurdle in Daniel's project. Like him, many have become disillusioned and cynical about working as architects. Some have completely withdrawn from society, some have given up their practice all together, some have even gone 'over there' (*nach drüben*). In the context of East German social history, it should be noted that going 'over there' or 'across' specifically refers to emigrating to West Germany – the ideological and political 'Other' of East Germany throughout the Cold War period. This brief reference to emigration to West Germany at the beginning of *The Architects* thus establishes an important dichotomy: while the film continuously comments on a lack of freedom and creative choice by the architects, emigration to the West is presented as an alternative for disillusioned individuals despite not precisely knowing what lies behind the Wall.[3]

In the film Daniel eventually succeeds in gathering a team of six architects willing to help him in designing the cultural centre. They are confronted with the monumental task of their assignment when they first visit the future site of the cultural centre in the midst of vast grey housing blocks. A shot in which the architects' backs are turned towards the camera as they look upon the estate highlights the juxtaposition between the dullness of the existing society and the possibilities offered by the cultural centre. The fact that the architects work in a team further helps to establish a central theme in the film: while the disillusioned individual might seek to emigrate or escape to the West, the architects stay put in order to embark on a project that shall aide the wider community as a whole. In other words, rather

Figure 3.1: Daniel and his team of architects on the future site of the cultural centre.

than pursuing a project for individual gain, or even more extreme, pursuing the desire for freedom by leaving the GDR, the architects are in the pursuit of a project for the greater good of their community. Here, *The Architects* apparently embraces socialist themes such as one of the mantras of the governing party, the SED, which proclaimed: 'The force of the masses resides within their amalgamation around the Party'[4] (Vorsteher 1997: 90). The film introduces the complex party politics of the GDR near the beginning, when Daniel is asked by a representative of the SED if he wants to become a 'comrade' (*Genosse*). Unlike the romanticized representation of the community as articulated by the SED, however, Daniel flatly turns down the offer in front of the visibly annoyed Party official with a decisive 'I do *not* wish to do so'.

The architects' deep felt suspicion towards the Party officials comes to a climax when a more experienced member of staff is ordered from the head office to oversee the group's activities. Immediately, Daniel's colleagues suspect that he is from the notorious STASI, the secret police of the GDR. Later in the film, one of the architects actually attacks this individual in the office and accuses him of sabotage in light of the continued failures of the project. Apart from this literal representation of suspicions towards the regime, the Party critical subtext in *The Architects* can also be observed in the way the group of architects interact with each other. As the leader of the project, Daniel assumes the role of a passive chairman, sitting back while his team continuously disagree with each other and argue over the plans. In other words, rather than recreating the top-down power structure of the Party, the architects recreate a constantly shifting form of democratic exchange that inevitably leads

Figure 3.2: A stone-faced representative of the SED hears that Daniel does not wish to become a member of the Party.

to friction and argumentation. By doing so, the architects effectively create a democratic microcosm within the rigid structure of authoritarian Stalinism in the GDR.

The architects' self-proclaimed goal is to create a vibrant and innovative space that stands in contrast to the dreary and depressing looking mass housing estates commonly found on the outskirts of East German cities. The architects proposed ambitious plans for the cultural centre, which should include a bowling alley, a cinema – thus cleverly referring to the ontological space in which *The Architects* would ultimately be seen in – and a Vietnamese restaurant.[5] In short, the proposed plans for the cultural centre subtly imply the architects' own hopes and desires for cultural diversity. Just as Daniel feared however, the team of architects consistently encounter restrictions and resistance from their superiors and high-ranking Party apparatchiks. Fully aware of the ensuing failure of the project, the architects become increasingly frustrated and voice their concerns to Daniel who is negotiating for understanding and leniency with his superiors. Under the heavy weight of state regulation and interference, Daniel's relationships with his friends, colleagues and his own family begin to suffer and deteriorate.

The central plot of *The Architects* thus establishes a powerful set of binary oppositions that continuously work against each other: the idealistic architects versus their conservative superiors, the plans for a vibrant cultural centre versus the grey mass housing estates, the individual desire for cultural diversity versus the reality of living in the GDR. A poignant scene also establishes this confrontation on a visual level: separated by a large conference table, the architects sit across their superiors who heavily criticize their idealistic and

Figure 3.3: Boardroom meeting with portrait of the General Secretary of the SED Erich Honecker above the top of the table.

'utopian' plans. The architects have to endure a very public shellacking, as one idea after another is ripped apart. An important detail in the scene, a portrait of the General Secretary of the SED Erich Honecker above the top end of the table signifies that the watchful eye of the Party is ever present (see Figure 3.4). Importantly, in the shot Honecker's image is situated on one side of the table at which members of the Party are sitting, while his eyes are directed towards the architects on the other side of the table. In as much Honecker's gaze signifies the relentless culture of surveillance and control in the GDR, the fact that it is a black-and-white drawing, and not a colour photograph for instance, equally functions as an allegory for an increasingly outdated mode of a political system.

Architectural utopia as counter-hegemony

Reflecting a significant political shift in GDR long before the first pieces of the Wall were hammered out, *The Architects* is full of references to a people's desire for ideological renewal and political change. This is particularly well exemplified in a scene in which Daniel confronts the supervising architect, the same person who was earlier suspected to work for the STASI, about drastic changes to the initial plan. The man replies: 'I have ten years more experience than you. This project is unviable for now'. Daniel angrily replies: 'Nobody asked for your opinion'. The man returns: 'I do my part where *one* needs me'. Daniel presses the man: 'Who is *one*'? To which the man replies: 'Management, my party'. Daniel, now infuriated

Figure 3.4: Daniel confronts a senior architect and member of the SED.

by the man's arrogance, throws the new sketches down and angrily shouts: 'We'll see if your party backs such stupidity'.

Later in the film, when Daniel has to justify his plans to yet another superior, he says the following: 'You want facts? Let's tell it like it is. The standard facilities you prefer were designed ten years ago. But in the meantime, something has changed hasn't it'? Here, these references to a new type of architecture which surpasses the old paradigm of constructing with standardized designs functions as a symbol for political change. The architects' desire to build a vibrant cultural centre not only refers to an architectural renewal, but also a desire to overcome outdated modes of thinking.

In the history of DEFA, there are a number of films that appear to represent a subtle critique of the political system through the means of metaphors. The film historian Wolfgang Gersch points out that between 1971 and 1973 films that initially received backing from DEFA were later regarded as too critical of the GDR. As Gersch points out, this apparent relaxation of ideological restrictions on DEFA productions occurred after the resignation of General Secretary of the Socialist Unity Party and Honecker's predecessor Walter Ulbricht in 1971: 'For a moment, freedom [*freiraum*] appeared to have surfaced. It lasted for three movies and then fell apart once these movies came out in 1973' (Gersch 2006: 140–41). Referred to by Gersch as *Aufbruchsfilme*, or literally, films of departure, these include *Die Legende von Paul und Paula/The Legend of Paul and Paula* (Heiner Carow, 1973) and *Die Schlüssel/The Keys* (Egon Günther, 1972). In the latter film, keys given to young lovers by a Polish couple who lent them their flat in Krakow signified to the citizens of the GDR a society that since the erection of the Wall in 1961 they were metaphorically locked out of. Gersch analyses the key as a metaphor in relation to the representation of Poland as following:

> The declaration of love to the neighbouring country [Poland], with its spontaneity, dignity and fantasy, was the unspoken search of an opposite of the GDR whose rigid and militant formalism defrauded life itself. The hope of the film, which evoked the desire for freedom and free travel, laid outside, and as such, Poland did not simply signify Poland, but it signified the rest of the world. (2006: 146–47)

DEFA films such as *The Keys* thus established the significance of metaphors which later films such as *The Architects* equally make use of. My point is that in both cases, the metaphor is applied as a narrative technique in order to express a government critical subtext. Here, the metaphor fulfils the function as a language of the politically repressed.

With its depressing representation of the workplace and mass housing estates, *The Architects* also evokes comparisons with the DEFA film *Das Fahrad/The Bicycle* (Evelyn Schmidt, 1981). Gersch describes *The Bicycle* as part of a series of films made in the early 1980s that represented filmmakers' total lack of hope for the GDR. Gersch writes that: 'In a country of small-minded people something akin to a second dictatorship emerged: a dictatorship of parochialism (*Beschränktheit*). It is a horrific product of a system that made people feel locked in, patronized, assimilated and scared' (2006: 178). In Gersch's observations, the German word for parochialism, *Beschränktheit,* which literally translated

Figure 3.5: Daniel and his wife Wanda (Rita Feldmeier).

refers to a state of being enclosed by a barrier (*Schranke*), implies that the cultural and intellectual disintegration of the citizens of the GDR is closely associated with the inability to travel freely and, literally, cross the *barrier* to other cultures and countries. In *The Architects* the association between feeling physically but also intellectually locked in consistently emerges when Daniel's wife Wanda (played by Rita Feldmeier) complains about 'dumbing down' in the small housing estate flat that they share with their young daughter. Daniel's plan for a vibrant cultural centre is not only motivated by his professional ambition, but also his desire to improve his family's life.

Wanda's frustration with her environment, the lack of cultural stimulation, space and intellectual exchange is an important aspect of the movie. Wanda's disillusionment vis-à-vis Daniel's tentative enthusiasm for the project is neatly represented in a scene in which they both look at each other's reflection in their bathroom mirror. The mirror – not a single sheet of glass but separated into three parts – signifies that Daniel and Wanda fail to see each other as they are, but rather, that they are beginning to see each other only as fragmented reflections.

With Wanda's increasing frustration and the architects' attempts to counteract cultural claustrophobia, the writer of the screenplay for *The Architect* Thomas Knauf sought to capture the difficulties incurred by his generation – a generation that was born before the Berlin Wall was built in 1961. Despite growing up under the insular ideology of the GDR, Knauf's generation was aware of the possibilities of a united Germany and deeply frustrated about the direction of their country as he points out: 'Two years before the end of the GDR, I seriously began to reflect on my life. For me this was already the endgame' (Poss 2006: 462). The architects' frustration with their superiors and with party officials is therefore representative for a far wider reaching frustration felt by a generation.

Here, it is important to note that the architects' continuous frustration with their superiors is not only a narrative device for the cinema, but it also reflects the real conditions faced by an architect practicing in the GDR. The architectural historian Frank Betker argued that in the GDR city planning and architecture was, in contrast to engineering, politically devalued to such an extent that, as a profession, it was unrecognizable (Betker 2005: 28). In his book on East German architecture, Betker argues that architects worked under considerable pressure from the Party to build structures favourable to the socialist ideology:

Any impression of individuality in mass housing developments had to be avoided. It did not matter then that some architects would watch extremely carefully at any savings they could make and build more resourcefully. The use of equally shaped, recyclable 'type projects' made of standardized elements, which were also an intrinsic part of industrial scale buildings, was downright sacrosanct. (2005: 339–40)

The type of building referred to here by Betker is commonly known as *Plattenbau* – a German word combing the words 'plates' and 'building', or a building made of large, prefabricated concrete slabs. In many ways the format of the *Plattenbau* represents the architect's nightmare

Figure 3.6: Mass housing estates in *The Architects*.

as every building needs to be designed from rigid, pre-produced concrete walls with specific unchangeable dimensions. The consequence of building with such a methodology is that in the GDR mass housing estates looked generic, homogenous and unrecognizably the same.

While the mass housing estates represent an outdated and oppressive form of Stalinist socialism, the architects' aspirations for the cultural centre represents the desire of a generation for urban renewal and cultural diversity. Yet this desire is not solely manifested in building a cultural centre in the midst of a dysfunctional housing estate, but rather, the cultural centre acts as a symbol for hope and a new beginning. This hope is best represented in a scene in which the architects celebrate the early success of their project. Asked by a group of alternative-looking teenagers what they are celebrating, one of the architects replies: 'The beginning of a new GDR architecture'. In other words, the cultural centre symbolized a new beginning, not only for the housing estate, but for the whole of GDR architecture, and by extension, for the whole country.

With Daniel and his team of architects continuously fighting against their oppressive superiors and those associated to the Party, the provocative plans for the cultural centre function as a counter-hegemonic discourse within the film. The political theorist Chantal Mouffe summarizes the dynamic between hegemony and counter-hegemony as follows:

The articulatory practices through which a certain order is established and the meaning of social institutions is fixed are 'hegemonic practices'. Every hegemonic order is susceptible of being challenged by counter-hegemonic practices, i.e. practices which will attempt to disarticulate the existing order so as to install another form of hegemony. (Mouffe 2005: 18)

Following this schema, in *The Architects* the large structures of the mass housing estate represent the hegemony of the state, the Party and the so-called 'planned economy' (*Planwirtschaft*) of the GDR. In contrast to that, the innovative and visionary ideas for the cultural centre brought forward by the architects represent an attempt to deconstruct the existing order, even to create a space that might challenge the master narrative of the Party. In the film this is expressed in a brief discussion about footpaths on the estate: the architects agree that rather than superimposing a rigid matrix of paths onto the existing structure of the estate, the new plans for the cultural centre should take into consideration the natural flow of people. In other words, similar to the counter-hegemonic space proposed by the architects, the natural footpath represents the universal desire to choose one's own direction in life whether this is geographically, ideologically or politically. It is to this extent that Peter Kahane's film is deeply political and steeped in symbolism.

DEFA's internal power struggle

The witty and slightly opaque political symbolism in *The Architects* can be explained by analysing the films production history. In line with the ideological agenda of the Socialist Unity Party, DEFA films were to represent antifascist, socialist and communist ideals as well as love for the GDR (Brummel 2010: 39). In other words, it was the artist's obligation to rear socialist citizens. Filmmakers who veered off from the SED ideology of social realism, either risked the withdrawal of funding, censorship, or they risked their films being banned all together. At a historically important junction for East German cinema, the Eleventh Plenum of the SED's Central Committee in December 1965 launched 'a scathing attack on artists, singling out the DEFA feature film studio for especially harsh criticism' (Feinstein 2002: 151). In the following months, the SED banned twelve pictures that were deemed unfavourable to the regime.

Despite this apparently rigid system of power that seeped from the SED through to DEFA, the history of East German cinema also underwent phases in which films that were subtly critical of the regime received financial backing and subsequently made it to the movie theatres. As pointed out above, one such period occurred between 1971 and 1973, while the early 1980s similarly saw a number of films that painted a bleak and depressing picture of the GDR. *The Architects* thus fits into a history of films, such as *The Legend of Paul and Paula*, *The Keys* or more recently *The Bicycle*, which subtly critique the living conditions in the GDR.

Emerging out of a discourse of films that critically engage with the social conditions of growing up under a repressive and isolated political system, Peter Kahane belonged to a group of filmmakers and writers who wanted a 'departure from any form of taboo-making' at DEFA. In 1988, Kahane co-authored a manifesto with other aspiring yet increasingly disillusioned filmmakers and writers who argued:

> Uniformity and the average characterize the majority of our films. It is our responsibility, through a sharpening of perception to engage in the process of treating reality, where the result is not predetermined. What counts is to rediscover the pleasure of a provocative viewpoint. (Schenk 2006)

Reiterating the frustration of filmmakers of his generation, in August 1988 Kahane gave an interview in which he attacked DEFA for failing to support filmmakers of his generation as he points out: 'We were treated as the new generation, as little apprentices. In truth we were not really wanted' (Schenk 2006). Proposing an exposé of *The Architects* to DEFA in 1986 was, as Kahane says, a 'last attempt in which I wanted to free myself from everything which I had experienced'. Herrmann Zschoche (born 1934), who was initially shortlisted as potential director for *The Architects*, recognized the conflicts of a younger generation and turned down the project.[6]

At the time, the General Secretary of DEFA was Hans Dieter Mäde (born 1930) – a man considered loyal to the SED regime and who held his position for 13 years. Reflecting a larger movement towards 'Openness' (*Glasnost*) and 'Restructuring' (*Perestroika*) emerging from the Communist Party under the leadership of Mikhail Gorbachev in the Soviet Union, the SED's control over DEFA began to unravel. As a sign of how rapidly Mäde was losing control over DEFA, *The Architects* was finally granted full funding in 1988. In an interview, Peter Kahane reflects on his experience with DEFA:

> We had the screenplay accepted right before Christmas 1988. And of course I hoped we could start shooting real soon. It was remarkable that we had imposed our will. There were many arguments against DEFA producing it. But the balance of power had already started to shift. They [DEFA] were under pressure. Our project had a lot of support. (Kahane 2006)

As of early 1989, since even films with a government critical subtext such as *The Architects* received DEFA's support, Mäde's position became untenable. The ideological power struggle within DEFA is neatly reflected in the fact that despite the film receiving official support, at the same time, the actual production of it was consistently stalled and delayed. Even before filming for *The Architects* could begin, in June 1989 Kahane gave an interview in the premier film journal of the GDR in which he argued for the complete abolishment of cinematic censorship under DEFA. Kahane said: 'The gulf between the daily experiences of our potential viewers and the experiences represented in our films is enormous' (Oehmig 2008: 23). In his interview, and what can only be considered as another affront to the aging DEFA leadership, Kahane emphasized that his industry is suffering from a generational conflict which suffocates any new developments and ideas (Oehmig 2008: 23).

While Mäde was still in office, a replacement was found in the reformer Gerd Golde. In late summer 1989, Mäde finally announced his resignation 'due to health reasons' (a commonly used code in the GDR for a dismissal resulting from an internal political revolt). In response to a new generation of filmmakers such as Kahane, even the GDR's very own Secretary of Culture Hans-Joachim Hoffmann felt it was necessary to distance himself from the previous DEFA leadership in a speech he gave at the inaugural festivity for the new DEFA leadership on 8 September 1989.[7] Rather than customarily addressing the obligations of the artist to produce works in the name of the Party, the socialist cause or the people of the GDR, Hoffmann said:

> We live in a time of many changes. More than ever, film will have to help people in their lives. Help in the search of happiness and fulfilment. (Poss 2006: 347)

The new General Secretary of DEFA Gerd Golde meanwhile emphasized in his inaugural speech that the new management wishes to promote better communication, exchanges of thought and dialogue (347). As Ingrid Poss points out, the dialogue that DEFA sought to promote, however, was already expanding at a fast pace, on the streets, throughout the whole country: 'When 6500 people met at the Monday Demonstrations on 25 September 1989, that was only the beginning and the end of the GDR could not be stopped' (347). Staying true to his reconciling words, the new General Secretary of DEFA Gerd Golde finally sanctioned the production of films, which were previously stalled for political reasons (Brummel 2010: 87). Filming for *The Architects*, precisely one of those films, which was, despite being initially approved by DEFA, consistently stalled, could finally begin on 2 October 1989.

There are several important parallels between the main character in *The Architects* Daniel and the filmmaker Peter Kahane. Like his protagonist, Kahane (born 1949) was nearing his forties when the film was initially proposed to DEFA. Like Daniel, Kahane had to grapple with the strictures of a restrictive bureaucracy governing his profession. Like Daniel's proposal for a cultural centre, Kahane's movie had to fit into government policy and an ideological agenda. In short, Daniel's frustration with the apparatuses of his profession represents Kahane's very own frustration working as film director in the GDR.

In the film, this ideological conflict is subtly referred to in an ongoing discussion amongst the architects about the importance of a movie theatre in the cultural centre. After the various cutbacks to the architects' plans, however, the movie theatre is eventually combined with an assembly hall suitable for party congresses. As they are being told by those in power, Daniel and his team have to 'compromise'. In *The Architects*, this compromise signifies the very restrictions under which filmmakers such as Peter Kahane had to operate. The constant meddling with the architects' plans by more superior architects or members of the Party thus functions as a powerful metaphor for filmmakers fighting for artistic freedom in the GDR. Like the architects represented in the film, filmmakers had to grapple with the ideological restrictions superimposed by the Politbüro. *The Architects* is therefore a deeply self-referential movie which uses the architects' struggle to equally represent the struggles of aspiring filmmakers working under a repressive system of control.[8]

The vanishing of the border

At times, the division between fiction and reality in *The Architects* appears rather blurred. Filmed in a quasi-documentary style, with very little artificial lighting and a bleak range of colours, the film can easily be read as a representation of reality rather than a representation of fictional characters and events. The format of the film also appears to lend itself to the family drama that is slowly unfolding as Daniel is more and more consumed by his failing project. Importantly, the collapse of Daniel's family is foreshadowed by a public sculpture proposed for the cultural centre with the title 'Family in Stress'. Like all the other innovative ideas for the cultural centre, the management demands that the sculpture should be changed because 'a depiction of stress is no field for dedicated socialist artists.' Rather than displaying a 'Family in Stress', they suggest 'Family in Socialism' to reflect a more hopeful and idealistic theme. The film thus comments on the gulf between a romanticized version of socialism and the harsh reality of living in an oppressive state.

The tension between two conflicting perspectives – a 'Family in Stress' and 'Family in Socialism' – is best encapsulated in an argument between Daniel and his wife Wanda. Wanda has met a Swiss man and she has made the decision to leave the GDR as she cannot cope with living there any longer. In an emotionally charged scene, Wanda tells Daniel: 'There's more to life than our humdrum existence. The endless repetition day after day. Our love died of monotony and you didn't even notice'. Commenting on the chronic shortages of basic goods in the GDR, Wanda continues: 'There is nothing that positively surprises me anymore. For years it's always the same groceries in the store, the only surprise lies in the fact that except for a shortage of milk, onions have suddenly become scarce'.

In trying to convince Wanda to stay so that he can continue to see their daughter, Daniel says: 'You should know that I see similar problems. Yet I am trying to do something about them. Only through action can you change things'. Wanda meanwhile is completely disillusioned and cannot imagine a better life in the GDR. Daniel tries to convince Wanda by saying: 'But things are changing. Everywhere. Hope for change only exists if you are actively engaged'. Wanda meanwhile replies: 'Hope. I simply have no time to hope for something new'. With that statement it becomes clear that Wanda has made her decision that she will leave the country with their young daughter. In effect, Daniel's doomed project has lead to the complete breakdown of his family. Later in the film, faced with the unavoidable consequences of putting the plans of the cultural centre before his family, Daniel's wife eventually emigrates to Switzerland with their daughter. In an emotionally loaded scene, Daniel hugs his daughter for what he believes will be the last time. In the background a sign reads *'Ausreise'*, or 'Emigration', further emphasizing the dramatic split of the family this scene captures.

Figure 3.7: Daniel says goodbye to his daughter at a border crossing.

As the director Peter Kahane reflects, the scene was shot in the beginning of October 1989 while more and more East Germans were leaving for the West. The crew received permission to shoot the scene at the Friedrichstrasse border crossing, yet were given strict guidance on what could and could not be filmed. Importantly, the scene was not allowed to include any people who are actually in the process of emigrating. As a result, the crew had to intermittently stop the steady flow of people leaving for the West, and then get their own actors to replicate what is already happening in reality. As Kahane remembers, filming the scene in the fictional format of cinema seemed 'absurd' because what the film was trying to capture was in effect already taking place (Kahane 2006).

It is important to briefly situate *The Architects* in a historical context. Unable to contain the widespread dissent amongst its people, the tightly controlled borders of the GDR began to crumble in the summer of 1989. In August 1989, Hungary opened its border to Austria for East German refugees desperate to leave the Eastern bloc. The images of East Germans storming through a half-opened border gate and dodging sharp barbwire have in the meantime been imprinted into the Germany psyche. Beginning in September 1989, the 'Monday Demonstrations' in the city of Leipzig attracted more and more people ardent to make their voices heard. Under the motto 'We are the people' (*'Wir sind das Volk'*), these demonstrations grew from a few hundred to 300,000 participants by late October 1989 (see for example Glaeser 2000). Overshadowing these acts of political dissent was the 40th anniversary of the GDR on 7 October 1989. Mikhail Gorbachev arrived in East Berlin for what was supposed to be joyous celebrations of a fully functioning socialist state. Instead, the celebrations marked what can only be regarded as a political farce in which the dissent and even deep-felt hate against the SED could not be hidden any longer. In a desperate effort to save the regime from its impending end, the Politbüro ousted the General Secretary of the SED Erich Honecker who ruled the GDR for nearly two decades. Much like the ideological power struggle taking place at DEFA earlier that year, Honecker was forced to resign on 18 October 1989.

As a result of the tumultuous changes amongst the top brass of the SED, the distribution of power at the very heart of the government was descending into chaos. The reshuffling of important government officials caused a major vacuum of power that would prove terminal for the GDR. This became most apparent at the famous press conference hosted by the newly assigned government spokesperson Günter Schabowski on 9 November. Shortly before the press conference, Schabowski was given a short note which articulated several changes with regard to travel permissions for East German citizens. These changes were to take effect the following day so that border guards could prepare for the growing number of people leaving the country. Schabowski however was not fully informed about when the changes were to take effect, and when asked to confirm when exactly the new rules would be implemented, Schabowski replied with hesitation: 'As far as I know ... effective immediately, unhesitatingly' ['*Das tritt nach meiner Kenntnis ... ist das sofort, unverzüglich.*' (Timmer 2000: 283)].

Because of Schabowski's unusual choice of words, in later years the awkward phrasing 'immediately, unhesitatingly' (*sofort, unverzüglich*) would become a commonly understood reference to that very press conference. It represents the chaos of those days – a chaos that is still veiled in the bureaucratic yet also confusing language of the regime. Within minutes, Schabowski's statement was broadcast via the major TV networks and news agencies. The first parts of the Berlin Wall were to be hammered away that very night.

On the set of *The Architects* meanwhile, these rapidly unfolding events led to rather comical circumstances. Kahane recalls an incident on the evening of the Schabowski press conference when an American news network approached his lighting crew:

> They asked us what we would do now that we are free. Then we looked at each other in disbelief. ... We thought the Americans had lost their marbles. (Kahane 2006)

As Kahane recalls, the existence of the Wall, that ultimate signifier of a divided Germany, was simply unquestionable, and anyone who doubted it was declared insane: 'Nothing was as certain as death and the Wall'. It was only later that night that Kahane and his crew found out that indeed, the border was not only open, it was also quickly vanishing.

At this moment in time, the uncanny slippage between reality and fiction in *The Architects* is also reflected in Kahane's fear (even though it was unfounded) that his film crew would emigrate to the West, much like Daniel's wife and daughter emigrated to the West in the film. The rapid erosion of many parts of the Berlin Wall in the coming days and weeks led to another unforeseeable problem on the set of *The Architects*: a key scene which included the

Wall was yet to be filmed. The filmmakers thus had to search for a part of the Wall that was still intact and unmarked by the joyous celebrations in order to replicate the structure's status as signifier for division, while in reality, it was quickly becoming a signifier for unity. In the film, the scene unfolds as following: Daniel receives a phone call from his daughter who is on a class trip in West Berlin. She asks him what clothes he is wearing and they arrange to 'see each other' an hour later at, what sounds like, a well-known meeting spot. Instead of meeting face to face, however, Daniel ventures to an observatory deck next to the Brandenburg Gate and looks towards an adjacent platform on the other side of the border in the West. Standing next to several others who try to identify friends and family members in the distance, Daniel's gaze traverses the notorious strip of death (*Todesstreifen*) between East and West Germany in order to find his daughter. He opens his jacket to show the blue sweater he is wearing to help his daughter to identify him. Tragically, they fail to see each other.

The scene at the Wall is deeply symbolic for the open wounds of a divided Germany. A people, with the same culture, language and history, forcefully separated by a concrete and heavily protected structure that tore apart friends, families and, like in Daniel's case, parents and their children. It is here that *The Architects* turns from a movie about a generation's disillusionment with the political system to a movie about the utter tragedy of a brutally separated Germany. In that sense, *The Architects* appears to be at the very forefront of a massive political change that was taking place on the ground at the time. The constant slippage between reality and fiction, between documentary and narrative cinema is the very symptom of producing a film that not only seeks to be capture an ongoing debate

Figure 3.8: Daniel tries to see his daughter on the other side of the border.

Figure 3.9: West Germans looking through the Brandenburg Gate towards the East.

on political change, but also, that seeks to be part of that very debate. In addition to being produced at the very moment when the border between East and West Germany was rapidly eroding, the very format of the film, its subversive political message and witty symbolism also appears to erode the border between narrative cinema and documentary.

A footnote to history?

At the end of the film, the architectural plans for the cultural centre has undergone so many changes that by the time construction begins, the plans bear little resemblance with the initial draft. Rather than creating an aesthetic contrast to the Soviet-style housing estates it is surrounded by, the cultural centre itself becomes an architectural failure. The allegorical decline of the project comes to a climax when at a ceremony for the construction of the cultural centre, Daniel realizes that he has been abandoned by his colleagues, friends and his own family. The bleakness of Daniel's psychological disposition is exemplified by the grey mass housing estates to the background of the shot. The dominance of the red stage decoration and the flag of the GDR signify Daniel's sacrifice for the Party, the socialist cause and his country. It is at this moment that Daniel is confronted with the realization that he had to pay a bitter prize for a project that was not worth its sacrifices.

The deeply pessimistic vision explored in *The Architects* is best exemplified in an earlier montage of environmental shots underpinned by the high-pitched music from a children's

Figure 3.10: Daniel at a ceremony for the construction of the cultural centre.

choir singing the socialist anthem *Unsere Heimat* (*Our Homeland*): 'Our Homeland is not only the cities and villages; Our Homeland is also all the trees in the forest, Our Homeland is the grass in the meadow ...' The lyrics evoke the patriotic concept of *Heimat* by alluding to the beauty and diversity of the natural world. In complete contradiction to the lyrics of the song, however, rather than representing nature, the camera joins Daniel on a bleak car journey from the centre of East Berlin to the mass housing estates on the edge of the city. Importantly, just as the volume of the children's voices increases, the first short of the montage is a tracking shot filmed from the car driving in parallel to the Wall. The oblique looking Wall, the deserted streets, even the heavy dust that appears to cling onto the surfaces of buildings creates a shocking contrast to the children's joyful voices. The lyrics combined with the tracking shots documenting Daniel's viewpoint conjure a meaning all together different: rather than showing a homeland with trees and forests, it shows a homeland with decaying buildings, polluting cars and smoky chimneys. Importantly, the montage ends with a shot of a T-junction in the mass housing estate suggesting that this is, literally, the end of the road for Daniel. In other words, the housing estate is cinematically represented as a geographical, cultural and political dead end.

Commercially *The Architects* was a flop. The screenwriter Thomas Knauf recalls that when the film first came to the cinemas in May 1990, critics accused the filmmakers for cleverly producing a government critical film when the end of the GDR was already sealed (Poss 2006: 464). Partially as a result of a poor critical reception, *The Architects* only had a very short run in the cinemas and quickly faded into the archives. The gloomy and hyperrealist

Figure 3.11: Daniel's view driving from city centre East Berlin to the outskirts.

perspective on pre-unification GDR, particularly towards the final scenes of the film, simply did not fit into the greater narrative of a people celebrating their newfound freedom. The literary historian Stephen Brockmann has argued that 'by the time the film was released in the spring of 1990, the political community to which the film had addressed itself hardly even existed any more' (Brockmann 2010: 231). Instead, Brockmann writes, *The Architects* 'became a historical footnote' (231). Film historian Seán Allan similarly argues in reference to several East German films, including *The Architects,* produced towards the collapse of the regime: 'Needless to say, by the time the majority of these films were released, they were overshadowed by events on the political stage' (Allan 2003: 18). Allan concludes that 'events were happening so fast that the cinema – in common with perhaps all the arts in the GDR – was simply unable to keep pace' (18).

Brockmann and Allan appear to agree that the film itself is considered to be a reflection of a social condition, which was changing so rapidly that by the time the film was completed, the social conditions themselves have changed. In other words, the film is too late in capturing a process that is, or already has, occurred. While in the fictional narrative Daniel becomes increasingly pessimistic, in reality, a wave of optimism and political activism swept over the country. This complex mismatch between fiction and a representation of real social conditions is discernable in a brief conversation between Daniel and the last member of his team about to abandon him. Clearly referring to the growing number of people joining the 'Monday Demonstrations' at the St. Nicholas Church in Leipzig in October 1989, Daniel's colleague says: 'Today we are only a few, and we still need the protection of the Church. But there are many people who have no fear any longer. And one day, we will take to the streets'. Daniel is drunk and angrily retorts: 'What's wrong with you? Don't you get it? No one will take to the streets here'.

Even though *The Architects* appears to respond to the swiftly changing political climate, with Leipzig as the epicentre for growing dissent, Daniel's premonition that no one will take to the streets has been proven incorrect by history. While on one hand the film appears to adapt to and reflect the social conditions of the GDR, on the other the filmmakers consciously appear to use the fictional format of narrative cinema to represent Daniel's downward spiral into depression. *The Architects* therefore does both: it engages with reality while at the same time, conscious of the cinematic medium, it produces meanings autonomous of, even contradictory to, reality.

Figure 3.12: Daniel angrily proclaims that no one will take to the streets.

As case study, *The Architects* puts into question to what extent cinema can be regarded as a reflection of a social condition, a notion which was initially established by the Marxist critic Siegfried Kracauer. As pointed out by the film historian James Chapman, Kracauer argued 'that the disturbing themes and violently dislocated imagery in films such as *Das Kabinett des Dr. Caligari*, *Nosferatu* and *Dr. Mabuse, der Spieler* reflected the psychological trauma of the period following the First World War and revealed the unconscious disposition of the German people towards authoritarianism as the only answer to the social problems of the time, thus, he suggested, anticipating Nazism' (Chapman 2003: 27). In his classic book *From Caligari to Hitler: A Psychological History of the German Film*, Kracauer writes in this famous passage:

> Irretrievably sunk into retrogression, the bulk of the German people could not help submitting to Hitler. Since Germany thus carried out what had been anticipated by her cinema from its very beginning, conspicuous screen characters now came true in life itself. (Kracauer 1969: 272)

Kracauer sought to establish that the cinematic text helps to locate a psychological trauma that would come to a climax in the horrors of the Third Reich. Yet as James Chapman points out, Kracauer wrote about Weimar Republic cinema immediately after WWII thus giving him the benefit of hindsight and historical perspective (Chapman 2003: 27–30). Equally, the many American films that were popular in the Weimar Republic are not accounted for in Kracauer's theory, which only focused on a narrow selection of movies that might have suited a particular argument. The historian of German cinema Anton Kaes concludes that 'Kracauer's trajectory from the fictional tyrant Caligari to the all-too-real Hitler is a bold and problematic construct, manifesting his strong belief in the social power of the cinema to influence perceptions and mould opinions' (Kaes 1992: xi). Similarly, as outspoken critic of Kracauer's reflectionist model, Graeme Turner writes:

> Film does not reflect or even record reality; like any other medium of representation it constructs and 're-presents' its pictures of reality by way of the codes, conventions, myths and ideologies of its culture as well as by way of the specific signifying practices of the medium. (Turner 1999: 152)

Following Turner's argument, rather than regarding the film as capturing a history unfolding in front of the camera, what needs to be recognized is that cultural products are creating new meanings in their own right. This newly produced meaning, once consumed via the cinematic apparatus, thus functions as agent of social and historical change. In the case of *The Architects*, by the time cinemagoers watched the movie, a critique of the GDR's isolated and repressive political system became a forlorn conclusion. Yet my point is another. Rather than the film itself, I argue that the complex production history of the film must be regarded as an agent of social change which ultimately resulted, at least partially due to a new generation of filmmakers such as Peter Kahane, in a change of regime at DEFA even before the first crowds gathered in Leipzig. In other words, not necessarily the film as such, but the production of the film is in itself an active force in the dismantling of an ideology.

Conclusion

With the benefit of historical hindsight, *The Architects* appears to capture a social process that was happening so rapidly that the film was consistently lagging behind. Yet, a more accurate analysis, one that pays attention to the use of metaphors and codes, one that pays attention to the ideological struggle with regard to the film's funding, one that pays attention to the film's subversive political message reveals that *The Architects* played an integral part in a social process that eventually led to a change in leadership at DEFA and, ultimately, the collapse of the GDR. Any criticism that the film was belatedly trying to catch up with the ideological shifts in the latter stages of the GDR fails to recognize that the film itself is encapsulating a process of deep reflection and political debate that was repeated all over the country and culminated in the demise of the GDR.

The Architects is a profoundly self-referential film representing the conditions of filmmaking in an ideologically controlled and constantly surveyed environment. In that sense, not only did the internal power struggles at DEFA affect and delay the actual production of the film, these dynamics have actually become subject of the film itself as the architects' plans are consistently turned down or changed. The state's interference with the architects' plans thus functions as a metaphor for a variety of larger social problems in the GDR: a lack of freedom, disillusionment about the future and the omnipresent power of the state via a culture of regulation and surveillance.

Uniquely situated at the precipice of political and ideological change, *The Architects* was first written, then proposed to DEFA, consistently delayed and then finally produced as the GDR was nearing its demise. Far from reflecting the dissolution of ideological and geographic borders between East and West Germany, however, *The Architects* is in itself an active constituent of this dissolution in its own right. *The Architects* therefore does not simply *coincide* with the political shifts taking place in the GDR, nor does it belatedly capture a social process that was rapidly developing in the country, but rather, *The Architects* functions as a powerful symbol that even when faced with a strict system of censorship, surveillance and control, the outdated systems that the film put into question can be overcome.

References

Allan, S. (2000), '1989 and the Wende in East German Cinema: Peter Kahane's *Die Architekten* (1990), Egon Günther's *Stein* (1991) and Jorg Föth's *Letztes aus der Da Da eR* (1990)', in S. Taberner (ed.), *German Monitor: 1949/1989, Cultural Perspectives on Division and Unity in East and West*, Amsterdam: Rodopi.

—— (2003), 'DEFA: A Historical Overview', in S. Allan and J. Sandford (eds), *DEFA: East German cinema, 1946–1992,* Oxford: Berghahn Books.

Berghahn, D. (2005), *Hollywood behind the Wall: The cinema of East Germany,* Manchester: Manchester University Press.

Betker, F. (2005), *'Einsicht in die Notwendigkeit': Kommunale Stadplanung in der DDR und nach der Wende (1945–1994),* Stuttgart: Franz Steiner Verlag.

Brockmann, S. (2010), *A Critical History of German Film,* New York: Camden House.

Brummel, S. (2010), *Die Werktätigen in DEFA-Spielfilmen: Propaganda in den Filmen der DDR,* Hamburg: Diplomica.

Chapman, J. (2003), *Cinemas of the world: Film and society from 1895 to the present,* London: Reaktion.

Feinstein, J. (2002), *The Triumph of the Ordinary: Depictions of Daily Life in East German Cinema 1949–1989,* Chapel Hill: University of North Carolina Press.

Gersch, W. (2006), *Szenen eines Landes: Die DDR und ihre Filme,* Berlin: Aufbau.

Glaeser, A. (2000), *Divided in Unity: Identity, Germany, and the Berlin Police,* Chicago: University of Chicago Press.

Institut für Regionalentwicklung und Strukturplanung (2000), *Vom Baukünstler zum Komplexprojektanten: Architekten in der DDR,* Erkner: IRS

Kaes, A. (1992), *From Hitler to Heimat: The Return of History as Film,* Cambridge: Harvard University Press.

Kahane, P. (2006), *Die Architekten.* DVD.

Kracauer, S. (1969), *From Caligari to Hitler: A Psychological History of the German Film,* Princeton: Princeton University Press. First published 1947.

Mouffe, C. (2005), *On the Political,* London: Routledge.

Oehmig, R. (2008), *'Überholt' von der Geschichte? Drei DEFA-Spielfilme im Blickpunkt,* Norderstedt: Books on Demand.

Poss, I. (2006), *Spur der Filme: Zeitzeugen über die DEFA,* Berlin: Ch. Links.

Schenk, R. (2006), Programme notes accompanying the DVD *Die Architekten* (trans. J. White).

Schittly, D. (2002), *Zwischen Regie and Regime: Die Filmpolitik der SED im Spiegel der DEFA-Produktionen,* Berlin: Ch. Links.

Timmer, K. (2000), *Vom Aufbruch zum Umbruch,* Göttingen: Vandenhoeck & Ruprecht.

Turner, G. (1999), *Film as Social Practice,* London: Routledge.

Vorsteher, D. (1997), *Parteiauftrag: Ein Neues Deutschland,* Leipzig: Koehler & Amelang.

Notes

1   I would like to thank the anonymous reviewers of this edited collection for their invaluable feedback.

2   For an in-depth analysis of the SED's ideological agenda and DEFA film productions, please refer to Dagmar Schittly's German language book *Zwischen Regie and Regime: Die Filmpolitik der SED im Spiegel der DEFA-Produktionen.*

3 Later in the film the assumed freedom in the West is continuously discussed by Daniel and his wife Wanda.

4 All translations from German to English except where otherwise noted are mine.

5 Vietnam not only represents a state which shares an ideological affinity with the GDR, but also the proposed Vietnamese restaurant might function as an exotic and colourful space within the mass housing estate in which its inhabitants can embark on a culinary journey while travel and crossing borders to neighbouring nation-states itself is widely restricted.

6 In 1994, Zschoche directed the German TV movie *Natalie – Endstation Babystrich/Natalie – Final stop child prostitution*. Coincidentally, this author worked as an extra on the film set.

7 Hoffmann, himself considered a reformer, fell out of favour with the SED and was subsequently spied on by the STASI.

8 For DEFA censorship, please refer to Joshua Feinstein's book, *The Triumph of the Ordinary: Depictions of Daily Life in East German Cinema 1949–1989.*

Chapter 4

How to Win the Cold War: Borders of the Free World in *Guilty of Treason* (1950) and *Red Planet Mars* (1952)

Kimmo Ahonen
University of Turku

From Stettin in the Baltic to Trieste in the Adriatic an Iron Curtain has descended across the Continent. [...] The Communist parties, which were very small in all these Eastern States of Europe, have been raised to pre-eminence and power far beyond their numbers and are seeking everywhere to obtain totalitarian control.[1]

On 5 March 1946 Winston Churchill defined the political geography of post-war Europe in his speech at Westminster College in Fulton, Missouri. Churchill's 'Iron Curtain' speech held a grim view of the division of Europe, and it fuelled the ongoing debate over the threat of international communism in the United States. The following year, in March 1947, the Truman Doctrine finally articulated the clash between the superpowers (Gaddis 2005: 94–95). The Soviet Union detonated its first atom bomb in August 1949, accelerating the discussion of Soviet espionage in the United States. Simultaneously, with the onset of the Cold War came intensified anxiety over domestic communist subversion in the United States.

The House Committee on Un-American Activities (HUAC), which had been investigating communist influence in Hollywood since 1938, opened the hearings of 'friendly' and 'unfriendly' witnesses regarding a group soon to be known as the 'Hollywood Ten', in October 1947. The Committee's investigations started the era of the 'Red Scare' in Hollywood, which continued up to the mid-1950s (Fried 1990: 73–79). Scholarly debate over the issues of McCarthyism and Soviet espionage in the United States has remained lively in post-Cold War American historiography. The debate is highly politicized, reflecting the struggle between conservatives and liberals in contemporary American academia (Ahonen 2006: 140–42). The Red Scare and communist influences in Hollywood are also a matter of heated scholarly dispute (Gladchuck 2007: 1–4; Radosh and Radosh 2005: 235–42).[2]

Hollywood films had an enormous impact on the audience's perceptions of the Cold War conflict. Popular culture was instrumental in keeping the American audience terrified by the communist menace (Hendershot 2003: 6–7).[3] Thomas Doherty (1988: 15) has estimated that between 1948 and 1954 Hollywood released some forty anti-communist films; most of these were usually low-budget films, shot with a relatively unknown cast. The first one was a spy-story, *The Iron Curtain* (William A. Wellman, 1948), which borrowed its title from Churchill's speech (Swann 1995: 52). *The Iron Curtain*, which was based on Igor Gouzenko's revelations of a communist spy ring formed to steal nuclear secrets in Canada, paved the way for the semi-documentary style that was typical of future anti-communist films. However, *The Iron Curtain* did not appear out of the blue in 1948: Hollywood had already been at war with communism for three decades prior to that, with the exception of the years 1941–45 (Shaw 2007: 2, 11–15). In the late 1940s and early 1950s, heightened Cold War fears gave new dimensions to the cinematic representation of communism. Anti-communist films defined the border between 'us' and 'them', between the free world and the communists. It was a geopolitical as well as a mental border.

This chapter deals with representations of communism and Eastern Europe in American anti-communist films of the early 1950s. Two films are examined more closely: *Guilty of Treason* (Felix E. Feist, 1950) and *Red Planet Mars* (Harry Horner, 1952), both of them B-budget films without any major film stars. The former is a political drama situated in contemporary Hungary and partly based on real-life events; the latter is a highly imaginative science fiction film about messages from Mars and their political consequences on Earth. Both films depict life behind the Iron Curtain, but they do so in very different ways. Despite their genre differences, both films deal with the question of communism and religion in Eastern Europe. Dianne Kirby (2003: 1–3) emphasizes the particular importance to the USA of the religious dimension of the Cold War. The USA's crusade to promote democracy was interwoven with its pretensions of protecting Christianity against atheistic communism. As Tony Shaw (2007: 106–7) has pointed out, religion constituted an integral part of the cultural Cold War. In many Hollywood films of the 1950s, (Christian) religion became discursively associated with liberty and 'Western civilization', which were juxtaposed with the atheism and totalitarianism of communism.

I examine *Guilty of Treason* and *Red Planet Mars* in conjunction with contemporary sources, and analyse how these films in particular deal with America's scope for action in fighting against the communist regime in Eastern Europe. I also look at the ways in which the films portrayed the Cold War as a religious conflict. In addition to discussing the films in the context of the film production of their own era, I also compare them to anti-Nazi propaganda films made during the Second World War, such as *Hitler's Children* (1943). In what ways did *Guilty of Treason* and *Red Planet Mars* define the border between free and totalitarian Europe?

Guilty of Treason and the case of Cardinal Mindszenty

The communist menace was a useful tool for HUAC in its 'red-hunting' in Hollywood. In order to justify its own actions, HUAC needed communists to be perceived as fearsome and powerful enemies (Booker 2007: 67–68). The political pressure of HUAC on its own, however, is an inadequate explanation for Hollywood's output of anti-communist films. For a variety of reasons, many filmmakers voluntarily contributed to the fight against the ideological enemy. Some of them, such as Leo McCarey, who directed *My Son John* (1952), were in fact ardent anti-communists (Shaw 2007: 43–44). For Emmet Lavery, the scriptwriter of *Guilty of Treason*, the screenplay offered the possibility to project his personal vision of the communist menace. McCarey and Lavery were both Catholics, and religion played an important part in their disgust with communism.

Figure 4.1: Charles Bickford plays Cardinal Mindszenty in *Guilty of Treason*.

Guilty of Treason, directed by Felix E. Feist, was intended as a topical comment on the intensification of the Cold War in Eastern Europe. It tells the story of Cardinal Mindszenty's heroic struggle against the communist regime in post-war Hungary. József Mindszenty (1892–1975) was an influential Catholic cardinal, who became the head of the Roman Catholic Church in Hungary after WWII. Mindszenty overtly opposed the Communist Party's attempt to take over the schools and religious institutions, and the Catholic church played a major role in the struggle against the Sovietization of Hungary as well as other parts of Eastern Europe (Czetz 2007: 169–73). The attack against the church was not directly dictated by Moscow: Hungarian communists had some autonomy in their struggle against 'reactionary' church leaders such as Mindszenty. Nonetheless, the Hungarian Communist Party, led by hardline Stalinist Mátyás Rákosi, willingly operated according to the framework established by the Kremlin (Kenez 2003: 889).

In December 1948, Cardinal Mindszenty was arrested and accused of treason and conspiracy against the communist government. During his five-week arrest, Mindszenty was forced to sign a confession concerning his counter-revolutionary action, and some two months later he was sentenced to imprisonment for treason.[4] The name of Cardinal Mindszenty became the symbol of Hungarian resistance to communist power; Peter Kenez (2003: 888), on the other hand, argues that the legacy of Mindszenty remains ambiguous in post-communist Hungary because of his conservative social and religious views.

During 1948–49, *The New York Times* (8 Feb 1949: 3) and *The Washington Post* (4 Feb 1949: 1) closely followed the Mindszenty case as well as similar cases in Bulgaria and Czechoslovakia, where clergymen were also accused of treason against the communist government. Homer Bigart of *The Washington Post* reported on 12 December 1948 that Hungary was the most depressing case of the Soviet Union's Eastern European satellites. The Catholic church was the toughest adversary of Rákosi and the communist regime, and Bigart rightly predicted that Rákosi would soon start a major showdown against Mindszenty in order to complete his seizure of ideological power (Bigart 1948: M1&M2). Rákosi, who proved to be a ruthless dictator, launched showcase trials against his political enemies in 1949. Communist ideology was taught in state schools, and the state took over control of almost all religious schools (Czetz 2007: 175–78).

The coverage of the Mindszenty trial in the American and British media helped to establish the cardinal's image as the prototype of the clerical martyr persecuted by the communists.[5] (Shaw 2007: 110; Carruthers 2009: 137). At the same time that *Guilty of Treason* premiered in the USA, in February 1950, an American businessman, Robert A. Vogeler, was imprisoned for espionage in Hungary – exactly one year after the Mindszenty trial. Vogeler was the first American to face trial behind the Iron Curtain; while his sentence did not stir up religious sentiment in a same way as the Mindszenty case, it gave rise to discussion of Truman administration's 'weak' foreign policy (Carruthers 2009: 137–39, 172).

Emmet Lavery was a distinguished playwright and scriptwriter who had served as President of the Screen Writers Guild (SWG) during the HUAC investigation in Hollywood in the autumn of 1947, when witnesses were questioned over their alleged communist views and affiliations. Many Hollywood filmmakers defended the Hollywood Ten against HUAC's investigations, which were considered to be a witch-hunt. Lavery, however, thought that the Hollywood Ten, who refused to cooperate with HUAC, had harmed the SWG by linking it with the Communist Party (Radosh and Radosh 2005: 164). Lavery's firm attitude against the Hollywood Ten shows that he was critical towards the Hollywood left, and his anti-communist script can be seen as a logical extension to of this view.

In November 1949 Lavery published an article in *The New York Times* in which he described the writing process of *Guilty of Treason*. Certainly the article can be seen as an advance advertisement for the movie, which at this point was still in production. Nevertheless, Lavery's depiction of the general theme of the film is intriguing, in that he deals overtly with the film's political objectives. According to Lavery, the producers did not originally have any intention of writing a story about Hungary. They developed a story about Soviet Russia, based on the Overseas Press Club's book *As We See Russia* (1948), until the central theme of the film was provided by the arrest of Cardinal Mindszenty in December 1948.

Lavery explained the significance of the title of the film as follows: 'those who were "guilty of treason" were the accusers of the cardinal, the men who, by a political finesse, had taken over Hungary and had turned it into a satellite of the Soviet Union'. Even though the film was fictional, Lavery emphasized that it was founded on fact: even the fictional characters and episodes of the story would reflect, in relation to Mindszenty's experience, 'an accurate picture of Budapest in transition'. Lavery also lamented the political difficulties involved in making the film, which were aggravated by 'continuing attacks' upon the filmmakers in *The Daily Worker* and *The People's World*. Both newspapers adhered to the Communist Party line, and Lavery was thus claiming that American communists had tried to impede the making of the film (Lavery 1949b: 5).

Unusually enough, Lavery's screenplay was published by the *Catholic Digest* in 1949, an American Roman Catholic monthly magazine. The anti-communist and pro-Catholic emphasis in Lavery's text may have pleased the editors of the *Digest*. *Guilty of Treason* focuses on Mindszenty's arrest and trial. The protagonist and narrator, however, is an American journalist Tom Kelley (Paul Kelly), who has come to Budapest to investigate the Mindszenty case. Kelley meets a Hungarian schoolteacher, Stephanie (Bonita Granville), who is secretly involved with a Soviet colonel Alex (Richard Derr). Stephanie, encouraged by the example of Cardinal Mindszenty, openly resists the communist takeover of the schools, which eventually leads to her imprisonment and torture.

How did *Guilty of Treason* define the geopolitical borders of post-war Europe?

In Lavery's script, the mission of Soviet Communism is total domination over Europe. This view of Stalin's ever-increasing thirst for power was shared by many American politicians, conservatives and liberals alike (Fried 1990: 58). It was also shared by Hannah Arendt. In her influential study, *The Origins of Totalitarianism* (1948), she emphasized that totalitarian regimes pursue global rule as their ultimate goal because otherwise they might lose the power they have already seized (Arendt 1994: 90). The question of Soviet threat is raised already in the opening sequence of *Guilty of Treason*. The film begins with a Soviet 'newsreel' of a military parade, in which the aggressive narrator announces that Soviet Communism will aim at world revolution:

Today we salute the Union of Soviet Socialist Republics, which together with her neighbors, is the greatest force for peace that the world has ever known. Poland is with us, Czechoslovakia is with us, Germany is with us, China is with us!

Soviet communism had extended its sphere of influence, so that it now controlled Eastern Europe, and was supporting the communist takeover of China. To camouflage its ugly power politics Soviet rhetoric used beautiful words, such as 'peace'. In Lavery's shooting script, the narrator's opening monologue had originally been even more extensive: 'those who are not with us are against us ... and those who are against us are traitors ... they are guilty of treason and must be eliminated accordingly' (Lavery 1949a: 17). The reason for cutting the text could have been the length of the newsreel scene – it was already over one minute – but it could have been the pomposity of Lavery's text as well.

Guilty of Treason depicts Hungary as having turned into a totalitarian police-state, where local communists dutifully obey orders from the Kremlin. The Soviet Commissar Belov (Roland Winters) is depicted as the puppet-master of Hungary's Communist Party. He is a soft-spoken but unscrupulous fanatic, who gives instructions to the party elite as to how Mindszenty's reputation can be discredited by a smear campaign. Lavery's shooting script describes Belov as 'a substantial echo of Vishinsky' (Lavery 1949a: 20). The script's reference to Soviet Foreign Minister Andrei Vyshinsky, though not explicitly stated in the film, shows how Lavery tended to connect his fictional characters to real-life persons. Furthermore, Mátyás Rákosi is portrayed in the film as 'Vice-Premier Rakosi' (Nestor Paiva), who obediently follows his instructions from Belov.

In the final scene of *Guilty of Treason*, the protagonist Tom Kelley presents a warning to the audience. He mentions the Marshall Plan and the Berlin airlift: these are practical manoeuvres promoting the cause of liberty against Soviet expansionism. Thus the situation in Hungary is connected to the general scheme and strategic setting of the Cold War conflict. Kelley looks straight into the camera and proclaims that 'we're living in a time when liberty is everybody's business, and either there's liberty for everyone, or there's no liberty at all'. This form of direct address, in which the protagonist declares his message overtly to the audience, was a highly exceptional stylistic device in mainstream Hollywood films. Charles Chaplin had utilized it in his anti-Nazi satire *The Great Dictator* (1940). Both Chaplin's emotional speech about peace in *The Great Dictator* and Kelley's geopolitical lecture in *Guilty of Treason* serve as a summons to action, even though the enemy is different.

The idea of defending the cause of liberty against dictatorship was also the essential message of the Truman Doctrine, according to which the choice was between two alternative ways of life: between Western democracy and totalitarianism. The latter relied upon 'terror and oppression, a controlled press and radio, fixed elections, and the suppression of personal freedoms' (12 March, 1947. DWP: 111–15).[6] *Guilty of Treason* proclaimed that communism could be contained, and that the United States should be active in the struggle against a communist takeover in Western Europe.

Interestingly, however, the proclamation of liberty contradicts the film's analysis of the situation in Hungary. *Guilty of Treason* is trying to prove that the brutal communist regime has a stranglehold on Hungarian society. At the end of the film Cardinal Mindszenty is in prison, the heroine Stephanie is dead and the protagonist Kelley is back in the United States to lecture on the menace of communism. The cause of liberty has been lost in Hungary, but the film does not offer any alternative scenario to remedy the situation. It was this pessimism that distinguished *Guilty of Treason* from many other anti-communist films of the era. It was also one of the few films in which the story was located behind the Iron Curtain. *The Red Menace* (1949) and *I Married a Communist* (1950) deal with communist espionage and subversive activities in the United States. *The Iron Curtain* is set in Canada, but contains a similar view of sinister communist infiltration. *The Iron Curtain* and *The Red Menace* have happy and uplifting endings, where the protagonists escape from the communist spy ring. *Guilty of Treason* did not offer such relief to the audience. Instead, it suggested that Hungary, like Eastern Europe in general, was already a province of the Soviet Union.

The critical reception of *Guilty of Treason* was mixed. In his negative review, Richard L. Coe of *The Washington Post* was not happy with the romantic aspects of the film and argued that the protagonists were just stereotypes (Coe 1950: 14). Thomas M. Pryor of *The New York Times* was also critical of the film, but nevertheless praised Emmet Lavery for a creditable reportorial job; he concluded that 'despite its shortcomings, *Guilty of Treason* is an important picture'. According to Pryor, the film 'does help to bring into the clearer focus the modus vivendi of communistic imperialism' (Pryor 1950: 26). The film's political importance thus superseded its artistic weaknesses.

For Hungarians, the film offered a lot of sympathy, but did not promise a US-supported counter-revolution. Europeans, however, were not the target audience of the film, which was released only in Belgium, Portugal and Italy. The film's main purpose was to warn American audiences about the dangers of communist dictatorship. As Thomas M. Pryor of *The New York Times* put it, '*Guilty of Treason* serves as a sharp warning that the lights are dim once more in Europe and may go out altogether at any time' (Pryor 1950: 26). The film also worked as a request to Western Europe for help in the global struggle against communism, and, more implicitly, as a request to foster domestic anti-communist mission in the United States. *Guilty of Treason*, which depicted Cardinal Mindszenty as a persecuted victim of the communist government, can be interpreted as reflecting Emmet Lavery's Catholic anti-communism. Its ideological content also had interesting connections with Lavery's wartime scripts.

'Red fascism' behind the Iron Curtain

Guilty of Treason equated Soviet-dominated communism with Hungary's alliance with Nazi Germany during WWII. In his article for *The New York Times*, Lavery described the general theme of the film by linking the communists of the Kremlin to the Nazis, and emphasizing that their dictatorship was no better than that of their 'one-time collaborator', Adolf Hitler (Lavery 1949b: 5). Despite their propaganda, Lavery's arguments as to the similarities between Nazi Germany and Stalinist Russia resemble some conclusions reached in recent Cold War historiography (Gaddis 2006).[7] There is a connection between anti-Nazi, anti-Japanese and anti-communist films, in that Emmet Lavery also wrote the scripts for *Hitler's Children* and *Behind the Rising Sun* (both 1943 and directed by Edward Dmytryk).

The label of 'fascism' was very widely – and wildly – applied in political rhetoric on both sides of the Iron Curtain. In the Soviet Union the term was used pejoratively against Social Democrats and other revisionist variants of orthodox Marxist-Leninist doctrine. At the same time, the analogy between communism and Nazism was very commonly drawn in American anti-communist rhetoric, which often depicted communism as 'red fascism' – just another version of totalitarianism, and actually even more dangerous (Gleason 1995: 80–88). Hannah Arendt, for example, compared the aims and methods of Nazi Germany and Stalinist Russia and identified terror as the very essence of both Bolshevist and National-Socialist dictatorships (Arendt 1994: 78).

Guilty of Treason was similarly claiming that the Nazis and the communists alike used terror and torture in Hungary to promote their ideological ends. It encouraged the audience to regard Nazism and communism as two sides of the same coin. In *Guilty of Treason*, Mindszenty frequently emphasizes that he had fought against both Nazi and communist power. In his last sermon, he declares that he has always sought to fight 'against tyranny in all forms and under all labels'. One totalitarian regime has been replaced by another, but Mindszenty continues to defend his staunch Catholic faith. In anti-communist rhetoric, communism was also described as a bastardized form of religion, with its own hagiography and doctrines. *The Washington Post*, for example, compared Stalinism to religious fanaticism. According to the article, published in February 1951, communists worked from a closed system of beliefs and were fanatically devoted to advancing the party's cause. To them the word of the Kremlin was an article of faith, and did not permit questioning: 'there is but one God, and Stalin is his prophet' (*The Washington Post*, 11 Feb 1951: B3).

Through the character of the Soviet Colonel Aleksandr Melnikov (Alex), Emmet Lavery depicted the inner conflict of the faithful communist, confronted with the difference between communism's ideals and the brutal reality of the party dictatorship. The self-contradiction of his internal world is revealed in a scene in which the portrait of Stalin is visible behind the stone-faced Alex (see Figure 4.2). Big Brother is, literally, watching his choices: Alex is a tragic figure who is caught between his love for Stephanie and his loyalty to the party. In the end he chooses the party: the life of the individual is utterly meaningless compared to 'the welfare of the state'. Even though he is an ardent believer in the party's cause, Alex's anti-Nazism and his affection for Stephanie are shown in a favourable light.

According to Cyndy Hendershot (2003: 42–44) *Guilty of Treason* differentiates between individual Russians and the Soviet system. The sad love-affair between Stephanie and the Alex distinguished the film from many other anti-communist films which portrayed all communists as ruthless, gangster-like murderers (Sayre 1982: 82–83). The critic Bosley Crowther, for example, argued in his review of the anti-communist science-fiction film *The Flying Saucer* (1950) that Russians and communists were 'a handful of thick fellows who move slowly and act unspeakably dumb' (Crowther 1950: 36). The portrayal of Alex in *Guilty of Treason*, in contrast, is more nuanced and complex. Through the ambiguous portrayal of Alex's character, the film seems to be arguing that good Russians are trapped in the prison of the communist dictatorship. The distinction is explicitly stated in Lavery's script when, in discussion with Kelley, Mindszenty distinguishes between the Russian

Figure 4.2: Big Brother Stalin is watching Alex (Richard Derr).

people and the communist ideology. He does not condemn Russians 'as a race or as a people', but he criticizes the police state in which they are 'enslaved' (Lavery 1949a: 48).

The portrayal of the Cardinal in *Guilty of Treason* as a harassed victim, forced to admit his guilt in the courtroom, was related to emerging anxieties about communist brainwashing techniques. These fears were later intensified during and after the Korean War, when stories of 'brainwashed' American prisoners of war were widely discussed in the US media (Carruthers 2009: 175). In *Guilty of Treason*, Mindszenty is presented as a tragically heroic priest, who is willing to make sacrifices for his religious beliefs. Mindszenty's and Stephanie's physical and mental torture is portrayed explicitly, and the scene in which Stephanie is tortured contains powerful religious symbolism (see Figure 4.3). Stephanie is depicted as a Hungarian patriot, who eventually becomes a crucified victim of the communist-led secret police. The director, Felix E. Feist, had previously directed several crime movies, and the visual style of film noir is also present in *Guilty of Treason*: the low-key lighting, and the sharp contrast of dark and light in the torture sequences resemble film noir.

The dialogue between Mindszenty and Kelley, which takes place on Mindszenty's farm before his arrest, is one of the key sequences of the film. The cardinal explains the tactics

Figure 4.3: Stephanie (Bonita Granville) is tortured by Hungary's communist-led secret police.

of the communist government in taking over the educational system, and defines the ideological difference between the competing forces of communism and Christian faith:

> Mindszenty: As long as I am responsible in any degree for those schools, we shall teach there the Gospel according to Jesus Christ, not the Gospel according to Karl Marx ... or Commissar Stalin. On this point I will not yield.

> Kelley: Is there no chance to some compromise ... to some agreement

> Mindszenty: What chance is there for an agreement between Christ and Anti-Christ? (Lavery 1949a: 47–48)

Mindszenty is drawing a line against the spread of communism: faced with the forces of evil represented by the communists, there can be no negotiation. The corresponding image of Mindszenty as a saint-like, principled man of faith can also be found in the American media coverage of the Mindszenty trial. For example, *The Washington Post* quoted Cardinal Francis Spellman, who called Mindszenty a victimized martyr and denounced communists as 'ghoulish men of slaughter who worship the gods of Stalin and Satan' (7 Feb 1949: 1).

Interestingly, *Hitler's Children*, which was filmed six years before *Guilty of Treason*, contained a very similar dialogue, and in both films Bonita Granville played the tragic heroine. Both films place a love story behind enemy lines, and the parallels between Lavery's scripts are strikingly obvious in the sequence where Anna (Granville) escapes the Nazis and finds refuge in the church. In his sermon, the German bishop (H. B. Warner) boldly criticizes the Nazi ideology:

> For the time has come, my friends, when you must choose, for once and for all, between the gospel of Christ, and the gospel of Hitler. There can be no compromise between what is right and what is wrong.

While the enemy is different, Lavery uses almost identical language to describe the enemy's totalitarian and atheistic ideology. In both films, the concept of individualism is juxtaposed to the totalitarian state ideology, in which the life of the individual has meaning only in relation to the welfare of the system. The individual is merely a cog in the machine; if he does not function without friction, he can be eliminated. In *Hitler's Children*, the bishop tells the Nazi Major (Gavin Muir) that all people are free before God and have inalienable rights. Major answers with a fanatical look in his eyes – and in words that resemble those of Alex in *Guilty of Treason* – that if he must choose between Christianity and the state, he is glad to choose the state; he adds that when the time is right, the Nazis will break with Christianity completely. In *Guilty of Treason* the Russian commissar Belov also shows his distaste for Christianity in declaring that all religions are inevitable enemies of the Soviet state. Hence Mindszenty and 'the faith that is with him' must be destroyed (Lavery 1949a: 67).

Richard L. Coe noted the resemblances between *Guilty of Treason*, *Hitler's Children* and *Behind the Rising Sun* in *The Washington Post*: 'one is fully alive to the parallels between the three attacks on the enemies of personal liberties' (Coe 1950: 14). The narrator's voice in *Hitler's Children* depicted Berlin before the Nazi seizure of power, describing it as a pleasant place full of laughing and smiling people. Similarly, in *Guilty of Treason* Kelley's voice painted a nostalgic picture of Budapest in the 1930s as a place where 'East meets West', and where everything seemed as 'light and gay as the whipped cream of the coffee' (Lavery 1949a: 22–24). In both films, the civilized atmosphere of an old European city has been transformed into the grim reality of totalitarian surveillance and control.

In one respect, *Guilty of Treason* is crucially different from most of the anti-communist films of its time. In films dealing with communist subversion in America, the danger of communist 'infiltration' was typically wildly exaggerated. These films can be seen as a by-product of the anti-communist hysteria that swept over America in the early years of the Cold War. However, *Guilty of Treason* was at least partly a different case, since the communist takeover of Eastern Europe was an indisputable fact. Its depiction of the Mindszenty trial and of communist power in Hungary is close to the conclusions of the post-Cold War historiography of Hungary. Another anti-communist film, *Red Planet Mars*, also differs from the others in that it does not focus on revealing the (real or imagined) threat of communism in either the United States or Europe: instead, it envisioned a world beyond the Cold War.

Red Planet Mars and the religious revival

The Cold-War warriors of Hollywood, such as Eric Johnston and Ronald Reagan, aimed at eliminating subversive themes from the screen and promoting positive virtues of American democracy (May 2000: 203). *Red Planet Mars*, directed by Harry Horner, indeed offered a positive alternative to communism. *Red Planet Mars* has been considered one of the most peculiar among the anti-communist films of the period (Warren 1982: 87; Bagh 2009: 304–5). The scriptwriters John L. Balderston and Anthony Veiller were experienced Hollywood professionals, but the film had a tangled plot structure, with, as the critic of *Box Office* (24 May 1952) put it, 'more switches than a railroad yard'. According to the *Monthly Film Bulletin* (Oct 1952: 140–41), the film was 'an almost pathological curio', and even the usually positive *Variety* (14 May 1952) described it as a 'hard-to-take piece of nonsense'. [8] Despite its complicated plot, *Red Planet Mars* delivered an explicit and clear-cut religious and political message to the audience.

The scientist Franz Calder (Herbert Berghof), an ex-Nazi now working for the Soviet Union, has invented a machine making it possible to make contact with Mars. Simultaneously, the American scientist couple Chris and Linda Cronyn (Peter Graves and Andrea King) is picking up transmissions from Mars. In these messages Mars is described as a utopian planet; the Martians do not need any fossil fuels. These messages cause an economic crisis in the Western world. As a depression reigns, the communist leaders in the Kremlin celebrate the decline of Western societies. Suddenly, however, the tone of the messages changes, and it appears that Mars is a Christian society, ruled by a supreme authority. This leads to a religious revival on earth and a new revolution in Russia. The Russian people overthrow the communists and crown an Orthodox patriarch as their new ruler.

According to *The New York Times*, the propaganda nature of *Red Planet Mars* was noted – curiously enough – in the Soviet periodical *Art of the Cinema*, where G. Avarin dealt with the new boom of science fiction films in Hollywood; he argued that these films were just another example of American imperialism. To Avarin, *The New York Times* wrote, the purpose of these space films, of which *Red Planet Mars* was mentioned as one example, was to 'incite hatred' against the Soviet Union and the people's democracies (6 Feb 1954: 1, 3). In *Red Planet Mars*, the Soviet regime is indeed portrayed as repressive and totalitarian, and the Russian communist leaders await a sign of weakness to start a war and 'build the New World in the ruins of the West'. In order to bring down the Russian people's uprising, a Soviet General plans a mass population transport, and is prepared to foster a famine to promote his ends: 'Let twenty or thirty millions of these sheep die, and see how long their religious faith lives' (*Red Planet Mars*, Final Script 1951: 82).[9] Thus the communists in the Kremlin are portrayed as cynical oppressors, ready to sacrifice the lives of millions of people to maintain their power. As in *Guilty of Treason*, the communist rulers in *Red Planet Mars* overtly despise religion and try to eradicate the authority of the church from society.

Many American politicians constantly referred to the idea of ruthless communists aiming at world domination. John Foster Dulles, who later became Secretary of State in Eisenhower's administration, discussed the nature of communism in his book *War or Peace* (1950). According to Dulles, the Russian people were not the USA's true enemy; it was the relatively small and fanatical Soviet Communist Party, which maintained 'despotic political power in Russia and elsewhere' (Dulles 1950: 5–6). Both *Guilty of Treason* and *Red Planet Mars* contained corresponding arguments: the main adversary was the communist elite, not the ordinary Russian (or Hungarian) people. In *Red Planet Mars* the Russian people are described as noble and religious peasants, who eagerly listen to the Voice of America (VOA); inspired by the messages from Mars, they start a revolution against communist dictatorship. In the film, the VOA, which was the US government's official broadcasting service, played a crucial role in the spiritual awakening of the Russian people. The film thus presents religion as a key factor in successful American radio propaganda broadcasting to the Socialist countries.

In its portrayal of Russian people, *Red Planet Mars* resembled *The North Star* (Lewis Milestone, 1943), Hollywood's wartime anti-Nazi film, in which Ukrainian peasants are fighting against the invading Nazi troops. In Hollywood films produced during 1942–45, the years when America was actively involved in the war, depictions of the Soviet Union underwent a dramatic transformation from an enemy into a valuable partner. HUAC later used pro-Soviet films, such as *The North Star*, as evidence of the growing communist influence in Hollywood (Shaw 2007: 23–24; Sayre 1982: 57–68). In both *The North Star* and *Red Planet Mars* humble peasants were depicted in an admirable light, even though the attitude of the two films toward the Soviet Union was the reverse. The first was anti-Nazi, the second anti-Soviet, but both were anti-dictatorship films.

Red Planet Mars argues that the Iron Curtain is the border between Christianity and Atheism, but that it is not a stable one. Even though the communists have taken over Russia and Eastern Europe, their dominance is on shaky ground. The majority of Russians oppose the Communist Party elite, which is able to sustain its position only by promoting terror and oppression. When the revolution against the communist regime begins, the peasants dig out the old Orthodox symbols that have previously been banned. The film argues that communist power in Eastern Europe is only temporary, and that it can be reversed, not militarily but by spiritual means and by supporting resistance against the communist dictatorship. The President of the United States (played by Willis Bouchey, who resembled the future president Dwight D. Eisenhower) announces that US foreign policy is now 'following the Star of Bethlehem'.

The Second World War and the Cold War were increasingly perceived in America as wars of faith against other faiths, of the American way of life against other ways of life,

Figure 4.4: The critic of the *Monthly Film Bulletin* noted the resemblance between the president (Willis Bouchey) and Dwight D. Eisenhower. The 1952 Republican presidential primaries, however, had not yet begun when *Red Planet Mars* was shot.

of Christianity against a diabolical enemy. This 'return to religion' was a major post-war phenomenon (Ellwood 2000: 2, 9; Whitfield 1991: 80–81). The polarity between Christianity and atheism was crucial to the anti-communist rhetoric of the 1950s. The communist ideology was considered to be 'the vision of Man without God', as the well-known anti-communist Whittaker Chambers put it in *Witness* (1952) (Chambers 1969: 9). Dulles also emphasized that Soviet communism starts with an atheistic, 'godless' premise, and suggested that the Americans should reject totally 'the Marxian thesis that material things are primary and spiritual things only secondary' (Dulles 1950: 8, 259). In a way, *Red Planet Mars* fulfilled this demand by showing that Marxist materialism could not satisfy the spiritual needs of the Russian people. Simultaneously, however, the film hints that Western consumer culture, which aims only at the growth of material welfare, is also wrong. Communism and Nazism are external menaces to the USA, but the film also suggests that excessive confidence in scientific progress and a lack of faith threaten to undermine the western democracies from within.

Red Planet Mars combines stereotypical characters from anti-Nazi and anti-communist films – rowdy Nazis and cynical communists. The Nazi scientist Franz Calder is depicted as a war criminal who, during the Second World War, performed grisly human experiments. *Red Planet Mars* draws an analogy between communists and Nazis, but – unlike *Guilty of Treason* – it also explains that they represent essentially different threats. At the end of the film, Calder meets the Cronyn couple in their laboratory and declares that Lucifer is his hero and that he wants to demolish Christianity.

Hendershot (2003: 58–59) argues that even though *Red Planet Mars* portrays communism as a false religion, it is the Nazis, not the communists, that are the true embodiment of evil. Hendershot claims that Nazism is projected as an even more powerful enemy than communism because it has incorporated Christian faith into its political ideology. Linda Cronyn, however, represents the antithesis to both ruthless communists and evil Nazis. She is portrayed as an intelligent women scientist, who admires her husband and ardently believes that the religious messages from Mars represent divine guidance. The Cronyns represent an American marriage based on equality, whose harmonious family life is contrasted to

Figure 4.5: Nazi Scientist Calder (centre) reveals his anti-Christian ideology to the Cronyn couple.

Calder's anti-religious bitterness. Their death, caused by the furious Calder, is presented as an act of martyrdom, and the President of the United States praises them as the patron saints of the new religious world order. In recent American political culture the phrase 'New World Order' is, paradoxically enough, anathema to the Christian right, who identify it with a (UN-led) one-world government. In *Red Planet Mars*, however, it represented the hope of the better future.

Red Planet Mars, which ends with the words 'the Beginning', announced that a spiritual awakening was necessary in the ongoing struggle between Marxist materialism and Christianity. It is a rare example of a utopian science-fiction film, ending in a situation in which mankind has reached peace and happiness. Nevertheless, it does not indicate what kind of social order would prevail after the global religious revival has swept the world. It merely prophesizes that both atheist communists and Nazis can be defeated through reliance on Christian principles. After the collapse of the totalitarian forces, the world will be ruled by a spiritually renewed American democracy. Thus *Red Planet Mars* can be interpreted as a Cold War utopia.

Conclusion

Red Planet Mars and *Guilty of Treason* define the conflict between communism and American values in religious terms. Both films deal with the menace of communism and portray communist rulers as ruthless oppressors, who use terror and violence to promote their ends. They argue that the Iron Curtain formed the border between freedom and tyranny in Europe and emphasize that Soviet-dominated communism was essentially an atheistic ideology, which aimed at expanding its dominance and sphere of influence in Europe. In spite of these similarities, however, the films offer two almost diametrically opposed views of the outcome of the Cold War.

For contemporary audiences, *Guilty of Treason* presented a rather pessimistic view of American possibilities of acting behind the Iron Curtain. The film's view of Eastern Europe is for the most part quite disconsolate; it also does not promise much help or comfort to the countries behind the Iron Curtain. The film seems to accept the border of the Iron Curtain as an indisputable fact, and the picture of the Eastern European police state is very bleak; this is not surprising, considering the anti-communist ideology that the film aimed at promoting. What is surprising, however, is the film's view of the USA's role and scope for action in Hungary. The communists had crushed the opposition and taken over control in Hungary, and all the United States could do was keep the hope of liberty alive among the suppressed Hungarians. Consequently, *Guilty of Treason* does not suggest any alternative scenarios, such as the rollback of communism or a revolt of oppressed peoples in Eastern Europe.

If *Guilty of Treason* defines the Iron Curtain as a stable border, *Red Planet Mars* presents a very different kind of scenario. Unlike *Guilty of Treason*, *Red Planet Mars* was not tied to real-life events; it was a science-fiction film, and the filmmakers could thus offer speculative answers to topical political questions. Thus *Red Planet Mars* announces that the Cold War can be won through a global religious revival. It delivers a utopian-like view of liberated Eastern Europe.

Religion is in an important part of both films, but its function is different. Thus the comparison of the films highlights the multidimensional ways in which anti-communist films integrated Cold War propaganda and religion. Both films define communism as an essentially atheistic belief system, which oppressed Christians in Eastern Europe. Both Stephanie and the Calder couple are prepared to sacrifice themselves for the cause of liberty, and their martyrdom underlines how the struggle against political enemies was at the same time a fight in the defence of Christianity. Both films represent Eastern Europe as governed by a small and cruel group of Communist Party leaders, all of whom obey orders from Moscow. Furthermore, both films distinguish sharply between individual Russians (or Hungarians) and the Communist Party elite. Although their analysis of the situation behind the Iron Curtain is similar, their conclusions are different: while in *Guilty of Treason* even the most religious individuals, such as Cardinal Mindszenty, were losing the struggle against communist domination; *Red Planet Mars* told the audience that a profound political and spiritual change in Eastern Europe was not only conceivable but almost inevitable. The Iron Curtain could be torn down by means of a global religious revival.

Guilty of Treason and *Red Planet Mars* contain opposite view of the USA's possibilities of changing power structures in Eastern Europe. In *Guilty of Treason* the Iron Curtain is an unambiguous border against the enemy ideology; in *Red Planet Mars*, it is a border that can be crossed and demolished by a spiritual awakening. The view of *Guilty of Treason* can be called 'realistic': the United States should contain the spread of communism, but it could not really change the situation in Eastern Europe. The Cold War conflict seemed to be a permanent landscape in the international politics. *Red Planet Mars* suggests a far more idealistic approach, where the suppressed majority of people in Eastern Europe are simply awaiting a sign to start a counter-revolution against their communist governments. In a way, the latter approach can be said to resemble the ideology of Ronald Reagan.

Ideologically, Reagan was a product of early Cold War antagonisms; his anti-communism was rooted in his experience as a film actor in the Red Scare era in Hollywood (May 2000: 211–12, 269). During the early stages of his presidency in the 1980s Reagan was vocal in his support for dissidents in the Soviet bloc, since he believed that the struggle against the 'evil empire' could be won. Reagan escalated the Cold War conflict and emphasized that the United States should encourage democratic change in communist regimes.

In his address to the British Parliament on 8 June 1982, Reagan referred to Winston Churchill's Iron Curtain speech. Unlike Churchill in 1946, however, Reagan envisioned that the collapse of communist regimes in Eastern Europe was foreseeable. Eventually, 'the march of freedom and democracy will leave Marxism-Leninism on the ash-heap of history'. According to Reagan, the ultimate determinant of the Cold War would not be weapons but 'a test of ideas, a trial of spiritual resolve'. Reagan's rhetoric could have been taken from *Red Planet Mars*, in which the President of the United States cherishes the idea of a global process of democracy and religious revival. When the messages from Mars turn into religious instructions, the president announces: 'I pray particularly that behind the Iron Curtain, where our eyes are not permitted to see, men will open their hearts to the message of peace and the promise that their leaders have so long denied them' (*Red Planet Mars*, Final Script 1951: 75). Thirty years later, in a similar vein, Reagan declared that the Cold War was about to end. Reagan's choice of words would have pleased the scriptwriters of *Red Planet Mars*:

> Let us be shy no longer. Let us go to our strength. Let us offer hope. Let us tell the world that a new age is not only possible but probable. (Address to Members of British Parliament, 8 June 1982)

References

Ahonen, K. (2006), 'Anticommunism in the United States in the 1950s: Post-Cold War Interpretations', in A. Cimdiṇa and J. Osmond (eds), *Power and Culture: Hegemony, Interaction and Dissent*, Pisa: Pisa University Press, pp. 131–45.

'Archbishop of N.Y. Thinks Mindszenty Was Drugged and Tortured by Reds', *The Washington Post*, 7 Feb 1949, p. 1.

Arendt, H. (1994), *Totalitarianism. Part Three of the Origins of Totalitarianism*, San Diego, New York & London: A Harvest Book. First published 1948.

Bagh, P. v. (2009), *Lajien synty. Elokuvan rakkaimmat lajit. Esittelyssä 147 genre-elokuvan helmeä*, Helsinki: WSOY.

Bigart, H. (1948), 'Catholic Church in Hungary Biggest Obstacle to Reds', *The Washington Post*, 12 Dec 1948, pp. M1&M2.

Booker, K. M. (2007), *From Box Office to Ballot Box. The American Political Film*, Westport, Connecticut & London: Praeger.

BoxOffice, 24 May 1952, Production files, clippings: *Red Planet Mars*. The Academy of Motion Picture Arts and Sciences, Margaret Herrick Library, Los Angeles (AMPAS).

Carruthers, S. L. (2009), *Cold War Captives: Imprisonment, Escape, and Brainwashing*, Berkeley: University of California Press.

Chambers, W. (1969), *Witness*, Chicago: Henry Regnery Company. First published 1952.

Coe, R. L. (1950), 'Romance Obscures Mindszenty Story', *The Washington Post*, 11 May 1950, p. 14.

Crowther, B. (1950), 'Ready, Aim, Fire!', *The New York Times*, 5 Jan 1950, p. 36.

Czetz, B. (2007), 'The Relationship Between the Catholic Church and the Communist Party in Hungary', in A. Cimdiṇa and J. Osmond (eds), *Power and Culture: Identity, Ideology, Representation*, Pisa: Pisa University Press, pp. 167–80.

Doherty, T. (1988), 'Hollywood Agit-Prop: The Anti-Communist Cycle 1948–1954', *Journal of Film and Video*, 40: 4 (Fall), pp. 15–27.

Dulles, J. F. (1950), *War or Peace*, New York: Macmillan.

Ellwood, R. S. (2000), *1950: Crossroads of American Religious Life*, Louisville, Kentucky: Westminster Knox Press.

'Final Act in Drama', *The New York Times*, 8 Feb 1949, p. 3.

Fried, R. M. (1990), *Nightmare in Red. The McCarthy Era in Perspective*, Oxford University Press: New York and Oxford 1990.

Gaddis, J. L. (2005), *The Cold War*, London: Allen Lane.

Gladchuck, J. J. (2007), *Hollywood and Anticommunism. HUAC and the Evolution of the Red Menace 1935–1950*, New York & London: Routledge.

Gleason, A. (1995), *Totalitarianism. The Inner History of the Cold War*, New York & Oxford: Oxford University Press.

Hendershot, C. (2003), *Anti-Communism and Popular Culture in the Mid-Century America*, Jefferson, North Carolina, and London: Mcfarland.

Kenez, P. (2003), 'The Hungarian Communist Party and the Catholic Church, 1945–1948', *The Journal of Modern History*, 75: 4 (December), pp. 864–89.

Kirby, D. (2003), 'Religion and the Cold War – An Introduction', in D. Kirby (ed.), *Religion and the Cold War*, Basingstoke: Palgrave, pp. 1–22.

Lavery, E. (1949a), *Guilty of Treason. Shooting Script by Emmet Lavery*. Catholic Digest/Freedom Productions.

—————— (1949b), 'Footnotes on Film of the Mindszenty Trial', *The New York Times*, 27 Nov 1949, p. 5.

May, L. (2000), *The Big Tomorrow. Hollywood and the Politics of the American Way*, Chicago & London: University Press of Chicago.

'Mindszenty Admits Some Guilt But Not Treason', *The Washington Post*, 4 Feb 1949, p. 1.

Monthly Film Bulletin, 225:19, Oct 1952, pp. 140–41.

President Harry S. Truman's address before a Joint Session of Congress, 12 March, 1947,*The Dynamics of World Power. A Documentary History of United States Foreign Policy 1945–1973. Volume 1, Part 1, Western Europe*. General Editor A. M. Schlesinger, Jr. New York: Chelsea House 1983 (DWP), pp. 111–15.

Pryor, T. M. (1950), 'Mindszenty Trial Reviewed as Film', *The New York Times*, 11 Apr 1950, p. 26.

Radosh, R. and Radosh, A. (2005), *Red Star Over Hollywood. The Film Colony's Long Romance with the Left*, San Francisco: Encounter Books.

Red Planet Mars, Final Script. Dated: Nov 29 1951, UCLA Arts Library, Special Collections, Box 742 (The script was written by John L. Balderston and Anthony Veiller).

Ronald Reagan, Address to Members of the British Parliament, June 8 1982, http://www.reagan. utexas.edu/archives/speeches/1982/60882a.htm. Accessed 7 May 2012.

'Russian Press Gives Space to Space to Capt. Video', *The New York Times*, 6 Feb 1954, pp. 1, 3.

Sayre, N. (1982), *Running Time. Films of the Cold War*, New York: The Dial Press.

Shaw, T. (2007), *Hollywood's Cold War*, Edinburgh: Edinburgh University Press.

'Stalinism Has a Strength of a Religion', *The Washington Post*, 11 Feb, 1951, p. B3.

Swann, P. (1995), 'International Conspiracy in and around the Iron Curtain', *The Velvet Light Trap*, 35 (Spring), pp. 52–60.

Variety, 14 May 1952, Production files, clippings: *Red Planet Mars*. The Academy of Motion Picture Arts and Sciences, Margaret Herrick Library, Los Angeles (AMPAS).

Warren, B. (1982), *Keep Watching the Skies! American Science Fiction Movies of the Fifties. Vol. I 1950–1957*. Jefferson, North Carolina: McFarland.

Whitfield, S. J. (1991), *The Culture of the Cold War*, Baltimore & London: The Johns Hopkins University Press.

Winston Churchill, 'Sinews of Peace' address at Westminster College in Fulton, Missouri on March 5 1946, http://www.historyguide.org/europe/churchill.html. Accessed 7 May 2012.

Notes

1   Winston Churchill, 'Sinews of Peace' address at Westminster College in Fulton, Missouri on March 5 1946.

2   John Joseph Gladchuck (2007: 1–4) argues the 'Reds' in film industry posed no real threat to the security of the United States, and that HUAC betrayed the constitution in its ultraconservative witch-hunt of Hollywood's left. Ronald and Allis Radosh (2005: 235–42) have reached the opposite conclusion. According to them, most of the Hollywood Ten were committed members of the Communist Party and admirers of the Soviet system.

3   At the same time, however, Hollywood films offered ways to criticize, question, or even laugh at Cold War rhetoric. For example, *The Day the Earth Stood Still* (Robert Wise, 1951), can be interpreted as implicit critique of Cold War hysteria.

4   Mindszenty stayed in prison until he was temporarily liberated by the uprising of 1956. When Soviet troops invaded Hungary, he escaped to the American embassy, where he lived until 1971.

5   The image was so powerful that five years later the Mindszenty Case was the subject of another fiction film, *The Prisoner* (UK, Peter Glenville, 1955), which was commercially more successful than *Guilty of Treason*.

6   President Harry S. Truman's address before a Joint Session of Congress, 12 March, 1947. DWP: 111–15.

7   John Lewis Gaddis (2005: 10–14), for example, argues that Stalin's goal was to dominate the continent as thoroughly as Hitler had tried to do, although Stalin followed no fixed timetable or method to achieve the goal.

8   *BoxOffice*, 24 May 1952, AMPAS; *Variety*, 14 May 1952, AMPAS; *Monthly Film Bulletin*, no 225, Vol 19, Oct 1952: 140–41. *Red Planet Mars* was based on a play *Red Planet* (1932) written by John L. Balderston and John Hoare.

9   In the script, the description of the transfer of population is stated more explicitly: 'Ukrainians to the Caucasus ... Lithuanians to the Urals ... Georgians to the Baltic provinces'. However, this additional comment has been cut from the film. Red Planet Mars, Final Script 1951: 82.

Chapter 5

Crossing Over: On Becoming European in Aki Kaurismäki's Cinema

Sanna Peden
The University of Western Australia

Aki Kaurismäki's films depict marginalized characters making the most out of their lives in bleak, urban surroundings. These marginal spaces are witness to a sudden geopolitical shift at the end of the Cold War and the subsequent gradual redefinition of Europe. I appropriate Thomas Elsaesser's term 'double occupancy' to examine how Kaurismäki's cinema reflects the changing borders and identity formations of Europe. Double occupancy is a flexible term, but at its core is the idea that cultures and identities are in constant flux, characterized by overlaps and contradictions, and that the history of one nation is entwined with that of another. In my analysis I consider how the idea of Europe 'occupies' space in Kaurismäki's cinema.

I focus on Kaurismäki's London-set film *I Hired a Contract Killer* (1990) and the nostalgic road film *Pidä huivista kiinni Tatjana/Take Care of Your Scarf, Tatjana* (1993). In many respects, these films represent very different aspects of the director's work: while *I Hired a Contract Killer* is already by virtue of its setting, cast and language an international undertaking, *Take Care of Your Scarf, Tatjana* is an expression of specifically Finnish nostalgia. However, both films are concerned with issues of belonging, identity and the end of the Cold War. Both films are also set in liminal spaces that contribute to the films' broader interrogation of real and metaphorical borders, such as those between life and death, past and present and East and West.

The representation of space in both films is characterized by Kaurismäki's familiar aesthetic, and the marginal locations on screen are often subject to competing claims over their identity: whether they are repositories of national memories or whether by their stylized liminality they are anything but. By drawing on the concept of double occupancy I argue that while the spaces in these films are subject to a host of claims over their role with respect to national identity, in the context of the fundamental shifts in Europe's borders at the time of the films' production, Europe itself becomes an occupier of the screen space. *I Hired a Contract Killer* and *Take Care of Your Scarf, Tatjana*, then, serve to interrogate the changing form of Europe and the place of national belonging in a post-Cold War world. Ultimately, the negotiation of spatial, temporal and emotional boundaries in the films reveals the emergence of a new, doubly occupied European reality.

Place in Aki Kaurismäki's cinema

The Finnish auteur director Aki Kaurismäki has for almost 30 years made films which contemplate and critique aspects of belonging and identity. His films are highly stylized: Henry Bacon (2003: 92) argues that while some locations are recognizable to locals, Kaurismäki's Helsinki appears off-kilter and 'displaced'. Kaurismäki's diegetic world, sometimes referred to as Akilandia, is internally consistent in its displacement and almost instantly recognizable. Best known for his 2002 film *Mies vailla menneisyyttä/The Man Without A Past*, Kaurismäki has been instrumental in putting Finland on the cinematic map, both in terms of critical recognition and as a cinematic place in itself.

Kaurismäki's films are replete with anachronistic objects and old-fashioned music. They exude an indeterminate sense of pastness, a temporal displacement reinforced by the films' particular representation of space. Satu Kyösola (2004: 50) has referred to the archival nature of Kaurismäki's cityscape, drawing attention to the fact that filming locations have often been demolished or repurposed soon after being captured by Kaurismäki's camera. In an interview in 1996, the director stated that he wished to 'document everything that is beautiful', and said that everything beautiful was under threat in Finland. He went on to say that earth-movers have always followed at the crew's heels, but that this was due not to his decision to seek out such sites, but to a coordinated effort to 'destroy Old Finland' in favour of becoming a 'Euro-worthy High-Tech society' (Lindqvist 1996: 14). As the comment suggests, Kaurismäki has been vocal in his opposition to Finland's European Union membership. Indeed, in a characteristically polemical statement published just days before Finland's 1994 referendum on EU membership, Kaurismäki explained his opposition by stating that Finland had not striven towards national independence for 'three thousand years' in order to become nothing but a 'market area' for a 'huckster' (Anon 1994: n.p.). While in the course of this essay I approach 'Europe' as an idea and a conceptual framework rather than as the European Union or any real geographical space, it is worth keeping in mind the director's objection to more formal political Europeanization processes, as this does have an impact on the way Kaurismäki's screenspaces respond to the redefinition of post-Cold War Europe in the broader metaphorical sense.

Kaurismäki's disenchantment with societal change – not only processes of Europeanization specifically but also the increasing influence of global capitalism at the expense of comprehensive welfare networks and genuine social compassion is reflected in the run-down, desolate spaces on screen. Sirpa Tani (2007) draws attention to the way the settings reflect the characters' identities and statuses, pointing out that Kaurismäki's protagonists are both physically and psychologically in the margins of society. Kaurismäki's disillusionment with contemporary society also finds expression in a stylized yet critical nostalgia: for Tytti Soila certain choices of settings in Kaurismäki's films are inherently nostalgic and signal in themselves social, and specifically national, transition. Soila notes that the '[u]biquitous and pleasantly anonymous' cafeterias – like the ones the protagonists in *Take Care of Your Scarf, Tatjana* frequent on their drive to Helsinki – are a 'reminder for post-war Finnish audiences of the shared past' (2002: 196). Crucially, Soila (2002: 197) argues that Kaurismäki's 'cinematic space [...] is constructed as *critical space* allowing the interrogation of political, social and economic power structures'.

In a similar vein Pietari Kääpä discusses locations in Kaurismäki's films as corresponding to Michel Foucault's *heterotopias,* buildings and delimited areas that somehow encode social transition or transgression. Heterotopias are places that invert and challenge 'lived spaces that have a normalizing, banal function within a cultural formation', places which by their existence expose the compulsion to control society and imagine the nation (Kääpä 2006: 5). Delivered as a lecture in 1967 but not published until 1984, Foucault's essay 'Of other spaces' posits certain criteria for heterotopias, spaces that arise out of the tension between public and private space. These criteria include an element of containment and exclusion and a specific relationship with the passage of time. Foucault's examples include libraries and museums as sites for protecting material against the ravages of time, prisons and boarding schools for containing a threat to conventional society (such as crime or adolescent sexuality) and theatres and cinemas for providing alternatives to everyday reality, if only momentarily (Foucault 2008: 18–21). As Michiel Dehaene and Lieven De Cauter (2008: 5) point out, Foucault's heterotopias were 'important institutions of the city'; not so much places that questioned social order, but places whose impressive presence suggested that social order did not occur naturally.

Kääpä extends the Foucauldian original to apply more broadly in Kaurismäki's cinematic world: here the roads, the bars and edges of the city are also heterotopian sites, marked by transience and outsidedness. Given Kääpä's broad use of the term heterotopia, the places he refers to are closely linked to what Andrew Nestingen (2001: 167) calls Kaurismäki's 'non-places', emphasizing their non-national role as 'social spaces that are cut off from the national past'. The French anthropologist Marc Augé introduced the concept of non-places in his treatise on 'supermodernity', proposing that such spaces are located outside national imaginaries and are instead symbolic of an increasing individualization of reference: Nestingen draws on Augé's conceptualization of contemporary spaces to argue for the transnationality of Kaurismäki's films, and their self-aware distantiation from the national past.

Keeping in mind these disparate readings of space in Kaurismäki's cinema, from the nationally nostalgic to critically transnational, I approach the depiction and manipulation of space in *I Hired a Contract Killer* and *Take Care of Your Scarf, Tatjana* through Thomas Elsaesser's concept 'double occupancy'. Elsaesser (2005: 108, 110–11) proposes the term as a 'counter-metaphor for Fortress Europe', emphasizing the plurality of identities across Europe whilst also acknowledging that not all identities are equal, that plural identities are subject to hierarchies and power struggles. Elsaesser writes that he

> want[s] the term to be understood as at once tragic, comic and utopian. Tragic, because the reality of feeling oneself invaded, imposed upon, deprived of the space and security one thinks one needs [...] a state of pathos, disempowerment and self-torment. Comic,

in the way one considers mistaken identities as comic, that is, revealing ironies and contradictions in the fabric of language and its signifiers. And utopian, insofar as under certain conditions […] it opens up ways of sharing the same space while not infringing on the other's claims. (2005: 110–11)

Double occupancy is clearly a very flexible concept, and although it has not yet been widely used in film studies it is open to a range of uses. For example, Senta Siewert (2008: 206) applies the term to her analysis of the soundscapes of *Gegen die Wand/Head On* (Fatih Akin, 2004), arguing that 'double occupancy helps develop an audiovisual analysis that fully apprehends the combination of cinema and popular music'. In Siewert's analysis double occupancy refers to the sampling and mixing of disparate music styles, the creation of 'sonic memories' that tie together characters and places on screen and the audience's 'multi-occupied' state in relation to the film, as viewers in all likelihood share some but not all of the reference points and musical codes of the film (Siewert 2008: 204, 205).

In my analysis I understand the films' spaces in the first instance as doubly – or, indeed, multiply – occupied by competing and mutually constitutive claims from national nostalgia to non-place. What I am interested in, however, is the way in which these spaces come to be further 'occupied' by the redefinition of European borders at the end of the Cold War. I take the cue for my analysis in part from Rosalind Galt's and Luisa Rivi's work on post-Cold War European cinema. Galt and Rivi approach post-Cold War films from different perspectives: Rivi seeks to understand the role of European film industries in the development of a supranational European space and identity, while Galt prioritizes close textual analysis in exploring how cinema takes stock of such geopolitical shifts. They are nevertheless united in a desire for analyses of European cinema that approach Europe not as a homogenous entity but as a process of spatial and temporal imagining. Rivi (2007: 3) agitates for a conceptualization of post-Cold War Europe that acknowledges the 'persistence of the nation-state' without vilifying it, while also taking into account 'heterogeneity and the idea of overlapping communities', ultimately leading to a 'post-Cold War Europe that is neither dualistic nor postnational'. Galt (2006: 4–5) sees the analysis of cinematic space as crucial to such an understanding of Europe, and calls for film writing which 'takes on the logic of cartography' to come to terms with the way in which post-Cold War European cinema 'speak[s] both of and from the changing spaces of the continent […] coarticulating cinematic space and geopolitical space', or the way in which the shifts and challenges of European identities are mapped on to the screen.

In my analysis I consider how the post-Cold War Europeanization process finds metaphorical expression in Kaurismäki's screenspaces. My intention is not to imply that these metaphors would necessarily be deliberate references on the part of the filmmaker, but that if we are to understand the profound impact the end of the Cold War had on European identities and the idea of Europe itself it is necessary, following Galt, to 'begin from the image, moving from the space of the frame to that of geography' (2006: 231) and approach the screen as a representational space that can not only directly comment on the geopolitical shifts of its time, but can also be inhabited–occupied–by those same shifts. I argue that the spaces in *I Hired a Contract Killer* and *Take Care of Your Scarf, Tatjana* come to be occupied by an approaching Europe in the heterogeneous, metaphorical sense of Galt's and Rivi's models, albeit without optimistic underpinnings: the Europe on the horizon in these films is unstable, fragmented and potentially destructive. If understood in terms of an encroaching European space, the many crossings of real and metaphorical borders in *I Hired a Contract Killer* and *Take Care of Your Scarf, Tatjana* can be seen as reflections on the possibilities as well as the precariousness of the geopolitical shifts of the late 1980s and early 1990s.

No fatherland? Belonging in a new world order in *I Hired a Contract Killer*

I Hired a Contract Killer is set in London, and shows the lonely Frenchman Henri fail at suicide, hire a hardened criminal to kill him only to regret the transaction on meeting Margaret, a friendly flower seller. Henri and Margaret are driven further into the margins of society as they try to prevent the killing, finally finding an unexpected ally in the killer's own body, weakened by cancer. Paul Newland (2007) argues that Henri's loneliness and troubled existence are 'echoed, and indeed informed' by his dilapidated, liminal, 'dead' environment, and that the film emerges as a celebration of the 'detritus of the city – both architectural and human'.

Claire Monk (2009: 268, 275) considers the film's 'transtextual' relationship to other visions of the city, arguing that Kaurismäki's London 'is more a socio-historic and psychogeographic composite than a spatially coherent rendition of the capital'. The effect is similar to Kaurismäki's distinctive vision of Helsinki: 'the imaginary world of the films both is and is not that city' (Bacon 2003: 92). Indeed, while all of Kaurismäki's urban settings are very similar, *I Hired a Contract Killer* draws from and contributes to a vast catalogue of imagery and narratives of London in particular. At the same time, because of the film's aesthetic similarity to Kaurismäki's other works the film carries a residual 'Finnish' quality: for example, Finland's pre-eminent film critic Peter von Bagh argues that with *I Hired a Contract Killer* '"Kaurismäkiland" was created on foreign soil – but [it is] still genuinely Finnish' (see foreword in Hukkanen 1997: 6; see also Kääpä 2004: 92–93). The film had a multinational cast and crew, was coproduced by Finnish, Swedish, West German, French and British companies and was shown in film festivals around the world, including in London, New York, Belgrade and Hong Kong ('I Hired a Contract Killer' 2002: 509, 512), and the casting of Jean-Pierre Léaud as Henri was a clear tribute to Léaud's celebrated work in films of the French New Wave. The very fabric of the film, then, is doubly occupied by a range of national cinematic traditions as well as international film commerce.

Given the competing claims as to the nature and identity of the film, *I Hired a Contract Killer* is an interesting point of departure from Kaurismäki's Finland-based films, and provides a rich opportunity for analyses of place and belonging in the director's work. For example, Pietari Kääpä (2004: 91) argues that Kaurismäki's cinema communicates 'a transcending of national origin, where the national question becomes a moot point', citing as examples Henri's displacement and Margaret's comment that 'the working class has no fatherland'. Indeed, Kaurismäki's films have always maintained a critical view of constructions of nationhood. However, when examined in terms of Europeanization and double occupancy, *I Hired a Contract Killer* emerges specifically as a reflection of the transition in global identity coordinates and the idea of Europe at the end of the Cold War.

I Hired a Contract Killer was filmed between 26 March and 4 May 1990 (Anon 2002: 511). The film, then, arises out of a moment of rapid and fundamental change in world politics, following the fall of the Berlin Wall, revolutions in Eastern Europe and the Malta Summit in 1989, but before the official unification of Germany or the breaking up of the Soviet Union and Yugoslavia. As Rosalind Galt (2006: 1) notes, in the early 1990s, '[f]or the first time since the end of World War II, the borders of Europe were disconcertingly unstable'. This geopolitical instability is metaphorically reflected in Henri's social marginality, the film's dilapidated settings, and Henri's transient state between life and death.

Henri works as a clerk at the royal Waterworks. During breaks he sits apart from his colleagues, who share a laugh at another table. Henri is so marginal in his work environment he manages to only just squeeze into the frame of the scene itself (Figure 5.1 and 5.2). Clearly this is a man who does not belong, who has no friends and who, when gone, would not be missed. Later we see the only entries in his address book are his workplace and an already crossed out, deceased relative. When he explains to Margaret that he is 'not used to talking' she responds that that much was clear: his accent may mark him as a foreigner, but his abrupt mannerisms also reveal him as a man unaccustomed to friendship and casual chats. Yet while he does not belong, he is not outside national specificity. Instead, he negotiates his existence between his French past and British present as best he can. In a move that mimics the common practice of situating a film in a particular city by depicting iconic landmarks, the camera momentarily rests on a miniature Eiffel tower on Henri's desk. The item is a souvenir in its material sense, a cheap trinket, but it is also a more literal souvenir, a memory of who he is and where he comes from. He may have left France because he was not particularly 'liked' there, but the image, the ideal, the souvenir of France stays with him. At the same time he also follows certain quintessentially British codes: at home he drinks tea and eats scones, at the Honolulu Bar he orders a ginger ale, a beverage more appropriate to the adventures of the Famous Five than the underworld-frequented establishment. Henri's day-to-day life, then, is doubly occupied by the symbols and practices of his two homelands.

The Eiffel tower does not just 'set the scene' for Henri internally, as his Frenchness has a definite influence on his place in society. When Henri is made redundant, his supervisor appeals to his understanding: the foreigners must be the first ones to be let go. A Turkish worker waits in line after Henri, also due to receive as a departing gift a flimsy five-pound watch that does not work. When Henri does finally find a friend it is another Frenchman, the proprietor of 'Vic's French Hamburgers' at Hampstead cemetery. Being doubly occupied is clearly problematic, as a plurality of identity coordinates prevents one from having full access to society, from Henri and his Turkish colleague now having

Figure 5.1: Henri's social marginalization.

no 'occupation' at all to Vic inhabiting the finest example of a heterotopian non-place: a hamburger bar in a cemetery. It is telling that only as Henri travels to the very margins of the city to hire his own killer, he experiences a curious kind of courtesy denied him in otherwise respectable society: criminals try to convince him of the joys of life ('we don't work either, look at us, we're still happy'), and while his manager at the Waterworks steadfastly refused to do so, the crime boss gives him his 'two weeks' notice' as a matter of course. In these scenes double occupancy moves fluidly between tragedy and comedy: Henri's perfunctory dismissal is tragically unfair in that through his 'foreignness' he is positioned as the occupier, as if his displacement and isolation in the city were intended in malice. A further tragedy briefly inhabits the screen in the unrealized romantic aspirations of his forlorn landlady, who retreats to smoke in isolation when Henri takes his leave. At the same time the ironies of Henri's experience – the discrepancy of the two weeks' notice, the watch that does not work – allow for a comic mode to seep into his doubly occupied existence. Eventually the killer's philosophical decision to carry out the hit whether it is still required or not – 'nobody wants it, but die they must' – hints at the utopian possibilities of double occupancy, as he finds a way to fulfil his mission without harming Henri. However, the necessity of death returns tragedy to the frame: Henri has survived but not resolved his existential crisis.

The film is set in a host of public places, such as streets and bars, and once Henri has hired the contract killer he spends much time in transitional, border spaces such as corridors and stairwells, first waiting for and then evading death. He is frequently positioned at a doorway or

Figure 5.2: The remains of the Honolulu Bar.

a window, belonging nowhere in particular. On Margaret's advice he returns to the Honolulu Bar to cancel the assassination, but arrives too late, as the bar has already been demolished.

The rubble left behind reflects the dismantling of established social and political structures at the time of the film's making, leaving Henri in what Soila (2002: 197), in discussing Kaurismäki's cinema more broadly, refers to as 'a limbo between the demolished worldview of the former Soviet Union and an onrushing Euro-Americanism'. There is a similar effect when Henri seeks refuge at the cemetery, first working at the hamburger bar, then plotting his escape from Britain with Margaret, and finally in coming face to face with his assassin, Harry, in a decaying old church building. The graveyard is a border space, marking a transition between life and death, old world and new. The mixing of national codes at the cemetery represents the tentative unification of Europe, of parties brought suddenly closer together, unsure of what their new proximity will bring.

There is a curious parallel between Henri and his intended assassin: indeed, as Harry is a nickname for Henry the similarity of their names already invites further comparison. Both are in a sense doubly occupied by life and death, frequently marked by suggestions of their demise. Harry's double occupancy is more literal, as the cancer spreads and takes control of his body. He is weak, he coughs up blood. Henri's resolve to die is first shown in similarly definite terms, such as when he nails instructions to the killer on his apartment building door. As one of Henri's attempts at suicide had failed when the hook he had affixed to support his noose came loose form the wall, his decision to hammer the notice to the door revisits the imagery of his hanging attempt. While Henri's own will to die dissolves on meeting Margaret, he remains marked for death. For example, when he and Margaret part, she presses her lips on his forehead, leaving a bright red mark reminiscent of blood, a bullet wound. However, Henri wipes the mark away in a gesture suggesting relief, of wiping sweat off one's brow: there is still hope.

There are other similar instances where Henri metaphorically evades death. For example, Henri and Margaret sit down to play cards to the accompaniment of the radio playing 'Ennen kuolemaa' (Before Death). While Henri goes to the local shop, Harry arrives. The killer and his mark miss each other in a choreography of lifts and stairwells: it is not yet their time. As Harry and Margaret sit down to wait for Henri's return, the two are separated by a vase of dead roses. Meanwhile, Henri buys cigarettes and fresh flowers: the suggestion is of renewal rather than impending doom. Still, Henri and Harry's endgame at the cemetery must end in death, as the setting itself suggests as much. Henri darts through the literal space of death hoping to evade his killer, with no luck. Harry finds him soon enough. The two stand facing each other, one the negative of the other.

Harry wears a pale overcoat and a high-necked black shirt, where Henri's coat is black and collar white. While Henri faces an external threat, Harry is consumed from within by his illness. Faced with the prospect of a slow decay into death, Harry chooses instead to turn the gun on himself, as a stunned Henri looks on in silence. Given the geopolitical instability of the time of the film's making, it becomes possible to read the confrontation between these two literal opposites as an allegorical reference to the contemporary tension between dominant ideologies, a contest between the East and the West. That Henri is the

Figure 5.3: Harry and Henri come face to face.

confused witness to Harry's, his ostensible double's, self-destruction can be seen to reflect the West's ambivalent relationship to the fall of European communism: a self-preserving elation mingled with bewilderment over how to redefine one's identity in a post-Cold War world.

Seen in the context of an emerging European identification, the interplay of life and death comes to represent a negotiation of a new geopolitical occupation. From this perspective it is not difficult to see Henri's fraught emergence from the limbo of the cemetery – he is almost run over by Margaret's taxi – as a reflection of a new and still unstable world order. Indeed, the demolition of the Honolulu Bar, the pivot point between life and death, already suggested a fundamental paradigmatic shift in Henri's world view. Keeping in mind the ongoing geopolitical shifts of the time of the film's making, Margaret's comment that 'the working class has no fatherland' can no longer be taken on face value in its original Marxist sense. Instead the quote, delivered as it is in front of a partly torn down wall mere months after the fall of the Berlin wall, emerges as an acknowledgement of the end of the Cold War, the failure of Soviet communism and the prospect of an increasingly European future, for better or for worse.

The ostalgic road trip: Revisiting the in-between in *Take Care of Your Scarf, Tatjana*

Where *I Hired a Contract Killer* deals with the shock of the end of the Cold War, *Take Care of Your Scarf, Tatjana* reflects on Finland's position in the newly defined Europe. The film is set in the past, 'in a fictitious sixties' (von Bagh 2006: 154). While the aesthetics of the film are similar to Kaurismäki's other films, there are explicit references that tie the film to the specific time period: for example, Reino is keen to emphasize his belonging to the rocker subculture of the era and he makes reference to a sporting trip to Czechoslovakia in 1962 and the cost of purchasing a Volga car. *Take Care of Your Scarf, Tatjana* represents a peculiar kind of ostalgia once removed. Ostalgia refers to the nostalgic reflection of the communist past in German popular culture, such as in the films *Good Bye Lenin!/Goodbye, Lenin!* (Wolfgang Becker, 2003) and *Sonnenallee* (Leander Haußmann, 1999). Much like nostalgia, ostalgia is generally viewed as a complacent approach to history, one that valorizes the retro aesthetics of the GDR and ignores or glosses over the negative aspects of the regime. However, some commentators have suggested that ostalgia can instead have a critical function, in that it promotes 'the kind of critical distance necessary to reflect on current conditions' (Enns 2007: 477, see also Cooke 2005).

While 'ostalgia' as a term is of a more recent coinage, '[n]ostalgia became a defense [sic] mechanism against the accelerated rhythm of change and the economic shock therapy' in the former eastern bloc by the early 1990s (Boym 2001: 64), and it was not unusual for films of the period to address the changing world order with a mixture of critical perspective and nostalgia: examples include *Kolya* (Jan Svérak, 1996) and *Underground/Podzemlje* (Emir Kusturica, 1995). *Take Care of Your Scarf, Tatjana* can be seen as an expression of a Finnish variant of ostalgia in this critical mode, as the film returns to Finland's much-debated position in-between or doubly occupied by the two power blocks during the Cold War as a response to the geopolitical changes of the 1990s. Indeed, Pietari Kääpä (2010: 214) suggests that the film's valorization of Soviet and Baltic connections should be read as 'an allegorical anti-EU statement, which, in tandem with the nostalgic qualities of the narrative, suggests concrete dissatisfaction with the contemporary moment'. When considered in terms of double occupancy, the film's critique of the contemporary moment is evident, first, in the way the male protagonists negotiate norms of Easternness and Westernness and, second, in the depiction of space and travel in the film.

By the end of the Second World War, Finland had lost the Continuation War fought against the Soviet Union, and large areas of land along the border had to be ceded to the victor. As a result of the losses incurred in the war, Finland had to negotiate a new national identity which took into account both the psychological and economic impact of its diminished land area and subsequent influx of refugees from the ceded areas. The variety of products required for the payment of war reparations exceeded Finland's immediate post-war production capacity, and so Finland's industrial sector was forced to develop rapidly (Karisto et al. 1997: 57). By the time the final war reparations had been paid the Finnish economy had shifted in focus from primary production to secondary industry. Large-scale urbanization followed in the 1960s, again accompanied by changes in Finnish national identity (Karisto et al. 1997: 67). The first generation urban population moved from the traditional closely-knit rural communities with distinct regional identities to the cities and industrial centres, often with the effect of creating a sense of displacement.

While these internal shifts took place Finland sought to maintain a delicate balance in its foreign policy, professing a neutral and mediating role between the East and the West. Abroad Finnish neutrality was not always considered credible, but it was a crucial aspect of Finnish national narratives nonetheless. The end of the Cold War saw the dominant narrative of Finland being perched in-between the East and the West challenged. Christopher Browning has argued that since the end of the Cold War Finnish historiography has sought to emphasize Finland's Western qualities and to position Finland's Cold War in-betweenness as an unsatisfactory compromise:

> Of particular emotive appeal has been the notion that after the historical parenthesis of the Cold War Finland has finally *come home* to the West, the most concrete and symbolic manifestation of which has been Finland's membership in the EU. (Browning 2002: 47)

Take Care of Your Scarf, Tatjana was made in the second half of 1993 and released in early 1994. At the time when the film was being made there was much debate about Finland's potential membership of the European Union, and the Westernizing narrative identified by Browning was forming. The Maastricht Treaty had established the European Union of twelve member states in 1992, and shortly afterwards Finland had submitted an application for EU membership. There was close scrutiny of the membership negotiations throughout 1993 (see for example Jokelin 1993, Väisänen 1993), and as Finland was also due to have a presidential election in January 1994, the candidates' attitudes towards the EU and NATO were an important part of the campaign coverage. At this pivotal point in the Finnish national narrative *Take Care of Your Scarf, Tatjana* returns to the Cold War, to a now endangered national space in-between the East and the West.

In the film two surly and insecure Finnish men start on an improvised road trip: Reino, an alcoholic mechanic, is amenable to an extended test drive in the countryside proposed by Valto, a coffee-addicted dressmaker, who has locked his employer-mother in a closet in a moment of anger. Along the way the men decide to help an Estonian and a Russian woman get to Helsinki, and a cautious romance forms between the two pairings, Tatjana and Reino and Klavdja and Valto. It is in these timid cross-border affections that Kaurismäkian ostalgia operates in the comic mode of double occupancy, as the men repeatedly fail to interact with the women in satisfactory ways: nervous of physical contact and embarrassed by affection, the men are unable to live up to the romantic potential and sexual liberation implicit in the road movie genre. It is not so much a case of mistaken identities or even language barriers: the women's openness to romance is clear enough, but the men's caricaturish reticence stands in the way of romantic fulfilment.

In one scene, set in the ruins of a barn, Klavdja and Tatjana get up to dance while Reino and Valto remain seated, resorting to their copious intake of caffeine and alcohol for comfort. Later the four attend a formal dance, ostensibly as couples. Again Klavdja and Tatjana dance together, while the men steadfastly avoid eye contact and concentrate on their drinks. The musicians on stage perform a song which lends the scene exceptional irony: the lyrics tell

Figure 5.4: Valto and Reino drink, Klavdja and Tatjana dance.

the story of a Russian woman, Anjuska, who rejects 'Bolshevik' men and dances instead with her passionate Finnish suitors. Klavdja in particular is quick to compare Valto and Reino to Slavic men, reminiscing about her many dance partners and commenting pointedly that 'our men are talkative ... they take their wife or girlfriend to a fancy restaurant'.

If Reino and Valto fall short of the standards of Eastern masculinity, their performances of Westernness are equally flawed. Ewa Mazierska and Laura Rascaroli (2006: 22) draw attention to the pair 'clumsily adapt[ing] certain elements of the American "road ethos": clothes, gestures and expressions'. Reino in particular takes great pride in being a rocker, and gets into scuffles over the right to be considered an authentic member of the subculture. Yet the affectionate and sympathetic treatment of the men's idiosyncrasies suggests that they are not failures at being Western or Eastern but exemplars of almost utopian modes of double occupancy. The men's in-betweenness is forged out of their particular blend of Eastern and Western markers and attributes: in this vision of a past Finland, the alcohol-fuelled bravado of a provincial rocker is not in the least incompatible with a chaste affection for a slight Estonian woman, and the borders that exist between the men and women are emotional rather than material, political or even linguistic. This material borderlessness is emphasized by the fact that the eventual real border-crossing to Estonia is underplayed into meaninglessness, with Valto and Reino seemingly able to enter the country without passports, visas, or passing through customs. That the film depicts this eastbound freedom of movement at a time when much was being made in the media of the Finns' prospect of similar freedom within the European Union serves as a cogent example of the way Kaurismäki uses the pseudo-historical setting of the film to critique the Europeanization discourse of 'the contemporary moment'.

During their drive south ruins and dilapidated buildings dot the countryside, a reminder of a country in the grip of structural change. Reino also makes several references to 'ruins', for example in discussing his financial situation and the state of a man he had assaulted: in one case he mentions a trip to Czechoslovakia, where his fellow travellers chose to visit local sights – ruins – instead of focus on demolishing the tour group's stockpile of vodka, much to Reino's amazement. The repeated evocation of ruins serves a similar function as the depiction of demolished buildings in I Hired a Contract Killer, in that it draws attention to the irrevocable changes being wrought on society, both in terms of the historical period of structural change depicted on screen as well as the early 1990s Europeanization context. Given Kaurismäki's comments about the destruction of 'Old Finland' for the purposes of becoming 'Euro-worthy', the references to 'ruins' in the film tie in not only with a regular theme of Kaurismäki's cinema but also with the director's Eurosceptic public statements.

The depiction of travel, and specifically travel with no particular obstructions, is particularly relevant to the film's critique of the European project. Iina Hellsten (1996: 190–92) has studied the representation of the EU in Finnish mainstream media, and notes that Finland's EU membership was often conceptualized as an inevitable development, with the EU being referred to as a 'destination' and a natural end-point to the national 'journey'. Christopher Browning's identification of the already mentioned 'homecoming' motif in the post-Cold War Europeanization discourse also fits this broader tendency. Again, given the context of the film's production and Kaurismäki's sensitivity to processes of Europeanization in Finnish society, the protagonists' drive to Helsinki in *Take Care of Your Scarf, Tatjana* can be seen to reflect Finland's steady move towards the EU: in effect the journey itself is 'occupied' by Europe. That the foursome's journey will end in separation ties with the view at the time that Eastern elements of society had to be downplayed and recent history rewritten from a different perspective for Finland to be properly Europeanized. Here double occupancy becomes distinctly tragic, and reveals the inherent fraudulence of having to choose between the East and the West and building an identity based on implausibly neat distinctions.

When the protagonists finally arrive in Helsinki, Reino and Valto make a last-minute decision to see Tatjana and Klavdja further along on their journey, and the men board the ferry. Klavdja catches a train back home on her own, and Reino decides to stay in Estonia with Tatjana, leaving Valto to return to Finland by himself. The final sequence, showing Valto's stoic but lonely return home, is particularly telling of the film's ostalgic critique of Finland's European trajectory. During Valto's drive home the image is suddenly occupied by an alternative reality: Valto drives his car in through the window of a café, with Reino, Klavdja and Tatjana still his passengers.

Valto orders a small coffee at the counter, and turns back to look at his car: this time it is undamaged, out in the open and without his travelling companions. The very literal 'breaking of the frame' and Valto's longing for his lost friends reflect the sudden shift in

Figure 5.5: Breaking the frame.

the era's geopolitics, the shattering of old certainties and the rejection of the East in the Europeanization discourse of the 1990s. The surrealism of the fantasy sequence continues when Valto arrives home: without a word he releases his mother from the cupboard, sets himself by the sewing machine again and the two get on with life as usual. It is as if the intervening adventure had never happened, and the scene can be seen to reflect the contemporary view that Cold War Finlandization and Finland's close ties with the Eastern bloc were an unfortunate 'parenthesis' (Browning 2002: 47) in the country's history. The final scene leaves the viewer with a profound sense of dissatisfaction over Valto's inability to hold on to any of the relationships formed over the course of the film.

Conclusion

The end of the Cold War led to a radical shift in global identity coordinates. Over time, 'this traumatic overturning of spatial categories was augmented with a more gradual, although by no means painless, redefinition [of Europe]' (Galt 2006: 1). *I Hired a Contract Killer* and *Take Care of Your Scarf, Tatjana* arise out of this highly unstable moment in recent history, and the films' spaces are 'occupied' in different ways by this process of redefinition. In the case of *I Hired a Contract Killer,* the European moment occurs suddenly, with the protagonist Henri left uncertain about his place in the world. In *Take Care of Your Scarf, Tatjana,* the Europeanization process is already underway, and the protagonists' road trip reflects the steady progression towards a newly-defined Europe. In neither case is the prospective European future a particularly positive one. While Henri is able to start his life anew with Margaret, his hold on life is still tenuous and his direction unclear, suggesting an uncertain future as Europe begins to establish its new borders. Valto's failure to hold on to or learn from his relationships reflects a critique of Europeanization narratives in the Finnish national context. Ultimately, the crossing of both real and metaphorical borders in the films reflects the problems and possibilities inherent in the development of a new 'doubly occupied' Europe.

In Kaurismäki's more recent films, such as *The Man Without A Past, Laitakaupungin valot/Lights in the Dusk* (2006) and *Le Havre* (2011), Europe no longer haunts the borders and transitional spaces of the city, and is instead firmly established in the centres of power and commerce. In the Finnish-set films the Westernizing narrative has also taken hold: in telling juxtaposition with the cross-cultural romances of *Take Care of Your Scarf, Tatjana* the security guard Koistinen in *Lights in the Dusk* is frightened of and hides from three passing Russians. The security company he works for is named Western Alarm, the name serving as an ironic label for the cause of Koistinen's anxiety. The French-set *Le Havre* is, in turn, a striking critique of the xenophobic fears that characterize Fortress Europe. Where *I Hired a Contract Killer*'s Henri is made redundant on account of his foreignness, in *Le Havre* outsiders inspire even greater suspicions: when the frightened Idrissa manages to evade immigration officials, newspapers leap to the conclusion that the child must be an armed and dangerous Al Qaeda operative. The European occupation of Kaurismäki's screenspaces, a process that began during the geopolitical instability of the immediate post-Cold War years, continues, then, even as the initial instability that gave rise to it abates.

References

Anon (1994), 'Miksi Pekka Räty sanoo EU:lle "kyllä" ja Aki Kaurismäki "ei"?', *Ilta-Sanomat*, 13 October.

—— (2002), 'I Hired a Contract Killer', in S. Toiviainen (ed.), *Suomen kansallisfilmografia 10. Vuosien 1986–1990 suomalaiset kokoillan elokuvat*, Helsinki: Edita & Suomen elokuva-arkisto, pp. 509–16.

Bacon, H. (2003), 'Aki Kaurismäen sijoiltaan olon poetiikka', in K. Ahonen, J. Rosenqvist, J. Rosenqvist and P. Valotie (eds), *Taju kankaalle. Uutta suomalaista elokuvaa paikantamassa*, Turku: Kirja-Aurora, pp. 88–97.

Boym, S. (2001), *The Future of Nostalgia*, New York: Basic Books.

Browning, C. S. (2002), 'Coming Home or Moving Home? "Westernizing" Narratives in Finnish Foreign Policy and the Reinterpretation of Past Identities', *Cooperation and Conflict*, 37: 1, pp. 47–72.

Cooke, P. (2005), *Representing East Germany since Unification: From Colonization to Nostalgia*, Oxford and New York: Berg.

Dehaene, M. and De Cauter, L. (2008), 'Introduction. Heterotopia in a Postcivil Society', in M. Dehaene and L. De Cauter (eds), *Heterotopia and the City. Public Space in a Postcivil Society*, London and New York: Routledge, pp. 3–9.

Elsaesser, T. (2005), *European Cinema: Face to Face with Hollywood*, Amsterdam: Amsterdam University Press.

Enns, A. (2007), 'The Politics of *Ostalgie*: Post-Socialist Nostalgia in Recent German film', *Screen*, 48:4, pp. 475–91.

Foucault, M. (2008), 'Of Other Spaces', in M. Dehaene and L. De Cauter (eds), *Heterotopia and the City. Public Space in a Postcivil Society*, London and New York: Routledge, pp. 13–29.

Galt, R. (2006), *The New European cinema: Redrawing the Map*, New York: Columbia University Press.

Hellsten, I. (1996), 'Ovi Eurooppaan vai etuvartio Venäjälle? EU-metaforiikkaa Helsingin Sanomissa ja televisiossa', in L. Åberg, U. Kivikuru, M. Alastalo, P. Aula, J. Hakkarainen, H. Heikkilä, I. Hellsten and T. Mörä (eds), *Kansa euromyllyssä. Journalismi, kampanjat ja kansalaisten mediamaisemat Suomen EU-jäsenyysprosessissa*, Helsinki: Yliopistopaino - Helsinki University Press, pp. 178–208.

Hukkanen, M.-L. (1997), *Shadows in Paradise. Photographs from the Films of Aki Kaurismäki*, Helsinki: Otava.

Jokelin, R. (1993), 'Brysselin neuvotteluissa on sovittu tähän mennessä noin kolmannes asiakohdista. Suomen kannalta tärkeimmät kysymykset ovat avoinna tai niitä ei ole otettu edes puheeksi. Suomen kansan Euro-kortit', *Helsingin Sanomat*, 12 December.

Kääpä, P. (2004), '"The Working Class Has No Fatherland": Aki Kaurismäki's films and the Transcending of National Specificity', in A. Nestingen (ed.), *In Search of Aki Kaurismäki: Aesthetics and Contexts,* Ontario: Aspasia Books, pp. 77–95.

—— (2006), 'Displaced Souls Lost in Finland: the Kaurismäkis' Films as Cinema of the Marginalised', *WiderScreen,* 2, www.widerscreen.fi/2007-2. Accessed 13 November 2012.

—— (2010), *The National and Beyond. The Globalisation of Finnish Cinema in the Films of Aki and Mika Kaurismaki,* Bern: Peter Lang.

Karisto, A., Takala, P. and Haapola, I. (1997), *Matkalla nykyaikaan. Elintason, elämäntavan ja sosiaalipolitiikan muutos Suomessa,* Porvoo, Helsinki and Juva: WSOY.

Kyösola, S. (2004), 'The Archivist's Nostalgia', in A. Nestingen (ed.), *In Search of Aki Kaurismäki: Aesthetics and Contexts,* Ontario: Aspasia books, pp. 46–62.

Lindqvist, A. (1996), 'Katse, sen varaan minä rakennan', *Katso!,* 6, pp. 14–15, 78.

Mazierska, E. and Rascaroli, L. (2006), *Crossing New Europe. Postmodern Travel and the European Road Movie,* London and New York: Wallflower Press.

Monk, C. (2009), '"Where I Come From, We Eat Places Like This For Breakfast": Aki Kaurismäki's *I Hired a Contract Killer* as Transnational Representation of Local London', *Journal of British Cinema and Television,* 6: 2, pp. 267–81.

Nestingen, A. (2001), *Why Nation? Globalization and National Culture in Finland, 1980–2001, Scandinavian Studies and Comparative Literature,* Washington: University of Washington.

Newland, P. (2007), 'A Place to Go? Exploring Liminal Space in Aki Kaurismäki's *I Hired a Contract Killer* (1990)', *WiderScreen,* 2, www.widerscreen.fi/2007-2. Accessed 13 November 2012.

Rivi, L. (2007), *European Cinema after 1989. Cultural Identity and Transnational Production,* Houndmills, Basingstoke and Hampshire: Palgrave Macmillan.

Siewert, S. (2008), 'Soundtracks of Double Occupancy. Sampling Sounds and Cultures in Fatih Akin's Head On', in J. Kooijman, P. Pisters and W. Strauven (eds), *Mind the Screen. Media Concepts According to Thomas Elsaesser,* Amsterdam: Amsterdam University Press, pp. 198–208.

Soila, T. (2002), 'The Face of a Sad Rat: The Cinematic Universe of the Kaurismäki Brothers', in Y. Tasker (ed.), *Fifty Contemporary Filmmakers,* London and New York: Routledge, pp. 195–204.

Tani, S. (2007), 'Takapihojen estetiikka: tilat ja paikat Aki Kaurismäen elokuvissa', http://www.orimattila.fi/kirjasto/index.php?option=com_content&task=view&id=195&Itemid=88. Accessed 3 February 2012.

von Bagh, P. (2006), *Aki Kaurismäki,* Helsinki: WSOY.

Väisänen, P. (1993), 'Suomi aikoo ottaa maatalouden esille heti neuvotteluissa', *Helsingin Sanomat,* 1 February, http://www.hs.fi/arkisto/kayttoehdot.

Chapter 6

Looking for Alternative London: *The London Nobody Knows* and the Pop-Geographical Borders of the City

Kari Kallioniemi
University of Turku

Mike Sarne's *Joanna* (1968), according to pop enthusiast Bob Stanley, is 'the ultimate swinging London film' (Stanley 2011) full of delightful clichés depicting 1960s London. Joanna is an art-school student at the Royal College of Art and travelling around London in search of love. *Joanna* was London's answer to *La Dolce Vita*, a freewheeling and picaresque portrait of youthful life in the city, complete with Fellini-esque touches (Campion 2011: 3). With its art-nouveauish titles, its irreverent style reminiscent of slapstick comedy, its fashion statements related to Swinging London and green parks in full bloom (Stanley 2011), *Joanna* is the cinematic encapsulation of the Swinging Sixties. It even includes a foppish aristocrat, Lord Peter Sanderson (Donald Sutherland), taking Joanna and her swinging London crowd on a trip to Morocco.

In its dream-like euphoria *Joanna* reflects the world of 1960s London and the mythology of the swinging decade. There is a long tradition of depicting London in film either as a glamorous and glorious place, often approaching the tired cliché, or as a city darkened by its almost forgotten past and (invisible) borders.[1] The most famous (if not the first) identification of Swinging London (Gilbert 2006: 3) occurs in an article in *Time* magazine from April 1966:

> This spring, as never before in modern times, London is switched on. Ancient elegance and new opulence are all tangled up in a dazzling blur of op and pop […] The guards now change at Buckingham Palace to a Lennon and McCartney tune, and Prince Charles is firmly in the long-hair set. (Halasz 1966: 32)

This technicolour dream of Swinging London was a much welcomed antidote to the grimness of the London past as depicted in the cinema; but it also created the often ridiculed pop-cultural view of London as the ultimate pop city. This picture of London as a swinging city was challenged by documentaries depicting an alternative view. One remarkable instance was the television film *The London Nobody Knows* (Norman Cohen, 1967). This was an exceptional documentary: made in the atmosphere of Swinging London but not trying to celebrate it, it showed the forgotten and neglected back of the swinging capital. The tour of London, narrated by the well-known actor James Mason, offered a fascinating look at the remnants of a bygone age before the capital's extensive redevelopment in the late 1960s and 1970s.

It was also a social-realist comment on the euphoric sentiment of late-sixties British pop-culture. That is why it has also influenced more recent films seeking the visible and invisible borders of London and trying to translate them into alternative documentaries. *Saint Etienne Presents Finisterre* (Paul Kelly and Kieran Evans, 2003), according to St Etienne's main founder Bob Stanley, was an open homage to *The London Nobody Knows*. It was an audiovisual hymn to London, taking the form of a journey from the suburbs to the heart of the city (Stanley 2003), with a score by the dance-music pioneers of the St Etienne troupe. The group strolled through the English capital seeking its almost mysteriously hidden corners and neglected borders. With director Julian Temple, the London pop-group Madness created a visual tribute (*The Liberty Of Norton Folgate*, 2009) to their working-class roots, once again celebrating the forgotten and hidden London also immortalized in songs from the album by the same title. This film returned to the places and atmosphere of *The London Nobody Knows*, accompanied by Madness' elegiac songs about London.[2]

In this chapter I discuss *The London Nobody Knows* in the light of the current debate over the relationship between popular culture (more specifically popular music) and the urban scene. How are Swinging London and its representative films connected to the idea of the other side of London, dealt with in *The London Nobody Knows*, and to its psycho-geography in British pop culture? How are the complexly layered pop-geography of London and its soundscape reconstructed by such works as *Finisterre* and *The Liberty Of Norton Folgate*?

The London Nobody Knows and the pop-geographical imagination

It is difficult to find a more appropriate documentary from the end of the 1960s than *The London Nobody Knows*, which attempts to point a critical eye – with a serious undertone – at the one-dimensional craze of the Swinging Sixties. Because of its cult status, derived from late-night viewing on television (Stanley 2003) and from its recent rediscovery and release as a DVD, the documentary has been gathering accolades as a rare look at the last remnants of Victorian London, which disappeared quickly in the late 1960s. The clichéd London of red double-decker buses, miniskirts and pop-stars gets a quick glance in the documentary, but its main interest lies in the images of London it provides, as portrayed by the illustrator, writer and leading architectural figure Geoffrey Fletcher (1923–2004) in his book *The London Nobody Knows* (1962). Fletcher's quirky portrayal of London did not want to focus on the London of famous landmarks, but on 'the tawdry, extravagant and eccentric … the whimsical' (Cruickshank 2011: 6).

In the film, the veteran actor James Mason (1909–84) takes a leisurely walk around London, unofficially asserting and recording the boundaries of its hidden alleys and places, eerily transmitting messages from people of previous eras of the swinging city (Figure 6.1). Mason himself was not born in London – he was trained in architecture at Cambridge, and later joined the Old Vic as an actor in London; but it can be said that he took a personal interest both in the architecture and in the exuberant people of a city on the verge of disappearance.

Figure 6.1: James Mason taking a leisurely walk around The Roundhouse, one of the 'Victorian images from the past' in *The London Nobody Knows*.

The film starts in slapstick mode, showing a building site 'blooming' with new modernist skyscrapers reaching up to the sky; this gives way to a melancholy soundtrack, mourning the passing of old London. This is a very explicit comment on the rapid and often aggressive post-war reconstruction of London. The camera then descends from the sky and finds Camden Street, where Mason starts his journey. He first enters the dilapidated Bedford Theatre, the favourite theatre of the music-hall superstar of the early twentieth century Marie Lloyd, wondering at the deteriorated interior of the place and its uncanny atmosphere. He then visits the Victorian public gents' lavatory, which is decorated with a goldfish aquarium, and meets the last old-fashioned lamplighter, before finally visiting the locations of the Jack-the-Ripper murders in Spitalfields.

These places are for Mason 'crumbling images of the past', in which the 'Victorian loo is quite a work of art' and 'like Rome, London has its catacombs' in the form of horse tunnels. All of this refers to 'the architectural uncanny', a term coined by Anthony Vidler, which according to Lawrence Phillips refers to the psychological power of buildings and their place in the rise of great cities. In London this power represents above all the rise of the empire, of industrialism and of the Victorian city and the destruction of the Blitz, creating places for 'excursions in the secret history of London' (Phillips 2006: 2, 6).

In *The London Nobody Knows*, this secret history is also uncovered by reminding viewers not only of lost London places but also of marginal Londoners. These sad examples of the neglected world of the swinging frivolity are to be found in East End cafés, on the premises of the Salvation Army (itself one of the symbols of East End noir in London films, Brunsdon 2007: 161–76) and in winos looking defeated or catatonic in grubby streets while the wind blows eerily behind them. These scenes are occasionally interrupted by a comical look at the egg-breaking factory near the Thames, depicted in the slapstick style of Swinging Sixties movies, and by buskers in fancy costumes providing reminiscences of street entertainment before the Swinging London era.

The London Nobody Knows, however, attempts to avoid Swinging Sixties whimsicality. For this reason it is pervaded by the ethos of 1960s social realism, underpinned by an almost macabre melancholy; again using grim symbols – Salvation Army marches, undertakers' shops and graveyards – as challenging the Swinging London dreamscape. Among the bulldozers and ruins, the always suave James Mason concludes the film by saying that 'after all, most of Victorian London was rather hideous'; it is now giving way to optimistic post-war city redevelopment.

The London Nobody Knows can be included among television documentaries mourning the passing of old London and its (architectural) secrets. Poet Laureate John Betjeman (1906–84) specialized during his career in trying to save various landmark London buildings, but he also became a cult celebrity by giving televised strolls around uncanny London – often inspired by his poems connected to London places. In television documentary *Metro-Land* (Edward Mirzoeff, 1973), Betjeman gives a guided tour of the Metropolitan Line, from Baker Street in London to Verney Junction in Buckinghamshire, visiting architectural and other oddities in the area but also looking for 'the hidden eccentricities of Home Counties English life'.

One model for *The London Nobody Knows* can be seen in the short-lived craze for television documentaries in the early 1960s, in which famous actresses introduced their favourite cities by personifying the places with their star quality.[3] Especially Elizabeth Taylor's *Elizabeth Taylor in London* (1963) followed the tradition of representing London as a romantic place connected firmly to its history, exemplified in such John Barry songs as *London at Dawn (Including Westminster Bridge by William Wordsworth)* and *Lovers and Browning (Including Portuguese Sonnets by Elizabeth Barrett Browning)*, but also in patriotic speeches like *The Fire of London* and *Churchill Speech*.

The literary-historical influence behind *The London Nobody Knows* is obviously Charles Dickens. James Mason's journey evokes the atmosphere of the old Dickensian London, and it is reasonable to expect that both Fletcher and Cohen were aware of Dickens' essays about London, especially his *Night Walks* (1860). Here Dickens reveals his older and jaded views of the metropolis and 'broods on the dark soul of the city … peering into theatres after the audience has left, encountering drunks and wandering the streets with thoughts of crime and sin' (Orford 2010: x). There is a long history of constructing an image of London as monstrous and threatening (Phillips 2006: 3), strengthened by a 'dickensian imagination', linked to theories and ideas concerning place- and site-specific popular culture, musical and cinematic movements that are powerful, geographically described mythologies which turn real cities into imaginary places.

From the days of Charles Dickens, London – as the first modern imperial centre and industrialized city – has been an especially fertile site for (popular) cultural imagery and mythology. Its places and spaces have been transformed into urban sanctuaries by this 'imaginary geography', created by film, tourism and travel-writing.[4] Tony Mitchell has described this phenomenon as the fetishizing of localities. In this process a place becomes a constructed landscape of collective aspirations, mediated through the complex prism of popular culture in which the locality becomes a fetish which disguises globally dispersed forces (Mitchell 1996: 87).

These connections between 'real' and 'imagined' places are complex and nuanced; imaginary and real places are often so intrinsically intertwined in the body of works of popular culture that the pop-geographical map seems to be more multi-layered and 'real' than can be contained within the one-dimensional concept of locality. Thus the term 'pop geography' can easily be applied in cases where the relationship between geography and popular culture is analysed, imagined or re-imagined.[5] The relationship between a city and its inhabitants comes close to psychogeography, with its notion of the point where psychology and geography meet in assessing the emotional and behavioural impact of urban space. This is measured both through imaginative and literary responses and on foot by walking the city (Coverley 2010).

It is arguable that psychogeography creates both traditional and unconventional ways of seeing not only London but all of England, its cities and Englishness itself as (pop-) geographical constructions.[6] For example: a simple overview of Britain shows the country as passing through a number of historical periods, which uncannily parallel the geographical map – 'rural', 'industrial', 'imperial', 'suburban', 'tourist' and 'multicultural' (Storry and Childs 1997: 8–14) – at the same time revealing romantic and not so romantic aspects of the environment in every period. If the idea of 'English supremacy', constituted by the British Empire or the English nation, is linked via geography as a historical narrative to construct London, then the place is seen through a power-bloc model dominated by the south of England, and not recognized through many layers of pop-geography. London as a national/regional construction is then most strikingly defined by the history of royalism, empire, global financial banking and the North-South divide. This is easily connected to other traditional ways of seeing London, for example in terms of suburban/metropolitan and countryside/city dichotomies.

It is therefore the history of London which most strikingly signifies London as a place, London places and also London localities. This is also the case in the narrative of *The London Nobody Knows*: London is seen through its (hidden) places, borders, localities and buildings; it is either under construction or its alternative heritage is hidden in uncanny corners, streets, backyards and tunnels. The fetish of landmark/heritage/museum London (Brunsdon 2007: 21–38) is thus in constant tension with 'rubbish London' (Smith 2002: 26) and local 'peripheral' London.

In this connection a number of scholars, among them Iain Chambers, have recognized 'that for many observers much in the modern city and in the wake of industrialism has been considered foreign and distinctly "unBritish"' (Chambers 1986: 17). In this connection, the city space is not a familiar space in terms of Englishness, but is foreign, monstrous and threatening. Simon Frith therefore links the spirit of (pop-) Englishness to suburbia: 'Because of its increasing marginality Britain is an essentially suburban, not metropolitan society' (Frith and Horne 1987: 181).

For Frith the rhetoric of class and street and grit is itself the product of suburban dreams and suburban needs. Suburban culture, whether shaped by pop or by the BBC, is a white south-eastern English culture; ultimately it describes an urban phenomenon, the media domination of London, a concentrated site of both political and cultural power. Suburban culture seems essentially middle-brow, in part because the literature of suburbia has been predominantly middle-brow, as in the no-nonsense poetry of John Betjeman (Frith 1997: 269–71), which is forever mourning, wandering and seeking the forgotten and neglected spaces and places of Englishness in London.

Thus most of London metropolitanism is also part of this 'suburban dreaming'. James Mason's journey through *The London Nobody Knows* is one which seeks that sense of English London; not the London of global migration, entertainment or even the wide range of British nationalities visible in London. Apart from the lonely black woman standing on the doorstep in Petticoat Lane, *The London Nobody Knows* rarely visualizes London as a place of global immigration; the only time this occurs is when Mason visits the Huguenot houses in Spitalfields, originating from the seventeenth century.

This sense of Englishness in London is easily associated with its rock-shrines, scattered around the city. This is an essential part of the pop-geography of London. Marc Bolan and Freddie Mercury, for example, are enshrined at Barnes Common and Earls Court respectively (Perry 1996: 2–3). While ordinary tourists visit places like Liverpool's Beatles Museum and London's Rock Circus (now closed), more passionate pop-pilgrims make their way to the shrines of their stars. These might include the tree which claimed the life of Marc Bolan in a car accident, or the location of the phone box which was on the cover of David Bowie's *Ziggy Stardust* (ibid: 2–3). These might be located in the city, in suburbia or even in the countryside reflecting the power of relics to blur or destroy the concrete or mental borders between those places. It can be said that museum London and marginal London coalesce to some extent through popular culture tourism and rock shrines. This is clearly seen when instead of 'epic' places or museums people choose to romanticize the intimate atmosphere of rather grubby spots. One example: the *Good Mixer* pub in Camden, famous for its Britpop clientele and its impenetrable grittiness, became a place of pilgrimage for the Britpop generation in the 1990s.

By this means the traditional concepts of geography overlap and become intertwined with pop-geography, leading to continual interaction between local and national, between city, suburbia and countryside and between periphery and centre. This can be seen as a new reading of the city, which is now more aware of its links to different kinds of 'English dreaming' through pop-geography. It is thus not difficult to understand why *The London Nobody Knows* became a cult-film; it was due to the entrepreneurs of this pop-sensibility.

The London Nobody Knows and London in the pop-cultural imagination

London itself has been reinvented on several occasions by this sensibility. It has been used frequently both as a filming location and as a film setting, from the Victorian London of Charles Dickens to crime and spy films, science fiction and recent romantic comedies like

Notting Hill (Roger Michell, 1999) and *Bridget Jones' Diary* (Sharon Maguire, 2001) (Brunsdon 2007: 111–16). Songs about London, most notably The Kinks' *Waterloo Sunset*, Ralph McTell's *Streets of London* or The Clash's *London Calling,* vividly reflect the kind of geographical imagination at work in pop music in this connection (Fact 1995: 46–47; Dalton 1993: 12–13).[7]

One interesting example of the imagining of London through pop music was offered by *Uncut* magazine's CD of the month entitled *London Pride!* in May 2009. The CD offers a rich trip through London-related music and London in the musical imagination: from Noel Coward's ode to indestructible London during the Blitz (*London Pride*) and calypsonian Lord Kitchener's praise of London from the point of view of an immigrant in the early 1950s (*London is The Place for Me*) to Robyn Hitchcock's psychedelic elegy to disappearing London (*Trams of Old London*) and the punk version of *Streets of London* by the Anti-Nowhere League, expressing the angry dissent of a Londoner of the early 1980s in Thatcherite Britain.

Many of the foreign film-makers who have dealt with notions of Englishness (such as Michelangelo Antonioni, Roman Polanski and Stanley Kubrick) have tried to avoid presenting a particular vision of London in their films (Brunsdon 2007: 10–14). This has often meant criticizing the features that supposedly typified Swinging London – although this view is the subject of continuing fascination. Supposedly this fascination arose from the dream of doing away with all cultural borders and thereby creating a classless society, with its eccentric bohemianism, high-spirited lifestyle and the convergence of tradition and modernity. London thus became a historical cultural symbol, not for its Englishness but for the sentiment which linked 1960s London to a radical European urban heritage:

> In this century, every decade has had its city. *The fin de siécle* belonged to the dreamlike round of Vienna, capital of the inbred Habsburgs and the waltz. In the changing 20s, Paris provided a moveable feast for Hemingway, Picasso, Fitzgerald and Joyce, while in the chaos after the Great Crash, Berlin briefly erupted with the savage iconoclasm of Brecht and the Bauhaus [...] In the uneasy 1950s it was the easy Rome of *la dolce vita.* Today, it is London. (Halasz 1966, 32)[8]

In her influential article Piri Halasz designated the image of London as the mythological city of the world's youth, which became a dominant model of style, fashion, the social turmoil of rock-culture, pop-cultural tourism and a state of mind exemplified by pop. The hedonistic self-indulgence of Swinging London cognoscenti – the suddenly exalted legions of pop singers and artists, the fashionable young dress designers and interior decorators, hairdressers, fashion photographers, journalists and models – was described as 'classlessness', a 'New Aristocracy' or a 'New Class' (Booker 1969: 19). This group, colourfully portrayed in movies like *Joanna*, blatantly ignored the harsh realities of London depicted in *The London Nobody Knows.*

Although London was perceived in terms of its heritage factors, or 'the bus, the pub and Mary Poppins emerging from the fog' (Brunsdon 2007: 38–47; Shonfield 2000: 135), it was also sometimes seen in terms of the realities which formed part of London as an exotic locale, especially for the new pop generation: 'London was still (in early 1960s) a well-scrubbed landscape of white town houses, red telephone booths and double-decker buses' (Schaffner 1983: 3).

For outsiders, Britishness was still generally equated during the 1960s with London. It is thus understandable but unsettling, in *The London Nobody Knows*, to see the former Hollywood A-list star James Mason destroying this image of London as the epitome of Britishness although relieving the viewer to see the alternative with his suave and familiar voice. Mason himself starred in only one Swinging-London film, *Georgy Girl* (Silvio Narizzano, 1966), in which he played a wealthy widower trying to take part in the swinging social life of mid-1960s London. The category of 'Swinging London' movies is a disparate group of films, with a wide tonal range, usually seen as including *The Knack* (Richard Lester, 1965), *Georgy Girl* (Silvio Narizzano, 1966), *Darling* (John Schlesinger, 1965), *Alfie* (Lewis Gilbert, 1966), *Blow-Up* (Michelangelo Antonioni, 1966), *I'll Never Forget What's 'is name* (Michael Winner, 1967) and *Smashing Time* (Desmond Davis, 1967) (Brunsdon 2007: 35). All the signs of class, style, gender and region in these movies could also be viewed as signifying the ideals of the Swinging 1960s, and to be seen not only as coherent narratives, but as tapestries with a multitude of connotations (Sorlin 1991: 6–9; Murphy 1992: 139–41). Jon Savage sees these films not so much as celebrations of 1960s youthful affluence but more like documentaries capturing the lost moments of 1960s London in transition:

> The London of these films is almost unrecognizable from today's stasis: a city in transition, with its history becoming subsumed in a new cybernetic space. The images that you take away from these films are of the demolition of churches and constructing of new houses (*A Hard Day's Night*) (and) of underpasses and arrowed traffic signs (*Catch Us If You Can*). (Savage 1996: 304–5)

This imagery, linked to visions of demolition and construction, is inextricably bound up with recycled forms of the English pop world of the sixties. Both this imagery and *The London Nobody Knows* are also connected to a darker side of *Primitive London* (Arnold L. Miller, 1965), influenced by the jaunty 'Look at Life' movie *Mondo Cane* (Paolo Cavara and Gualtiero Jacopetti, 1962), in which Swinging London is a symbol for a world in turmoil hiding behind an all-encompassing frivolity. *Primitive London* was a once shocking mondo-style documentary that tried to reflect societal decay through the sideshow spectacle of 1960s London depravity. This was followed by a series of semi-documentaries in the same style, such as *London in the Raw* (Norman Cohen and Arnold L. Miller, 1964).

Primitive London shows the more or less direct influence of *The London Nobody Knows*, especially since Norman Cohen shared director credit. In *Primitive London* the camera follows London mods, rockers and beatniks and seedy Jack-the-Ripper re-enactments, also titillating viewers' preconceptions as to sinful London life by following flabby men in the sauna. All of this reflects the sensationalist style which reveals London as a suburban fantasy of the permissive 1960s, with stories of strip-clubs, exotically risqué variety shows, beatnik 'art lovers' and sordid wife-swapping parties – all representing the typical 'sohoised' fantasy of a London of free sex and confusion caused by 1960s social change.[9]

These documents and Swinging London films thus share a similar imminent sadness, reflecting the death of Swinging London as an ideal (Melly 1970: 172–77; Savage 1996: 307). There is a psychogeographical feeling about the melancholy aspects of London which permeates both *The London Nobody Knows* and certain Swinging London films; this distinguishes them from 'the underlying perversity, fetishism and camp sado-masochism of Bond-films and Swinging London-era send-ups like *Modesty Blaise* (Joseph Losey, 1966) and *Barbarella* (Roger Vadim, 1968)' (Melly 1970: 174).

When the Swinging London highbrow movie sought to expose the empty hedonism of the times, for example in the alienated voyeurism of fashionable photography of *Blow-Up,* it became apparent how quickly the Swinging London pop style was becoming obsolete and passing away (Richards 1997: 156–57; Savage 1996: 307; Murphy 1992: 140, 148). In this connection, documentaries like *The London Nobody Knows* seem to be better at capturing the momentary spirit and 'pop-geographic feeling' of mid-60s London.

Finisterre as an homage to *The London Nobody Knows*

It is thus quite reasonable that musicians influenced by the rich heritage of British pop, but without personal experience of the 1960s and Swinging London, would find documentaries like *The London Nobody Knows* fascinating in imagining the pop-geography of London. This was manifested by Bob Stanley, founding member of the dance-group St Etienne, when he recalled in *The Guardian* that 'when our band came to making our first film, *Finisterre*, Geoffrey Fletcher, the author of *The London Nobody Knows*, was our mentor, *The London Nobody Knows* our first point of reference' (Stanley 2003). *Saint Etienne presents Finisterre* (2003) was originally conceived as live visuals behind the band on their Finisterre tour, but in the end it was made into a documentary of modern-day London by the band's filmmaker and one-time band member Paul Kelly, who directed the film (Pulver 2008; O'Hagan 2005).[10]

From this starting-point, *Finisterre* became a pop-geographical meditation on changing London and its hidden and peripheral places, serving both ordinary and strange views of London. The psycho-geographical journey is narrated from a Londoner's perspective through a collage of sounds and images. From its beginning the journey expresses its gratitude to its inspirational source, citing Geoffrey Fletcher's *The London Nobody Knows* and its 'mysterious place names holding the key to your heart'. The trip starts in the morning mist of South Croydon station, before moving to Victoria, Tower Bridge, Spitalfields, Barbican and Hampstead Heath. The friendly and serious voice of the narrator Michael Jayston provides a commentary inbetween atmospheric St Etienne songs and reminiscences of pop-star and artist friends of the group commenting on living in London.

The narrator continues to explain his objective – 'to create an enthusiasm for the neglected and undervalued, even freakish' – again echoing Fletcher's original idea in his book. Some scenes indubitably echo St Etienne songs, videos and album covers, as shown in the portrayal of a playground with the 'cool kids of London'. London's rock landmarks, from the Water Rats Theatre Bar to Camden's Electric Ballroom, and modernist landmarks like the tower block of Highpoint, reinforce almost mystically the interdependence between London places and buildings, regardless of their history or cultural significance. In this connection heritage London is neglected, shown for example only by the wraithlike reflection of Piccadilly Circus in the window display of a commonplace souvenir shop. Instead of museum pieces, endless lists of menus in greasy cafes give a glimpse of everyday life in London. Only places like Cecil Sharp House in Primrose Hill, named for the folk-music collector, give a brief look at heritage London, with its southern England green and pleasant land – quickly to be forgotten when London's night life starts.

A 'green and pleasant land' is something which is not part of the vision of *Finisterre*. London is shown through what Iain Chambers has called 'the un-British element': grainy, gloomy and washed-out, its inhabitants messy and earthbound in their unattractive but mysterious banality. Thus *Finisterre* gradually mutates from its social-realist documentary mode to a tone poem about present-day London, reminding viewers of the legacy of 1960s films situated in London and of John Betjeman's oratories to the London of smog and tarmacadam, tower blocks and milk-grey skies. This seeming uneventfulness also recalls London's almost dadaist quirkiness, often emphasized in *The London Nobody Knows*. In an extended sequence filmed at Piccadilly Circus, for example, we see not the Circus but the visiting tourists, staring open-mouthed and filming the heritage London which is invisible in *Finisterre*. According to Andrew Pulver, Paul Kelly and St Etienne have created a 'preservation documentary' (Pulver: 2008) in homage to Geoffrey Fletcher; one in which London can be defined as a place by using what London psychogeographer Iain Sinclair has called "'liminal lands", neglected, in-between places in the heart of a fast-forward city, where another history, embedded, unofficial, murky, hangs heavy but invisible in the air' (O'Hagan: 2005).

This sense of liminality and hidden histories, lovingly captured in *The London Nobody Knows*, is enthusiastically transferred to *Finisterre* and updated by St Etienne's retro-modernist pop-geographical sensibility. St Etienne can be called London's village preservationist and musical laureate, in the same style as the Poet Laureate John Betjeman. Where Betjeman and Fletcher were mourning the post-war demolition of London and trying to save its architectural landmarks from the destruction of the post-war building frenzy, now at the beginning of the twenty-first century St Etienne is once again mourning the often too rapid redevelopment of the capital, rooted in the new cycle of financial globalization. Where James Mason announces quite optimistically at the end of *The London Nobody Knows* that we are happy to get rid of the hideous part of Victorian London, *Finisterre* reluctantly shares in this optimism. The film and its soundtrack are filled with a cool pessimism, strangely echoing the national inertia after the euphoria of revisited 1960s sentiment during the Blairite 1990s (Collinson 2010: 168), so often penetrating through British pop music of the early twenty-first century.

Madness, *The Liberty Of Norton Folgate* and the pop-geographical celebration of old London

If St Etienne is the melancholic chronicler of London life for the dance generation, the London group Madness, originating from the new-wave era of the early 1980s, is an exuberant group influenced by London's immigrant subcultures, musical traditions and youth cults.

The white negro and art-school dandy of London's rhythm and blues scene, with the mod subculture, invented London as the swinging city of the 1960s in terms of pop music. Unfortunately the interaction between black and white London teens (Hebdige 1981: 104–5) was not recognized sufficiently before the late 1970s and the innovation of groups like Madness. The hard-mod style, which tried to distinguish itself from the commercial styles of Swinging London, led to skinheads in the late 1960s (Fowler 1996: 158–9; Hebdige 1981: 52–59). Through these styles, and with an obsession with Afro-Caribbean music and continental clothing styles, it led to the post-punk styles of reggae and ska-influenced pop-groups like Madness.

The embodiment of these influences after Madness' 30-year career as the ultimate London band[11] was the album *The Liberty Of Norton Folgate* (2009), in which multiple non-English musical styles collide with British music hall and pop, celebrating the often forgotten or undervalued history of certain London landmarks in pop music. The album and accompanying musical document were an homage both to the bohemian side of London and to the cultural melting pot of Norton Folgate. During the nineteenth century this was a liberty located between the Bishopsgate ward of the City of London to the south, the parish of St Leonard Shoreditch to the north and the parish of Spitalfields to the east (Suggs 2010: 94, 196).

Suggs, the singer of Madness, explains in the booklet accompanying the CD/DVD that he found the idea for this concept album in the book *This Bright Field* (2001) by William Taylor. Taylor was a trainee vicar who was sent to Shoreditch by the bishop of Oxford 'in order to test his vocation. While he was discovering his ultimate vocation he also set about discovering the lives and history of the people and the area around Spittle Fields'. He got a job in the fruit market, worked in a pub and 'threw himself headlong into the social and political life of the locals'. From these experiences 'the charming book of anecdotes, local culture and dialogue, was written by a middle class man struggling to understand the alien culture of the working classes (of London) in their rawest form' (Suggs 2009: 1).

Giving more information concerning The Liberty of Norton Folgate, Suggs goes on to explain that it was 'built up as a collection of courts and alleyways off Bishopsgate, the Liberty of Norton Folgate in the 1700s had its own school, church, hospital and almshouses for destitute silk weavers [...] It was nevertheless a refuge for actors, writers, thinkers, louts, lowlifes and libertines, outsiders and troublemakers all' (Suggs 2009: 1) (Figure 6.2). All of this suggests that the book was an immediate inspiration for the group like Madness, always

Figure 6.2: The ghost-like reveller from the London past in the cover of *The Liberty of Norton Folgate*.

specializing in seeking out London's hidden mental and physical borders and celebrating its lively bohemian life.

The director Julien Temple is famous for his documentaries and film adaptations relating to London's musical and cultural life.[12] His document *The Liberty Of Norton Folgate* (2009), shot partly at the band's first live performance of the new material at London's Hackney Empire, is a collection of short stories and vignettes linked to Madness' performance of music drawn from the native and immigrant generations that have made London. The songs are performed attempting to imitate the authentic music-hall atmosphere of late nineteenth century London, in which characters from 'the old London' play pearly kings and queens, flower girls and Victorian circus jugglers. Between the songs, Suggs and Chas Smash of Madness take the viewer on a delightful theatrical jaunt through the secrets of London's past.

This journey attempts to recreate both the eeriness of the Dickensian underworld and the naughtiness of Victorian London, connected to the licentiousness associated with London life during and after the Swinging Sixties. The alternative heritage of London is celebrated by visual backdrops projected behind the band in the Hackney Empire. These concentrate on London life and history, with images of such local luminaries as William Blake, Karl Marx and Marie Lloyd, and of historic London landmarks and drawings by Blake and Edward Lear. Pictures of London club landmarks, especially in Soho (French House, Bar Italia and Colony Room Club), supposedly refer to Sugg's bohemian tête-à-têtes with local eccentrics in the television series *Sugg's Disappearing London*.

Madness celebrates a continuum of London-centred pop Victoriana, from British psychedelia to the Sex Pistols dressed as Dickensian urchins (Savage 1991: 61, 66, 232). Pearly kings and queens in the audience can be perceived as an homage to London's historical street life and music-hall past, also presented in *The London Nobody Knows*. This celebration of pop-Victoriana, however, does not signify for Madness the celebration of a superficial imaginary associated with 1960s Swinging London, but an acknowledgement of a longer heritage of London musical and cultural life, dating back to the days of *The Liberty Of Norton Folgate*. It is thus an homage to a London of cultural and historical diversities, pointing beyond the sometimes too simple pop-vision of the 1960s, to Huguenots and to Jewish and Bangladeshi immigrants in Brick Lane. Suggs formulates this legacy of *The Liberty Of Norton Folgate* in his book, *Suggs and the City: My Journeys Through Disappearing London* (2010), referring to Peter Ackroyd's obsessive work on London life and history: 'A perfect Ackroydian example of a strange social continuum, down through the ages, as an area passes hands again and again' (Suggs 2009: 2).[13]

In this connection, the influences on *The Liberty Of Norton Folgate* can be found in various sources. It is reasonable to assume, however, that *The London Nobody Knows* is one of the most important, mainly because in his quasi-autobiography of his life in London Suggs places special emphasis on the history of The Bedford Theatre on Camden High Street (Suggs 2010: 88–89). It is quite comfortably associated with another famous music hall theatre, The Hackney Empire, still retaining most of its original features and functioning as a popular theatre today, and featured as a concert locale in *The Liberty of Norton Folgate* (Suggs 2010: 94).

Before this historical connection, Suggs expresses gratitude to Norman Cohen's cult documentary. He fondly recognizes Fletcher's 'particular penchant for "off-beat" London' (Suggs 2010: 89) and a celebration of the quirky, unusual and downright bizarre places which make the city so special. Suggs also reminds readers that 'the streets of this London certainly aren't those which feature in the cliched images of the swinging 60s' (Suggs 2010: 89). In this connection he is really fascinated by James Mason's visit to Bedford Theatre and his reminisces about the story of Marie Lloyd, while the scene is soundtracked by 'a scratched 78 rpm recording of Lloyd singing the music-hall classic *The Boy I Love Is Up in the Gallery*' (Suggs 2010: 90). All of this indicates that both Geoffrey Fletcher's book and Norman Cohen's document have played a memorable role in Madness's (re)imagining of the pop geography of London.

Conclusion: The legacy of *The London Nobody Knows*

The London Nobody Knows, Finisterre and *The Liberty Of Norton Folgate* form a chain of (pop) documentaries which have critically broadened ideas as to how London can be portrayed as an antithesis to the euphoric images of the Swinging London of 1960s pop films. This has happened not merely by ignoring the 'English dreaming' of Swinging London and its fascination for a city's pop-geography, but by the acknowledgement of a longer heritage of London's musical life and a widening of its cultural borders. After all, London still remains one of those definitive places in the pop culture imagination, only strengthened by the bittersweet popcultural tributes of *Finisterre* and *The Liberty Of Norton Folgate*.

The need to bypass the celebration of (pop)heritage of London is associated with the desire to find alternatives to the limited borders of the (pop-)Englishnesses of the past. The influence of the cult documentary *The London Nobody Knows* is one such basis for a critical dialogue about the relationship between popular music and culture, and London; this has been extended by recent documentaries searching for London's pop-geographical borders, but also by the dramatic historical developments following the end of the Cold War era and the collapse of the Soviet bloc. In 1990s Britain this meant a shift toward neo-national and nostalgic canonizations of Englishness, often exemplified by the convergence of British pop, English literature and cinema as an ever-conquering postmodern Arcadian canon. This echoed an emerging English nationalism and regionalism, often ambiguously connected to each other, and the increasing devolution of the United Kingdom, which left London as a British capital vulnerably contemplating its role as a symbol of English nationalism and the past.

With the 2012 Olympics, the city once again experienced dramatic redevelopment; the body of work by Geoffrey Fletcher, Norman Cohen, St Etienne and Julian Temple are the most recent reminders of 'that other side of London' which disappeared five decades ago with Swinging London and its representative films. London's complexly layered contemporary pop geography, and its ever-widening connections to the soundscapes of British pop culture, are thus the latest unofficial descendants of *The London Nobody Knows*.

References

Ackroyd, P. (2001), *London: The Biography,* London: Vintage.

Booker, C. (1969), *The Neophiliacs. The Revolution in English Life in the Fifties and Sixties,* London: Pimlico.

Bracewell, M. (1997), *England is Mine. Pop Life in Albion from Wilde to Goldie,* London: Harper & Collins.

Brunsdon, C. (2007), *London in Cinema: The Cinematic City Since 1945,* London: British Film Institute.

Campion, C. (2011), 'Joanna', *The booklet accompanying DVD Joanna,* London: BFI, pp. 1–5.

Chambers, I. (1986), *Popular Culture. The Metropolitan Experience*, New York: Methuen.

Collinson, I. (2010), 'Devopop: Pop-Englishness and Post-Britpop Guitar Bands', in A. Bennett and J. Stratton (eds), *Britpop and the English Music Tradition,* Farnham: Ashgate Popular and Folk Music Series, pp. 163–77.

Coverley, M. (2010), *Psychogeography*, London: Oldcastle Books, Pocket Essentials.

Cruickshank, D. (2011), 'Foreword', in G. Fletcher (ed.), *The London Nobody Knows*, pp. 5–8. First published 1962.

Dalton, S. (1993), 'Ditty Old Town', in *New Musical Express* 22 May, pp. 12–13.

Du Noyer, P. (2009), *In the City. A Celebration of London Music,* London: Ebury Press.

Fact, F. (1995), 'Going Underground', in *VOX* July, pp. 46–47.

Fowler, P. (1996), 'Skins Rule', in C. Gillett and S. Frith (eds), *The Beat Goes On. The Rock File Reader*, London: Pluto Press, pp. 153–67. First published 1972.

Frith, S. (1997), 'The Suburban Sensibility in British Rock and Pop', in R. Silverstone (ed.), *Visions of Suburbia*, London: Routledge, pp. 269–79.

Frith, S. and Horne, H. (1987), *Art into Pop,* London: Methuen & Co.

Gilbert, D. (2006), '"The Youngest Legend in History": Cultures of Consumption and the Mythologies of Swinging London', *The London Journal*, 31: 1, pp. 1–14.

Halasz, P. (1966), 'You can walk across it on the grass', *Time* 15 April, pp. 32–42.

Hebdige, D. (1981), *Subculture. The Meaning of Style*, Suffolk: Taylor & Francis.

Laing, D. (2009), 'Gigographies. Where Popular Musicians Play', *Popular Music History,* Vol. 4, No. 2, Sheffield: Equinox Publishing, pp. 177–95.

Lewis, J. (2009), 'We are London', *Uncut,* May, pp. 50–59.

Melly, G. (1970), *Revolt into Style. Pop Arts in Britain*, London: Allen Lane.

Mitchell, T. (1996), *Popular Music and Local Identity. Rock, Pop and Rap in Europe and Oceania*, London: Leicester University Press, 1996.

Murphy, R. (1992), *Sixties British Cinema*, London: British Film Institute.

O'Hagan, S. (2005), 'Remember Lea', *The Observer,* 23 October, http://www.guardian.co.uk/film/2005/oct/23/popandrock?INTCMP=SRCH. Accessed 18 January 2012.

Orford, P. (2010), 'Introduction', in *Charles Dickens on London,* London: Hesperus Press Limited, pp. vii–x.

Perry, T. (1996), 'On the rock'n'roll tourist trail', *The Independent 24 Seven*, 19 June, pp. 2–3.

Phillips, L. (2006), *London Narratives: Post-War Fiction and the City,* London: Continuum.

Platt, J. (1985), *London's Rock Routes*, London: Fourth Estate.

Pulver, A. (2008), 'Welcome to the Pulverdome: Saint Etienne', *The Guardian,* 21 July, http://www.guardian.co.uk/film/2008/jul/21/4?INTCMP=SRCH. Accessed 18 January 2012.

Richards, J. (1997), *Films and British National Identity. From Dickens to Dad's Army*, Manchester: Manchester University Press.

Savage, J. (1991), *England's Dreaming. Sex Pistols and Punk Rock,* London: Faber & Faber.

—— (1996), 'Introduction', in *Time Travel. From the Sex Pistols to Nirvana: Pop, Media and Sexuality, 1977–96*, London: Chatto & Windus, pp. 1–11.

Schaffner, N. (1983), *The British Invasion: From the First Wave to the New Wave*, New York: McGraw-Hill.

Shonfield, K. (2000), *Walls Have Feelings*, London: Routledge.

Smith, M. (2002), *Trainspotting*, London: BFI.

Sorlin, P. (1991), *European Cinemas, European Societies 1939–1990*, London: Routledge.

Spoto, D. (1995), *A Passion for Life: The Biography of Elizabeth Taylor*, London: HarperCollins.

Stanley, B. (2003), 'The Naked City', *The Guardian*, 21 November, http://www.guardian.co.uk/film/2003/nov/21/history?INTCMP=SRCH. Accessed 18 January 2012.

—— (2011), 'Joanna – the ultimate swinging London film', *The Guardian*, 21 April, http://www.guardian.co.uk/film/2011/apr/21/joanna-swinging-london-mike-sarne?INTCMP=SRCH. Accessed 18 January 2012.

Storry, M. and Childs, P. (1997), *British Cultural Identities*, London: Routledge.

Suggs (2009), 'Introducing, The Liberty of Norton Folgate!', *Booklet of Madness Liberty of Norton Folgate*, Lucky 7003CD, pp. 1–2.

—— (2010), *Suggs and the City: My Journeys Through Disappearing London*, London: Headline Publishing Group.

Wolfe, T. (1968), *The Pumphouse Gang*, New York: Farrar, Strouse & Giroux.

Notes

1 Wartime documentaries celebrated the struggle of the Blitz, as seen in the short documentary *London Can Take It!* (Humphrey Jennings and Harry Watt, 1940), covering less than eighteen hours of the Blitz and its impact on London and its people. The Free Cinema documentary movement of the 1950s connected both social realism and heroism in the British documentary tradition – in representing everyday London life as well.

2 Patrick Keiller's films about London (*London*, 1994 and *Robinson in Space*, 1997) are also important examples of films seeking the hidden borders of London and accompanied by a 'high-brow' soliloquy by an anonymous narrator, played in this case by the actor Paul Scofield. However, I do not include them in this analysis, as they fall into the category of art films rather than documentaries. For close readings of them, see Brunsdon (2007: 28–33).

3 Grace Kelly, by then Princess of Monaco, took viewers on a tour of that principality, and Jacqueline Kennedy gave the world a visit to the White House (Spoto 1995: 212).

4 Typical examples are tourist pop-guide must-sees like the Abbey Road crossing in London made famous by the Beatles or the London Camden pub where members of Oasis and Blur have been known to imbibe. There have been many books presenting places related to London-connected cinema and rock culture, such as John Platt's *London's Rock Routes* (1985).

5 For example, Dave Laing uses popular music in his article *Gigographies: where popular musicians play*, mapping performance sites in order to understand the links between performers and their audiences and between music and its geographical, social, economic and cultural environments (Laing 2009: 177–95).

6 A wonderful example of this imagination is Song Map. It is a litho print of an imaginary street map made up of song titles and including a Spotify playlist of all the song titles included. The work was designed by Art and Design Group Dorothy. See http://www.wearedorothy.com/art/song-map-unlimited-edition. Accessed 17 January 2012.

7   Of course there is an enormous number of artists and songs related to London, from Ian Dury's London characters to the playgrounds, pubs and inner-city housing estates in Madness' songs of a bittersweet nostalgia for a London childhood. Songs named after London's underground stations, Morrissey's album name *Vauxhall & I*, and My Life Story's *Mornington Crescent* are also examples of this very exclusive imagination related to the specific places of London.

8   The new pop aristocracy of London loved to be referred to as the 'New Bohemia' or the 'fashionable intelligentsia', and to be compared to earlier upper-class youth cults like the Bright Young Things of the 1920s. Swinging London was thus seen by Tom Wolfe as a counterpart of the Regency era of 1811–20, another aristocratic reference point for pop London (Wolfe 1971: 156–70).

9   *Primitive London* was also exploited, but in a more stylized manner, by more obscure Swinging London films, such as *The Sorcerers* (Michael Reeves, 1967) or *Tonite, Let's All Make Love in London* (Peter Whitehead, 1968) (Brunsdon 2007: 53).

10   In addition to *Finisterre* and a whole repertoire of songs based on London in their twenty-year career, St Etienne has produced and/or inspired two other works – *What have you done today, Mervyn Day* and *This is Tomorrow* – plus short films about their favourite cafes in London that are about to vanish. *What have you done today* is the semi-fictional journey of a paper boy on his round around the flattened Lower River Lea Valley, the site of the 2012 Olympic village. *This is Tomorrow* is about the painstaking restoration of the Royal Festival Hall in London (Pulver 2008).

11   This connection to London had also been celebrated in the television series made by Madness' singer Suggs (*Disappearing London*, 2011 (2006)) and by the concept of the Madness box-set compilation, *A Guided Tour of Madness* (2011), covered with a London map and including a hiker's guide to the London of Madness.

12   One of the best examples is his undervalued cult-film adaptation (Julian Temple, 1986) of Colin McInness book *Absolute Beginners* (1959). It documents London's emerging youth cults and the relationships between natives and immigrants in late-1950s London, and predicts the fantasy world of Swinging London.

13   Writer and London aficionado Peter Ackroyd's massive book about London and its history, *London: The Biography* (2001), has been another influence on the concept of *The Liberty Of Norton Folgate* (Lewis 2009: 50–59).

Chapter 7

The *Cité's* Architectural, Linguistic and Cinematic Frontiers in *L'Esquive*

Jehanne-Marie Gavarini
University of Massachusetts Lowell and Brandeis University

Recent events in France such as the *affaires du voile islamique* that resulted in bans on the burka and headscarf, repeated riots, the expulsion of several hundred Roma and Nicolas Sarkozy's announcement that prayer on the street should be prohibited, have put the country in the limelight of international news. This has raised questions regarding French freedom of expression, hospitality, multiculturalism, secularism, the integration of immigrant populations and national identity. Most of these events and issues directly concern the population of, and are geographically located in, the *banlieues*, the poor and segregated suburbs that are home to immigrants – many of them from the former French colonies. The *banlieues* are liminal and complex border areas located on the edge of French cities. They are spaces of social marginalization that are in constant flux.

Cinema and the *banlieues* were born around the same time and the two have cross-pollinated ever since. The *banlieues* have been a source of inspiration for numerous filmmakers whose work contributes to the large archive of images of these neighbourhoods. French research on *banlieue* representation often refers back to early films such as that of the Lumière brothers and point to a continuum in French cinematic tradition. However, this approach does not always reflect the specificity of a new film genre known as *cinéma de banlieue* (*banlieue* cinema) that appeared in the mid-1990s and presents a very different vision of today's *banlieues*. In contrast, Anglophone studies of French *banlieue* cinema have a tendency to bypass films shot before 1980, which are for the most part generated by white directors and do not represent today's multi-ethnic *banlieue* population. Anglophone scholarship most often emphasizes issues such as violence, drugs and sexism that have been identified as *banlieues* problems. These studies also focus on the representation of frictions between French authorities and the population of the *banlieues*.

This chapter considers and combines these two different approaches. I underline how Abdellatif Kechiche's *L'Esquive/Games of Love and Chance* (2004), a low-budget film (450,000 Euros) that won four César awards including best film, best script, best director and best female emerging actress participates in the continuum of *banlieue* representation. This film represents the youth of a *grand ensemble* – also euphemistically called *cité* –in a Parisian *banlieue*. Kechiche's protagonists are shaped by the design and geographic location of their neighbourhood.

The *grands ensembles* are housing estates constructed from enormous concrete blocks called *barres* that physically and culturally demarcate the separation of the *banlieues* from mainstream culture and French affluent society. These estates house a large immigrant population and are commonly associated with current ethnic and class divisions in France. *L'Esquive* emphasizes architecture to convey that the *grand ensemble* is a self-contained micro society that becomes both refuge and prison to its inhabitants. Therefore, in order to fully analyse and understand this film, it is necessary to consider the historical background and comprehend the decisions that led to the construction of the *grands ensembles* in the 1950s and 1960s. In this chapter, I examine the evolution of the physical space of the *banlieues* along with the demographic transformations that France experienced after World War II. I look at films created both before and after 1980 and also *banlieue* and *beur* cinema as useful tools to ascertain *L'Esquive's* specific position within the longer continuum of French cinematic tradition.

Post-war urban developments: *les grands ensembles*

In the early years of the twentieth century the need to improve living conditions drove urban planners to rethink the city in radical ways. A new architectural vision based on purity of form and the belief in the cleansing power of the Modern Project was born. An early example, Le Corbusier's 1925 *Plan Voisin* was to replace the narrow and dark streets of nineteenth century Paris. This project involved levelling the right bank of the Seine River and replacing it with an orthogonal grid of eighteen cruciform skyscrapers set into a landscape of parks, grass and trees. Le Corbusier's buildings were often inspired by his two favourite references: the cruise ship and the monastery. They were designed as isolated objects that would be artificially implanted on the terrain without consideration for the site or its social fabric (Panerai, Castex and Depaule 2009: 131–41).

The *Plan Voisin* was not implemented. However, Le Corbusier's *Cité Radieuse* in Marseille, was the source of inspiration for the *grands ensembles,* the high-rise housing estates that became the landmark of the *banlieues*. The *Cité Radieuse* was a vertical island built on *pilotis*, or concrete pillars, and physically floating in space. This type of self-contained housing development was supposed to replace the traditional city. It comprised housing units with individual garden loggias, as well as indoor streets, shops, a roof garden and other communal facilities. The *Cité Radieuse* virtually became the model for the *banlieues* and *grands ensembles*. These new *cités* were conceived in contrast with the old cities perceived, at the time, as outdated and inhuman. As François Tomas explains, these modern projects created a decisive break in architectural and urban planning as well as in the appreciation of cities. Tomas (2003: 14) argues that the *grands ensembles* symbolized not only the victory of hygiene and whiteness, of light and comfort, but also the perspective of a future where social progress would contribute to the reduction of diseases, the decrease of delinquency and possibly even the eradication of domestic disputes.

L'Esquive, which was shot in the Cité des Francs-Moisins, a neighbourhood in Saint-Denis on the outskirts of Paris, offers a direct cinematic comment on the *grands ensembles*. The film is shot mostly outside and it uses the *cité* as a set, revealing the detrimental effects of modern ideology and urban planning on today's *banlieue* population. The architectural background presents a viewpoint that diverges from 1960s propaganda for 'hygiene and whiteness'. The large buildings of the *cité* have aged poorly; they are decrepit and show numerous signs of neglect. However, *L'Esquive,* which revolves around the end-of-year school production of Marivaux's eighteenth century play *Games of Love and Chance* by a group of high school students, does not depict the *banlieue's* space solely in a negative way. The film also brings the viewer's attention to an outdoor amphitheatre where the protagonists endlessly rehearse scenes from the play. The teenagers, who meet in this public space before and after rehearsals, have heated arguments at times, but they also discover their passion and desires as budding actors. Although ominous buildings are always present in the background, the open space of the amphitheatre provides the protagonists with room to breathe and invent themselves beyond the physical confinement of their *grand ensemble.*

The film presents the space of the outdoor amphitheatre in a somewhat positive manner, yet Kechiche's representation of this *banlieue* is far from the early blind seduction for the *grands ensembles* described by Jean-Noël Blanc (2003: 44). Indeed, the initial utopian fervour and enthusiastic response for these new neighbourhoods did not last. Tomas specifies that the *grands ensembles* projects were re-evaluated sometimes before being completed. Further, he states (2003: 9) that one of the problems with the conception and critique of the *grands ensembles* was that on one hand sociologists and geographers privileged the role of users and neglected the forms, while architects were interested in the forms per se. Although they reflected the prophecy of twentieth century architecture pioneers, the *grands ensembles,* for the most part, left out the positive aspects of early architectural visions such as Le Corbusier's roof gardens that would have participated in making the *banlieues* more livable. Instead, Tomas (2003: 23) specifies that although it was later denied that the spatial marginalization of the *grands ensembles* was intentional, they were built on cheap or free land, cut off from the cities and far from view.

This type of isolation from the rest of the world is exemplified in *L'Esquive.* In this film, the teenage protagonists are confined to their neighbourhood, the Cité des Francs-Moisins, a large urbanization project that was erected from the ground up in 1973. The *cité* was completed over the course of three years. It was conceived as a single plan to replace an infamous slum of the same name. Originally, these types of emergency housing developments were supposed to provide temporary apartments to palliate the need of immigrant populations who lived in insalubrious hotels and shantytowns (Bernard 1993: 73). However, the *grands ensembles* sprouted all over France. These high-rise concrete buildings became the undisputable models for low-income housing and a permanent feature of the *banlieues.*

The physical space of the *banlieues:* a tradition in cinematic critique

In the 1950s and 1960s, the enormous *grands ensembles* began to fill up the countryside cutting through space like fortresses. They spread on the edges of towns and cities and engulfed all signs of nature. The bucolic *banlieues* with their popular *guinguettes* and relaxing riverbanks represented by the Impressionists and early French cinema were rapidly disappearing. Images from films like Marcel Carné's *Nogent, Eldorado du dimanche/Nogent* (1929), which depicts Parisians deserting the city and descending onto the *banlieue* to relax and enjoy numerous summer activities along the Marne River, were becoming a mere celluloid memory.

The *grands ensembles* replaced the city centre model of the past and became a symbol of the opposition between tradition and modernity. In the popular imaginary, the modern urban transformations of the *banlieues* represented the excitement of modern innovations but also brought forth nostalgia, anxiety and criticism. Cinema of the 1950s and 1960s such as the films of Jacques Tati illustrate these urban transformations and the anxiety they generated. In *Mon Oncle/My Uncle* (1958), Mr Hulot repeatedly goes over the physical border of an ancient crumbling stone wall that separates his old neighbourhood from the tower blocks of the new suburbs. Tati shows the transition from one world to the other, from a city and civilization to another[1] (Millot 2003: 27). Tati's critique of the blandness of modernity and its standardized lifestyle culminates in *Play Time* (1967), a film in which sterile and homogeneous architecture creates social alienation. Although he might not address the low-income housing estates per se, Tati focuses on high-rise buildings to question the confusion and disorientation introduced by modern architecture and new design. *Play Time* shows 'the spectacularization and reification of life itself through a shot of identical flats seen through their glass front' (Marie 2001: 261).

Jean-Luc Godard's *Deux ou trois choses que je sais d'elle/Two or Three Things I Know About Her* (1967) provides another early examination of the negative impact of modern urban planning. The film focuses on the setting of the *banlieue* to address the challenges faced by working class people who both literally and symbolically prostitute themselves as a way of coping with the demands of consumer society and capitalist ideology. Godard shows the drastic transformation that France experienced after World War II. His depiction of the urban landscape with its eternal cycle of demolition/reconstruction, its empty lots, ruins and construction sites represents the social and economic expansion of the 1960s. Katherine Shonfield (2000: 118) states:

> the sense of Godard's film is not just that Paris has been atomized into objects: it is that it is decimated. Despite the ambiguities of his camera, the figure of the prostitute is first and foremost the victim of the ruthless practices of international capital, symbolic of the body of Paris, and indeed France herself.

In *Deux ou trois choses que je sais d'elle*, buildings are seen from the outside before the camera goes inside and subsequently turns them into volumes, or objects that are examined from within. Protagonists travel between the outside world and domestic interiors. The film also presents the city through windows; Godard is interested in showing that the world exists both from within and without. Influenced by modern theories on architecture, he writes (Godard 2006: 81) that buildings are both objective and subjective entities. Therefore, although he questions the urbanization projects of the 1960s in this film, Godard shows his obvious fascination for their idealized geometric forms. This propensity for modernity and abstraction is accentuated by the conceptual nature of the film, which, for instance, blurs the boundary between Marina Vlady's role as Juliette Jeanson and her real-life identity.

In contrast with Godard's film, Kechiche prefers a realistic approach that accentuates the impact of the *banlieue* on today's young population. Unlike the characters of *Deux ou trois choses que je sais d'elle*, *L'Esquive's* teenagers do not travel to Paris. They are confined to the location of the Cité des Francs-Moisins. The film's numerous outdoor shots and careful framing of the characters transform the setting from mere background into a subjective space. The *cité* creates visual and physical boundaries for the protagonists. The *banlieue* is not solely an external location that supports the work of the actors; the director's attention to the environment transforms the set into a critical element of the *mise-en-scène*.

In *L'Esquive*, the *banlieue* appears inescapable. Numerous close-up shots create a sense of entrapment within the frame. The film's images reinforce the fear of imprisonment felt by the protagonists and the audience alike during an unjustified police attack on the youth. Low camera angles define the physical space of the *banlieue* as overpowering; they draw attention to large housing developments, lines of mailboxes, tiled lobbies, bars on windows and numerous fences. All these grids and boxes refer to the idea of '*la barre*', the concrete landmark and basic building block of the *grands ensembles* and *cités*. The boxes and visual obstacles in the film are barriers that remind the audience of prison cells. This parallels the experience of the young Krimo (Osman Elkharraz) whose father is in jail. Moreover, '*la barre*' is the symbolic border that isolates and separates the *banlieue* from the rest of the world.

Figure 7.1: The silhouettes of Krimo (Osman Elkharraz) and his friend Fathi (Hafet Ben-Ahmed) appear in front of the set of the Cité des Francs-Moisins.

Figure 7.2: Fathi (Hafet Ben-Ahmed) is discussing male-matters with his friend Krimo (Osman Elkharraz).

Kechiche's understanding of the *cité* departs from Godard's view of the *banlieue*. Writing about *Deux ou trois choses que je sais d'elle*, Godard uses the architectural term *grands ensembles* as metaphor. For this director, the expression not only evokes the large geometrical apartment blocks that shape the modern landscape of French suburbs; it also alludes to the mathematical ensemble theory. The protagonists' singular experiences are part of larger structures and laws beyond them – the 'ensemble' laws (Godard 2006: 80). Godard's application of this mathematical concept to the *banlieue* is an intellectual exercise in line with his oeuvre. It situates him – and by extension his viewer – as outside his subject, an observer who does not belong in the *banlieues*. This type of preoccupation with abstraction is another manifestation of the director's modernist approach. Kechiche takes a very different position. *L'Esquive* follows the teenagers in their daily routine. Camera viewpoints and close-up shots bring the viewers at the centre of the scenes. This style creates a sense of intimacy and belonging that is lacking in Godard's remote gaze and intellectual exercises.

In addition, in spite of its political awareness, Godard's film does not acknowledge the immigrants, mostly men from the Maghreb and other former French colonies, who built the *banlieues* during the 30 years of post-war economic expansion. Although Godard's choice of Marina Vlady[2] as an actress could signify that France is a melting pot of immigrants and their children; for the most part, the population of the film appears as white, French-speaking and quite homogeneous. In this way, the film does not anticipate the multi-ethnic neighbourhoods depicted in *L'Esquive*. At one point, in *Deux ou trois choses que je sais d'elle*, a child who has just arrived from Algeria is asked a couple of questions to which he responds, but he is not in the camera's visual field. Interestingly, along with the director who whispers his commentary as soundtrack throughout the film, this child is the only person whose presence remains off screen. This lack of visual representation of a newcomer to the country conforms to the blindness of French ideology of the 1960s and the systematic invisibility and erasure of non-white immigrants from mainstream culture, an approach that remained for the most part unquestioned until the 1980s.

Cultural background: the *banlieues*

As Philippe Bernard (1993: 67–84) explains, immigration laws have followed the whims and political agendas of successive governments in France. For instance, foreigners were enlisted to fight in World War II, only to subsequently become victims of racist persecutions and be forcibly returned to their countries of origin. Afterwards, the Nazis' need for manual labour brought back to France a wave of Algerian recruits. During the *Trente Glorieuses* (1945–74), there was a large influx of immigrants due to reconstruction demands. At first, the immigrant workers were expected to go back to their countries of origin by both conservative governments and companies that thought of them as disposable. However, despite anti-immigration laws and financial incentives from the French government to encourage returns to countries of origin, families joined the male immigrant workers who had originally come to France alone. For the most part, this immigrant population settled in the *banlieues* and serious antagonism and hostility ensued. In this way, France transformed itself into the multi-ethnic – and not always well-integrated – society that Kechiche represents in *L'Esquive*.

The French *banlieues* are stigmatized and commonly blamed for social ailments such as violence, crime and drug problems. This was demonstrated in the summer of 2005 when Sidi-Ahmed Hammache, an 11-year-old boy, was accidentally shot in La Courneuve (one of the *banlieues* on the Paris outskirts). Nicolas Sarkozy, who was then Minister of the Interior, assumed that the crime was a consequence of gang rivalries and, as if the *banlieues'* populations were just nuisance or refuse to be disposed of, publicly announced that the neighbourhood would be cleaned up with Kärcher (a brand name for a high-pressure cleaning device). In reality, the incident was neither related to drug trafficking nor gangs. The bullet was directed at a young man of Comorian origin. The two Maghrebi brothers who tried to kill him were infuriated with this young man's interracial relationship with their sister. Sarkozy's comment was one in a series of blunders; he had used degrading vocabulary towards his constituents on repeated occasions. In particular, Sarkozy is remembered for referring to youth in the *banlieues* as riff-raff (*racaille*).

A few months after the Kärcher incident, riots spread from the Paris *banlieues* to nearly 300 cities throughout France signifying that the tensions in the *banlieues* had reached alarming levels. Three weeks of riots resulted in thousands of burned cars, hundreds of burned buildings and thousands of youths arrested. The situation has not improved for youths in the *banlieues* and a high level of tension and despair prevails. This is illustrated in a scene of *L'Esquive* where the viewers become witnesses to an unwarranted and violent police attack on the youth. As rightfully pointed out by Carrie Tarr (2007: 137) in this scene, one of the youth's

> copy of the Marivaux text is first assumed to contain illegal substances and then used to hit her. The sequence, which ends ironically with a close-up of the battered book, is in vivid contrast with the ensuing performance sequence, showing how the legitimacy of the adolescents' attempt to access bourgeois culture is denied in the wider world.

Beur and *banlieue* cinema

Kechiche's representation of the abuse of power by French police is not unusual. Tensions with institutions of the French Republic, along with the struggle for belonging of *banlieues* youth, have become the subject of numerous cinematic representations, so much so that in the 1990s the term *banlieue* cinema became commonly used to describe these films. According to Myrto Konstantarakos (1999: 160), the *banlieue* film is the first type of film since the Western that 'takes its name from a geographical feature'. Some of the directors of *banlieue* cinema are white and did not grow up in the *banlieues*. However, a large corpus of films comes from ethnic minority directors, in particular second-generation children of Maghrebi immigrants such as Kechiche. Unlike Jean-Luc Godard's allegories and representations of abstract concepts, these filmmakers' work derives from their personal experience. Their films, which often describe the typical difficulties of everyday life in the *banlieues,* have been brought together under the category of *beur* cinema, a genre that intersects and overlaps with *banlieues* films.

Beur cinema is part of a movement for self-representation that started in the early 1980s when children of Maghrebi immigrants began to identify as a group. They organized to denounce their exclusion from mainstream French culture as well as the negative stereotypes and racism plaguing their lives. In 1983, the anti-racism organization *SOS Racisme*, called for a 'march against racism and for equality' from Marseille to Paris. This march, which was soon called *La Marche des Beurs* by the media, gathered tens of thousands of people. A *Beur* is someone whose parents are immigrants from the Maghreb and who has grown up and been educated in France. The word *beur* most probably originates in *verlan*, a popular and coded way of speaking, which consists of inverting syllables. *Beur* is believed to be an inversion of the word *Arabe*. Although it is not universally accepted, it is a term used to identify French youth of Maghrebi origin, many of whom live in the *banlieues*.[3] The term appeared in the late 1970s. It has become so commonly used that it has been integrated into French dictionaries and is followed by its own back-slang inversion *rebeu*, a term that is now – along with words such as *rabza* and *rabzouz* – increasingly replacing the older term *beur*. As Sylvie Durmelat (1998: 193) demonstrates, words such as *beur* come from the inventiveness of everyday language and represent a bridge between the oral/popular and mainstream/dominant cultures.

Beur protagonists played an important role in the instigation of *banlieue* cinema, which in the 1990s repeatedly featured *black, blanc, beur* male trios. One film in particular, Mathieu Kassovitz's *La Haine* (1995), drew international public attention to the hardships experienced by multi-ethnic *banlieues* youth. The film was the subject of numerous studies, which contributed to its iconic status. *La Haine* reflects the drastic changes that have taken place in the *banlieues* since the 1960s and represents the new multicultural face of France. However, as Carrie Tarr (2005: 62–72) argues, this film reflects the privileged background and social position of its white director and white actor Vincent Cassel, who, out of the three main actors of the film, was the only one to receive a nomination for a César for his role as Vinz. Tarr explains that the film favours the white character and adds 'La Haine structures two *beur* youths into the narrative, only to use them in ways which deny them an active role' (2005: 71).

Writing about both *La Haine* and *Métisse,* another film by Kassovitz that examines race and miscegenation, Tarr adds that although Kassovitz is interested in representing multi-ethnic youth, 'this liberal integrationist vision is a one-way crossing of racial boundaries, and the complex hybrid identities of the ethnic others in these two films are much less adequately explored' (2005: 72). She also explains that this represents a 'different discursive position' in contrast to the work of non-white film directors who speak from their own experience. In particular, directors of Magrehbi origin counteract negative stereotypes by presenting a *beur*-centred perspective. Tarr (2005: 49) states '*Beur* cinema similarly suggests both agency in the production of representations by this particular ethnic minority and a challenge to the dominant representations of "Frenchness" and "otherness"'.

Hamid Naficy (2001: 100), who describes the films of immigrant directors as 'accented' cinema, explains that by means of their 'organizational and textual counterpractices, the [accented] filmmakers are transformed from displaced subjects into active agents of their own emplacement'. Naficy (2001: 98) applies the concept of accented cinema to *beur* cinema, which, he says, 'embodies the accented style more in its themes, characters, and structures of feeling than in its style of visualization or narration'.

This is certainly true of *beur* and *banlieue* films that raise questions about specific issues concerning immigrants and their children. For instance, in *Wesh Wesh qu'est-ce qui se passe?* (Rabah Ameur-Zaïmeche, 2002), the main protagonist, Kamel (Rabah Ameur-Zaïmeche), has been subjected to the *double peine,* or double sentence. He has had to serve prison time both in France and Algeria because, although he grew up in France, he does not have French citizenship. Returning to his family's apartment building in the *banlieue,* he faces the impossibility of finding work due to his status as both former prisoner and illegal immigrant.

In Yamina Benguigui's *Inch'allah dimanche/Inch'allah Sunday* (2001), Zouina (Fejria Deliba) leaves her native Algeria to join her husband who is virtually a stranger to her. They were separated ten years before when he found work in a provincial French town.

Zouina is subjected to the harassment of her Algerian mother-in-law who does not respect her and has extremely traditional and sexist values. She is also the object of the racist stupidity of her new white French neighbours who display hostility and animosity towards her throughout the film. This film focuses on a female perspective and gives agency to Zouina despite the difficult situation she is facing and although all the odds seem to be stacked against her. These two *beur* films, in addition to numerous others, represent the voices of immigrants and expose the extreme difficulties they encounter due to racism, xenophobia and invisibility.

Deportation is another important theme in *beur* cinema because children of immigrants who do not have French citizenship can be deported to the countries of their parents where they have never set foot before. In *Origine Contrôlée/Made in France* (Ahmed Bouchaala and Zakia Rahri, 2001), the three protagonists Youssef (Atmen Kelif), Sonia (Ronit Elkabetz) and Patrick (Patrick Ligardes) are on the verge of being deported to Algeria. However, Patrick is not an Algerian. He is a French man who has been confused for an Algerian transsexual by the police. The film's use of mistaken identity is a traditional comedy style that in this case underscores the xenophobic nature of a blind and arbitrary police decision. The film is not limited to issues of immigration. It examines other forms of oppression such as trans-phobia. Patrick realizes what it means to be poorly treated because of one's difference. He also has to resolve his own conflict around trans issues when he realizes that Sonia, with whom he has fallen in love, is a male-to-female transsexual.

Jeunesse Dorée (Zaïda Ghorab-Volta, 2001) draws attention to the *banlieues* by giving a camera to its two young female protagonists Gwenaëlle (Alexandra Jeudon) and Angela (Alexandra Laflandre). They go on a road trip throughout France after winning a grant from a neighbourhood association. Their unusual project is to take photographs of isolated apartment buildings in the landscape. *Jeunesse Dorée* begins with Gwenaëlle's viewpoint, a 360-degrees aerial shot from the window of her apartment building. Beyond the towers of her *cité*, the horizon expands to include more groups of apartment buildings and *grands ensembles*. This environment does not create easy lives for the protagonists. The film exposes some of their difficulties such as the abuse they face at home but does not dwell on them. Instead it shows the characters' friendship and solidarity. It focuses on positive experiences such as their joy when they hear that their photo project is going to be funded. *Jeunesse Dorée* is a road movie, but it is also about two young women from the *banlieue* who, against the odds, discover the world through their artistic perception. As they travel and take photographs, the film's numerous still images of apartment buildings stop the movement of the camera. This generates questions regarding the visible presence of these buildings in the film, and by extension the landscape of the *banlieues*. The agency of the protagonists is made clear by the diegetic noise of the camera shutter that accompanies each photograph. It reminds the viewers that the photographs are the vision of the young female protagonists, their documentation of their journey. Although the beginning of the film explicitly shows how these young women cannot wait to leave their environment, the nature of their photo project emphasizes the influence of the *banlieue* environment on the protagonists' development and psyche.

Docufiction

The depiction of tower blocks and apartment buildings in *Jeunesse Dorée* is a recurring theme in films by a generation of directors such as Abdellatif Kechiche who have grown up in the *banlieues*. An accomplished actor and director, Kechiche comes from an underprivileged family who immigrated to France from Tunisia when he was six years old. Although he does not like labels, and is careful not to be typecast as a *beur* filmmaker, Kechiche's films correspond with Naficy's (2001: 22) description of an accented style.

> They are also created in a new mode that is constituted both by the structures of feeling of the filmmakers themselves as displaced subjects and by the traditions of exilic and diasporic cultural productions that preceded them. From the cinematic traditions they acquire one set of voices, and from the exilic and diasporic traditions they acquire a second.

L'Esquive, which represents the voice of children from multi-ethnic backgrounds facing issues of identity and integration, reflects Kechiche's own double belonging. The film neither perpetuates the usual negative stereotypes of delinquent *banlieue* youths, nor creates totally positive images of the *banlieues*. It presents a multi-dimensional group of young protagonists with problems typical of their age group such as relationships, love, breakups and rivalry. These young people are establishing their identity while facing a culture and society that are not always inclusive.

L'Esquive underlines how the subtext of Marivaux's eighteenth century play, *Games of Love and Chance,* about the difficulties of escaping one's social condition, still applies to contemporary French society. The viewers' attention is not captured through conventional narrative form. The interactions between the teenage protagonists constitute the main structure of the film and are more important than a storyline. *L'Esquive* exposes its young protagonists' struggle with belonging and their complex relationship with their French cultural heritage. The visual and spoken languages of the film are markers of these tensions.

Although very few scenes take place in a classroom, *L'Esquive* shares common themes with Laurent Cantet's *Entre les murs/The Class*, which received the *Palme d'Or* at the Cannes Film Festival in 2008. The latter is based on a middle-school teacher's semi-autobiographical book. François Bégaudeau who wrote the book also collaborated with Cantet on the script and plays the role of the teacher in the film. *Entre les murs* represents the daily life of a group of students within the four walls of their classroom. In *L'Esquive*, the walls of the *cité* are the protagonists' boundary and they become their symbolic frontier. In both films, the camera penetrates the walls of an enclosed space and follows the protagonists throughout their day. This entering of a semi-private space combined with the use of non-professional actors and naturalistic style transforms, to some extent, the two directors into ethnographers and brings a documentary quality to their films. By extension their viewers become non-participant observers.

Linguistic barriers and language creativity

David Lepoutre (1997: 51–70) notes that although the teenagers of the *grands ensembles* express the desire to escape what they perceive as their prison, not surprisingly they also construct imaginary fantasies about their neighbourhoods. They are emotionally invested in these spaces where some of them were born and all of them have accumulated numerous memories. Lepoutre demonstrates how the spatial separation of the *cité* allows for territorial identification.

This is illustrated in *L'Esquive*, which opens in the middle of a sentence with the words 'I am going to fuck their mother' (*je vais niquer leur mère*), and continues with 'sons of a whore' (*fils de pute*). These words instantly immerse the audience in a heated discussion between teenage boys. No full explanation is provided for this discussion. However, in the midst of the chaos of insults and hatred, the viewer gathers that the verbal attacks concern another group of young men from 'the wrong' neighbourhood.

Although the boys seem legitimately upset, their emotional display also appears like a routine, talking for talking's sake. These young men's show of anger and masculinity, their performance for one another, is what matters. This use of language is sustained throughout the film, which presents the teenagers' verbal expression in extreme ways. Handheld camera shots add a sense of chaos and instability and accentuate the anger and strong feelings of the teenagers who appear extremely tense. They spend a great deal of time being upset and screaming at one another.

The protagonists' accents, tone and speed of delivery along with their use of slang make for an intense language that at times resembles a dialect more than the language of the French *Académie*. The teenagers' way of speaking includes creative grammar and syntax; it incorporates *verlan* and imports expressions from Arabic. As Annie Longatte (1999: 69) explains, children of Maghrebi immigrants often speak a vernacular Arabic at home, which is different from the dialectal Arabic spoken in the countries of their parents. This language is perceived as the '*mélange*' spoken by immigrants in opposition to the 'pure' classical Arabic taught in school. The pattern and habit of mixing languages are carried over into the French spoken by teenagers. Further, Longatte (1999: 75) speaks of these children's use of different codes depending on their interlocutors. They alternate between diverging and converging codes to signify respectively distance and their non-belonging status (in particular when they address their parents and authorities' representatives), or their complicity with one another. In convergent codes, the integration of segments of their parents' native language into conversations in French is a way to acknowledge their common experience of double belonging. This language codification allows the youth to acknowledge their roots and signify their intentional identification with a specific ethno-cultural group.

The *banlieue* children, who might speak a different language at home, suffer from a double alienation. It is likely that the majority of French children struggle with literature from the past. Nevertheless, the language of the eighteenth century play by Marivaux that they are studying becomes a third or fourth language for the teenagers of the *banlieue*. The language they speak in the film is so different from conventional French that it can be perceived as symptomatic of their exclusion and marginalization. In *L'Esquive*, Kechiche establishes a contrast between the raw language spoken by his young protagonists and the eighteenth century play that they are rehearsing. However, Kechiche uses language to signify both the fracture in the children's identity and their belonging in the continuum of French culture. The film exploits Marivaux's refined and nuanced use of words to create a parallel between the *préciosité* of the eighteenth century text that, at times, sounds like jargon, and the language developed by the youths of today's *banlieues*. Kechiche reclaims Marivaux's writing and uses it as counterpart to the teenagers' speech. This confirms that languages are in constant flux. They are live material that gets transformed and changes rapidly.

L'Esquive's teenagers have little apparent contact with contemporary French society outside of their life in the *cité*. The film focuses on the protagonists' discovery of the language of eighteenth-century France to addresses issues of assimilation and belonging. The teenagers are fully committed to Marivaux's text. They tirelessly rehearse the same scenes on their own and ask themselves and their teacher insightful questions about theatre and their roles in the play. Thus the film builds connections between its young characters and mainstream culture through Marivaux's text. It also shows the teenagers' irreverence for mainstream French and demonstrates their linguistic creativity through the freedom they take with language. This creative use of language is spreading rapidly beyond the world of immigrant children of the *banlieues*. The increasing adoption of *verlan* and Arabic expressions by mainstream French people is evidence of the impact that the *banlieue* teenagers have on today's French language.

Marivaux's text might represent the struggle for acculturation but it is also an important cultural artifact that opens doors to the young protagonists' imaginations. Lydia (Sara Forestier), who acts the part of Lisette in Marivaux's play, is completely affected by her role. Her stage costume is of critical importance to her. Early in the film, the audience watches her bargaining with the tailor who has created the period outfit. Lydia might be penniless, but she is determined to get the dress. She is so overwhelmed by its beauty and power that she wears it throughout the *cité* – at times under a jean jacket – in spite of her friends' judgement and horrified comments. The film underscores the strange displacement of this ostentatious costume from the past during a conversation between Lydia and her friend Zina (Hajar Hamlili). Shots of Lydia and Krimo contrast with reverse shots of Zina framed by her apartment window with her two young siblings.

In Marivaux's play, Lisette is actually a servant who disguises herself as her mistress. Lydia's performance of Lisette, who in turn is performing her mistress, is a *mise en abîme* that enables both the subservient character and the young actress to transcend their social condition.

Figure 7.3: Lydia (Sara Forestier) and Krimo (Osman Elkharraz) pay a visit to Zina (Hajar Hamlili) to show off Lydia's stage costume.

Lydia fully embraces Lisette's part. The double trans-vestment of Lisette and Lydia allows these characters to cross class borders and transgress the economic and social codes by which they are supposed to abide. Wearing Lisette's dress in the *cité*, Lydia discovers her wish to become an actress. Acting transports her into the world of the imaginary. She is transformed and allowed access to dreams beyond her class status and the walls of the *banlieue*.

On the other hand, Lydia's male counterpart Krimo shows signs of distress. Originally not cast in Marivaux's play, Krimo falls for Lydia, the 'film's and the play's blonde, blue-eyed fully *française* heroine' (Nettelbeck 2007: 314), as he watches a rehearsal of one of the play's love scenes. Subsequently, in order to engage with Lydia during rehearsals, Krimo trades items of merchandise for the part of the young actor who plays Arlequin. But acting as Arlequin does not allow him to fulfil his dream. Critics (Vinay Swamy 2007: 65–66; Nettelbeck 2007: 314) agree that Krimo's acting stint reveals his lack of integration in French society. Swamy states 'For education, thus far promoted by the Republic as a means of successful integration … seems to have failed in this instance to include the likes of Krimo into the national fold'. Although he uses the play to declare his love to Lydia, he does not succeed in pursuing her and unlike some of the other teenagers in the film, he does not seem able to escape his condition.

Krimo becomes increasingly morose as Lydia keeps evading[4] his love and advances. Ilaria Vitali (2009: 6) explains that Lydia is not willing to drop the theatrical mask, the secret passage that opens up a parallel dimension beyond the walls of the *cité* for her. Furthermore, Vitali (2009: 10) adds: 'as long as she performs the Marivaudian role, she remains outside the sphere of action of other kids from the *banlieue*, beyond power struggle, values and rules established by the *cité*' (my translation).[5]

Krimo, in the same manner as Marivaux's Arlequin – a servant who is passing for his master Dorante – has to perform a role that he does not master.[6] Vitali points out that Arlequin's role takes away the slang of the *cité* from Krimo and creates a language void (*vide langagier*) that leads him to walk out of the rehearsal and abandon acting altogether. Krimo is able to flee the stage but his inability to act confirms his confinement in reality and reinforces the impossibility of escaping his social position. His body and his psyche belong in, and cannot get away from, the *cité*.

Figure 7.4: Krimo (Osman Elkharraz) is watching the play from outside the auditorium.

At the end of the film, Kechiche accentuates Krimo's multiple exclusions by making him watch the performance of the play from outside the building. He is seen through a window, his face framed by metal mounts. More than ever, the viewers witness his loneliness, confinement and isolation. Swamy (2007: 66) states 'Krimo's failure, thus played out, implies that the school has also failed in nurturing and integrating our protagonist' and further, although 'the film portrays the adolescents as perfectly capable of being culturally competent, their "successful" cultural performance might not necessarily tell the whole story of their place within the national space'.

Krimo floats unanchored within the walls of the *cité* like one of the sailboats pictured in a collection of watercolour paintings sent by his father, that he carefully pins on his bedroom walls. These drawings are vehicles that provide father and son with different, possibly better worlds. Could the boats be floating on the Mediterranean Sea that separates France from the father's country of origin? Nevertheless, the imaginary space of the paintings does not provide a real escape from Krimo's feeling of imprisonment. This situation resembles other *banlieues* films, which often emphasize how these neighbourhoods do not provide their youth with the necessary tools to thrive in society. Although he appears to have a supportive mother (of all the teenagers represented in the film, his mother is the only parent we see and his apartment is the only one penetrated by the camera), Krimo suffers from unfulfilled needs. In the same manner as many other immigrants who have landed in the *cité*, Krimo lacks feelings of belonging. Apart from his academic education, the *cité* does not offer him the basic building blocks of identity formation. Nettelbeck (2007: 313) states that although

Kechiche's work is considered 'too soft' by some critics, his films depict France as a country that 'fails to safeguard its most vulnerable inhabitants' (2007: 311).

Krimo, along with other *banlieue* youth, is subjected to the social and cultural voids created by the *grands ensembles,* which were built either on wastelands or in the place of razed neighbourhoods where all signs of history had been obliterated. According to Françoise Choay (2006: 131–43), the living quarters of the *grands ensembles* positioned away from administrative centres become ghettos with minimal vital organs. The architects and planners of the *grands ensembles* did not provide anything new to replace the absent urban cultural markers of the past. Choay explains that until the twentieth century, monuments participated in identity formation and facilitated the integration of the self into a community. Monuments were erected as reminders of events, people, communal beliefs and rites. With time, as they lost their power on live memory – along with their identification value – they would be integrated into an abstract memory system to become historical monuments. The latter served as signs or illustrations; and functioned as visual support to the ordering of time. Monuments that represent shared institutional practices contribute to collective memory and facilitate community building. They capture time and appropriate space.

Modernity puts a stop to the construction of monuments. This is particularly true of the *grands ensembles* that provide neither new nor historical monuments around which the population can rally. Furthermore, Choay considers the constructed world as a language that constitutes a consubstantial way, and provides the means to coexist socially. In the *banlieues,* the landmarks that used to form the spatiotemporal identity of old cities are lost. Choay's ideas confirm that the architecture of the *banlieues* creates visual poverty and a cultural void, which for young people like Krimo, make the anchoring of identities very difficult.

Cultural and cinematic frontiers

L'Esquive's focus on architecture and language underscores the social fractures and cultural rifts produced by the low-income housing estates of the *banlieues.* The emphasis on the visual decrepitude of buildings, the accent on bars and orthogonal grids of *L'Esquive* show the physical and psychic deterioration of the *banlieues.* Run-down tower blocks, dark hallways and dilapidated staircases have replaced the architecture of spectacle found in Tati and Godard's films. Graffiti has been substituted for the background advertisements for consumer society items used by these filmmakers. This reflects the actual physical setting of the *banlieues* and documents how the authorities that constructed the *grands ensembles* have been neglecting them.

Although *L'Esquive* depicts the struggles and entrapment experienced by youth in a *grand ensemble*, it does not focus solely on the negative impact of this environment on its population. Beyond the façade of their antagonisms and rough verbal exchanges, the youth are portrayed as having important and tight relationships. When they face adversity, their friendships and solidarity with one another are unquestionable. This sense of community is what allows them to invent their own language and cultural expressions that seep through the walls of the *cité*. The *banlieue's* linguistic influence on mainstream French signifies that languages are positively contagious; culture can neither be imposed nor contained; and acculturation is a two-way process.

Through the use of Marivaux's play, *L'Esquive* demonstrates how the protagonists' complex identities are shaped by the Republic's school system, as much as by their multicultural experience and life in the *banlieue. L'Esquive's* emphasis on the play underscores how education enforces both French tradition and the dominant culture in the multi-ethnic *banlieues* schools. Endlessly rehearsing scenes from Marivaux's play together and on their own, *L'Esquive's* protagonists overcome their difficulties with this eighteenth century text. Thus they affirm their will to belong. Despite the long history of antagonisms and lack of support from successive governments, the population of the *banlieues* is here to stay. The youth's resilient spirit rises above and beyond the physical barriers of the *cité*. In the face of isolation and adversity, their creative language continuously transforms and expands. This echoes the determination of *banlieue* and *beur* filmmakers who have used their personal experience to bring great innovations to the screen. Kechiche offers a testimony to the active participation of young people from the *banlieue* in contemporary French culture and heritage. This, in itself, is a trope for *L'Esquive*, a film that in addition to belonging in *beur* and *banlieue* cinema undoubtedly needs to be considered in the long French cinematic history and tradition.

Acknowledgements

I would like to thank Tamsin Whitehead for her careful reading of this text and very helpful comments.

References

Bernard, P. (1993), *L'Immigration*, Paris: Le Monde-Éditions.

Blanc, J.-N. (2003), 'Le consensus sur les grands ensembles, ou le grand malentendu', in F. Tomas, J.-N. Blanc and M. Bonilla (eds), *Les grands ensembles: Une histoire qui continue ...*, Saint Étienne: Publications de l'Université de Saint Étienne, pp. 44–96.

Choay, F. (2006), *Pour une anthropologie de l'espace*, Paris: Éditions du Seuil.

Durmelat, S. (1998), 'Petite Histoire du mot *beur* ou comment prendre la parole quand on vous la prête', *French Cultural Studies*, 9: 26, pp. 191–207.

Godard, J.-L. (2006), *Documents*, Paris: Éditions du Centre Pompidou.

Konstantarakos, M. (1999), 'Which Mapping of the City? *La Haine* (Kassovitz, 1995) and the *cinéma de banlieue*', in P. Powrie (ed.), *French Cinema in the 1990s: Continuity and Difference*, Oxford: Oxford University Press, pp. 160–71.

Lepoutre, D. (1997), *Coeur de Banlieue,* Paris: Éditions Odile Jacob.

Longatte, A. (1999), 'Pratiques langagières de la deuxième génération de l'immigration', in E. Ruhe (ed.), *Die Kinder der Immigration/Les Enfants de l'immigration,* Würzburg: Königshausen & Neumann, pp. 65–81.

Marie, L. (2001), 'Jacques Tati's *Play Time* as New Babylon', in M. Shiel and T. Fitzmaurice (eds), *Cinema and the City: Film and Urban Societies in a Global Context,* Oxford: Blackwell Publishers, pp. 257–69.

Millot, O. (2003), 'La Banlieue au cinéma', in O. Millot and P. Glâtre (eds), *Caméra plein champ - La banlieue au cinéma, le cinéma en banlieue,* Paris: Éditions Creaphis, pp. 19–33.

Naficy, H. (2001), *An Accented Cinema: Exilic and Diasporic Filmmaking,* Princeton and Oxford: Princeton University Press.

Nettelbeck, C. (2007), 'Kechiche and the French Classics: Cinema as Subversion and Renewal of Tradition', *French Cultural Studies,* 18: 3, pp. 307–19.

Panerai, P., Castex, J. and Depaule, J. C. (2009), *Formes urbaines de l'îlot à la barre,* Marseille: Éditions Parenthèses, Collection Eupalinos, Série architecture et urbanisme.

Shonfield, K. (2000), *Walls Have Feelings: Architecture, Film and the City,* London and New York: Routledge.

Swamy, V. (2007), 'Marivaux in the Suburbs: Reframing Language in Kechiche's *L'Esquive* (2003)', *Studies in French Cinema,* 7: 1, pp. 57–68.

Tarr, C. (2005), *Reframing Difference: Beur and Banlieue Filmmaking in France,* Manchester and New York: Manchester University Press.

———— (2007), 'Reassessing French Popular Culture: L'Esquive', in D. Waldron and I. Vanderschelden (eds), *France at the Flicks: Trends in Contemporary French Popular Cinema,* Newcastle: Cambridge Scholars Publishing, pp. 130–41.

Tchetche-Apea, P.-D. (2000), 'Révéler la citoyenneté des banlieues', in H. Hatzfeld (under the direction of), *Banlieues: villes de demain 'Vaulx-en-Velin au delà de l'image' séminaire de 5ᵉ année mars-mai 1998,* Lyon: École d'architecture, pp. 73–90.

Tomas, F. (2003), 'La place des grands ensembles dans l'histoire de l'habitat social français', in F. Tomas, J.-N. Blanc and M. Bonilla (eds), *Les grands ensembles: Une histoire qui continue ...,* Saint Étienne: Publications de l'Université de Saint Étienne, pp. 7–43.

Vitali, I. (2009), 'Marivaudage ou tchatche? Jeux de masques et travestissements linguistiques dans L'Esquive d'Abdellatif Kechiche', *Francofonia Studi e Ricerche sulle Litterature di Lingua Francese,* 56, pp. 3–16.

Notes

1 'Ce que Tati nous montre, c'est la transition d'un monde à l'autre, d'une ville et d'une civilisation à l'autre, le passage du centre ville (ou centre village) au quartier moderne ...'

2 As mentioned in the film, she is of Russian origin.

3 Sylvie Durmelat cites Nacer Kettane: 'even though the word *beur* comes from the back slang word for *Arabe* [...] it does not mean the same as the academic definition of the word "*arabe*". *Beur* evokes a geographical and cultural space at the same time as a social space, the

space of the *banlieue* and French proletariat' ('quand bien même beur vient du mot Arabe en verlan […] il n'a rien à voir avec la signification académique du mot "arabe". Beur renvoie à la fois à un espace géographique et culturel et à un espace social, celui de la banlieue et du proletariat en France') (1998: 198).

4   The title *L'Esquive* means to evade.

5   'tant qu'elle joue le rôle marivaudien, elle est hors de la sphère d'action des autres "banlieusards", hors des rapports de force, des valeurs et des règles établies par la cité'.

6   In the play Dorante and Silvia exchange roles with their servants Arlequin and Lisette. This is a stratagem they use to test one another in an arranged marriage situation. During the course of the play, the masters are confused by their feelings. They realize their attraction for one another while thinking that they are getting involved with a servant. In the meantime, the reverse situation is taking place between Lisette and Arlequin. While they incarnate their masters, the audience is aware of Lisette and Arlequin's status as servants because they are not fluent in the language and manners of the upper class. In the end, both servants and masters realize the travesty and can happily marry within their social rank.

Chapter 8

Between Hamburg and Istanbul: Mobility, Borders and
Identity in the Films of Fatih Akin

Jessica Gallagher
The University of Queensland

R oughly half-way through Fatih Akin's acclaimed *Gegen die Wand/Head-On* (2004), a plane descends into Istanbul. The film's main female character, Sibel, makes her way through the airport and past the border control. She barely resembles the woman whom audiences had met earlier in Hamburg, with her hair now cut short and her clothing dark and shapeless. The expression on her face is pained and sorrowful. In Akin's *Auf der anderen Seite/The Edge of Heaven* (2007), Nejat, the male protagonist, watches as a coffin is unloaded from a plane in Istanbul. He has accompanied the body from Germany, and he too looks troubled and unhappy. There are more dissimilarities than likenesses between these two characters, but both are Turkish-German and both have made this trip unwillingly, because of the actions of others.

Transnational journeys are comparatively uncommon in films about members of the Turkish diaspora in Germany. Most films in the past have depicted characters from Turkish origins as being static and/or confined to a small number of designated spaces. Thus these two films by Akin represent a shift in Turkish-German cinema – the arrival in Istanbul denotes new spaces and places for characters and, potentially, greater freedom of movement. A number of scholars have commented favourably on the travelling protagonists in Akin's films, suggesting that they are emblematic of a new phase in the representation of the Turkish-Germans. Yet, if this is the case, why do Sibel and Nejat seem so lost on arrival? With reference to the history of Turkish immigration, this chapter will consider the significance of transnational movements in films which focus on the Turkish diaspora in Germany, and will argue that the increased mobility of characters continues to demonstrate the limitations of a hybrid Turkish-German identity and existence, and cannot be viewed as positively as some have suggested. The chapter will also explore how borders are framed in recent Turkish-German cinema and the role they play in highlighting some of the struggles that second-generation Turks face today, four decades after Turkish foreign workers began arriving in Germany.

The Turkish diaspora in Germany

Whilst a lengthy examination of the ongoing complexity of the relationship between mainstream German society and the Turkish diaspora cannot be accommodated here, a short overview is of use to this discussion. The complicated German-Turkish relationship can be traced back to the early 1960s, when Turkish workers began arriving in Germany as

Gastarbeiter ('guest workers') to help ease the labour shortages during the post-World War II economic boom. The *Gastarbeiter* were originally accepted as a temporary workforce that would eventually go home, but, as the Turkish-German poet Zafer Şenocak remarks, '[w]hat at first appeared to be a harmless economic phenomenon soon developed into a momentous social phenomenon. The so-called guest workers violated the rules of hospitality, settled down, improved their economic status and became immigrants' (2000: 87). With the economic downturn of the early 1970s, the West German government placed a ban on the recruitment of foreign labour, but permitted *Gastarbeiter* who were already in the country to stay and to continue to bring their families into Germany. By the following decade it became clear that a large proportion of these guest workers were in Germany to stay. In these two decades, West Germans faced large-scale unemployment for the first time since the war and there was almost immediately a change in attitude towards the *Gastarbeiter*.

Today there are three generations of Turks living in Germany, and whilst the first generation is approaching retirement, the younger generations are now working in a variety of fields and 'are beginning to write their own history, create their own place and voice their own expectations about what it means and what it should mean for Turks to live in Germany' (Horrocks and Kolinsky 1996: xviii). Many second- and third-generation Turkish-Germans have had only limited experience of Turkey, and though they may still identify with elements of their parents' and grandparents' Turkish cultural and national identities, the younger generations have established a new identity based on their own experiences and affiliations. Within Germany's larger cities, the Turkish community has created new diasporic cityscapes with essentially self-sufficient suburbs. The expatriate Turkish community is one of the longest-established and largest immigrant groups in Germany and has at times been the focus of resentment and violence. For example, shortly after German reunification, the Turkish diaspora in Germany became a focal point of international media due to violent attacks. In two separate incidents a number of Turkish women and children were killed during arson attacks on their homes. The crimes were condemned by the broader German society, but the events highlighted the fact that in the public imaginary Turks often represented an identifiable cultural and social 'Other'. This chapter is concerned with the cinematic representation of members of this diaspora, and whilst filmic narratives cannot necessarily be seen as a mirror of social reality, it is against this socio-cultural background that the discussion on national and cultural borders in recent Turkish-German cinema is devised. Turkish-German cinema is generally defined as films produced by filmmakers from Turkish origins which focus on the lives of members of the Turkish diaspora in Germany.

Turkish-German cinema since the 1970s

The relationship between the broader German society and the Turkish diaspora has been the subject of a number of Turkish-German films, as have the physical borders and spaces that separate the two peoples and nations. The films which focused on the lives of the *Gastarbeiter* and their families in the 1970s and 1980s, labelled the 'cinema of the affected' (Burns 2006: 133) or the 'Kino der Fremdheit' ('cinema of alterity') (qtd in Berghahn and Sternberg 2010: 28), presented minority characters, in accordance with popular (mis)conceptions, as victims of incompatible 'Turkish' and 'German' ways of life. The 'cinema of the affected' is commonly associated with the works of New German directors such as Helma Sanders-Brahms and Hark Bohm, as well as Turkish-German filmmaker Tevfik Baser (Burns 2006: 133), and tended to depict minority characters as silent, static and disadvantaged, often by concentrating on the first generation and on spatial confinement. For example, Baser's *40m² Deutschland/40m² of Germany* (1986) centres around a young woman called Turna who is brought to Hamburg-Altona after an arranged marriage, and promptly imprisoned by her husband Dursun in their small apartment. Turna's only view of the outside world is through the small window from which she can look onto a courtyard and neighbouring street, but even from here she experiences cultural intolerance and bigotry. Turna's brief experiences with Germans signify that she is not only trapped by her husband, but 'has been incarcerated twice over: in her role as a Turkish woman and secondly, as an immigrant in an alien society' (Burns 1999: 749). When Turna finally escapes the confines of the apartment in the final scene, after Dursun dies, it is made clear that her protracted isolation has left her fearful of and unable to communicate in this alien country.

In his subsequent film, *Abschied vom falschen Paradies/Farewell to False Paradise* (1988), Baser again pursues the 'trope of imprisonment' (Burns 2006: 131). In the film, a young Turkish woman called Elif has been incarcerated for killing her abusive Turkish husband. Imprisonment in the German jail is presented as a vast improvement on the abuse and confinement that Elif had suffered living with her husband in Hamburg, as she is finally able to learn German, and even makes friends with fellow inmates. However, after learning of her imminent deportation, Elif tries to commit suicide – preferring to take her own life rather than be returned to Turkey and face the retribution of her husband's family. Both *40m² Deutschland* and *Abschied vom falschen Paradies* present, as Daniela Berghahn comments, 'sombre, claustrophobic depictions of the plight of Turkish women, suffering from oppression' (2006: 142). Both films highlight the extreme confinement of first-generation characters in Germany: Turna can barely cross the threshold of her apartment, and Elif cannot endure the thought of having to cross the border back into Turkey.

A new generation of Turkish-German cinema began to emerge in Germany from the mid- to late 1990s, associated chiefly with young German filmmakers of Turkish origin such as Thomas Arslan, Fatih Akin and Yüksel Yavuz. The films, including *Geschwister-Kardesler/Brothers and Sisters* (Arslan, 1996), *Dealer* (Arslan, 1998), *Kurz und Schmerzlos/Short Sharp Shock* (Akin, 1998) and *Aprilkinder/April Children* (Yavuz, 1998), attracted considerable interest from critics and audiences, so much so that in 1999 one reviewer announced that 'the New German Cinema is Turkish' and praised these films as rejuvenating the German film landscape (Kulaoglu 1999: 8). This 'new cinema' focuses predominantly on the lives of the second-generation Turkish youth in Germany, and has been praised by scholars as a movement away from the representation of Turkish *Gastarbeiter* as victims to a representation of 'the pleasures of hybridity' that shows transnationality in a more positive and good-humoured light (Göktürk 2001: 131). The notion of hybridity has become a common and generally positive concept in discussions about minorities or diasporas in the context of multifaceted identities which have evolved from the straddling of borders or cultural heritages (see Hall 1993; Shohat and Stam 1994; Naficy 2001). These ideas about identity and hybridity are central to recent Turkish-German cinema, with filmmakers exploring alternatives to the one-dimensional identities typical of the first-generation figures through the depiction of younger characters who pursue identities which are influenced by more contemporary discourses about 'Germanness', 'Turkishness' and 'Turkish-Germanness'. Scholars have generally viewed this shift in positive terms. For example, Deniz Göktürk suggests that, by resisting restrictive identity politics and focusing on the potential of hybridity, 'filmmakers have begun to tackle migration and cultural clashes with a sense of humour and irony' (2001: 149). Akin has commented on the dual elements of his own cultural identity and productions, stating that

'we look at Germany through our family's perspective as a Turk and we look at Turkey as a German. Therefore we do contain both identities; as a filmmaker, it is a rare change for me to be able to grasp both cultures from inside; but at the same time, it also brings a sense of not belonging to anywhere'. (qtd in Durmus 2006: 6)

The availability of space, increased mobility and how these might be linked to the articulation of hybrid identities have also been a focus of discussion. Unlike most of their predecessors, who were trapped in claustrophobic domestic spaces and limited by social and cultural barriers, the characters in more recent films are young, appear to enjoy greater choice in terms of their identities and lifestyles and are continually on the move, both within the multi-ethnic neighbourhoods and, in some instances, across national borders. Many of the more recent Turkish-German films are, perhaps unsurprisingly, set in the well-known multi-ethnic neighbourhoods of Germany's larger cities, such as Hamburg-Altona and Berlin-Kreuzberg. In the films, characters regularly take to the streets, where it is possible to see the impact that the Turkish diaspora has had on the German streetscapes, for example the Turkish restaurants and Turkish newsstands. A number of scholars have also commented on the increased movement of characters, arguing that the shift to exterior spaces signifies greater liberation and confidence. For example, Rob Burns suggests:

[O]ne indication of the freedom migrants increasingly enjoy is the cinematic spaces they now inhabit: No longer trapped within hermetic domestic spaces or other sites of confinement, they now tend to be situated in a multiplicity of urban and metropolitan environments where frequently they can demonstrate a new and confident mobility. (Burns 2007: 11)

However, not all commentators would necessarily agree that the increased space and movement in the films represent a positive shift from the earlier productions. For many characters, 'their search for identity is always accompanied by a search for roots and for a safe haven where they can remake themselves' (Durmus 2006: 6). The continuing restrictions on Turkish-German characters are repeatedly demonstrated in recent Turkish-German films by borders both within Germany and between Germany and Turkey. The limitation of space and the borders in Germany's urban centres were the focus of an earlier article (Gallagher 2006); this chapter will concentrate on the border between Germany and Turkey through analysis of border spaces and crossings in Fatih Akin's films.

Crossing borders in Fatih Akin's films

Fatih Akin is arguably the most recognized Turkish-German filmmaker and, following the critical acclaim of *Gegen die Wand*, commercially the most successful. Travel between Germany and Turkey is a significant feature in Akin's films, and a point of differentiation from many other Turkish-German productions, in which characters speak about leaving Germany and returning to Turkey, but the actual trip and what awaits characters when they arrive are rarely shown. In the majority of Akin's more recent films the journey, arrival and time spent in location are integral components in the narrative trajectory and in the development of the characters. Furthermore, border crossings occur in both directions, with Turkish characters travelling to Hamburg and German and Turkish-German characters making their way to Istanbul. It is this traffic at and across borders in Akin's films, but particularly in *Gegen die Wand* and *Auf der anderen Seite*, the first two films of his 'Love, Death and the Devil' trilogy, that is the focus of this chapter.

As Berghahn comments, Akin's films 'exhibit most of the characteristics associated with "accented cinema," [...] which has been identified by Hamid Naficy as an aesthetic response to displacement through exile, migration or diaspora' (2006: 141). Naficy interprets accented films 'as sites for intertextual, cross-cultural, and transnational struggles over meanings and identities' (1996: 121). Due to the duality of the filmmakers' own identities, the subject matter of accented cinema is not confined to a single culture, nor does it accept a simple notion of national identity. The framework of Naficy's accented cinema is useful for this discussion of Akin's work, because the iconographies that characterize accented cinema, including claustrophobic interiors and/or transitional spaces, multilingual and alienated or lonely characters who perform identity, wandering or displacement and a preoccupation with unbelonging, are also common features of Akin's films (2001: 289–92). Similarly, the border crossings and travels of Akin's protagonists reflect the same motivations as are common to many accented filmmakers and their characters. As Naficy writes:

They cross many borders and engage in many deterritorializing and reterritorializing journeys, which take several forms, including home-seeking journeys, journeys of homelessness, and homecoming journeys. However, these journeys are not just physical and territorial but are also deeply psychological and philosophical. Among the most important are journeys of identity, in the course of which old identities are sometimes shed and new ones refashioned. (Naficy 2001: 7)

Akin's earlier films *Kurz und Schmerzlos* and *Im Juli/In July* (2000) thematise barriers within Germany, and the borders between Germany and Turkey. In *Kurz und Schmerzlos*, characters are unable to cross the symbolic divide that exists between multi-ethnic and mainstream suburbs. The spatial restrictions reflect similar limitations in terms of identity, with the main character, second-generation Turk Gabriel, struggling with the dualities of his hybrid identity. In the film, Gabriel sees little option but to leave his family home in Altona after succumbing to the violence of the street. His friends are all dead and he himself has killed an Albanian drug boss. Fearful of retribution and with no other German space presented as an option, Gabriel views Turkey as the only possible destination. However, crossing the national borders and returning to this imagined homeland is problematic. Gabriel's departure for Turkey indicates his ongoing exclusion from the Turkish-German space of Altona, as well as from German society as a whole. As Stan Jones notes: 'The plot's logic means that Gabriel has become dislocated. He has to flee to Turkey, which may still be a "Heimat," but now signifies a place of refuge and enforced anonymity, akin to exile' (2003: 84). There is no suggestion that Gabriel has spent any significant time in Turkey in the past. The country that Gabriel has imagined represents a kind of utopian space and, as Berghahn comments, 'a country which combines the best of both worlds: traditional Turkish village life and the westernized Turkey as a tourist destination' (2006: 151). Audiences are not privy to Gabriel's arrival in Turkey and therefore are left only guessing as to whether he will be able to create a legitimate life for himself in Turkey and whether this journey will provide him the redemption he now seeks.

Akin's popular romantic comedy/road movie *Im Juli* is structured around journeys from Hamburg to Istanbul. The film presents the tale of a conservative German schoolteacher called Daniel, who after a chance encounter with a beautiful Turkish-German woman called Melek decides spontaneously to follow her from Hamburg to Istanbul and confess his love for her. Daniel is joined on his journey by the free-spirited Juli (who has fallen in love with him), and finds that his travel through south-eastern Europe is more difficult than initially expected. Along the way, he is beaten up, seduced, drugged, robbed and imprisoned at the Turkish border, but through the hospitality of strangers, including the Turkish-German character Isa (who turns out to be romantically involved with Melek), Daniel manages to reach Istanbul and find the happiness that he was looking for – albeit with Juli, who must overcome numerous obstacles on her own journey to Istanbul.

As a European road movie, *Im Juli* is primarily about negotiating borders, and the concrete imagery of boundaries and maps is central to the film. Scholars have generally commented favourably on the presentation of border crossings and journeying in the film. For example, Burns suggests that '[w]hereas in the "cinema of the affected" boundaries are fixed, static and frequently impenetrable, here they are either easily removable obstructions or liminal, transitional spheres where new identities can or indeed have to be constructed' (2007: 13). Similarly, Göktürk remarks that '*Im Juli* reminds us of the liberating pleasures of cinema, of its potential in projecting fantasies of travel [...] and performing national identities with self-conscious irony' (2002: 255). However, most commentators have concentrated on the travels of the 'German' characters, Daniel and Juli, and largely overlooked the film's key border crossing, which is made by the 'Turkish-German' character, Isa. This crossing is significant for a number of reasons. It is Isa's travel which ultimately precipitates the journeys of the other three characters – Melek is on her way to Istanbul to meet him, Daniel is following Melek and Juli is following Daniel. Isa, like so many of Akin's characters, is making the transnational journey not by choice, but because of the actions of others and to resolve difficult questions of belonging. Isa is travelling from Germany to Istanbul because he is returning his dead uncle's body to Turkey. When he is stopped at the Turkish border with Daniel and the body is discovered, the two are arrested (see Figure 8.1), and Isa explains to Daniel that his Uncle Ahmed had come to Germany to visit the family, and had enjoyed being there so much that he decided to stay illegally. When he died of a heart attack six months later, the family decided that, given his lack of legal status in Germany, he would have to be smuggled back into Turkey, and the only real option was to be returned across the border in a macabre manner in the boot of Isa's car. As Isa informs Daniel: 'We couldn't go the official route because my parents had an illegal corpse in their basement. [...] And since I am the youngest and I'm on vacation, I got stuck with all this crap'. It is noteworthy that Isa's journey appears to run smoothly until he reaches the Turkish border and is arrested by border guards. Ultimately, the border crossing into Turkey was not one that Isa or his Uncle Ahmed had wanted to make. Whilst the narrative of *Im Juli* may explore the interconnectedness

Figure 8.1: Isa and Daniel in prison at the Turkish border (Reproduced courtesy of Senator Film Verleih).

of Europe and question the need for rigid national borders and boundaries, the film's key border crossing is nevertheless characterized by loss and dislocation.

Travel between Germany and Turkey is a key feature of Akin's subsequent films *Gegen die Wand* and *Auf der anderen Seite*, which form part of his 'Love, Death and the Devil' trilogy. The trilogy is said to be Akin's response to Rainer Werner Fassbinder's FRG Trilogy, comprising the films *Die Ehe der Maria Braun/The Marriage of Maria Braun* (1979), *Lola* (1981) and *Veronika Voss* (1982), in which Fassbinder traced the history of post-war West Germany through the lives of three women. Like Fassbinder's productions, Akin's *Gegen die Wand* and *Auf der anderen Seite* are connected thematically rather than in a narrative sense. The films deal with different characters and plotlines, but each presents a story about Turkish-Germans living in Germany and explores the impact and significance of when characters make the journey back to Turkey. Both films present the negotiation of national and cultural identities, intercultural and intergenerational relationships and the search for somewhere to belong. As Thomas Elsaesser comments, '[w]hat the troubled relationship between West Germany and its Nazi past was to Fassbinder, Akin seems to imply, is to him the no less troubled negotiation between "assimilated" Turks in Germany and their homeland' (2008: 36).

Trapped in border spaces

In 2004, *Gegen die Wand* was celebrated by the German media as the first German film in eighteen years to win the coveted prize for Best Film at the Berlin International Film Festival. Its success was simultaneously hailed by Turkish critics as a triumph for contemporary Turkish cinema (see Majica 2004: 22; Gülfirat 2004: 219). For the most part, scholars have commented positively on the characters' movements across national borders. Göktürk remarks that

> [t]he characters in *Head-On* have multilocal affiliations and frequently travel across borders. They show little concern with the problems of acculturation [...]. *Head-On* proposed a dynamic perspective on traffic in and out of a "Germany in Transit" – fundamentally reshaped by transnational migration, European integration and economic globalisation. (Göktürk 2010: 216)

According to Randall Halle, the film exposes 'a routine of travel and contact that is not a matter of being in-between,' and depicts 'a new order of cultural and geographic mobility' (2008: 167). Similarly, Adile Esen argues that in *Gegen die Wand* 'second generation Turkish-German characters [...] chose Turkey as a new "homeland" yet at the same time are conveyed as void of the struggles with national belonging via citizenship or otherwise' (2009: 22). Scholars have also suggested that the journey from Hamburg to Turkey provides characters a means of finding redemption (see Burns 2009: 15; Berghahn 2006: 155). Certainly, the main characters in *Gegen die Wand* (which begins in Hamburg) repeatedly transgress or traverse socio-cultural or geographical borders to discard or refashion their identities. Sibel attempts suicide to escape her conservative, devout family, and Cahit attempts suicide to escape his alienation from mainstream German society. The pair meet in a psychiatric facility after these attempts fail, and a doctor foreshadows that they will have to make drastic changes, including possibly leaving Hamburg, if they want to continue to live, when he tells Cahit: 'If you want to bring your life to an end just do it. But you don't have to die for that. Bring your life here to an end and move away. Do something useful [...]. If you can't change the world, change your world'.

Sibel and Cahit initially attempt to outmanoeuvre social norms by deciding to marry, but agreeing to grant each other emotional and sexual autonomy. This marriage of convenience demonstrates the lengths that Sibel, in particular, will go to in order to secure her continued place within the family, and by extension the Turkish diaspora in Germany, by manipulating the cultural boundaries she abhors. At first the marriage and marital home in Hamburg-Altona offer a kind of neutral safe haven from which Sibel and Cahit are able to straddle the metaphorical border between the Turkish community and a more modern mainstream German society, and to enjoy a more 'hybrid' lifestyle. However, the strategy leads to a fragile and dubious existence, in that once the characters' pretence is revealed, the consequences are severe. For Cahit, this attempt to subvert cultural and social boundaries results in incarceration when he kills one of Sibel's sexual partners in a jealous rage, and then (after his release from prison) a border crossing from Germany to Turkey, a nation to which he had expressed little affinity and where he has essentially no ties. Sibel is disowned by her family after the manslaughter and, fearful of their retribution, is forced to flee Hamburg for Istanbul. There she seems initially bent on self-destruction and, in a moment of self-loathing and complete desperation, nearly loses her life again when she picks a fight with a group of Turkish men and is left beaten and stabbed on the street. When Cahit travels to Istanbul to find Sibel, he discovers that she has moved on with her life. She is in a relationship and has a daughter, and although she still has feelings for him, Sibel is unable or unwilling to leave this new life for him.

Throughout the film, but particularly during the latter half, Sibel and Cahit frequently find themselves in border spaces, such as airports, bus stations and hotels. Although such locations are often associated with wanderlust, freedom and adventure, these transitional and transnational sites are for Cahit and Sibel, as Naficy asserts is the case with many characters in accented cinema, 'not just rhizomatic points of linkage to other points in an abstract network of relation and commerce as they are for transnationals and cosmopolitans' (2001: 246). In many accented films, these border spaces strongly represent displacement, homelessness and the search for identity and belonging. As highlighted previously, when Sibel is at the airport in Istanbul, she is almost unrecognizable (see Figures 8.2 and 8.3).

She has cut her hair very short and donned dark and shapeless clothing, as if to acknowledge that her pursuit of a fluid Turkish-German identity has failed and she must now face a physical border crossing that she had never wanted to make. Her enforced presence in this border space highlights her dislocation and sudden homelessness, and essentially signals an end to her life in Germany. In Istanbul, Cahit lives in a hotel

Figure 8.2: Sibel in Hamburg (Reproduced courtesy of Wüste Film).

whilst waiting to see Sibel. According to Naficy, '[m]otels and hotels allegorize exilic and diasporic transitionality' (2001: 253). The anonymous, rented room, which serves only as a site of transition, represents another non-aligned border space where Cahit is positioned between two worlds – his old life in Germany behind him and his new life in Turkey

Figure 8.3: Sibel on arrival in Istanbul (Reproduced courtesy of Wüste Film).

yet to begin. In many ways, the scenes of Cahit's sojourn at the hotel reinforce his social isolation and homelessness. At the end of the film, Cahit leaves Istanbul alone on a bus. In many accented and diasporic films buses, along with trains, are vehicles and symbols of dislocation and rootlessness. Naficy writes that these 'vehicles provide not only empirical links to geographic places and social groupings but also metaphoric reworkings of notions of travelling, homing, and identity' (2001: 257). Cahit is travelling alone because he is without family, without fixed abode, uncertain of his identity and national and cultural affiliation, and still seeking a place where he belongs. The fact that he is travelling to Mersin, his birthplace, may indicate a desire to start over, but the fact that the viewers do not see his journey or his arrival implies that Cahit's voyage is likely to be a long, if not endless, one. The final scene is of course reminiscent of Gabriel's return to Turkey in *Kurz und Schmerzlos*, where audiences are left to wonder whether any relief or redemption awaits the male protagonist when he finally arrives at his destination.

It is significant that both characters effectively have no choice about making the journey from Hamburg to Istanbul. The failure of the performed marriage has left both Sibel and Cahit essentially exiles, in that there is no longer a space in Germany available to them. For Sibel this is evident after her brother chases her down the street in Altona: it is clear that if she remains, her family will kill her. When Cahit is released from jail, he returns to Altona, but he is unwilling or unable to interact with previous companions, acknowledging that the life which he had there is now over. Sibel and Cahit are both expelled from Germany and have little choice but to seek refuge in Turkey. However, this does not represent a homecoming for either character, because neither has any real prior connection with Turkey. As Akin comments:

'The characters in my films do not in fact hail from Turkey. They come from Germany. Turkey is something foreign to them [...]. And what they have in common is that they are engaged in a quest. The quest for a better life. [...] What they are seeking – but cannot find – in their country of origin is redemption'. (qtd in Burns 2009: 16)

The spaces and images of Istanbul presented in *Gegen die Wand* are markedly different from those seen earlier in *Im Juli*. As the director notes:

'My film *Im Juli* shows the view of Moritz Bleibtreu: the Bosporus, the bridges and all the beauty. Now I have tried to capture the view of the people in Istanbul, to show that Istanbul is also an extremely tough city and can also be an extremely ugly city'. (qtd in Farzanefar 2003: 12)

Rather than the bright, warm city that 'German' characters of *Im Juli* encounter, Istanbul for Sibel is presented as bleak, violent and lonely. The opposing experiences of Daniel from *Im Juli* and Sibel reflect perhaps the important difference between visiting a space and having to belong to it, for Daniel can re-cross the border and return to Hamburg at any time, whereas Sibel cannot. For Sibel, life in the Turkish metropolis is presented initially as claustrophobic, and then dark and dangerous as she attempts to resume the life that she had wanted to live in Hamburg. She likens the city to a jail in a letter to Cahit, writing: 'Istanbul is a colourful city. Full of life. The only one who isn't alive is me. All I do is try to survive. [...] You got the harder lot. But prison is the only thing that I can think of if I think of my life here'. Hence Sibel's move from Hamburg to Istanbul does not symbolise liberation or an expansion of geographical options, but the exact opposite. As Berghahn notes: 'Sibel's initial experience of life in Istanbul shows that she is as estranged from contemporary Turkish culture as she was from the traditional Turkish family life back in Hamburg' (2006: 154).

Throughout the film, Akin transports his audience from Hamburg to Istanbul through the scenes with the Roma orchestra, where the narrative is momentarily suspended and viewers are taken to the shores of the Golden Horn. As Burns comments, '[i]n part a Brechtian device for dividing the film into acts, these musical sequences, through which the spectator, as it were, makes repeated journeys to Istanbul, also serve as a means of stitching together the promiscuity of geography' (2009: 18). Akin has commented on the scenes, stating: 'I wanted to break the traditional narrative form. [...] I wanted to install a filter to show: Hey, this is just a story' (qtd in Bax 2004: 3). However, the continued interruptions also and perhaps more importantly highlight the divide between the two nations, serving to maintain the status quo in terms of representation of Turkish migrants and culture in German cinema and the popular imaginary. Tradition keeps breaking in on the lives of the characters. The singer embodies a cliché – the subordinated and unhappy female. The fact that she continues to appear throughout the film intimates that female subordination and unhappiness are inescapable and that leaving Germany for Turkey is unlikely to have a positive ending for Sibel. It remains difficult to present the lives of young Turkish-Germans without repeated reference to the past, to traditional customs or to an imagined homeland.

In *Gegen die Wand*, travel from Hamburg to Istanbul does not represent greater liberation for characters as this journey is made for the stark lack of any other options. As the title indicates, Sibel and Cahit crash literally and figuratively into walls throughout the film in both Germany and Turkey. They are forced to flee Hamburg and seek refuge in Istanbul, and it remains to be seen whether either character will enjoy any lasting salvation. Identity remains a key driver for characters, with their travelling and positioning in numerous transitional sites highlighting a continued struggle with the negotiation of their hybrid cultural identities.

A new phase in migration or a persistence of the past?

In *Auf der anderen Seite*, all of the main characters make the journey from Germany to Turkey. As in *Im Juli* and *Gegen die Wand*, the film begins with a situation now familiar to Akin's audiences – a lone man in a car driving somewhere. This time the man is Nejat, a second-generation Turk from Hamburg, who is on his way to Trabzon, on the Black Sea, to find his estranged father, Ali. Ali has been deported from Germany following his manslaughter of Turkish prostitute, Yeter, whom he killed in a drunken, jealous rage. Nejat puts his life as a professor of German literature on hold to travel to Turkey and make amends for his father's crime. He hopes to find Yeter's daughter Ayten, and pay for her education, but during the search he finds himself taking over a German bookstore in Istanbul. Unbeknown to Nejat, Ayten, who is a member of a Kurdish resistance group in Turkey, has travelled to Hamburg to escape persecution and imprisonment and to find her mother. Unable to find Yeter, she meets a German student, Lotte, who welcomes her into her family home, and the two women quickly fall in love. When Ayten is caught by German authorities and sent back to Turkey, Lotte follows to try and fight for her release, unwittingly also becoming a go-between for the Kurdish activists. Not long after arriving in Istanbul, Lotte is murdered by a group of Turkish youths. Her mother, Susanne, travels from Hamburg to Istanbul to mourn the loss of her daughter and to take up her cause of freeing Ayten. Here she also meets Nejat and becomes his flatmate for a time.

Auf der anderen Seite has been praised by scholars as presenting a new Europe and a new phase of migration, one where it is possible to travel in both directions because ethnic and national borders have been suspended or removed (see Burns 2009: 19 and El Hissy 2009: 186). In addition to blurring borders, critics have also suggested, the film 'champions understanding between cultures, without distinction of race or nationality' (De Barros 2007: 1). For example, Ekkehard Knörer suggests that the film remains purposefully ambivalent as to whether 'the "other" is meant to now be the German, Turkish or Turkish-German' (2008: 16). *Auf der anderen Seite* is also said to be Akin's most political film, and as Maha El Hissy comments, it 'deals with questions about illegal migration and the right to asylum in Germany, the political resistance in Turkey and with the possible consequences of the accession of Turkey to the EU' (2009: 180). The film's English title was *The Edge of Heaven*, but its literal translation 'On the Other Side' more accurately emphasizes Akin's presentation of difference, separation, otherness and, to some extent, physical distance between the core characters and the spaces that they travel between and inhabit. In the film, the characters are on the other side of generations, social norms, the law, but also of cultural and national divides. The movement of characters across these borders is a significant feature of the film.

Nejat, arguably the main protagonist, has been described as 'a paradigm of integration' (Jähner 2007: 31). Critics have suggested that, unlike other representatives of second-generation Turks, Nejat is 'completely integrated and at home in Germany, having successfully made the tricky transition from working-class immigrant housing complex to a life as an intellectual, complete with high-ceilinged, book-lined apartment' (Elsaesser 2008: 36). However, as the film begins with and repeatedly returns to Nejat's travels through Turkey, it is apparent that his 'integration' into German society may not be all that it seems. Nejat's life in Germany is depicted as a solitary one. He lives alone, is not in a relationship and spends his weekends travelling to and from Bremen to visit his elderly Turkish father. When Nejat is depicted with Ali, they 'are visually framed at a remove from the rest of German society' (Silvey and Hillman 2010: 108). When the pair are shown eating ice-cream outside the Bremen train station, they are the only people sitting down, while everyone else moves busily around them. They do not interact with mainstream German society, and are positioned visually as outsiders. The fact that Nejat may not be comfortable with his position as a second-generation Turk in Germany is also alluded to in a scene at his university. During a lecture, Nejat is framed on one side by a map of Europe, which includes Turkey, and then on the other side by a map of Germany. He stands in the middle, suggesting that the 'caught between two worlds' motif common in early Turkish-German films may not be as far removed as some would suggest (Silvey and Hillman 2010: 108). Furthermore, during his time in Germany, Nejat is frequently depicted travelling on trains or trams. Michel de Certeau has described travelling by train as '[a] travelling incarceration [...], a module of imprisonment that makes possible the production of an order, a closed and autonomous insularity' (1984: 111). This preference for the suspended animation of the train, a vehicle which, according to Naficy, often represents dislocation and rootlessness, is reminiscent of previous second-generation Turkish characters in *Geschwister-Kardesler* and *Der schöne Tag/A Fine Day* (Arlsan, 2001), and it highlights Nejat's feelings of disassociation and disconnection from mainstream German society and foreshadows his likely need for ongoing travel (2001: 257). Nejat travels to Istanbul out of a sense of obligation, and as for Sibel the journey is not one that he had wanted to make. This is evident in the pained expression on his face as he watches Yeter's coffin being unloaded from a plane after arrival in Turkey (see Figure 8.4). Yet, it seems probable that Nejat's journey is also motivated by his unease with his hybrid existence in Germany and a desire to find somewhere that he belongs. In this way, the film, as Katja Nicodemus comments,

> delivers the debate on integration a nice punch line when Nejat, who as professor of German studies has drawn the super joker so to speak in the migrant social scale, suddenly discovers a sense of home and wants to stay in Istanbul. (Nicodemus 2007: 40)

Figure 8.4: Nejat watches as the coffin is unloaded in Istanbul (Reproduced courtesy of Artificial Eye Films).

Nejat crosses the border to Turkey, but when he arrives he feels, embraces and really articulates his 'Germanness'. In Istanbul, Nejat surrounds himself with pieces of Germany – he buys a German bookstore, takes on a German flatmate and appears to speak more German than he does Turkish. The irony of this situation is noted by the bookstore's previous owner when he remarks: 'That would be funny, if a Turkish professor of German from Germany ends up in a German bookshop in Turkey'. Nejat's travel and decision to remain in Turkey seem underpinned by unease with his hybrid identity and his continuing search to balance its two cultural elements – 'German' and 'Turkish'.

Ayten's travel across national divides is also the result of a struggle with cultural identity and lack of national 'home'. As a Turkish-Kurd and member of a political resistance group, Ayten has experienced persecution because of her cultural identity, heritage and beliefs. She is forced to flee Turkey for fear of imprisonment or worse and in doing so is required to take on the false identity that essentially renders her stateless. Ayten can 'be viewed not only as an example for mobility, but also for homelessness. Neither in Germany nor in Turkey does she have a home' (El Hissy 2009: 183). In Hamburg, Ayten must rely on the kindness of strangers and is taken in by Lotte. Lotte's mother Susanne is less than thrilled with her daughter's new houseguest and metaphorically establishes borders between herself and Ayten when she talks about setting rules in one's own house in the context of an argument about Turkey's possible entry into the European Union. She is quick to put Ayten in her place, stating: 'I don't want you to talk like that in my house. You can talk like that in your house'. As Burns notes, 'in the context of post-war Turkish-German relations, the political resonance of a discourse on notions of host (country) and guest (worker) is all too apparent' (2009: 19). Perhaps unsurprisingly, Ayten, like Nejat, is positioned as an obvious outsider in Germany. Shortly after arriving in Hamburg, she is depicted walking alone around a university campus. During the scene she is framed in front of a poster promoting 'rebel studies', playing on contemporary clichés about members of the Turkish community in Germany as something to be feared, as violent criminals linked to terrorist activities. Furthermore, the scene points to the extreme differences between life in Germany and Turkey. As Silvey and Hillman comment, '[t]he irony here emerges that in Germany political rebellion can be studied in the abstract, whereas in Turkey it comprises everyday life for Ayten' (2010: 108). Hence Akin's characters continue to 'betray remnants of the cliché figures and relationships' common to Turkish-German productions of the late 1990s, with the scenes depicting Turkish characters in Germany highlighting that 'transnationalism does not necessarily or immediately erase divisions' (Silvey and Hillman 2010: 108).

Auf der anderen Seite offers a rather sober examination of the political and social borders which still exist between Germany and Turkey. Unlike the tongue-in-cheek border crossings that audiences witnessed in *Im Juli*, where time in a country could be bought and the ramifications of being without citizenship documents were negligible, the policed border controls at the airports into Germany as well as the scenes in the German courts clearly highlight the continued significance of being on the wrong side of national divides and subtly critique the treatment of asylum seekers by German officials. When Ayten pleads for asylum in Germany, her application is rejected by the court as officials state that in light of Turkey's application for membership of the European Union, Ayten need not fear political persecution or torture when she returns. Ayten is expelled from Germany and sent back to a Turkish prison. And after Ali is released from prison, he is also deported from Germany. On arrival in Istanbul he is accompanied by police through customs. He shakes his head as he is led over the symbolic border back into Turkey.

In *Auf der anderen Seite*, characters demonstrate a global awareness and freedom of movement uncommon to Turkish-German films in the past. Travel between Germany and Turkey occurs in both directions – pointing to some extent to an evolving interchange between the two cultures and nations. However, characters are not as at ease with their hybrid identities as some critics have suggested. During the scenes in Germany, Turkish-German characters are frequently depicted alone and set away from mainstream German society. The characters' discomfort with their hybrid identities appears a key motivator in their decisions to travel abroad and yet they exhibit an equal lack of ease with these identities when they arrive. Characters continue to frequent border spaces which point, as in *Gegen die Wand*, to a sense of displacement, homelessness and the search for identity and belonging. And as in *Gegen die Wand*, the film's final scenes leave the audiences guessing as to whether redemption, salvation or peace awaits any of the remaining characters. Ayten has betrayed her activist comrades out of her remorse for Lotte's death and desire for freedom. This is likely to have dire consequences. Nejat is still on the move. The film ends with him waiting on the beach for the return of his father. As Elsaesser comments, '[t]he Black Sea, where Nejat is waiting in the last shot, is still calm, but as the fishermen tell him, here you cannot trust the weather' (2008: 37).

The journey continues

In Akin's more recent films, the space available has extended well beyond the claustrophobic domestic environments of the earlier 'cinema of the affected' and the confrontational multi-ethnic neighbourhoods in Germany's larger cities in the Turkish-German films of the 1990s. Characters now travel across national divides between Germany and Turkey, but this mobility does not signify any significantly greater liberation or freedom for characters. Border crossings in Akin's films are strongly associated with loss and dislocation. Both *Gegen die Wand* and *Auf der anderen Seite* depict protagonists who must embark on physical and metaphorical journeys because they have been expelled from Germany and/or compelled to make the journey to Turkey by the violent actions of others. Most are looking for redemption and a new life, but for the majority it seems unlikely that this salvation will be found in Turkey.

Throughout *Gegen die Wand* and *Auf der anderen Seite*, characters frequently find themselves in border spaces, spaces which point to their ongoing displacement, homelessness and struggle with the negotiation of their hybrid cultural identities. The final scenes in both films suggest that the main characters remain restless and on the search for somewhere to belong. Sibel hurriedly packs a suitcase, then suddenly stops and sits down alone on the bed. Her face is unreadable, as she slowly bows her head towards the ground. Nejat's face is equally expressionless as he sits and looks out to sea waiting for his father to return. Akin has commented that he feels strongly about completing his 'Love, Death and the Devil' trilogy. It remains to be seen whether the last instalment will see Turkish-German characters at ease with their hybrid identities. In the future, movement and encounters across national borders may well result in greater options and spaces for Turkish-German characters, but for the time being it seems that there is still a long journey ahead.

Acknowledgements

The author is grateful to Dr Geoff Wilkes for his ongoing counsel and assistance with the revision of this chapter.

References

Bax, D. (2004), 'Ey, das ist nur eine Geschichte', *tageszeitung*, 11 March, p. 3.

Berghahn, D. (2006), 'No place like home? Or impossible homecomings in the films of Fatih Akin', *New Cinemas*, 4: 3, pp. 141–57.

Burns, R. (1999), 'Images of Alterity: Second Generation Turks in the Federal Republic', *Modern Language Review*, 94, pp. 744–57.

—————— (2006), 'Turkish-German Cinema: From Cultural Resistance to Transnational Cinema?' in D. Clarke (ed.), *German Cinema Since Unification*, London, Continuum, pp. 127–49.

—————— (2007), 'Towards a Cinema of Cultural Hybridity: Turkish-German Filmmakers and the Representation of Alterity', *Debatte*, 15: 1, pp. 3–24.

—————— (2009), 'On the streets and on the road: identity in transit in Turkish-German travelogues on screen', *New Cinemas*, 7: 1, pp. 11–26.

De Barros, M. (2007), 'Fatih Akin's cinema: a step closer to integration', *Cafe Babel*, http://www.cafebabel.co.uk/article/22521/fatih-akins-cinema-a-step-closer-to-integration.html. Accessed 7 August 2011.

De Certeau, M. (1984), *The Practice of Everyday Life* (trans. S. Rendall), Berkeley: University of California Press.

Durmuş, O. D. (2006), 'Fatih Akin's Cinema: A World without Borders', *Internet-Zeitschrift für Kulturwissenschaften*, 16, p. 6.

El Hissy, M. (2009), 'Transnationaler Grenzverkehr in Fatih Akins *Gegen die Wand* und *Auf der anderen Seite*', in H. Schmitz (ed.), *Von der nationalen zur internationalen Literatur: Transkulturelle deutschsprachige Literatur und Kultur im Zeitalter globaler Migration*, Amsterdam: Rodopi, pp. 169–86.

Elsaesser, T. (2008), 'Ethical Calculus', *Film Comment*, 44: 3, pp. 34–37.

Esen, A. (2009), *Beyond 'in-between,' travels and transformations in contemporary Turkish-German literature and film*, Ann Arbor: ProQuest.

Farzanefar, A. (2003), 'Migrantenkino heißt jetzt Mittelmeerkino', *Berliner Zeitung*, 9 August, p. 12.

Gallagher, J. (2006), 'The limitation of urban space in Thomas Arslan's "Berlin Trilogy"', *Seminar*, 42: 3, pp. 337–52.

Göktürk, D. (2001), 'Turkish Delight – German Fright: Migrant Identities in Transnational Cinemas', in D. Derman, K. Ross and N. Dakovi (eds), *Mediated Identities*, Istanbul: Bilgi University Press, pp. 131–49.

—— (2002), 'Beyond Paternalism: Turkish German Traffic in Cinema', in T. Bergfelder, E. Carter and D. Göktürk (eds), *The German Cinema Book*, London: bfi, pp. 248–56.

—— (2010), 'Sound Bridges: Transnational Mobility as Ironic Melodrama', in D. Berghahn and C. Sternberg (eds), *European Cinema in Motion*, New York: Palgrave Macmillan, pp. 215–34.

Gülfirat, S. (2004), 'Was türkische Blätter über Sibel Kekilli schreiben', in F. Akin (ed.), *Gegen die Wand: Das Buch zum Film*, Colgone: Kiepenheuer & Witsch, pp. 219–20.

Hall, S. (1993), 'Culture, Community, Nation', *Cultural Studies*, 7, pp. 349–63.

Halle, R. (2008), *German Film After Germany: Toward a Transnational Aesthetic*, Urbana: University of Illinois Press.

Horrocks, D. and Kolinsky, E. (1996), 'Introduction: Migrants or Citizens? Turks in Germany between Exclusion and Acceptance', in D. Horrocks and E. Kolinsky (eds), *Turkish Culture in German Society Today*, Oxford: Berghahn Books, pp. x–xxviii.

Jähner, H. (2007), 'Bildung macht sexy', *Berliner Zeitung*, 27 September, p. 31.

Jones, S. (2003), 'Turkish-German cinema today: A case of study of Fatih Akin's *Kurz und schmerzlos* (1998) and *Im Juli* (2000)', in G. Rings and R. Morgan-Tamosunas (eds), *European Cinema: Inside Out. Images of the Self and the Other in Postcolonial European Film*, Heidelberg: Winter, pp. 75–91.

Knörer, E. (2008), 'Der Muff des Humanismus', *tageszeitung*, 29 April, p. 16.

Kulaoglu, T. (1999), 'Der neue "deutsche" Film ist "türkisch"? Eine neue Generation bringt Leben in die Filmlandschaft', *Filmforum*, 16, pp. 8–11.

Majica, M. (2004), 'Kontrollierte Konfusion', *Berliner Zeitung*, 11 March, p. 22.

Mandel, R. (1989), 'Turkish Headscarves and the "Foreigner Problem": Constructing Difference through Emblems of Identity', *New German Critique*, 46, pp. 27–46.

Naficy, H. (1996), 'Phobic Spaces and Liminal Panics: Independent Transnational Film Genre', in R. Wilson and W. Dissanayake (eds), *Global Local: Cultural Production and the Transnational Imaginary*, Durham: Duke University Press, pp. 119–40.

—— (2001), *An Accented Cinema*, Princeton: Princeton University Press.

Nicodemus, K. (2007), 'Zwei Särge und die Liebe', *Die Zeit*, 14 December, p. 40.

Şenocak, Z. (2000), *Atlas of a Tropical Germany: Essays on Politics and Culture* (trans. L. A. Adelson), Lincoln: University of Nebraska Press.

Shohat, E. and Stam, R. (1994), *Unthinking Eurocentrism*, London: Routledge.

Silvey, V. and Hillman R. (2010), 'Akin's *Auf der anderen Seite* (*The Edge of Heaven*) and the widening periphery', *GFL-journal*, 3, pp. 99–116.

Chapter 9

Transnational Heroines: Swedish Youth Film and Immigrant Girlhood

Heta Mulari
University of Turku

I'm not Swedish! Don't you get it? I'll never be Swedish, no matter how much I want to be.

This is the outburst of 18-year-old Nazli Kashani, the female protagonist of *Vingar av glas/Wings of Glass* (Reza Bagher, 1998), to her boyfriend. In this Swedish youth film, Nazli (Sara Sommerfeld) is negotiating between two intertwining identities. With her friends and in job interviews she calls herself by a Swedish name, Sara Lundström, to hide her Iranian background. At home she rebels against her father's rules about curfews, drinking, suitable boyfriends and appropriate clothes. Through Nazli's character, *Vingar av glas* visualises certain themes – youthful rebellion, heterosexual romance, conflicts within a circle of friends and with the older generation – that ever since the birth of the youth film genre have been highly common in cinematic portrayals of youth (Biltereyst 2007: 9–10; Driscoll 2011: 2). In addition, the film comments on the contemporary debate over immigrant youth, particularly immigrant girls and girlhood. In Sweden, media discourses on immigrant youth have been highly gendered: concerns about immigrant girls have frequently focused on topics such as veiling, family strictness and gender equality (Brune 2006: 148–79; Eduards 2007: 58–64; Reimers 2005: 141–60). In this chapter, I focus on images of immigrant girls in Swedish youth films at the turn of the millennium. I discuss the cinematic immigrant girl as a symbol of social and cultural change and anxiety: through the individual identity struggle faced by these girls, cultural differences and tensions are negotiated.

European film theory of the past couple of decades has shown a growing interest in the relevance of ethnicity and the experience of diaspora in films and filmmaking practices. As several film scholars have noted, European film industries have been characterized by an increasing number of filmmakers with an immigrant background, who have focused on themes of diaspora, exile and being in-between (Naficy 1999: 5–6; Shohat and Stam 2003: 1–2). As film scholar Rochelle Wright argues, in Sweden the turn of the millennium coincided with the introduction of the concept of 'immigrant film', which became a topic of media attention and critical debate (Wright 2005: 55–56; see also Tigervall 2005; Gustafsson 2006: 187). Film critics have frequently applied the concept of 'immigrant film' in review journalism and popular literature, where it has been linked in particular to the portrayal of young people and generational conflicts.[1] The concept, however, can and should be critically analysed, since it brings together relatively different films under a common, simplifying umbrella term, often linking immigrant themes to the filmmaker's background alone (see for example Gustafsson 2006: 187).

Here, rather than referring to 'immigrant films', I look at youth films about immigrant girls in the context of youth film production, both in Sweden and internationally. As the Swedish film scholar Tommy Gustafsson has argued, the late 1990s and early 2000s were marked by the emergence of a 'young youth film' – films made by young filmmakers who often used new digital technologies. These filmmakers frequently portrayed themes of cultural differences and clashes through young (female) protagonists (Gustafsson 2006: 171–76). Internationally the volume of youth film production has grown considerably since the late 1980s. Youth film as a genre has been divided into various overlapping sub-categories, including teen comedy, teen horror and teen films that include more explicit social or political criticism (Driscoll 2002: 216–34; see also Driscoll 2011: 56–61). Historically, since the 1950s the commercial youth film has looked at youth from a multidimensional viewpoint: on the one hand these films are an essential part of commercial youth culture, meant to entertain young audiences and engage them in youth-oriented consumer culture, while on the other they always include, at least to some extent, an educational point of view as well (Janson 2008: 127). Finally, they have often engaged in the critical debate over youth, generational conflicts and the future. Since the mid-1990s Swedish youth films have been characterized by political themes, such as sexual harassment, bullying, immigrant issues and youth anarchism.

As Catherine Driscoll has argued, scholarly work on youth and teen films continues to focus overwhelmingly on US teen films (Driscoll 2011: 149, see also Shohat and Stam 2003: 2). In girls' media studies the emphasis has been rather similar. The focus of this chapter is therefore on recent Swedish youth film production, more specifically on images of immigrant girlhood, bringing a new perspective to youth and teen film research. I mainly analyse *Vingar av glas* and *Bäst i Sverige/We Can Be Heroes!* (Ulf Malmros, 2002), but I also refer to other films that deal with immigrant youth and girlhood, including *Jalla! Jalla!* (Josef Fares, 2000) and *Hus i helvete/All Hell Let Loose* (Susan Taslimi, 2002). Finally, I look at these Swedish films in comparison to the British youth film *Bend It Like Beckham* (Gurinder Chadha, 2000), which tells the story of 15-year-old Jesminder, a girl with an Indian background who is struggling between her wish to become a professional football player and her family's demands that she adapt an Indian lifestyle – learn how to cook Indian dishes and prepare for marriage to an Indian boy. By examining these films together, I explore the possibilities of understanding the cinematic images of immigrant girls transnationally. While *Vingar av glas* and *Bäst i Sverige* are situated specifically in a Swedish setting and debate, they nevertheless follow the narrative structure of a youth film, including internationally familiar themes of rebellion, coming-of-age, the generation gap and falling in love (Shary 2007: 2). In short, these films challenge and re-imagine the relationship between national debates over youth and transnational cinematic images of girlhood in the context of youth film production.

In between, on her way

Vingar av glas portrays a young woman's rebellion against patriarchy and established traditions. Simultaneously the film illustrates the challenge of finding an identity in a new society while having cultural roots in another. The father's love conflicts with the daughter's need for freedom in this realistic film about contemporary Sweden. (Lagerström 2000)[2]

This excerpt is from Louise Lagerström's pedagogical guide to teaching media skills. These guides are published by the Swedish Film Institute's pedagogical department, School Cinema, advising teachers on the use of film in schools. Typically, the guides include a summary of the plot and a few topics to discuss with students in the classroom. As Malena Janson argues, these guides frequently address key themes that are central to Swedish democracy and education, such as social equality, gender equality, anti-violence and the importance of empathy (Janson 2008: 141). In the case of *Vingar av glas*, Lagerström advises teachers to focus on the themes of Nazli's rebellion against her parents, her struggle 'between two identities' and the multi-cultural Swedish society. While the article should be understood in the context of education, since *Vingar av glas* has been chosen as a School Cinema film, it is important to note how similar themes are visible in the press reception of the film as well.

As we see from the excerpt, Lagerström contextualizes *Vingar av glas* through the media discourse on immigrant girls: young women who are leaving their traditions behind and travelling towards the 'new' society (see for example Brune 2006: 164–67). She also emphasizes that the film is a realistic portrayal of contemporary Sweden. This type of commentary on realistic images of immigrant girls is apparent in the press reception of *Vingar av glas* as well. For example, the film was described and contextualized in *Helsingborgs Dagblad* as follows: 'immigrant girls who seek freedom and abandon their families and traditions. The topic is divisive – but director Reza Bagher confronts it directly in "Vingar av glas"' (Anon. 2000: 33).[3] Monika Tunbäck-Hanson argued in *Göteborgs-Posten* that '[youth] rebellion just becomes much clearer when it also includes challenging traditions, as in Nazli's case' (Tunbäck-Hanson 2000: 57).[4] This notion of a dualistic opposition – on the one side tradition, patriarchy and family, on the other a new society, freedom and independence – was one of the interpretative framings of *Vingar av glas*. These critics described Nazli, the young female protagonist of the film, as a sign of movement – it is her role to negotiate between the familiar and the strange, between the new and the traditional, between Swedish and 'immigrant' (see also Tigervall 2005: 75).[5]

Historically, this mediated image of immigrant girls' in-betweenness and negotiation between cultures and identities can be traced, as Paulina de los Reyes et al. have argued, to the construction of the modern Swedish welfare state and the ideologies of first and second wave feminisms.[6] The development of this discourse between 'us Swedes' and 'the others' can be described as discursive colonialism, where the modern welfare state has been (and still is) defined in contrast to 'the others'. While Swedish women have been represented through the success of second wave feminism, gender equality and economic independence, immigrant women have been connected to dependence, tradition, oppression and the private sphere (De los Reyes 2006: 36–37; de los Reyes, Molina and Mulinari 2006: 12–17; Reimers 2005, 142). Furthermore, as Sara Ahmed has argued, the identities of modern European nation states have been constructed to a great extent by comparison to the colonized others, who have been seen as dangerous, exotic and strange (Ahmed 2000: 3–10).

As Catherine Driscoll has argued, youth films often represent adolescence through difficult choices and negotiations over cultural identity, alienation and belonging (Driscoll 2011: 157; see also Shary 2007: 4). In addition, the familial culture is often defined in youth films as traditional, even old-fashioned, while the youth culture is portrayed as something new, alternative and desirable (Driscoll 2011: 155). In *Vingar av glas* these negotiations are addressed already in the opening scenes, as Nazli is introduced to the viewers. In the beginning of the film, Nazli cycles to the local church for a job interview. During the interview, however, the church staff notice that she has used a false name in her job application. When the minister and the secretary ask Nazli to explain, she replies: 'You know how it is. If you say that your name is Nazli Kashani, people think that you wear a veil. And then you don't even have a chance to get an interview.' After this confrontation Nazli walks out of the office, still jobless, and angrily cycles through the streets. On a bridge, she stops when she sees two young girls practicing roller-skating on a basketball court. One of the girls is wearing a long, dark veil. In the next scene, Nazli is at home having dinner with her father Abbas and her older sister Mahin. Over dinner Nazli and her father argue about her not eating enough and wearing inappropriate clothes. Soon, Abbas tells the daughters that he has found suitable young men for them to date and possibly marry.

In its focus on immigrant girls and young women, *Vingar av glas* is not unique in Swedish youth film production. In *Bäst i Sverige* (Ulf Malmros, 2002), 10-year-old Lebanese Fatima (Zamand Hägg) tries to adjust her life between the demands of her older brothers and her aspirations of becoming the best football player in Sweden. While the protagonist of *Bäst i Sverige* is Fatima's best friend Marcello (Ariel Petsonk), who dreams of a career as a pilot, the image of Fatima bears significant resemblance to Nazli. Fatima's older brothers keep a close eye on her and forbid her to play football or meet Marcello. When the brothers pick Fatima up at the football field they say, angrily: 'Fatima, look at yourself! The way you look! What would mom have said? So dirty, shitty, sweaty … Like a boy, her little princess!' Here rather similarly to *Vingar av glas,* the motherless girl character is contrasted to her family: the girl represents a wish to integrate into Swedish society, while her father or brothers want to maintain the values and traditions of their background (see for example Brune 2006: 164–67). For example, Marcello states to Fatima: 'You speak really good Swedish … But your brothers don't', and Fatima replies: 'No, they don't want to.'

In these two films, the football enthusiast Fatima and Nazli with her dreams of a motorcycle represent a typical view of girls and young women in the popular culture of the 1990s and early 2000s. They can be described as 'girl power girls', the young female heroines of the 1990s popular feminist movement and commercially oriented girl power. In the Swedish media culture of the 1990s and the early 2000s, references to the contemporary feminist movement became highly common. In the characters of Nazli and Fatima the attributes of mediated girl power heroines are combined with their non-Western backgrounds in several ways. A couple of critics also noted the influence of the popular feminist movement. Rebecka Liljeberg, for example, described Nazli in *Svenska Dagbladet* as 'strong, pretty and smart', but criticized the film for over-exaggerating and making Nazli 'not an ordinary girl but some kind of a super version' (Liljeberg 2000: 57).[7] Pia Huss, on the other hand, criticized *Bäst i Sverige* for its stereotypical portrayals of bullies and immigrant young people – both boys and girls. As she ironically put it: 'Marcello's new best friend Fatima is the best. Brave, sporty, takes the initiative, independent ...' (Huss 2002).[8]

Besides the popular feminist movement, the emergence of strong young cinematic heroines is linked to the wider phenomenon of girl-centred youth films and popular culture both in Sweden and internationally (Projansky 2007: 189–90).[9] During the mid-1990s, Swedish youth film production started to focus on girls and young women, due to a great extent to the financial weight of the Swedish Film Institute. The Institute started to channel financing to films about girls and to search for girl-centred manuscripts. Films such as *Fucking Åmål/ Show Me Love* (Lukas Moodysson, 1998), *Lilja 4-ever/Lilya 4-ever* (Moodysson, 2000) and *Hip hip hora!/Ketchup Effect* (Teresa Fabik, 2003) have also gained international recognition. What is common to these films is their overtly political, often feminist agenda about girl-related issues: lesbian relationships, trafficking, sexual harassment and young feminist anarchism. While the volume of girl-themed youth films increased, 'the girl' became the focus of several political debates during the 1990s and the 2000s.

Further, compared to earlier decades, the late 1990s and the early 2000s were characterized by a change in the representations of immigrant youth. In Swedish youth film production, the theme of immigrant youth had been addressed earlier, especially during the mid- and late 1990s. As Rochelle Wright argues, films such as *30:e November* (Daniel Fridell, 1995) and *Nattbuss 807* (David Flamholc, 1997) portrayed urban youth through violence, racism and criminality (Wright 2005: 61). These films commented on the rise of extreme right-wing movements in Sweden, usually focusing on confrontations between young skinheads and immigrant men. Immigrant girls and young women were often portrayed in minor roles. Another feature common to these films were the romances between immigrant and Swedish youth; the latter often had a background in the extreme right-wing movement. In *30:e November,* for example, the Peruvian girl Julia falls in love with a boy whose friends spend their free time in a skinhead group.

In the 1990s films, especially in *30:e November,* immigrant girls were usually portrayed as shy and quiet and without little if any knowledge of Swedish culture or language. Julia in *30:e November,* for example, does not speak many words of Swedish, and is a shy, reserved and almost exotic figure. Her life is strictly controlled by her family, especially her older brother. By comparison, Nazli and Fatima in *Bäst i Sverige* offer a different image of immigrant girls, marked by strength and rebellion. Already during those first scenes of *Vingar av glas,* the lyrics of the soundtrack song tell the viewer that she does not have to 'ask your permission'. Nazli responds to her father's orders by rebellion: going out, wearing miniskirts and meeting Swedish boys. Her tattoo becomes one of the most visible signs of her aim of independence from her family. Against her father's orders, she has the feminist symbol of a fist tattooed on her upper arm (see Figure 9.1). This symbol was used during the 1980s by the feminist network Grupp 8/Group 8. Through this action the film makes an important connection between the popular feminist movement and Nazli's Middle-Eastern background, thus widening the understanding of a Western young feminist.

However, not all cinematic images of immigrant girls and young women can be understood through rebellion and challenging parental authority. A good example of a more passive and reserved girlhood is the image of the Lebanese Yasmin (Laleh Pourkarim) in the comedy *Jalla! Jalla!* ('Hurry! Hurry!'). The protagonists of this highly successful film are two young men, Måns and Roro, who are best friends and who both have problems in their relationships. Roro has to hide his relationship with the ethnically Swedish Lisa from his family, since his father and grandmother want him to marry Yasmin. Måns, on the other hand, suffers from erectile dysfunction, resulting in a crisis in his relationship. Through Roro he meets Yasmin and falls in love with her. Yasmin's role remains relatively passive, as Carina Tigervall argues: '"The immigrant woman," Yasmine [sic], is portrayed as a powerless victim in the hands of a discriminating "immigrant culture"' (Tigervall 2005: 65; see also Gustafsson 2006: 189; Wright 2005: 64). Yasmin's older brother wants her to marry Roro, threatening to send her back to Lebanon if she refuses. The central theme of the film is thus similar to that of *Vingar av glas*, suitable boyfriends and a marriage, but the behaviour of the girl characters differs.

Through the characters of Nazli, Fatima and Yasmin, the films negotiate between two mediated images of girlhood: the Western popular feminist heroine and the immigrant girl,

Figure 9.1: Nazli with her new tattoo.

who has to challenge authority and tradition in order to fit the role of heroine. Importantly, in these films rebellious behaviour is viewed in a positive light – thus the Western powerful heroine becomes the norm against which the other girl characters are measured (see McRobbie 2007: 24–29). Especially in *Vingar av glas,* however, these two images are intertwined in several ways. Rather than presenting a straightforward journey from one culture to another, *Vingar av glas* explores a new subject position for a girl with multiple backgrounds and cultural influences. In all of these films, being an 'immigrant' girl means taking on the role of negotiator over questions of girlhood, sexuality and the girl's right to make her own decisions about hobbies, friends or boyfriends.

As the youth-studies scholars Sunaina Maira and Elisabeth Soep have argued, discourses of masculinity and femininity are deeply intertwined with narratives of the nation and of collective culture (Maira and Soep 2005: xxvii). Following their argument, it is essential to note how the image of a young woman in these youth films has become a symbol of cultural change and movement. In addition, the focus on girls expands the view of societal concerns, expectations and hopes about youth. Since the mid-1990s the focus in the public debate and in youth research has increasingly turned to girls, which in turn has meant changes in the public discourses of youth. At the turn of the millennium, two intertwining issues were widely debated in the Swedish press and in feminist studies: the harassment of (Swedish) girls, and arranged marriages and 'honour'-motivated violence against immigrant girls.

Mapping the difference: honour and reputation

If I had an arranged marriage, would he let me play football?

That is what Jess, lying on her bed in her small bedroom, asks the poster of David Beckham. 18-year-old Jess' future plans include becoming a professional football player in a women's league. Her parents strongly disapprove of her ambitions, and she has to hide her football career from them. In particular Jess' mother wants her to learn to cook traditional Indian dishes and to behave and dress 'like a proper young Indian lady'. As mentioned above, the theme of football is central in *Bäst i Sverige* as well, where Fatima has to practice football in secret from her elder brothers. In both films, playing football becomes a means for the young female protagonist to challenge both gendered boundaries and cultural stereotypes. Choosing football, historically a male-dominated sport, as a central theme of the films can be compared to Nazli's interest in motorcycles in *Vingar av glas.* Football and women's leagues were also frequently mentioned in the popular feminist literature of the 1990s. For example Anja Gatu says in the popular feminist anthology *Fittstim*: 'Chicks are good at football and football is good for chicks' (Gatu 2000: 160).

The contrasting between such activities as playing football or getting a motorcycle licence and arranged marriages or relationships is an important theme in *Vingar av glas, Bäst i Sverige* and *Jalla! Jalla!.* More generally, arranged marriages have been a recurring theme in

Western youth films about girls with a non-Western background, especially Muslim girls. Where *Bend It Like Beckham* and *Jalla! Jalla!* address the issue through humour,[10] *Vingar av glas* brings up a concern about immigrant girls' vulnerability. As the sociologist Ylva Brune has argued, the mediated image of (an immigrant) girl has, since the 1970s, been deeply intertwined with sexuality and relationships. The Swedish media debate has focused on the vulnerable status of immigrant girls, along with fears concerning the (violent) behaviour of immigrant boys.[11] During the 1990s and early 2000s there have been two major concerns with regard to immigrant girls: arranged marriages, and violence connected to questions of 'honour'.[12] At the same time, these issues have been signifiers of difference compared to girls with an ethnically Swedish background. In the discourses of honour and arranged marriages, Swedish society has often been perceived as egalitarian and lacking in gendered oppression (Honkasalo 2011; Ambjörnsson 2003); that is why these discourses need to be critically opened up and analysed.

Arranged marriages and girls' proper (sexual) behaviour are central already in the first scenes of *Vingar av glas*. Nazli's father Abbas Kashani wants to raise Nazli and her elder sister Mahin according to the wishes of their deceased mother. In order to fulfil this obligation, Abbas has started preparing his daughters for marriage with their cousins. While Mahin is happily in love with Hassam, Nazli protests and occasionally runs away from home to spend time with her friends and her Swedish crush Johan. Abbas' choice for Nazli is Hamid, who owns a video rental store. Hamid is portrayed in terms of economic success: he wears an Armani suit and is proud of his independence. Nazli accepts a job in Hamid's store to earn

Figure 9.2: Hamid and Nazli at the video store.

money for a motorcycle licence, but she frequently has to tell Hamid that she does not want to date him or get married (Figure 9.2).

In the following dialogue, Nazli and Hamid end up arguing about Nazli's behaviour.

HAMID:	Have you been with a guy, by the way?
NAZLI:	Yeah, of course I have.
HAMID:	But do you sleep with them or just mess around?
NAZLI:	That's my business.
HAMID:	Don't do that anymore, OK?
NAZLI:	It's not up to you to decide!
HAMID:	Well, if the two of us are a couple, then …
NAZLI:	Listen, I'll fuck anyone I want!

The confrontations culminate when Hamid gets drunk and tries to rape Nazli in the office of the video store. Before the rape attempt, Hamid and Nazli have been arguing about the way Nazli should behave and the importance of avoiding bringing shame to her family. In the following dialogue, Hamid's opinions change from compliments to judgement and violence.

HAMID:	I think you're the prettiest and finest of all the girls in the family … You are the sexiest, you … You're, like, free. That's what I think, really.
NAZLI:	Too bad.
HAMID:	Why?
NAZLI:	Because I don't give a damn what you think of me!
[…]	
HAMID:	You're a shame to your whole family, don't you see that? Even your idiotic dad knows it … You run around like a cheap little whore …

In the first excerpt, Hamid compliments Nazli for being pretty, fine, sexy and *free*. As he gets angrier, however, he combines these attributes with *shame* and acting 'like a whore'. The adjectives used in the dialogue – pretty, sexy, free, tough – have been frequently used, as noted, in the discourse about popular feminist girls. In this scene, on the other hand, prettiness, sexiness and freedom are combined with bringing shame to the family. Similarly, in *Jalla! Jalla!* Yasmin's brother Paul calls Roro's Swedish girlfriend a 'whore' and aims at keeping Yasmin safe from relationships with Swedish men (see Tigervall 2005: 58). The theme of suitable marriages and paternal control is addressed in *Hus i helvete* as well, where Iranian Minoo (Melinda Kinnamon), a young woman in her twenties, returns to Sweden for her sister's wedding after spending several years in the United States. Minoo's father had thrown her out of the house because she had had an abortion. When she returns to Sweden the father tries to control her clothing and behaviour, which Minoo strongly resists. Compared to *Vingar av glas* and *Jalla! Jalla!*, the tone of *Hus i helvete* is much darker and in its conclusion the film does not offer reconciliation between the generations or resolution of cultural conflicts. As Carina Tigervall has noted, the discourse of hatred towards women and 'macho culture' is often located in one character of the film; typically a young immigrant man, such as Paul in *Jalla! Jalla!* or Hamid in *Vingar av glas*. This stereotypical representation is one of the most problematic aspects in these films about immigrant youth: while young immigrant women are often represented as sympathetic, brave and independent, young men are viewed as a threat to gender equality (Tigervall 2005: 58, 91–92).

Hus i helvete was released in 2002, a year, as described by Rochelle Wright, of widespread media attention arising from the murder of a young Kurdish woman, Fadime Sahindal.[13] The infamous case of Fadime was a watershed that triggered a more polarized media debate over honour, violence and the status of immigrant girls (Wright 2005: 68). Shortly after the murder, 'immigrant girls' were turned into a political concept and a cultural symbol. In this discourse, the understanding of girlhood was split in two: Swedish (egalitarian) and non-Swedish (oppressed) (Lynggard 2010: 19; Eduards 2007: 58–59). The murder of Fadime was also mentioned in the pedagogical material concerning *Bäst i Sverige*. Anna Hedelius, for example, analyses *Bäst i Sverige* in the teaching guide as follows:

A notable case is the murder of the Kurdish girl Fadime Sahindal. In January 2002 she was murdered because her father couldn't accept her way of living. In the film Fatima's brothers want to keep their sister in order because they are, as they put it, 'worried about her'. (Hedelius 2002)[14]

In this excerpt Hedelius links the narrative of *Bäst i Sverige* and the protagonist Fatima to the destiny of Fadime and the established media discourse about immigrant and Swedish values, where 'immigrant' is characterized by patriarchy, inequality and oppression and 'Swedish' with gender equality and freedom (Reimers 2005: 142–46; Tigervall 2005: 53–55). Importantly, in this guide for teaching immigrant girls are not addressed directly: being an immigrant girl with a Muslim background is connected to familial control and the tragic murder of Fadime Sahindal instead.

In the discourse of immigrant girls and honour, the plight of immigrant girls is most often understood in a cultural context where the violence is seen as a distant feature of a 'different culture', of 'others'. Consequently, links and similarities between other forms of gendered power go unnoticed. A good comparison is the debate over girls' sexual harassment in the early 2000s, which was a topic of a few youth films as well. In 2003 two youth films premiered having to do with girls' harassment and bullying. These films, *Hip Hip Hora!* and *Fjorton suger/Fourteen Sucks* (Martin Jern et al., 2003) describe teen girls who are sexually harassed at school and at house parties (see Figure 9.3). They critically explore the discourse of reputation and practices of gendered harassment at school and in youth groups. The focus of these films, especially their closures, resembles the tone of contemporary popular feminist guidebooks and columns (see Skugge et al. 2000). Central to these publications was encouraging girls to stand up against oppression. At the end of *Hip Hip Hora!*, for example,

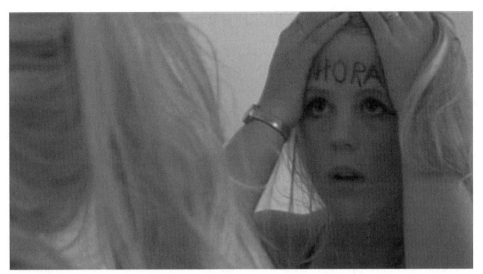

Figure 9.3: In *Fjorton suger*, someone has written 'hora' over 14-year-old Emma's forehead after a drunken house party.

the protagonist Sofie confronts the young man who has been harassing her and says, triumphantly: 'Damn whore? Is that all you can say? Damn, you should get a dictionary!'

In the press reception of *Hip Hip Hora!* and *Fjorton suger*, sexual harassment was understood as a severe societal problem that could no longer be ignored in the schools. Martin Jern, one of the directors of *Fjorton suger*, described the theme of the film in *Göteborgs-Posten* as follows:

> I was furious. Rape within a circle of friends wasn't considered rape. If the girl was too drunk, the excuse was 'But she didn't say no'. I think this is one of the most serious problems in our society. It's devastating for girls. (Helmerson 2004: 99)[15]

As seen in this excerpt, the view of Swedish girls as 'equal and free' is strongly challenged. Rather, Swedish society is seen as harmful, even devastating for girls and young women. As we have seen, in the debate over honour-related violence and arranged marriages girls with a non-Western background are often seen as victims – the opposite of Swedish girls, who are 'free and independent'. In the debate over girls' reputation and sexual harassment, on the other hand, Swedish girls are seen as in danger of victimization. Furthermore, in the harassment debate the blame is placed on the society, while in the discourse of honour the focus is usually on the girls' family and cultural background (see Honkasalo 2011: 29–30; Ambjörnsson 2003).

The egalitarian Nordic discourse is studied and challenged in the cinematic image of an adolescent girl. The image of a sexually harassed girl makes visible the crisis of the egalitarian society: she becomes the symbol of the new feminist critique of Sweden's image as 'the most equal country in the World'.[16] However, this critique is closely tied to nationality and ethnicity. In the discourse about immigrant girls, the understanding of an equal Swedish society prevails; these girls are understood as in need of its values and of being 'rescued'. Focusing on cinematic girlhood thus reveals inclusions and exclusions in the national discourse of gender equality. These cinematic images can most fruitfully be understood as *discursive encounters* between different understandings of girlhood (Ahmed 2000: 10). A 'normalized girlhood' is constructed intersectionally, through negotiations concerning culture, nationality and ethnicity.

Back to the wedding: transnational girl heroes?

The story of 'Vingar av glas' is universal. It is about a father with two daughters who are about to gain more independence. Things like that happen in every family with teenage children, but in this case there's one more difficulty – the clash between two cultures that function really differently. (Bagher 2000)

In this excerpt from the press release of *Vingar av glas*, director Reza Bagher first suggests that the narrative of teen daughters' rebellion and gaining independence has universal validity. He then foregrounds the clash between cultures as a special feature in the story of Nazli and her family: being an 'immigrant girl' brings an additional challenge to the process of growing up. Here the notion of a 'universal struggle' is important. While film critics and researchers have contextualized *Vingar av glas* in the Swedish debate, representations of immigrant girls should be analysed in the context of transnational youth film production as well. Images of immigrant girls, and related questions of vulnerability and in-betweenness, have become increasingly important in youth film production internationally. For example, as Savaş Arslan has argued, in Turkish cinema from the 1970s to the 1990s the young characters going through the process of Westernization and engaging in complex negotiations over cultural change were mainly female (Arslan 2007: 164).

Further, according to Sunaina Maira and Elisabeth Soep, popular representations of youth should be analysed through the intersections of youth cultures, national ideologies and global markets. As Maira and Soep argue, over the past couple of decades youth has become 'an ideological battleground in contests of immigration and citizenship' (Maira and Soep 2005: xix; see also Wiles 2007: 175–76). These 'contests' are visible in cinematic representations of youth on several levels. *Vingar av glas, Bäst i Sverige* and *Bend It Like Beckham*, for example, all express multidimensional young female subjectivities and clashes between cultures through the themes of food, music and participation in Western youth culture. In the early scenes of *Vingar av glas*, the main arena for arguments between Nazli and her father is the family dinner. Food is central to these scenes; Abbas tells his daughters to eat more so as to maintain the looks of a desirable young woman and not get an eating disorder.

In *Bend It Like Beckham,* Jess's mother wants her daughter to learn how to cook traditional Indian dishes and meet 'proper' Indian boys, rather than playing football and dreaming about David Beckham or her football coach Joe. The film scholar Sarah Projansky, who has studied the US reception of *Bend It Like Beckham,* has argued that food often becomes the marker of authenticity in the reception of films about immigrant girlhood. Consequently, the gaze becomes exotic, a form of 'culinary tourism' (Projansky 2007: 193–94).

In addition to food, cultural negotiation is also constructed in the soundtracks. *Bäst i Sverige* shows Fatima and Marcello both getting dressed in bright-coloured veils and playfully dancing to Lebanese music. In *Vingar av glas* the soundtrack combines independent female (feminist) artists and Iranian music, especially in the scene of Mahin's wedding celebration. The soundtrack of *Bend It Like Beckham* is a mixture of Western pop songs and bhangra songs, which have become widely popular in Britain. In the case of bhangra music, the genre in itself implies negotiations between Western popular culture and the Punjabi culture of Pakistan and India. Bhangra, developed in Britain in the 1980s by immigrants from the Punjab region, combines influences from Punjabi music and culture with various Western musical styles. Through music the young female characters are simultaneously negotiating with Western commercial youth culture and with their background located outside of it.

Through these similarities in the narratives, these films engage in the international debate over girls' power and agency that is specific to the popular cultural context of the late 1990s and early 2000s (Projansky 2007: 199; Aapola, Gonick and Harris 2005). In the discourse of girls' power and agency, popular feminist viewpoints are combined with societal concerns over girls' vulnerability and their need for empowerment. As Sinikka Aapola, Marnina Gonick and Anita Harris have argued, the popular media culture of the 1990s and 2000s contains two intertwining narratives concerning girls. They call these narratives 'girl power' and 'reviving Ophelia', the first referring to strong and independent 'can-do girls', the latter to 'at-risk girls', who are in danger of victimization (Aapola, Gonick and Harris 2005; Projansky 2007: 190–91). These two narratives are also deeply connected to class, ethnicity and nationality. Here, following Paulina de los Reyes, it is essential to note and analyse the meaning of ethnicity in concrete historical contexts (de los Reyes 2006: 31): in the cinematic images of immigrant girls, the struggle to become a (Western and middle class) 'can-do girl' involves extra difficulties.

Angela McRobbie has studied feminism and girlhood in girls' commercial media culture since the 1970s, and argues that the past couple of decades have seen the intensification of a highly conservative mode of young feminine empowerment. By this she means the strict division between Western young women, who are connected to change, modernity and freedom, and those girls and young women who have 'no access to Western freedoms' and who should be encouraged to culturally 'travel' to reach these possibilities. Girls' empowerment has been reduced to appearance-oriented consumer culture that worships romantic relationships and wealth (McRobbie 2007: 27–29). However, while Nazli, Jess and Minoo in *Hus i helvete* do strive to fit into the role of a Western 'can-do girl', these films look at this image critically as well. Nazli's ethnically Swedish friends are shown as shallow, appearance-oriented and in unhappy relationships. In *Hus i helvete*, the 'sexual freedom' Minoo has achieved in the US is presented through (unhappily) working as a stripper. Jess confidently confronts her friends when they ask her about having sex before marriage: 'Why sleep with boys you're not going to marry?' These films thus succeed in creating intersections between Western, consumer-oriented girl culture and various other cultural influences.

In all the films discussed in this chapter apart from *Bäst i Sverige*, a heterosexual wedding is shown as the key scene and watershed in the narrative of the young female protagonist's change and growth (see Figure 9.4).

The wedding scenes reveal the central tensions in the narrative. In *Vingar av glas*, it is at Mahin's wedding that Nazli reveals to her father that Hamid has tried to rape her; in *Bend It Like Beckham*, Jess gets her father's approval to go to the football game despite her sister's on-going wedding celebration. In both films, the protagonist girls are rebellious younger sisters who are compared with and contrasted to their elder sisters; the latter follow their parents' orders (especially about boyfriends and marriages) more closely. At the end of *Jalla! Jalla!*, the escape from the arranged wedding celebration of Roro and Yasmin brings the inter-cultural couples together in the same car, on their way to a new kind of future. As we have seen, *Hus i helvete* differs from the other films due to its darker tone; this is especially apparent in the wedding scene, where Minoo reveals to her family that she has been working as a stripper. Minoo's father gets furious and the wedding is ruined; the film does not offer any possibility of reconciliation, either between father and daughter or between cultures. Following

Figure 9.4: Nazli helps out in Mahin and Hassam's wedding.

Catherine Driscoll, heterosexual Western marriages 'blend local culture (including family culture) and global bridal culture'. In addition, they position girls and their families in a social context of class, ethnicity and culture (Driscoll 2002: 180–81). In the wedding scenes of these films, the younger sisters represent the image of Western feminine adolescence in the context of a wedding celebration, including non-Western traditions. Thus the wedding becomes a central moment in transnational girl culture.

Conclusions

At the end of *Vingar av glas,* Nazli proudly drives a motorcycle around the parking lot and in the streets: she has finally received her driving licence. Her father has come to congratulate her, and the relationship between daughter and father is shown – after all the confrontations and arguments – as warm and caring. The father even accepts Nazli's boyfriend Johan, although he turns away when Johan kisses Nazli in the parking lot. At the conclusion of *Bend it like Beckham,* Jess and her friend Jules are ready to travel to the US to train in football and study at a college. As Jess and Joe passionately kiss goodbye at the airport, the end of the film emphasizes reconciliation between generations and cultures in an optimistic, 'feel-good' sense. In both films, intercultural relationships underline the westernization of the young female characters; both of them nevertheless also succeed in maintaining their ties with the cultural background of their families (see Figure 9.5).

Figure 9.5: The reconciliation between Nazli and her father.

From the point of view of cultural history, the Swedish images of immigrant girls comment on the specific societal and historical context of the late 1990s and early 2000s. In comparison to the images of violent confrontations between immigrant youth and right wing extremists in the 1990s, the turn of the millennium was characterized by the image of a girl heroine which can be seen as a combination of several discourses, including the popular cultural fascination with 'strong girls', the feminist discussion concerning new, young subjects of the movement, and the heated debate over immigrant girls' vulnerability and oppression. Here it is important to observe how the notion of 'immigrant girl' has been widely connected with girls from the Middle East, especially those with a Muslim background. The difference compared to ethnically Swedish girls has been constructed through concerns about such topics as veiling and family strictness – themes that are frequently addressed in these youth films.

In viewing these youth films, it is essential to observe how the image of a young woman symbolizes social change and movement. *Vingar av glas, Bäst i Sverige* and *Bend It Like Beckham* all participate in the transnational field of commercial girl culture, where certain key themes – coming-of-age, rebellion and falling in love – are seen as universal (see Driscoll 2011: 149). These films not only internationalize female adolescence but also create a common understanding of what it means to be a young woman living in a Western society but with roots outside of it.

References

Aapola, S., Gonick, M. and Harris, A. (2005), *Young Femininity. Girlhood, Power and Social Change,* New York: Palgrave Macmillan.

Ahmed, S. (2000), *Strange Encounters. Embodied Others in Post-Coloniality,* London: Routledge.

Ambjörnsson, F. (2003), *I en klass för sig. Genus, klass och sexualitet bland gymnasietjejer,* Stockholm: Ordfront förlag.

Anon. (2000), '"Vingar av glas" blev ett lyft för Reza', *Helsingborgs Dagblad,* 26 October, p. 33.

Arslan, S. (2007), 'Projecting a Bridge for Youth. Islamic "Enlightenment" versus Westernization in Turkish Cinema', in T. Shary and A. Seibel (eds), *Youth Culture in Global Cinema,* Austin: University of Texas Press, pp. 157–88.

Bagher, R. (2000), *Vingar av glas. Press release,* Sonet Film.

Biltereyst, D. (2007), 'American Juvenile Delinquency Movies and the European Censors: The Cross-Cultural Reception and Censorship of *The Wild One, Blackboard Jungle* and *Rebel without a Cause*', in T. Shary and A. Seibel (eds), *Youth Culture in Global Cinema,* Austin: University of Texas Press, pp. 9–26.

Bredström, A. (2006), 'Maskulinitet och kamp om nationella arenor – reflektioner kring bilden av "invandrarkillar" i svensk media', in P. de los Reyes, I. Molina and D. Molinari (eds), *Maktens (o)lika förklädnader. Kön, klass och etnicitet i det postkoloniala Sverige,* Stockholm: Atlas akademi, pp. 182–206.

Brune, Y. (2006), '"Invandrare" i mediearkivets typgalleri', in P. de los Reyes, I. Molina and D. Molinari (eds), *Maktens (o)lika förklädnader. Kön, klass och etnicitet i det postkoloniala Sverige*, Stockholm: Atlas akademi, pp. 150–81.

De los Reyes, P., Molina, I. and Mulinari, D. (2006), 'Introduktion – Maktens (o)lika förklädnader', in P. de los Reyes, I. Molina and D. Mulinari (eds), *Maktens (o)lika förklädnader. Kön, klass och etnicitet i det postkoloniala Sverige*, Stockholm: Atlas akademi, pp. 11–30.

De los Reyes, P. (2006), 'Det problematiska systerskapet. Om svenskhet och invandrarskap inom svensk genushistorisk forskning', in P. de los Reyes, I. Molina and D. Mulinari (eds), *Maktens (o)lika förklädnader. Kön, klass och etnicitet i det postkoloniala Sverige*, Stockholm: Atlas akademi, pp. 31–48.

Driscoll, C. (2002), *Girls. Feminine Adolescence in Popular Culture and Cultural Theory*, New York: Columbia University Press.

——— (2011), *Teen Film. A Critical Introduction*, Oxford and New York: Berg.

Eduards, M. (2007), *Kroppspolitik. Om Moder Svea och andra kvinnor*, Stockholm: Atlas akademi.

Gatu, A. (2000), 'Flickor blir inte fotbollsproffs i Italien', in L. Skugge, B. Olsson and B. Zilg (eds), *Fittstim*, Stockholm: Atlas, pp. 146–63.

Gustafsson, T. (2006), 'Ett steg på vägen mot en ny jämlikhet' Könsrelationer och stereotyper in ung svensk ungdomsfim på 2000-talet', in E. Hedling and A-K. Wallengren (eds), *Solskenslandet. Svensk film på 2000-talet*, Stockholm: Atlantis, pp. 171–94.

Hedelius, A. (2002), *Filmhandledning: Bäst i Sverige*, Svenska Filminstitutet.

Helmerson, E. (2004), 'Tonårsångest i Fjorton suger - Filmen får Sonet att drömma om en ny Fucking Åmål', *Göteborgs-Posten*, 24 October, p. 99.

Higbee, W. and Lim, S. H. (2010), 'Concept of Transnational Cinema: Towards a Critical Transnationalism in Film Studies', in *Transnational Cinemas*, 1: 1, pp. 7–21.

Honkasalo, V. (2011), *Tyttöjen kesken. Monikulttuurisuus ja sukupuolten tasa-arvo nuorisotyössä*, Helsinki: Nuorisotutkimusverkosto.

Huss, P. (2002), 'Ulf Malmros, aktuell med Bäst i Sverige. "Jag älskar kufar och vardagsnissar"', Svenska Filminstitutet, http://www.sfi.se/PageFiles/7736/MALMROSULF.PDF. Accessed 10 September 2011.

Inness, S. A. (2004), 'Introduction. "Boxing Gloves and Bustiers": New Images of Tough Women', in S. A. Inness (ed.), *Action Chicks. New Images of Tough Women in Popular Culture*, New York: Palgrave Macmillan, pp. 1–20.

Janson, M. (2008), 'Fostran', in A. Koivunen (ed.), *Film och andra rörliga bilder – en introduction*, Stockholm: Raster förlag, pp. 127–43.

Johanson, R. (2000), 'Efter Reza Parsa och…', *Borås Tidning*, 27 October, p. 18.

Lagerström, L. (2000), *Filmhandledning: Vingar av glas*, Stockholm: Svenska Filminstitutet.

Liljeberg, R. (2000), 'Bland sexobjekt, stålkvinnor och töntar', *Svenska Dagbladet*, 29 January, p. 57.

Lindblad, H. (2002), 'Konsten att förena gammalt med nytt. Form och berättande', in S. Björkman, H. Lindblad and F. Sahlin (eds), *Fucking film. Den nya svenska filmen*, Stockholm: AlfabetaAnamma, pp. 99–110.

Lynggard, T. (2010), '"Immigrant girls" as a political symbol', *NIKK Magasin*, 3/2010, pp. 16–19.

Maira, S. and Soep, E. (2005), 'Introduction', in S. Maira and E. Soep (eds), *Youthscapes. The Popular, the National, the Global,* Philadelphia: University of Pennsylvania Press, pp. xv–xxxv.

McRobbie, A. (2007), *The Aftermath of Feminism. Gender, Culture and Social Change,* London: Sage.

Naficy, H. (1999), 'Introduction. Framing Exile: From Homeland to Homepage', in H. Naficy (ed.), *Home, Exile, Homeland. Film, Media and the Politics of Place,* New York and London: Routledge, pp. 1–16.

Projansky, S. (2007), 'Gender, Race, Feminism and the International Girl Hero. The Unremarkable U.S. Popular Press Reception of *Bend It Like Beckham* and *Whale Rider*', in T. Shary and A. Seibel (eds), *Youth Culture in Global Cinema,* Austin: University of Texas Press, pp. 189–206.

Reimers, E. (2005), '"En av vår tids martyrer". Fadime Sahindal som mediehändelse', in P. de los Reyes and L. Martinsson (eds), *Olikhetens paradigm. Intersektionella perspektiv på (o)jämlikhetsskapande,* Lund: Studentlitteratur, pp. 141–60.

Shary, T. (2007), 'Introduction. Youth Culture Shock', in T. Shary and A. Seibel (eds), *Youth Culture in Global Cinema,* Austin: University of Texas Press, pp. 1–6.

Shohat, E. and Stam, R. (2003), 'Introduction', in E. Shohat and R. Stam (eds), *Multiculturalism, Postcoloniality, and Transnational Media,* New Brunswick and New Jersey: Rutgers University Press, pp. 1–17.

Skugge, L., Olsson, B. and Zilg, B. (eds) (2000), *Fittstim,* Stocholm: Atlas.

Song, M. (2003), *Choosing Ethnic Identity,* Cambridge: Polity Press.

Tigervall, C. (2005), *folkhemsk film. Med "invandraren" i rollen som den sympatiske Andre,* Umeå universitet: Sociologiska institutionen.

Tunbäck-Hanson, M. (2000), 'Självklar och trovärdig debut', *Göteborgs-Posten,* 27 October, p. 57.

Wiles, M. (2007), 'Narrating the Feminine Nation: The Coming-of-Age Girl in Contemporary New Zealand Cinema', in T. Shary and A. Seibel (eds), *Youth Culture in Global Cinema,* Austin: University of Texas Press, pp. 178–88.

Wright, R. (2005), '"Immigrant Film" in Sweden at the Millennium', in A. Nestingen and T. G. Elkington (eds), *Transnational Cinema in a Global North. Nordic Cinema in Transition,* Detroit: Wayne State University Press, pp. 55–72.

Zachrisson, T. (2000), 'Vackert om olyckig kärlek', *Östersunds-Posten,* 27 October.

Notes

1 Filmmakers often mentioned in the discussion of immigrant film wave include Josef Fares, Reza Bagher and Reza Parsa. See Lindblad (2002: 45); Wright (2005: 55).

2 *Vingar av glas* skildrar en ung flickas uppror mot patriarkat och gamla traditioner. Samtidigt belyser den utmaningen i att finna en identitet i ett nytt samhälle, när man har sina kulturella rötter i ett annat. Faderns kärlek ställs mot dotterns frihetsbehov i en realistisk film om dagens Sverige. (Lagerström 2000)

3   Invandrarflickor som söker frihet och bryter med familj och traditioner. Ämnet är infekterat – men regissören Reza Bagher drar upp det till ytan i 'Vingar av Glas'. (Anon. 2000: 33)

4   Upproret blir bara så mycket tydligare när det som i Nazlis fall också innebär at bryta mot traditioner. (Tunbäck-Hanson 2000: 57)
    See about the reception narrative on immigrant girls challenging traditions and balancing between cultures: Zachrisson (2000) and Johanson (2000: 18).

5   As Sarah Projansky has argued, the dual opposites of 'tradition and family' vs. 'freedom-seeking girls' also characterized the US reception of *Bend It Like Beckham*.

6   In feminist historiography, the movement is often divided into three separate periods or waves. The first wave is most often situated in the late 1800s and the early 1900s, the second in the 1960s and 1970s, and the third in the 1990s. However, a number of scholars have criticized this division and pointed out continua and similarities between the waves. See Eduards (2007: 246–50); Henry (2004, passim).

7   stark, snygg och smart [...] inte är en vanlig tjej utan någon slags supervariant. (Liljeberg 2000: 57)

8   Marcello's nya vän   Fatima är så himla mycket 'bäst'. Modig, sporting, initiativrik, självständig... (Huss 2002)

9   Internationally, the 1990s meant introducing new strong heroines in youth television and films, such as *Buffy the Vampire Slayer* (1997–2003) and *Xena the Warrior Princess,* for example. See Inness (2004: 2–15).

10 In *Bend It Like Beckham*, Jess confronts her friends: 'Why sleep around with boys you're not going to marry?' An arranged marriage, or at least choosing a proper Indian boy as a husband, is not a problem for Jess, and she tells her friends that she does not want to bring shame to her family. This approach differs from the perspective of Swedish youth films, where the young protagonists have widely been represented through questioning their parents' authority as to suitable partners.

11 With regard to media concerns over immigrant boys, see for example Bredström (2006: 180). These gendered concerns about the potentially violent behaviour of immigrant boys and about girls in danger of victimization are common in English-speaking countries (Song 2003: 20).

12 The concept of 'honour' is problematic in many ways, as it is often used one-dimensionally in the media and the public debate. If sexual violence and harassment are explained through 'honour', the wider political dimensions often go unnoticed and the explanation of violence against immigrant girls becomes a 'cultural' issue, connected to the girls' background and family (Lynggard 2000: 16–19).

13 Fadime Sahindal had moved to Sweden from Turkey at a young age. Fadime's father murdered her after she had lived for several years away from home with her Swedish fiancée. What is special about Fadime's case is that she was an active presence in the Swedish media, giving interviews about immigrant girls, especially those with a Muslim background. In 2002, Fadime's tragic destiny became a media event that included several discourses about the oppression of immigrant girls, family-based violence and honour (Reimers 2005: 142–46).

14 Ett uppmärksammat fall är mordet på den kurdiska flickan Fadime Sahindal. Hon blev i januari 2002 mördad därför att fadern inte kunde acceptera hennes levnadssätt. I filmen är det Fatima's bröder som vill hålla ordning på sin syster för att de, som de säger, 'är rädda om henne'. (Hedelius 2002)

15 Jag var så arg. Våldtäkter inom kompiskretsen anses inte vara våldtäkter. Om tjejen var för berusad heter det 'Hon sa ju inte nej'. Jag tycker att det här är ett av de största samhällsproblemen. Man förstör unga tjejer. (Helmerson 2004: 99)

16 In 1995, the UN named Sweden as the most equal country in the World. Since then, the Swedish debate over women's power and feminism has been characterized by a discourse of achieved gender equality. In the late 1990s, activists of the third-wave feminist movement started to criticize this egalitarian discourse and point out its blind spots, such as girls' harassment or mediated beauty pressures (Skugge et al 2000).

Chapter 10

Family as Internal Border in *Dogtooth*

Ipek A. Celik
Bilkent University

reek filmmaker Yorgos Lanthimos' second feature film *Kynodontas/Dogtooth* (2009) received much critical acclaim in the international festival circuit, prestigious awards including *Un Certain Regard* at Cannes and nomination for the Foreign Language Film Academy Award. The low-budget film is set in a secluded country estate fenced in by a high bush-lined wall, affluent with luxuries such as a swimming pool and a large garden. Within the bounds of the property three young adults (Aggeliki Papoulia, Mary Tsoni and Hristos Passalis) are confined by their parents (Christos Stergioglou, Michele Valley) who are obsessively protective under the pretence of providing their children with proper education. To justify the confinement the parents feed the children with myths of monsters lingering outside the fence to attack them. The siblings are taught that they will be allowed to go out of the estate once their dogtooth falls, hence the title of the film.

This chapter reads the disturbing tale of a pathological family in *Dogtooth* as an allegory to internal borders in and of Greece, and in extension those in and of Europe – Greece being its periphery that serves as a centre both in terms of mythical origins and of intense confrontations with non-European foreigners (Balibar 2004: 1–2). I argue that the 'gated' family in Lanthimos's *Dogtooth* is a crucial commentary on the social problems that have emerged from the migratory confrontations that have preoccupied post-1989 Greece and Europe. *Dogtooth* does not explicitly deal with migration and population movements in Greece, yet the film captures a critical stance that is more extensive than just that of an oppressive family: the family in *Dogtooth* represents the protected zone of the 'inside' and the extent of protective measures that frequently takes a pathological shape, the fear of the foreign/outside which translates into xenophobia. The enclosed and incestuous family in the film is a trope for the increasing anxieties to protect the internal borders of Europe, an exclusionary turn in response to the changing composition of European society due to the dynamics of post-Cold War migration.

In what follows, I briefly trace the movement in Greek cinema from the 1990s, a period during which many works on migration were produced, to the mid-2000s when many young filmmakers focused on dysfunctional families – what I call a cinematic turn from the investigation of external to internal borders. Expanding on Etienne Balibar's theorization of 'internal borders' constructed within Europe anxious of its multicultural present (2004), I analyse the ways that the concept of family becomes a central allegory that defines and outlines these borders. *Dogtooth*, with its focus on a family that disciplines its borders through the protection of language, the control of communication technologies and an obsession with purity and hygiene, insightfully captures how external borders of a nation/civilization are reproduced internally.

From external to internal borders in Greek cinema

In 2006, the 47th Thessaloniki Film Festival had a retrospective on migration in Greek cinema which attested to the increasing number of Greek films on the topics of borders and migration. The festival organizers' selections reflected the fact that the post-1990s immigration films are considered as an extension of the longer tradition of Greek cinema on emigration, with well-known examples ranging from *America America* (Kazan, 1963), *Anaparastasi/Reconstruction* (Angelopoulos, 1970) to more recent major productions such as *Nhfes/Brides* (Voulgaris, 2004). The constellation of more recent films on immigration portrayed the identity challenge Greece was going through in the 1990s: a nation of emigrants (from the end of nineteenth century through the 1970s) has turned into one that attracts immigrants through the end of the twentieth century.

After 1989, with the collapse of Soviet socialism, Greece has become a host country for migration from neighbouring Balkan countries, primarily from Albania. Post-Cold War migration towards Greece has initiated demographic, social and cultural changes that shifted many coordinates of Greek society, especially regarding the country's place within the Balkans and in relation to the new and expanded Europe. Greek cinema of the 1990s has depicted such experience of confronting the other, revealing established borders (literal and metaphorical) that reinforce an unequal encounter of migrant from the Balkans with the Greek host. Katherina Zacharia describes the decade as 'repositioning of Greek cinema' as filmmakers responded to the challenges and anxieties associated with the increasing migrant presence in Greece: 'Greek cinema is attuned with the global fascination with cultural flows and circulations, syncretism and migrancy, engaging in the post-colonial discourses of multilayered identities and deterritorializations, and deconstructing dominant national discourses' (Zacharia 2008: 15).

Wendy Everett similarly describes the 1990s in Greek cinema as a period predominantly concerned with themes of 'immigration, borders (geographical and temporal), and problematic and unstable identities' (2005: 26). Everett highlights Theo Angelopoulos's leading role in the articulation of the path for both Greek and European cinema during the decade and describes Angelopoulos's films as 'key illustrations of the move from autobiography to journey narratives that marked films across Europe in the 1990s' (2005: 26). Soon after the collapse of the communist regime in neighbouring Albania Angelopoulos shot *To Meteoro Vima tou Pelargou/Suspended Step of the Stork* (Angelopoulos, 1991) and later *Mia Aioniotita kai mia Mera/Eternity and A Day* (Angelopoulos, 1998). The two philosophical inquiries on the solitude of humanity divided by borders were among the first works to depict then recent phenomenon of migration to Greece and the Greek-Albanian border. Migration and borders are explored by several Greek directors from various angles over the 1990s and early 2000s – the themes ranged from critique of leftist politics of migration [*Mirupafshim/ See You* (Korras and Vourpouras, 1997)], the hardships faced by illegal migrants on their way to Greece [*Ap'to Hioni/From the Snow* (Gortisas, 1993)], the victims of sex trafficking [*O dromos pros ti Dysi/The Way to the West* (Katzourakis, 2003)] and marginalized lives of minority youth in the ghettos of Athens [*Apo tin Akri tis Polis/From the Edge of the City* (Giannaris, 1998)]. These films introduced characters and themes that were, at the time, marginal to Greek cinema, and addressed the exacerbated identitarian anxieties of Greeks as well as social exclusion and xenophobia faced by migrants in Greece.

Within the framework of this recent legacy of migration films, when *Dogtooth* was premiered, it was seen an anomaly in Greek cinema.[1] The film has been compared to Michael Haneke's *Das weiße Band/The White Ribbon* (2009) in its perverse pedagogy or *Der siebente Kontinent/The Seventh Continent* (Haneke, 1989) that portrays a suicidal family. The director's style is described as one that is 'between Bunuel's surrealism and Haneke's surgical blade'[2] (Danikas 2009). Lanthimos's vision was deemed as closer to Austrian cinema rather than being part of Greek or Southern European tradition: 'with pristine clarity, refrigerated light and deadpan stabs of violence, it looks unmistakably like something by Michael Haneke or his Austrian contemporaries Ulrich Siedl and Jessica Hausner' (Bradshaw 2010).

Such comments dismissed a movement within Greek cinema towards the exploration of dysfunctional families, a common theme in recent Greek films made by young and upcoming directors. In a short retrospective on contemporary Greek cinema Steve Rose names this hard-to-define movement as 'the Greek Weird wave'. One of the filmmakers of the 'Weird wave' Athina Rachel Tsangari – director of *Attenberg* (2010), a film that portrays a 23-year-old girl isolated from the world apart from her strange relationship with her dying father – states that family is the recurrent theme to preoccupy Greece's new generation of filmmakers: 'It's a Greek obsession. The reason our politics and economy is in such trouble is that it's run as a family. It's who you know'[3] (Rose 2011). What marked the beginning of the era of unconventional and malfunctioning family films in Greek cinema is *Spirtokouto/ Matchbox* (Economides, 2002), a film that focuses on a Greek family in shreds. Offering a strongly contrasting situation compared to *Dogtooth*, the father of this family loses all control and authority in his relation to a capricious wife and disrespectful children.[4] More recently, *Strella/A Woman's Way* (Koutras, 2009) which premiered almost simultaneously with *Dogtooth*, also follows the trend. *Strella* shows the torturous path of a transsexual prostitute who ends up having a relationship with his long lost father.[5]

In short, towards the mid-2000s, a younger generation of Greek directors moved away from exploring migration, the arduous travels of illegal migrants and the xenophobia and exploitative working conditions they experience in Greece. Can this representational shift from the theme of migration or external borders of Greece and Greek identity to that of family be explained through the camera's withdrawal from the public and move into the private space? Despite appearances, I suggest that the younger generation of filmmakers in Greece do not turn significantly away from the route that Greek cinema took in the 1990s, its focus on external borders. The contemporary Greek filmmakers' emphasis on the family reflects a response to the increase, spreading and deterritorialization of such borders within the society. The pathological concern to protect the 'inside' carries the family to the core of 'internal borders' to be secured. In order to further clarify the larger social connotations of family implied in *Dogtooth* allow me to take a close look into the contemporary focus on the institution in Greece and Europe, and the policies that give family the status of an internal border.

The family as allegory

Lanthimos describes *Dogtooth* as a film that explores the obstinate desire to cling on to the idea of family and the obsession of raising children within this realm in a world where the concept of family is slowly disintegrating:

> To me it was basically thinking about the future of family – and if it's something that could stay the same forever and raise the children the same way […] and if such a thing is necessary […] what if, at some point, families were extinct? If that happened there would definitely be people that would really want to keep that as they know it, really try to keep their families together forever. I thought that people would go to extremes to maintain that. (Lanthimos in Anon 2010)

The director emphasizes the contrast between the aesthetics of the idyllic estate with the beautiful children and the 'horrible and tragic' pedagogy of the parents (Zelenko 2010). Lanthimos has been reluctant to offer social and political commentary on *Dogtooth* beyond his critique of the perverted sense of family that blindly protects itself. He prefers to leave the question of political allegory open to many interpretations that the audience would bring in: 'it is a political film, but I didn't start making as an allegory to political issues' (Adams 2010).

In parallel with the director's comments on his film the reviews so far focused on the film's original critique of the claustrophobic family life, the extremes of pedagogy and of suburban isolation. Roger Ebert of *Chicago Sun Times* writes: 'God help children whose parents insanely demand unquestioning obedience to their deranged standards', while *The Guardian* reviewer Steve Rose makes a tongue-in-cheek comment on the 'overprotecting parent syndrome': 'No wonder Greece is in economic crisis. Family life is plumbing drastic new levels of wrongness over there' (Rose 2010). Most reviews hint at the broader connotations of everyday power and control that overwhelms the household of *Dogtooth*: 'Everything in the family's world – from sex to language to the use of mouthwash – becomes subject to a precise ritual control that becomes all the more ludicrous the more solemnly its arbitrary diktats are observed' (Fisher 2011: 23). The reviews fleetingly hint at the film's allegorical potential, describing family in *Dogtooth* as 'a walled city state with its own autocratic rule and untellable secrets'

(Bradshaw 2010) or 'castle of xenophobic purity' (Azoury 2009), while they fall short of exploring the larger connotations of such strong statements.

What, then, are the larger connotations of family in today's Greece and Europe? In his review of *Dogtooth* Mark Fisher quotes Alain Badiou's critique that family has become once more the nexus of society in today's Europe: 'it is striking to see that as the century draws to a close the family has once more become a consensual and practically unassailable value' (Fisher 2011: 25). Family 'as an unassailable value' in Europe has been appearing in various levels that range from scientific conferences on the topic to popular culture and state policies. Major EU-funded conferences in the mid-2000s ['Families, Change and European Social Policy' (Dublin 2004), 'The Demographic Future of Europe – from Challenge to Opportunity' (Brussels 2006)] showed an upsurge of institutional interest both in population policies and the well-being of families. Demographic concern is commercialized in Swedish government sponsored Björn Borg advertisement campaign in 2001, which featured a group of midwives gathered in the hospital nursery with empty cribs. Sixteen midwives, each representing an EU member state, looked sternly at the camera in support of Borg's advice for the people of Europe:

> One quick, and you're home free! We have a bit of a delicate problem here in the Western world: there aren't enough babies born, if nothing drastic happens soon there won't be anyone who can work and put up for our pensions [...] Get to it! Fuck for Future.

In the realm of state policies a striking example is the former Italian Prime Minister Silvio Berlusconi's 2006 offer of a baby bonus to parents who had a second child. Those migrant parents who were accidentally sent baby bonuses were asked to return the money (Joyce 2008).

As the Berlusconi policy highlights, frequently at the centre of debates on family is an anxiety about not having enough of the 'right' babies born, a problem intimately connected to the growing presence of migrants and minorities of non-European origin. In Greece, journalist Tasoula Karaiskaki's article titled 'Dramatic Population Decline' rang the alarm bell as early as May 1995, soon after the first influx of migrants to post-Cold War Greece: 'We are doomed to turn into a state of foreigners unless every [Greek] couple has at least four children' (in Athanasiou 2003: 239). The connection between demographic anxiety and migration is more immediately felt in Greece due to the country's geographical position on the European border, open to so-called intrusions of illegal migrants. Being the country with the lowest 'native' birth rate and highest percentage of migrants in proportion to total population among other countries in Europe, there has been a growing nationalist public discourse of demographic crisis in Greece (Halkias 2003: 213). Hence, the Greek context provides a fertile ground to contemplate on the anxiety about the protection of family, and the nationalist concerns of a demographic crisis.

Etienne Balibar, in his book on the frontiers of post-1989 European identity, observes the intimate link between the concepts of family, nation and race: 'the interference of family politics [...] with the definition of the national "community" is a crucial structural mode of production of historical racism' (2004: 123). Balibar articulates how family becomes a predominant metaphor through which racial ideology is perpetuated in the nation: 'the racial community has a tendency to represent itself as one big family or as the common envelope of family relations' (Balibar and Wallerstein 1991: 100). The metaphorical link between nation and family (nation as family) is established through securing and promoting the genealogical link (nation/family protecting the purity of its blood). Such discourse inevitably excludes those groups who do not 'belong' to the genealogy.

Balibar calls this anti-democratic construction of the transnational space 'European apartheid': a zone that puts the migrant labour at the service of European citizens yet, much like a colonial regime, while it expects the workers who economically produce inside the EU border to reproduce, socially and sexually, outside the EU. Thus, Europe is constructed as an ever shifting borderland where the inside and the outside become ambiguous, and where the population and social welfare policies promote the social and physical reproduction of its hereditary insiders while discouraging that of migrants and minorities – as in the case of Berlusconi.

As the borders of Europe become ubiquitous the dynamics of 'inside' and 'outside' has undeniably changed: 'differential inclusion of European apartheid in the process of globalization no doubt explains why, more and more, the traditional figure of external enemy is being replaced by that of the internal enemy' (Balibar 2004: 172). The external borders of Europe are duplicated in the form of 'internal borders,' that stigmatizes and represses certain populations 'whose presence in European societies are nonetheless increasingly massive and legitimate' (Balibar 2004: x). As borders increase and become deterritorialized, what remains 'inside' shrinks while the obsessive protection of that realm inflates the concerns and measures of security and control, carried away from the geographical borderlines into the heart of public space:

> [B]orders are vacillating. This does not mean that they are disappearing. [...] on the contrary, borders are being multiplied and reduced in their localization and their function; they are being doubled, becoming borders *zones, regions* or *countries* one can reside and live. (Balibar 2002: 92)

In this realm, family (the right kind of family) becomes a frontier, an internal border in the core of society, to be protected from external intervention, controlled and disciplined in a way that promotes it to further close in on itself.

Disciplining the borders of the house

Dogtooth is Lanthimos's second solo feature film. Many critics were pleasantly surprised by the uniqueness of *Dogtooth*'s script and cinematography attained at such early stage in Lanthimos's career. After studying film in Athens throughout the 1990s he directed a number of TV commercials, music videos, short films and theatre plays, and contributed to the organization of opening and closing ceremonies of the 2004 Olympics in Athens. *Kinetta* (2005), his debut feature, screened at Toronto and Berlin film festivals, is the story of an odd group of three – a policeman, an employee of a photo shop and a hotel chambermaid – gathered in an old seaside resort restaging crime scenes of local women murdered by a serial killer. While the curiosity for strange experimentation of human behaviour in *Kinetta* prepares the way for the later film, the use of shaky handheld camera in the film sharply contrasts *Dogtooth*'s fixed shots that frame characters and carry the inescapable borders of the *mise-en-scène* into the cinematography.

Dogtooth is a film about the obsessive desire to wall out and protect the realm of family from outside corruption; a bordering and control mechanism that goes to such extremes that the family ends up becoming incestuous. How are borders of the household and family regulated in the film? One of the key ways that regulate the inside outside boundary beyond the closed gates of the mansion is the control of language and other forms of media and communication. All items in the house are carefully restricted with the only available media being a few medical books and homemade educational videos and cassettes that teach the grown up children incorrect definition of words.

The opening sequence of *Dogtooth* immediately establishes the boundaries of inside and outside by showing how communication and speech in the house is contained. There are no establishing shots providing a clue of the space and context. After the title shot, the camera is fixed on an old-fashioned cassette player (Figure 10.1). A finger presses the play button and we hear a woman's voice – that later we learn belongs to the mother. The recording slowly explains 'Today the new words are the following: sea … motorway … excursion … and carbine.' The camera cuts to a medium shot of a young boy in his 20s anxiously looking off screen while he listens to the tape. He stands in a minimally furnished bathroom with

Figure 10.1: The opening shot.

shampoo bottles that have no tags in the background, no written or spoken words/texts are available outside those that emerge from the cassette player.

Soon we hear the incorrect definitions affiliated with the words: 'the sea is a leather armchair with wooden arms … like the one we have in our living room … For example: Don't stand on your feet. Sit on the sea to have a quiet chat with me.' While the exemplary sentence commands obedience and passivity, the word of the outside realm 'sea' becomes contained in a word of an object that can be found in the house. Then the motorway is described as 'a very strong wind', and 'excursion' takes the meaning of 'very resistant material used to construct floors'. The lessons strategically replace the meanings of words that would be unknown for the listeners with objects familiar to them, convert the vocabulary that signifies movement to rigidity and immobility. Later we notice that even anything that uncontrollably passes by the house, will be turned into a home object: the parents convince that the planes flying by are toys that sometimes drop into the garden. This perverted pedagogy introduces us to a contained life, where the language describes a limited habitat, words of nature are limited to the ones that can be found in a garden and all other objects are bounded with the ones within a household. The erroneous teachings do not only erase the meaning of outside but also contain any possible communication with an outsider as the terms of speech between 'the insiders' and those on the outside would never be the same. Even the names of the characters in the household are reduced to their roles within the family, the father, the mother and the children.

As the homemade educational tape runs the jump cut first shows a girl, nearly the same age as the boy, and then a younger second girl, all beautiful and blond, healthy looking young people with similarly confused, anxious and unhappy looks on their faces. In separate frames that emphasize their isolation despite being in the same space, we are introduced to the main characters, the three siblings as they are homeschooled by their parents who record the day's lesson on cassette tapes. The door is shut, the window is closed with a curtain which gives the feeling of entrapment. The muted tones and domination of white in the bathroom, a colour scheme similar to other rooms in the house, give a hygienic and cold hospital feel. We are not only introduced to the siblings, but also to the mother through her voice in the recording. In the next sequence we meet the father in the same manner, first we hear his voice as he drives the car while the camera captures a blindfolded woman stiffly sitting in the passenger seat. Being introduced to the voices of the father and mother before the camera captures their figure increases their omnipotent presence and power over the other characters. Throughout the film, frequent use of sound bridges and voiceovers carry or insert the mother's and more often the father's voice to another scene where the parents are not physically present. Their omnipresent voices, which may be running in the siblings' heads, suggest an omnipotent control of their lives. Their voice presented both as on and off-screen sound makes the film itself take the role of the cassette player, the film becoming part of the homemade media that further encloses the narrative, accelerates the entrapment. Film becomes a meta-border within the frontiers of the household.

In *Dogtooth*, the pedagogy reinforces a cherished and contained inner world, a barrier that inherently limits communication with the outside world. What is more striking is that even the means of pedagogy refer to a border between them and the outside world. There is no media, TV, radio or even telephone except for the pedagogical tapes. Along with the voice recordings that enclose the realm of meanings into the household, the borders of the house are ensured by the only other media available in the house: the homemade videos of themselves. These videos provide rare entertainment which the siblings watch *ad nauseam*, they remember and reiterate every word and sentence (their own) that has been previously recorded. Hence, even their entertainment is watching videos of the inside, images turned inward in a vicious circle of entrapment repeated in the frame within the frame, by the camera within the camera. Communication is further bounded with memorized videos that refer only to what has happened inside the gates of the house (Figure 10.2).

The only person in the family to leave the mansion is the father who works in a factory. He occasionally brings home an employee of the factory Christina (Anna Kalaitzidou), the only person named in the film, to satisfy the sexual urges of the son and they mechanically go through the actions. The walls around the highly protected environment start shaking when the elder daughter blackmails Christina – who gives her little presents in exchange for oral sex – to lend the videotapes she has in her purse, copies of *Jaws* (Spielberg, 1975), *Rocky* (Avildsen, 1976) and *Flashdance* (Lyne, 1983). The elder daughter becomes obsessed with the films, often quoting them and re-enacting scenes. When the father finds out, after punishing both the daughter and Christina, determined to never let any other outsider have 'bad influence' on his family he assigns the elder sister to the 'task' of having sex with her brother.

The videotapes coming from and depicting the realm outside the house eventually shatter the extremely well orchestrated checks and balances of the cloistered realm. How would these

Figure 10.2: Watching homemade videos.

videotapes acquire such function, especially considering these films are three Hollywood blockbusters *Jaws*, *Rocky* and *Flashdance*? All three films came out during 1975–85, a decade of blockbuster hits and major publicity campaigns, of new technologies and special effects (Hoberman 1985: 34–59) when Hollywood started to 'invade' the global homes through the introduction of home entertainment, the VCR. Hence, these films represent an era of further globalization of Hollywood, from the global movie theatres into the global homes. Moreover, all three films show heroes winning against the odds – a deadly shark, an undefeatable fighter or the most competitive dance school rehearsal. The videotapes represent a window into another world, a utopian Hollywood world that has the capacity to challenge the idyllic space that the parents of *Dogtooth* provide their children. In comparison, the outside world of *Dogtooth*, the factory where the father works, for instance, presents no charms. Sharp geometric shapes, gray and pale tones contrast the delicately lit interiors of the family home, the beauty of a garden with well-trimmed plants and swimming pool. So only the videotapes have the capacity to challenge this protected zone with an offer of another idyllic world. In turn, the father reframes the function of the videotapes as punitive/educative rather than pleasurable by using one to beat the daughter on the head.

Another element of 'border control' in *Dogtooth* is the obsession with bodily hygiene and health consciousness, which includes concern about the son's sexual health which eventually leads to incestuous relationship. Hygiene and taking care of the body's health is a daily ritual and routine for the children. In the factory-like house (no wonder the father works as a manager at a factory) the kids have a regulated schedule of exercise, meals and they continuously drink freshly squeezed fruit juices. The son polishes his shoes before the nightly family dinner, washes his father's car diligently while the older daughter vacuums her room 'to keep the germs off.' The younger daughter, on the other hand, keeps track of the medicine and plays the family doctor while initiating strange games such as that of anesthetizing oneself.

Before the first sex scene between the son and Christina, the father makes sure Christina has taken a bath, and asks if she washed her hair. When the father enters the son's room and sees that he is working out, he patiently waits until the exercise is finished so the health routine is not broken. When the father leaves the room, the son and Christina start to take off their clothes dutifully, they lie on bed. They do not talk or kiss; sex is performed mechanically. They barely look at each other, they are focused on his penis which is their sole point of contact. The sexual encounter between the son and Christina consists of a single long take from a fixed camera set at about waist level at a steady distance from the characters as if a security camera is filming. As in all other scenes indoors – there are no tracking shots, the movement is captured only through jump cuts that give the sense of ruptured mobility, reflecting the cruel stillness in the lives of the characters. A result of this steadiness peculiar to this scene as well as some others inside the house is that the frame is constantly broken vertically by the characters, we see torsos without heads, fragmented bodies (Figure 10.3). Yet they never break the frame horizontally; while they break the edges of the frame, they never exit the frame. They enter the off-screen space only by using a door placed in the

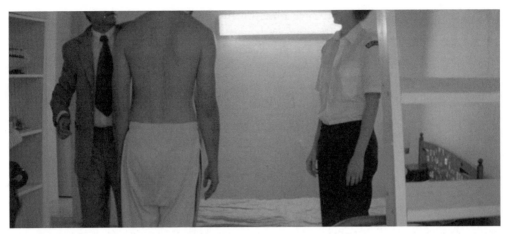

Figure 10.3: Fragmented bodies, preparing to have sex.

background. Hence the filmic frame that 'captures' them is never broken which enhances the feeling of confinement.

The camera in *Dogtooth* becomes a border in itself, skilfully articulating the limits of space and movement. Lanthimos's camera does not only imprison the characters in its static nature, it erases the possibility of off-screen space, the character's inability to break the frame horizontally makes the off-screen always contained by the screen space. In the framed/ bordered, protected and hygienic realm of the *Dogtooth* estate, after the contamination of the delicately balanced life of the family by the blockbuster videotapes, the urge to continue providing a healthy sexual life to the son leads to a complete enclosure of the house into an incestuous relationship. Inbreeding is prophesized when even the dog that will soon be brought into the house is introduced as something that the mother will give birth to. The parents' fixation on preserving the purity of the family goes to such extremes that it creates the absolute societal transgression: incest. Soon after the incestuous affair the daughter in desperation knocks out her own dogtooth. This is also one of the rare incidents when the fixed camera finally moves and tracks the older daughter who runs out in the garden at night, to her freedom or death. She hides in the trunk of the father's car. The ambiguous final shot shows the car parked in front of the father's factory, the daughter does not emerge from the trunk.

Conclusion

In an analysis of *Dogville* (von Trier, 2003) Thomas Elsaesser suggests that the film does not make an immediate reference to Europe's borders and immigration policies, but through 'abstractions and schematisms' it stages borders, 'what constitutes inside and out', and ideologies of exclusion (2005: 123). On a similar line of argument, we may contend that young Greek directors who produce films on dysfunctional families in the mid-2000s reconsider the meaning of borders and exclusions, a topic already explored extensively in Greek cinema of the 1990s, from a more abstract perspective, which is at the same time closer to the heart of the Greek society, the very nucleus of it: the family that becomes an internal border of a society through the obsession to discipline and control it.

It is plausible to draw some immediate connections between the internal borders of the family in the film and external borders supported by migration policies. The language containment in *Dogtooth*, for instance, eerily recalls the particular ways that preserving the national languages becomes a crucial concern through which borders of a nation are defined and protected from alien 'intrusions'. This practice displays itself in language tests that migrants and minorities have to pass in order to attain citizenship in many European countries. In the Netherlands, for instance, migrants take a two level test. Naturalization requires testing the command of the Dutch language. But another aspect reminding mediated pedagogies of *Dogtooth*, its enclosed video trainings and entertainments, is the pre-arrival exam on Dutch culture which requires (only non-Western migrants) to watch a training video entitled 'Coming to the Netherlands', a video that 'includes images of homosexual men kissing and of female nudity' (Etzioni 2007: 356) made to test the levels of tolerance of especially Muslims. While the tapes appear to train Muslims into European ways of life they only emphasize and reconstruct the assumed barriers between Muslims and Europeans. Just as *Dogtooth* establishes the function of videotapes both as a border within a border (homemade videos) and a utopian escape (three blockbuster films), the video trainings of migrants similarly construct Netherlands as a utopia and a border impossible to cross.

The concern with health and hygiene in *Dogtooth* also reminds how the physical boundaries of the nation are supported with 'symbolic borders (criminality, deviance, dirt, disease), a fictional preservation of racial purity against "alien contamination"' (Tzanelli 2006: 40). Keeping the body of the nation clean becomes another internal border. Nadia Serematakis, in an article written in the mid-1990s about public health panic in Greece due to migration, notes:

There appeared a series of media panic stories about waves of infections crossing Greek frontiers: AIDS, hepatitis B, cholera, embola, and the list goes on. Borders were leaking not only people but also contaminated and contaminating substances, old and new viruses. The border now represented an infection. This medicalization of the border and of mobile people pointed to new forms of violence emanating from this space. (Serematakis 1996: 510)

The obsession with hygiene becomes a part of the protection of the borders from various 'penetrations'. *Dogtooth* presents the extents that the protection of hygiene, both literal and metaphorical, from external intrusions leads to: the ultimate enclosure of family into inbreeding.

While such parallels between exclusionary migration policies and the film's representation of a pathologically inbreeding family may appear viable yet forced, *Dogtooth* certainly presents the affective dimension of the socio-political changes taking place due to migration and the threat to the national family, and to nation as family. In Lanthimos's microcosm the overly-protected beautiful bodies are doomed to be consumed by incest, violence and deformation; they burst open, close down, emotions are discharged through sudden impassioned action. The reproductive economy of the family closes in on itself. The obsessive protections and walls inherently undermine the goal to secure future healthy adults. Lanthimos deconstructs the idea of national/genealogical union by taking it to the extreme through borders and enclosure. His film is not a simple allegory of nation as a family in crisis; it is a film that explores the impossible experiment of protecting a community through the multiplication of borders around it. The end result shows myriads of ways that everyday violence gets produced in a xenophobic space. Lanthimos's grotesque realism dissects the politics of exclusion that surround the focus on protection of family and its values both in Greece and in Europe, seen from its border zone most vulnerable to migrant penetrations.

References

Adams, S. (2010), 'Interview: *Dogtooth* director Giorgos Lanthimos', *A.V. Club*, 25 June, http://www.avclub.com/articles/dogtooth-director-giorgos-lanthimos,42525/. Accessed 9 July 2011.

Aggelikopoulos, V. (2006), 'Ηοικογένεια είναι εργαστήριο φόβου', Interview with Sotiris Dimitriou, *H Kathimerini*, 15 January, http://news.kathimerini.gr/4dcgi/_w_articles_civ_1_15/01/2006_169740. Accessed 10 May 2011.

Anon. (2010), 'Interview: Yorgos Lanthimos', *New York Times*, 31 March, http://video.nytimes.com/video/2010/03/31/movies/1247467499699/interview-yorgos-lanthimos.html. Accessed 10 July 2011.

Athanasiou, A. (2003), 'Bloodlines: Performing the Body of the 'Demos', Reckoning the Time of the 'Ethnos', *Journal of Modern Greek Studies*, 21: 2, pp. 229–56.

Azoury, P. (2009), 'Grèce animale', *Libération*, 20 May, http://next.liberation.fr/cinema/0101568296-grece-animale. Accessed 10 July 2011.

Balibar, E. (2002), *Politics and the Other Scene*, London: Verso.

——— (2004), *We, the People of Europe?: Reflections on Transnational Citizenship*, Princeton: Princeton University Press.

——— and Wallerstein, I. (1991), *Race, Nation, Class: Ambiguous Identities,* New York: Verso.

Bradshaw, P. (2010), 'Film Review: Dogtooth', *Guardian*, 22 April, http://www.guardian.co.uk/film/2010/apr/22/dogtooth-review. Accessed 12 July 2011.

Danikas, D. (2009), Ελληνική πρωτοπορία, *Ta Nea*, 22 October, http://www.tanea.gr/politismos/article/?aid=4542444. Accessed 17 June 2011.

——— (2011), '*ΤΟ ΚΑΣΤΡΟ ΤΗΣ ΑΓΝΟΤΗΤΑΣ*: Καρμπόν *Κυνόδοντα*', *Ta Nea*, 03 March, http://www.tanea.gr/politismos/article/?aid=4621246. Accessed 15 June 2011.

Ebert, R. (2010), 'Dogtooth', *Chicago Sun-Times*, 7 July, http://rogerebert.suntimes.com/apps/pbcs.dll/article?AID=/20100707/REVIEWS/ 100709986. Accessed 9 July 2011.

Elsaesser, T. (2005), *European Cinema: Face to Face with Hollywood*, Amsterdam: Amsterdam University Press.

Etzioni, A. (2007), 'Citizenship Tests: A Comparative, Communitarian Perspective', *The Political Quarterly*, 78: 3, pp. 353–63.

Everett, W. (2005), 'Re-framing the Fingerprints: A Short Survey of European Film', in W. Everett (ed.), *European Identity in Cinema*, Bristol: Intellect, pp. 15–34.

Fisher, M. (2011), 'Dogtooth: The Family Syndrome', *Film Quarterly*, 64: 4, pp. 22–27.

Halkias, A. (2003), 'Money, God and Race: The Politics of Reproduction and the Nation in Modern Greece', *European Journal of Women's Studies*, 10: 2, pp. 211–32.

Hoberman, J. (1985), 'Ten Years That Shook the World', *American Film*, 10: 8, pp. 34–59.

Joyce, K. (2008), 'Missing the 'Right' Babies', *The Nation*, 14 February, http://www.thenation.com/article/missing-right-babies. Accessed 06 June 2011.

Rose, S. (2010), What Dogtooth's Overprotective Parents Learned from *Footloose* and *Finding Nemo*, *Guardian*, 24 April, http://www.guardian.co.uk/film/2010/apr/24/dogtooth-pushy-parents-guardian. Accessed 12 July 2011.

——— (2011), 'Attenberg, Dogtooth and the Weird Wave of Greek Cinema', *Guardian*, 27 August, http://www.guardian.co.uk/film/2011/aug/27/attenberg-dogtooth-greece-cinema. Accessed 12 January 2012.

Seremetakis, N. (1996), 'In Search of the Barbarians: Borders in Pain', *American Anthropologist*, 98: 3, pp. 489–511.

Tzanelli, R. (2006), 'Not My Flag!' Citizenship and Nationhood in the Margins of Europe (Greece, October 2000/2003)', *Ethnic and Racial Studies*, 29: 1, pp. 27–49.

Zacharia, K. (2008), '"Reel" Hellenisms: Perceptions of Greece in Greek Cinema', in K. Zacharia (ed.), *Hellenisms: Culture, Identity, and Ethnicity from Antiquity to Modernity*, Aldershot: Ashgate, pp. 321–54.

Zelenko, M. (2010), 'Rumpus Interview with Yorgos Lanthimos, Director of Dogtooth', *The Rumpus*, 25 June, http://therumpus.net/2010/06/ rumpus-interview-with-yorgos-lanthimos-director-of-dogtooth/. Accessed 9 July 2011.

Notes

1   In Greece there have even been accusations that Lanthimos plagiarized the Mexican film *El Castillo de la Purezza/Castle of Purity* (Ripstein, 1973), a film that depicts the story of Gabriel Lima who keeps his wife and three children locked for 18 years in a deteriorating colonial mansion under the pretence of protecting them from a corrupt world (Danikas 2011).

2   All translations from French and Greek are mine.

3   Tsangari and Lanthimos work together in many projects (Rose 2011): In *Attenberg* Lanthimos appears in the role of the experimental lover of the main character; Tsangari is the producer in Lanthimos's recent film *Alps* (Lanthimos, 2011).

4   Aggeliki Papoulia, the older daughter in *Dogtooth*, plays the rebellious daughter in *Matchbox*.

5   The recent focus on dysfunctional and 'abnormal' families is not limited to filmmaking in
    Greece. Sotiris Dimitriou, a famous short story writer and novelist who has produced most
    of his works during the 1990s and 2000s, has frequently explored families in the margins of
    Greek society, stories of mothers involved in incestuous relations with their sons or daughters
    committing matricide. In an interview the author describes family as 'a workshop of fear. A
    small army camp where one frightens the other. A pathological love is manufactured within
    the family, love that is reduced to malice, since it enslaves the other, leaves no space to breathe'
    (Aggelikopoulos 2006). Dimitriou associates family with claustrophobia, pathology and fear,
    feelings similar to being in an army. His careful choice of terminology such as workshop
    and manufacture also suggests a view of the body as a machine of enforced production.
    Dimitriou's description eerily recalls the way family is conceptualized in *Dogtooth*.

Chapter 11

Gendered Conflicts in Northern Ireland: Motherhood, the Male Body and Borders in *Some Mother's Son* and *Hunger*

Raita Merivirta
University of Turku

The geographical border partitioning Ireland came into existence with the passing of the Government of Ireland Act by the British Parliament in December 1920, at a time when the Anglo-Irish War was still being fought in the South. Two subordinate parliaments were to be established in Ireland: one in Dublin, the other in Belfast. The Northern Ireland parliament, Stormont, duly opened in June 1921. The war in the South ended with a ceasefire the following month. The subsequent Anglo-Irish Treaty created the Irish Free State in 1922, but retained the partition of Ireland whereby Northern Ireland remained a part of the United Kingdom. The border created a Northern Ireland which was two-thirds Protestant and one-third Catholic. An overwhelming majority of Protestants were Unionists, while most Catholics favoured an independent, united Ireland. In the following decades, the half a million Catholics who lived in Northern Ireland were discriminated against in the allocation of jobs and housing as well as over political rights by the Protestant majority, which ran the state. In 1968–9 the 'Troubles' started brewing in Northern Ireland when Catholic protest marches and Protestant parades turned into violent confrontations. In the early 1970s violence spread all over Ulster and the Irish Republican Army (IRA) started attracting new members. Many of the young Republican men who took up arms were consequently arrested and imprisoned for their actions. The Republican inmates saw themselves as prisoners of war and started protesting against being classified as 'ordinary' criminals in 1976. This chapter examines two films: Terry George's mainstream maternal melodrama *Some Mother's Son* (1996) and Steve McQueen's less conventional art film *Hunger* (2008). Both films depict the 'blanket' protest of the Republican prisoners in Long Kesh and the protest's escalation into a hunger strike in 1981. The focus of this chapter is on the gendered nature and bodily aspect of the conflict as depicted on screen. I examine how these films fit into or contravene the gender pattern of Troubles films.

Some Mother's Son and *Hunger* show a clearly gendered conflict even when they stir up traditional gender roles to some extent. *Some Mother's Son* shifts the perspective concerning the hunger strikes; while the strikes had previously been 'portrayed as a narrative of Irish male sacrifice' (Pettitt 2000: 261), George's film focuses on the struggles and sacrifices of two Northern Irish mothers. The film follows the mothers' rather active involvement in the conflict through their imprisoned Republican sons and examines the role of (Catholic) women in 'troubled' Northern Ireland. Peter Flynn (2000), in his discussion of gender roles in *Some Mother's Son*, concludes that the film 'offers a feminist recasting of nationalist female stereotypes': the suffering Irish mother, traditionally 'a symbolic, non-active figure of silent anguish is here transformed into an active agent of socio-political change.' I argue that what initially appears as a 'recasting of nationalist female stereotypes' turns out ultimately to be an endorsement of fairly conventional gender roles. In this chapter, I explore the representation of genders and gender roles in the two hunger strike films, with special attention to the portrayal of the Catholic Irish mother in *Some Mother's Son*.

Hunger deals with the same prison protest as *Some Mother's Son*, but with a very different focus. Here the Republican male inmates embody the contested nation and its geographical border, with their bodies thus functioning as the last frontier of the conflict. The male body plays a crucial role in the men's protest, in which the passive resistance so often associated with women becomes a central tool as well. Martin McLoone (1999: 29) notes that '[t]he question of women in Ireland, especially in relation to nationalism, Catholic teaching and imagery, and the discourse around women's bodies engendered by the abortion debate in Ireland' have been recurring themes in Irish film in the late 1980s and through the 1990s. While women's issues and bodies, along with masculinity in Irish films, have been discussed in critical discourse,[1] men's bodies, as displayed in Irish films, have not received much critical attention. In this chapter, I discuss the representation of the male body as a site of the conflict, the ultimate frontier, as well as the politics of the cinematic, nude male body in these films.

The 'Troubles' in Northern Ireland

Inspired by the civil rights movement in the United States, Catholic political organizers founded the Northern Ireland Civil Rights Association in 1968. The association organized protest marches demanding reforms, such as changes in housing allocation, anti-discrimination legislation and the disbanding of the B Specials, the armed and exclusively Protestant auxiliary force under the command of the similarly largely Protestant Royal Ulster Constabulary (RUC). In late 1968 and early 1969, these Catholic civil rights marches were attacked by Protestant mobs, the RUC and the B Specials, which inflamed the Catholic population. In August 1969, a Protestant parade in Derry sparked violent confrontations between Protestants and Catholics. The violence spread to Belfast and all over Ulster. Eventually, the Prime Minister of Northern Ireland had to ask London to send in troops to restore order.

The IRA was not a powerful entity at the time, but it soon reorganized itself in the face of attacks on the Catholic population. In late 1969 the IRA split into an Official and a Provisional wing, of which the former were more in favour of conventional political approaches. They were soon outnumbered by the Provos, who were Republican traditionalists and preparing for battle. In the summer of 1970, the newly elected Conservative government in Britain made concessions to Ulster Unionists, ordered curfews in Catholic areas and authorized the army to ransack and search Catholic homes for weapons. The Catholic population of Northern Ireland became disillusioned and felt attacked as a whole, further increasing the

IRA's popularity. Violent confrontations continued, and in February 1971 the IRA shot their first British soldier. In August the same year, the government introduced internment without trial in order to target the IRA. This policy did not spare the general Catholic population – Catholics with no IRA connections were also hauled in for questioning. Interrogation techniques included sensory deprivation, denial of food and sleep and the continuous playing of 'white noise' (see for example Coogan 2002). As Tim Pat Coogan (2002: 57) remarks, '[a]fter the internment blunder the Provisionals [...] went over to a new policy of not alone retaliation against the army and the Unionist government it backed, but to a war aimed at driving out the British and destroying that government'. While the British government responded to the deadly campaign as terrorism, the IRA saw their campaign in the North as a nationalist war against colonialism.

Due to the continued violence in Northern Ireland, Stormont fell in March 1972 and Northern Ireland was brought under direct British rule. In summer 1972 the first head of the Northern Ireland Office, Northern Ireland Secretary William Whitelaw, entered into secret negotiations with the IRA and made conciliatory moves. As a result, many detainees were released and 'special category status' was conceded to prisoners associated with paramilitary groups. 'Special category status' separated inmates jailed for paramilitary offences from 'ordinary decent criminals'. In effect, special category prisoners had won a sort of prisoner-of-war status. As McKittrick and McVea write, these prisoners

> responded to orders not from their warders but from their paramilitary "OC", or Officer Commanding. To a large extent they controlled their own compounds. They wore their own clothes, were not forced to work, and were allowed additional visits and parcels. (McKittrick and McVea 2000: 137–38)

In March 1976, the British Government's Northern Ireland Office instituted a policy of criminalization and withdrew the Special Category status. Thus the IRA and other paramilitary groups were denied any acknowledgement of political motivation: convicted IRA men were from then on treated as common criminals and were expected to wear prison uniforms and carry out prison work. The IRA prisoners in Long Kesh started campaigning for political-prisoner status. As J. Bowyer Bell (1993: 544) puts it, the Republican inmates saw themselves as prisoners of war,

> and to make them into criminals would also make Northern Ireland into a normal part of the United Kingdom. The argument was not really over conditions or details but over sovereignty, over the cause of the armed struggle. The Irish resistance was a public and private commitment to the reality of the Republic.

The blanket protest started in September 1976, when the first IRA man sent to Long Kesh after the ending of special category status refused to wear the prison uniform. Protesting Republican inmates wrapped themselves in blankets and were therefore kept locked in their cells. The prisoners embarked upon a 'no wash' campaign which soon escalated into a 'dirty protest'. Prisoners refused to leave their cells to wash or empty their chamber pots. Soon they started smearing their excrement on the cell walls.[2] The prison authorities then forcibly moved the inmates to steam-clean the cells and subjected the prisoners to forced baths and haircuts. Resistance was met with beatings by the guards. By 1978 there were 300 Republican prisoners 'on the blanket'. They received very little popular support, and the leadership of the IRA opposed the protest. Despite this, some of the prisoners decided to step up the protest by going on a hunger strike in 1980, and again in 1981. The newly elected Prime Minister Margaret Thatcher adopted a hard line, making it clear that she would not concede the prisoners political status. The first hunger striker to die was Bobby Sands, who passed away on 5 May 1981 – having been elected MP on the fortieth day of his hunger strike. The hunger strikers called off the protest in October 1981, following intervention by their families: once the men lapsed into a coma, the families could ask the authorities to revive them. Altogether ten men died.

The hunger strikes, gender and film

Hunger strikes have a long history, beginning from the Druids in Ireland. Coogan (2002: 28) notes that

> [d]uring the time of the Brehon laws, by which Ireland was governed prior to the coming of the Normans, one of the most telling ways to retaliate against a wrongdoer was for the affronted party to starve himself outside the guilty party's house.

W. B. Yeats, whose play about a bard's hunger strike, *The King's Threshold*, was first performed in Dublin in 1903, noted in 1922 that when he wrote the play 'neither suffragette nor patriot had adopted the hunger strike, nor had the hunger strike been used anywhere, so far as I know, as a political weapon' (Yeats 1926: 423). By the time Yeats made this comment, the situation had changed significantly: hunger strikes had become a political weapon used against oppressors by suffragist women as well as by male nationalists. While it was the former who started using hunger strikes for political purposes, it was (young) men who elevated the hunger strike to a powerful tool and a revered form of protest among Irish nationalists. During the Anglo-Irish War, Terence MacSwiney, a member of the IRA and Sinn Féin Lord Mayor of Cork, died in Brixton Prison on the seventy-fourth day of his hunger strike. MacSwiney and other prison protestors from the 1916–21 period joined canonized Fenian hero-figures from the late nineteenth century to inspire militant young Republicans.

The Republican movement has been seen as largely masculinized and the history of the Anglo-Irish conflict on the whole as generally male in character. John Hill (2006: 224) says of the conflict in Northern Ireland: 'Although it would be a mistake to ignore the role of (predominantly republican) women as perpetrators of paramilitary violence […], it is by and large male violence, and violent masculinity, that has sustained the "troubles". Indeed, nationalist movements are often masculinized projects. The fear of and anger at being 'emasculated' by colonial rule have driven many a nationalist movement, while women's issues – and oftentimes women themselves – have been relegated to the background. Cynthia Enloe (1989: 44) argues that 'nationalist movements have rarely taken women's experiences as the starting point [...] Rather, nationalism typically has sprung from masculinised memory, masculinised humiliation and masculinised hope.' Unsurprisingly then, the Republican movement, and the armed conflict between Republicans and the British/Unionists in Northern Ireland, have generally been portrayed on screen, too, as essentially male. Men, masculinity and violence have often figured centrally in these films; films focusing on women caught up in the conflict, such as Pat Murphy's *Maeve* (1982), are exceptions. Both *Maeve* and Murphy's second feature-length film, *Anne Devlin* (1984), make the point that rather than integrating women, the Republican movement allows them only a subservient position (see for example McIlroy 1993: 104; Byrne 1997: 70). Fidelma Farley (2001: 203) argues that 'the majority of films about the Troubles in Northern Ireland are concerned with male identity, particularly the relation between masculinity and violence.' Of films depicting the 1980–81 hunger strikes, *Hunger* and Les Blair's *H3* (2001) fall into the majority category, as all their main protagonists are male; *Some Mother's Son* and Maeve Murphy's *Silent Grace* (2001), in contrast, portray women and their stories. In the former two films, women play only minor and near-silent roles as mothers, wives and girlfriends. Furthermore, the male body increasingly dominates centre stage in these films; especially in *Hunger*, where the film's focus in the last phase is on the emaciated body of Bobby Sands. *Silent Grace*, on the other hand, takes as its subject Republican women prisoners who took part in the 'dirty protest' and hunger strike in Armagh jail.

Both *Some Mother's Son* and *Hunger* draw on the personal memories of the films' directors as well as on the experiences of the Republican prisoners. *Some Mother's Son* was co-written by Terry George and Jim Sheridan, makers of the controversial 1993 Northern Ireland film *In the Name of the Father*. While Sheridan directed their previous collaboration, he encouraged George, a Belfast native, to make his directorial debut with *Some Mother's Son*. In the early 1970s, George, a politicized young Catholic of nineteen who lived in a predominantly Protestant neighbourhood, was interned for several weeks. He was arrested again in 1975, when a gun was found in the possession of one of the passengers sharing a car with him. George served three years of a six-year sentence in the political status section of Long Kesh. He got to know 'many prisoners' mothers, as well as some hunger strikers who were in there at the time' (George in Crowdus and Leary 1997: 26). *Some Mother's Son* reflects some of his experiences. *Hunger* was co-written by Steve McQueen, a London-born filmmaker of Grenadan descent, and by theatre writer Enda Walsh; McQueen was eleven years old, growing up in West London, when Bobby Sands' hunger strike took place in 1981. For their script, they interviewed hunger strikers and prison officers in Northern Ireland. The hunger strike campaign had left a lasting impression on McQueen, who directed the film as his debut feature (Crowdus 2009: 22).

Despite the potentially highly political topic, both George and McQueen describe their films as non-political and essentially humanist. But while the two films share their subject, they differ greatly in their approach to depicting it. *Some Mother's Son* employs mainstream cinematic conventions, such as a linear narrative and sympathetic protagonists, and uses music to heighten the melodrama. *Hunger*, on the other hand, breaks with traditional narrative conventions especially in its soundtrack and visual techniques – something I return to below.

Gendered domains

Following the example of playwright Sean O'Casey, Troubles films, Hill (2006: 192) argues, have conventionally constructed a clear 'opposition between the public world of politics and violence (which is associated with tragedy and fatalism) and the private world of romance, home and domesticity (which is linked with the avoidance of politics and the possibility of "redemption")'. The former domain has generally been associated with men, the latter with women. This is also the case with *Some Mother's Son*. The film constructs two separate and gendered spheres, a public and political one for men and a private and domestic one for women, thus creating internal borders within the society. The former sphere affects the latter as politics and violence, both Republican and British, invade the private and traditionally feminine space of the home, drawing the largely apolitical middle-class single mother and schoolteacher Kathleen Quigley (Helen Mirren) into the male conflict.

Some Mother's Son begins with documentary footage of the newly elected Margaret Thatcher arriving at 10 Downing Street, quoting Saint Francis of Assisi: 'Where there is discord, may we bring harmony.' Thatcher's words frame the whole narrative, and their irony – the last sentence is heard as voiceover, while the image, as the caption informs us, is of a fishing boat on a lake somewhere in Northern Ireland in 1979 – is emphasized when in the next scene British troops blow up a bridge to isolate Republican communities. The action is part of the new Prime Minister's hard-line strategy against the IRA, consisting of three elements: isolation, criminalization and demoralization. While the story is set in motion by the implementation of the policy of isolation and the Republicans' violent objection to it, of the three points it is criminalization that is the main cause of controversy in this film.

While the film begins with images of the public, male world, as the work of Northern Irish fishermen is interrupted by the explosion of the bridge, Kathleen is introduced to us in her own home, emphasizing her domestic role as a single mother of three. The Troubles literally disturb the domestic sphere and disrupt the lives of women and children: we see the explosion reflected in the windows of Kathleen's kitchen and rattling the glass, behind which Kathleen's young son Liam and her grown-up daughter Alice (Geraldine O'Rawe) are also looking out (Figure 11.1). The conflict is brought into the Quigley home more directly when Kathleen's older son Gerard (Aidan Gillen), one of the aforementioned fishermen, comes home for breakfast after attending a secret IRA meeting. The other main protagonist of the

Figure 11.1: The peace of Kathleen's (Helen Mirren) home is disturbed by an explosion reflected on the window.

film, the working-class mother Annie Higgins (Fionnula Flanagan), is also introduced in a domestic environment of sorts disturbed by male politics; she is herding cows when her way is blocked by British troops. As a more political figure, Annie is involved in the struggle from the beginning, possibly because (as we later find out) British troops have killed her young son.

Unlike Kathleen, Annie is aware of her son Frankie's (David O'Hara) activities and approves of them, yet she herself mostly stays clear of the trouble. Trouble, however, finds her in her own home, after Gerard and Frankie retaliate for the destruction of the bridge by blowing up a jeep with a rocket launcher, killing a British soldier in the process. Shortly after this, the Higgins' Christmas dinner – which Gerard is also attending – is interrupted by British soldiers, who burst into the Higgins' living room in another instance of the public sphere invading the private one. Gerard and Frankie flee, gunfire ensues and in the end the young men are captured. They refuse to recognize the authority of the court, and once sentenced join the protest in the H-block, refusing to wear the prison uniform since they see themselves as prisoners of war. Annie and Kathleen, two quite different women, are united by their situation as mothers of imprisoned sons. The border between the gendered domains is blurred when the two mothers become involved in their sons' political struggle. Kathleen, however, still refuses to be politicized herself, even saying to Annie that her life would not change even if the British left. Ultimately, the women have to decide the fate of their hunger-striking sons and make difficult decisions, with a bearing on the Republican struggle.

The violent (male) conflict impacts young women's lives not only in their homes but also in their schools and workplaces. Annie's 15-year-old daughter Theresa goes to the same Catholic girls' school where Kathleen teaches. While Gerard, Frankie and other young IRA men are preparing to blow up the British troops' jeep, a group of teenage girl students are practicing traditional Irish dancing in Kathleen's classroom. The girls' feet, moving to traditional-sounding Irish music, are intercut with the explosion (Figures 11.2 and 11.3); the latter makes the classroom windows shatter and causes chaos and panic among the girls. When Gerard is subsequently convicted and jailed, Kathleen's 23-year-old daughter Alice resigns from her job in a bank; she feels that she is no longer trusted there, as the IRA has robbed the bank several times. Alice feels she cannot stay in Northern Ireland, and leaves the country. The film's Northern Ireland does not seem to have much to offer to young Catholic women: they can choose between suffering silently and accepting the traditional, domestic role of a mother, or leaving the country altogether. In these sequences, a clear contrast is again constructed between the genders. Alice's leaving Northern Ireland 'speak[s] volumes', as Brian McIlroy (2001: 80) points out, 'about the exclusion of women from this messianic-like struggle.'

The girls in Kathleen's school keep up the traditions of Ireland by dancing traditional dances; they are assigned the role of conserving, and passing on, traditional (feminized) Irish culture, whereas young men engage themselves in violent campaigns and wage war for their country. Interestingly, this particular gendered division of duties is a recurrent feature in nationalist narratives, which *Some Mother's Son* arguably is. The film's nationalist

Figure 11.2: The girls as keepers of tradition.

Figure 11.3: Frankie (David O'Hara) gets ready to blow up a British jeep in retaliation.

undercurrent can be seen in its celebration of Irish culture, old and new – the girls' dancing feet and the music by Riverdance composer Bill Whelan effectively bring traditional Irish culture to the fore, although mixed with the 1990s' commercial success of all things (or at least cultural products) Irish – but also in its gender roles. McClintock (1997: 92) writes of national narratives:

> Women are represented as the atavistic and authentic body of national tradition (inert, backward-looking, and natural), embodying nationalism's conservative principle of continuity. Men, by contrast, represent the progressive agent of national modernity (forward-thrusting, potent, and historic), embodying nationalism's progressive, or revolutionary, principle of discontinuity.

Women are expected to uphold traditions and pass them on to the next generation; in short, to keep the authentic national culture alive. Men are left with the task of bringing about progress and change and protecting the national community and its women and children, if need be with armed violence.

In *Some Mother's Son*, women also seem to enable the culture of violence by performing the traditional female role as expected. As Deniz Kandiyoti (1991: 429) argues, it is women who 'reproduce the boundaries of ethnic/national groups, who transmit the culture and who are the privileged signifiers of national difference.' The parallel images of dancing girls and armed young men attacking an 'occupying' army do emphasize the national difference of the Irish: on the one hand drawing a boundary between 'the Irish' and 'the British', on the other showing the conflict as a nationalist war against colonialism, which is how it was seen by the IRA. The dancing feet sequence was controversial and was much discussed in the Irish press. Andy White (1996: 14) noted in the *Irish Times* that the body (or the pieces of the body) of the killed British soldier are not shown, as the spectators 'will only hear the whistles of the new Celtic Dawn ushering its children over the hill of history into a new world of pipes and bodhrans and, above all, big synthesizer chords. For this is Irish Hollywood.' The implication here is that the film was targeted at (Irish-)American audiences. In this sequence, (Northern) Ireland is romanticized and political violence may seem well motivated. Films like this often arouse the fear that they might encourage fundraising for the IRA in the US. It is noteworthy, however, that despite its nationalist stance, *Some Mother's Son* does not endorse political violence but condemns it as destructive. The film is sympathetic to the cause but not to the means adopted. Significantly, though, the blame for those means is placed on the British, especially Thatcher.

When (male) politics fail to yield results – the British administrators and the leaders of the local IRA cannot come to an agreement about the terms of ending the hunger strike – Kathleen is spurred into action and saving her son. 'In this respect,' Hill (1997: 44–45) points out, '*Some Mother's Son* belongs to a longstanding tradition [...] of contrasting the "humanity" and "commonsense" of women to the unyielding and destructive fanaticism of men.' Significantly, Kathleen is drawn into politics through her role as a mother and she herself draws the line there. She does not approve of violence and is not interested in politics as such. Kathleen sees the killed British soldier as 'somebody's son like you're mine', as she says to Gerard, not as a political player or opponent. In contrast, Annie's home is political and a site where political ideology is passed on to the next generation; the Higgins home is therefore also void of redemption. In this film, the separation between the gendered domestic and political spheres is clearly desirable; this border is not supposed to be crossed. In this, *Some Mother's Son* does not differ from other Troubles films, of which Farley (2001: 204–5) writes:

> The repeated scenarios of public invasion of the private sphere in films set in Northern Ireland [...] do not signal a radical blurring of the division between the public and private spheres. Rather, what the films see as progress is the re-establishment of separate spheres, with the woman occupying her rightful place in the home as guarantor of domestic, and, by extension, social stability.

In *Some Mother's Son*, one woman above others has left her place in the home. Prime Minister Thatcher, the only woman on the British side, is presented as the unbending Iron Lady of the British Government and becomes the chief villain of the film. She is not just British and a political opponent of the protagonist; she is also a woman who, as a politician, has crossed the border between the gendered domains. This transgression results in death and destruction. Similarly, Annie's greater involvement in politics yields an unhappy outcome – the loss of her son.

Mother Ireland and her sons

As noted above, most nationalist movements – and here the Irish Republican movement is no exception – are masculinized projects, and as such have traditionally relegated women to the background or have allowed them to participate only in subservient roles. McClintock (1997: 90) argues that in nationalist movements '[w]omen are typically constructed as the symbolic bearers of the nation but are denied any direct relation to national agency'. Joanne Sharp (1996: 99) notes that '[m]any nations are figuratively female – Britannia, Marianne and Mother Russia come immediately to mind. In the national imaginary, women are mothers of the nation or vulnerable citizens to be protected.' In Ireland too, the trope of woman as nation 'has a long representational history' (Barton 2004: 113); it has been employed in literature, stage plays, films and the visual arts alike. The nation has been variously represented as Hibernia, Cathleen ni Houlihan, Shan Bhean Bhocht (Poor Old Woman) and Mother Ireland; she has been imagined as an old woman sheltering her sons in difficult times and a beautiful young woman needing help and protection from young Irish men willing to sacrifice their lives for her freedom. In particular, 'the figure of the suffering mother has a kind of iconic status' (Meaney 1998: 243) and the suffering mother was often equated with a suffering motherland. The symbolic imagining of woman as nation was partly a reaction to colonial discourse, in which British rule was represented as 'manly', while the Celtic was seen as feminine. While Englishness was equated with maleness, '[t]he cultural production of Irish Otherness [...] placed it on the feminine end of the representational spectrum' (Cullingford 1997: 159). Luke Gibbons (1996: 131) notes that 'female imagery' was used in Irish culture 'in poetry and popular protest' to turn 'the colonial stereotype against itself, positing an alternative "feminized" public sphere (imagined as a nation) against the patriarchal order of the state.' Furthermore, Irish nationalist writers 'asserted masculinity as the essential characteristic of the "Gael"' (Nash 1994: 236). The Irish nation may have been represented as woman, but women did not govern political realities in Ireland. It was men who were seen as active agents in the public domain.

In contrast to women, who are symbolic of the nation, Sharp (1996: 99) argues, '[m]en are incorporated into the nation metonymically. As the Unknown Soldier could potentially be any man who has laid down his life for his nation, the nation is embodied within each man and each man comes to embody the nation.' This is quite literally true in *Some Mother's Son* and *Hunger*: the naked, hunger-striking men not only lay down their lives for their nation, but come in fact to embody that nation in the process. Peter Flynn (2000) writes of *Some Mother's Son* that 'it is arguably the male characters – and the hunger-strikers in particular – who perform the symbolic (non-active) function of representing the nation'. I argue that in *Some Mother's Son* and *Hunger* the symbolic representation of the nation as female is replaced by a representation of the male body as embodiment of the nation and its contested geographical border. In other words, and in line with Sharp's argument, in these two films the nation is embodied rather than symbolized by the hunger-striking men. Furthermore, in contrast to the long Irish tradition of gendering landscape as feminine, in these two films it is men – Republican male prisoners – who take on the burden of embodying national geography. The bodies of these men become 'site[s] of political warfare' (McQueen in Crowdus 2009: 23), actual embodiments of the contested nation, its geographical borders and the last frontier of the struggle.

Though women had the central role of reproducing the nation's actual bodies, their own bodies and sexuality remained heavily controlled by the patriarchal order. It could still be said in the 1990s that '[t]he relationship between the female body and the idea of the nation in contemporary Ireland is central to the constitution and to the intersection of the Catholic church and the state in their control of women's reproduction' (Nash 1994: 229). Yet it is significant that motherhood was given high status in the Irish national imaginary. Conn Holohan (2010: 66) notes that 'the nationalist elevation of the female to the role of symbolic embodiment of the nation was realised in the person of the Irish mother'. Womanhood was almost reduced to motherhood, for as Holohan (2010: 70) remarks, 'the dominant image of womanhood within Irish [...] culture for the majority of the twentieth century was an idealised, desexualised motherhood.' The image of Mother Ireland was especially strong. Ruth Barton (2004: 114) writes that in Irish culture,

[t]he mother figure is alternately and simultaneously, Mother Ireland and the Virgin Mary, devoted and a-sexual, her own desires subsumed into the maternal. At the same time, she dominates the domestic space, often dislodging the emasculated male as head of the family.

In accordance with this, many Northern Ireland films have had strong and influential mothers. As Hill (2006: 237) puts it: 'Despite the critique to which the imagery of "mother Ireland" has been subject, the figure of the Catholic Irish mother has nonetheless continued to carry a strong resonance for recent Northern Ireland films.' *Some Mother's Son* is no exception to this tradition: its protagonists are strong Catholic mothers, devoted and asexual. Significantly though, and in contrast to most other 'Troubles' films, which have rarely focused on women, *Some Mother's Son* assigns the central roles to these two mothers and highlights their plight rather than that of the IRA men. Nevertheless, as shown in the very title of the film, the two women are first and foremost mothers and are presented in that role alone; even their political activism, in itself counter-traditional, serves only that role. Motherhood also subsumes any other possible aspects of womanhood. Even though the film offers a new gender focus, women are thus still cast in conventional gender roles.

While Kathleen and Annie in many ways fit the image of the traditional, strong, Catholic Irish mother trying to protect her children, the sons' fathers are largely absent. Gerard's father is actually dead, and Kathleen does not have a new man in her life. Frankie's father is seen in only one or two scenes, an old man leaning on his cane – he is in fact described in the screenplay as 'prematurely old, sickly' (George and Sheridan 1996: 42); he lets Annie run the household and Frankie take care of the politics. He makes no decisions, not even about whether or not Frankie should be saved. In contrast to strong and influential mother figures, Northern Ireland films often have absent, weak and/or ineffectual fathers, echoing a historical situation. The dominant position of the mother in the domestic sphere 'has been ascribed to a post-Famine tradition of Church domination whereby the priest won control of the household through his alliance with the mother [...] and, equally, to a history of failed revolutions' (Barton 2004: 114, see also Kiberd 1996: 380). In Troubles films, fathers and father-figures are central in passing on the violence from one generation to the next. Yet in these films, as Fidelma Farley (2001: 203) writes,

> the fathers themselves are very often absent, and those who are present are weak and ineffectual, unable to provide their sons with an effective and appropriate (i.e. non-violent) model of masculine authority. The only route for young men to the acquisition of masculine authority is through violence.

The sons in *Some Mother's Son* seem to hold fast to the cause and to political violence in their quest to achieve the masculine agency which the presence of the colonial power has denied them. When violence against the colonial oppressor is no longer possible, the young men resort to extraordinary measures and embark on a hunger strike. The male prisoners gain masculine authority, and control of the situation, by carrying the struggle against the British government and Prime Minister Thatcher to the last border, the body.

For a woman, taking a political and active role seems to have negative consequences, as shown by the cases of Annie and Theresa. The film seems to be saying that obstinacy, at least in women, is destructive and ultimately fatal. These two women are obstinate and cross the gendered domestic/political divide. Their actions, such as Theresa's defiant slowing down in crossing the road while British tanks and jeeps are waiting to use the road, are politically motivated. Barton (1999: 45) remarks that 'gender roles in the Troubles dramas have tended towards the conventional. The males are seen to be torn between conforming to and escaping from violence, while the female figures represent reason and conscience.' *Some Mother's Son* may show male gender roles as more flexible than some other Northern Ireland films, but proposes a fairly conventional gender role for those females who are less domestic and more political. They suffer from the consequences of their actions. Annie and Theresa's active resistance and their belief in the Republican cause mean that they eventually lose Frankie, since Annie cannot interfere with her unconscious son's hunger strike but has to let him die for the sake of their shared beliefs. Kathleen plays on the side of 'reason and conscience' and actually makes the decision to take her son off the hunger strike when it becomes possible on account of Gerard's slipping into unconsciousness. Having made this decision, 'Kathleen looks back over her shoulder and you get this sort of Mother Ireland sense of Annie being left with her daughter' as Terry George himself puts it (George in Crowdus and Leary 1997: 26). While Kathleen sides with reason and acts solely out of motherly concerns, thus saving her son, Annie takes on the symbolic role of Mother Ireland. She acts out of political motivation and therefore loses her son. Annie and Theresa are left mourning, whereas Kathleen can return to her domestic role as mother of three; even her daughter has returned home.

The display of the protesting male body

For nearly two decades there has been increasing interest in the representation of masculinity and male bodies on screen. The dominant approach, however, has been psychoanalytical; as Robert Davis and Tim Maloney (2009: 112) suggest, the focus has been less on 'what is actually on screen – including characters, their bodies, and their bodies' disposition in the overall mise-en-scene – than on […] the subjective experience of the spectator.' Current film theories concerning the male body often emphasize sexuality, desire or the viewer's pleasure in gazing at a male, but these approaches do not seem the most useful ones in examining the display of the male body in *Some Mother's Son* and *Hunger*. Here I look at the representation of the male body, of 'what is actually on the screen', in these two films. In 1993, Peter Lehman (1993: 172) noted that

> [n]arrative cinema in Japan and the United States (and indeed elsewhere) conventionally avoids showing the nude male. In the few exceptions, the nude male is usually involved in action (e.g. running or wrestling) or the view of his genitals is obstructed through the careful placement of objects in the composition.

More than a decade later, male nudity may not be quite so rare on screen – Lehman (2001: 38) notes that even 'the taboo against showing the penis is crumbling'; but films like *Hunger*, which display nude male bodies in realist, non-sexual, non-voyeuristic manner, yet directly and without trying to hide any body parts, are still fairly uncommon. Cinematic cultures differ greatly from each other in this respect, and as Lee Parpart (2001: 172) points out, 'the European art film has tended to enjoy a greater comfort level with displays of the nude male body than is generally found in Hollywood film.' In *Hunger*, a European art film, the naked male body is shown in context, naturally as it were, as it would exist in these inhuman prison conditions. McQueen does not feel the need to cover up the actors in blankets or restrict the camera's view to the upper body at points where the prisoners' naked bodies are integral to the story, but shows the inmates in their state of nakedness.

Significantly, *Hunger*, although it presents a naked male body, disrupts its erotic potential by the excessive realism with which the film is shot. The stench of excreta and rotting food, the sight of the unwashed bodies, the very real sense of the beatings and violence inside the prison – all these factors eat away at the eroticism of the candidly portrayed naked male body (Figure 11.4). Gary Crowdus (2009: 22) describes Steve McQueen's short films and videos from the early 2000s as 'semi-documentary in format'. Crowdus notes that the films aim at 'conveying a participatory, sensory experience of their subjects.' Similarly, *Hunger* offers viewers a head-on sensory experience of the protest. The sparse use of dialogue and music also serves this purpose. McQueen himself says that he 'wanted to have a movie where more or less the first forty minutes is in silence, so the viewer's other senses would come to the fore. (McQueen in Crowdus 2009: 24). The excessively realistic depiction of the protest, the camera's lingering on the naked male body and bodily fluids immerse the

Figure 11.4: Bobby Sands (Michael Fassbender) is taken to a forcible bath in *Hunger*.

spectators in a near-physical experience: in addition to hearing and seeing, the audience can imagine the smells in the prison, along with the pain inflicted on the prisoners by the guards and by the inmates themselves.

The only exception to the sparing use of dialogue is a 22-minute-long scene in the middle of the film, in which Bobby Sands (Michael Fassbender) informs a priest (Liam Cunningham) of his decision to go on a hunger strike. This scene is central in casting a critical light on the forthcoming hunger strike. The nationalist tradition of the celebration of blood sacrifice is questioned when the decision to go on hunger strike is depicted as tinged with stubbornness, pride and self-aggrandizement. In *Hunger*, the IRA prisoners' intransigence is shown shorn of heroism, the hunger strike stripped of honour and glory. Even the election of Sands as MP is curiously ignored. Sands is shown merely as a man who carries the battle to the extreme, and this perhaps for selfish reasons. His naked body becomes the last terrain where the battle is fought, and the camera follows meticulously how this particular embodiment of the nation falls apart.

Furthermore, and perhaps more importantly even, the excessive realism debunks the iconic images traditionally associated with the men's sacrifice – as Emilie Pine notes, 'the Christ-like images of protesting male prisoners, with heavy beards and long hair, wearing only a blanket' have dominated the remembrance of the hunger strikes (Pine 2011: 109). Unlike *Some Mother's Son* which uses verbal descriptions by Gerard instead of visual imagery, *Hunger* documents the whole bodily protest very carefully: from 'no wash' to living in a cell daubed with excrement and awash with urine, from beatings of the naked body to close-ups of the bed sores on Bobby Sands' back (Figure 11.5), and on to the final emaciation of the body.

The excessive reality of the film is evident here, too: Fassbender actually lost more than 23 kilograms for the last third of the film. He lived on berries and nuts for ten weeks,

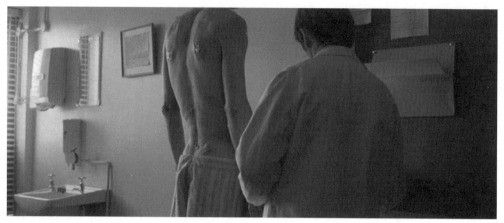

Figure 11.5: Hunger-striking Sands is weighed in in *Hunger*.

surviving the last four weeks on 600 calories a day (Maher 2008). The naked men sitting in dirty cells smeared with excrement and the actual emaciated body of the actor playing Sands (Figure 11.6) with cropped, gingerish hair – accurately depicted, in fact, as 'Sands had his hair and beard cut on the first day of his strike' (Pine 2011: 116) – disrupt the sanitised, iconic image of the hunger strikers. *Hunger* does forge a more traditional visual link between the sacrificial body of Christ and the body of Bobby Sands, however, when Sands is depicted in a position not unlike Christ on the cross. Significantly, this serves more as an acknowledgement of the tradition of depicting the protesters as Christ-like – yet without reverting to the iconic imagery of bearded, long-haired men – than as a continuance of that tradition. In contrast to the unresisting Christ, the naked and beaten-up Sands has forcefully

Figure 11.6: The emaciated body of Bobby Sands (Fassbender) in *Hunger*.

resisted a forcible haircut and bath before being carried in this position by the guards. When Sands then later on moves to passive resistance and hunger-striking, his decision is shown to be informed also by reasons other than self-sacrifice.

In contrast, *Some Mother's Son* to some extent reproduces the iconic images of the hunger strikers. When Gerard enters the prison, the inmates in the wing are 'on the blanket' and thus half-naked. Gerard shares a cell with Bobby Sands (John Lynch) who already has long hair and beard; as Gerard actually says in the film, he looks like Jesus Christ (Figure 11.7). Pine interprets Gerard's comment as 'a self-conscious acknowledgement of the Christ-like image generated by the blanketmen' (Pine 2011: 108). Terry George, who was 'criticised for mythologising Bobby Sands, for having one of the characters say "you look like Jesus Christ"', defended himself by saying: 'that was the reality of the situation. We've all seen the photographs, and they looked like that' (George in Linehan 1996: 11). However, in *Some Mother's Son* Sands continues to have long dark hair and beard until the end. At the moment of his death, his body is covered by a blanket up to the chin and only his pale, sunken face and dark hair is visible, framed by a pillow. Even if George was not aware of Sands cutting his hair when going on the hunger strike, the prisoners and strikers' Christ-like portrayal is not coincidental. George has said in an interview (Crowdus & O'Mara 1997: 25): 'A lot of the rural prisoners were very religious. They were all Catholic, and steeped in this sense of self-sacrifice – you know, the Christian thing of Christ giving himself up on the cross.' The prisoners, in particular Bobby Sands, are accordingly depicted as 'steeped in this sense of self-sacrifice' in *Some Mother's Son*. Sands does not have much

Figure 11.7: Bobby Sands (John Lynch) in *Some Mother's Son*.

screen time, but his almost mythological presence is felt throughout the latter part of the film. The iconic image of the long-haired, bearded and half-naked hunger strikers is left intact, and this is done mainly by shying away from the naked male bodies rather than examining or showing them.

As Jennie Carlsten (2007: 239–40) points out, in *Some Mother's Son* the starving bodies of the hunger strikers are largely absent from the screen: the protesters are covered in blankets most of the time. And while *Hunger* zooms in on the suffering male bodies, especially that of Bobby Sands, *Some Mother's Son* 'is remarkably restrained in its treatment of the actual physical debilitation of the hunger strikers themselves,' as McLoone (2000: 76) notes. Terry George (1996: 15) explains that the filmmakers left out 'the dismembered bodies of soldiers', 'the blanket protesters being wire brushed' and 'the maggots and lice in the cells' – shown by McQueen twelve years later – because 'films have boundaries'. Even without these images, *Some Mother's Son* was initially given an over-18 certificate, although this was later reduced by the Appeal Board. As Carlsten (2007: 240) notes, in George's film '[t]he death of Bobby Sands is depicted as symbolic rather than intimate and is intercut with scenes of a crowd outside the prison standing in vigil.' Thus the emphasis is 'on the reception of the event' rather than the event itself. I argue that this, too, continues to uphold the mythical status of the hunger strikers as something more than ordinary, mortal men.

Suffering (post)colonial male bodies

As a film focusing on male bodies, *Hunger* both resembles and differs from such 'body genres' as the action film and the male epic. Leon Hunt (1993: 69) has identified such features in male epics as 'insistence on violent spectacle, physical punishment and a contemplation of the male body'. *Hunger* shares in these, although the prisoners in the film are closer to lean, mean fighting machines than the usual buffed-up bodies of male epics. As the body genres, *Hunger* presents scantily clad (and even naked) male bodies, physical punishment as well as violent spectacles – some of them quiet ones as the close-ups show the starving male body wasting away. In such masculinist genres as the Western, the violence suffered by the male protagonist is a central part of the audience's experience. Paul Willemen (1981: 16) writes of Anthony Mann's Westerns that '[t]he viewer's experience is predicated on [...] the unquiet pleasure of seeing the male mutilated [...] and restored through violent brutality.' In *Hunger*, the physical pain of the prisoners does not encourage even unquiet pleasure in the audience but rather the realism of the film causes the spectators to feel the prisoners' pain. These scenes of suffering 'are not masochistic in that they encourage sympathy and or the experience of pain *per se* rather than pleasure in the audience' (Edwards 2008: 161).

Although pleasure is far removed from what is presented on screen in *Hunger*, there is a certain element of masochism involved in the hunger strikers' actions. Tim Edwards (2008: 161) suggests that 'masochism in movies' could be defined 'as the depiction of pain and or suffering as in some way positive, beneficial or pleasurable to the sufferer or audience.'[3] The prisoners' protest and hunger strike, though not pleasurable, are voluntary, willingly taken on, and they are depicted as something the prisoners think their cause can benefit from even when the IRA leadership disapproves. Attainment of personal glory may be part of the motivation, as Sands' dialogue with the priest reveals. Edwards (2008: 175) argues that

[t]he key defining feature of male masochism as it is presented in filmic media is that it is spectacle – set up to be looked at and to encourage emotional engagement, of whatever kind, and in some more particular cases to be quite spectacularly extreme.

In *Hunger*, the audience is invited to look and engage emotionally as the protesting and resisting male body is set up as spectacle; the spectacle first focuses on the actively resistant male body that makes forcible baths and mirror searches more difficult, and then on the quiet, passive suffering, hunger-striking male body slowly advancing towards death. Though slow and quiet, the death is 'spectacularly extreme'.

The spectacle of masochism is closely connected to the construction of masculinity in many films, especially of the body genres. Edwards (2008: 169) argues that

[c]lassical Hollywood movies, and particularly the [male] epics of the late 1950s, such as *Spartacus* and *Ben-Hur*, in many ways centrally and fundamentally construct masculinity around *heroism* which is then in turn dependent upon suffering, endurance and the spectacle of masochism for its resolution into happiness.

Interestingly, suffering, endurance and possibly even the spectacle of masochism are part of the mythology of militant Irish Republicanism. The canonized IRA hunger striker from the Anglo-Irish War, Terence MacSwiney, famously formulated in 1920: 'Victory is not won by those who can inflict the most, but by those who can endure the most.' In *Hunger*, however, the men construct their masculinity directly around suffering, endurance and the spectacle of masochism, which does not amount to heroism. The resolution into happiness is perhaps therefore also lacking.

In discussing filmic constructions of masculinity, Kirkham and Thumim note the

constant tension between control by the individual of his body (hence his identity) and the control by others (by those with access to power) of the individual's body – thus rendering it passive, subject. This tension is played out *on* the body, on its surface. (Kirkham and Thumim 1993: 25)

The hunger strikers in both films, and especially Sands in *Hunger*, are trying to break the prison's hold on their body, and thus also the British government's. Where action cinema emphasizes 'masculinity as performance' (Tasker 1993: 230), especially the latter part of

Hunger focuses on the inmates' inaction. The prisoners are committed to an active protest, which they execute in a highly disciplined manner, using passive resistance involving their bodies; it is here that the tension, the struggle, is played out, nowhere more than on Sands' body and skin at the end of both *Some Mother's Son* and *Hunger*. Nakedness might signal vulnerability and lack of authority; but in *Hunger* nakedness becomes a source of strength because it is voluntary. In prison where the inmates are required to wear uniform, wearing no clothes is an assertion of the individual's control over and politicization of their own body. Given the colonial connection and the older representation of the British as manly and the Celtic as feminine (see for example Cullingford 1997: 160; Meaney 1998: 246), the struggle for control of the prisoners' bodies is also a struggle for masculinity and for the control of Northern Ireland itself. Interestingly, the Republican prisoners prove their masculinity ultimately by using feminine methods (traditionally associated with the colonized). Especially in *Hunger,* Sands is shown to long to be a full man in the face of his oppressors, the British; this becomes evident when a childhood experience, of himself discovering his ability to lead and to bear the consequences of his actions, he has recounted to the priest is revisited when Sands is approaching the end of his life. With the hunger strike Sands longs to demonstrate his leadership qualities and endurance, which are central to his construction of masculinity.

On the one hand, these prisoners are specifically Irish fighters, who, unlike many an Irish man in British films, are highly controlled and not at all whimsical or unpredictably violent. In contrast to the British images of the 1970s IRA men as gangsters or simian-like brutes, the men in these hunger strike films display extraordinary bodily control. Regular exercise and hunger-striking point to the 'true' masculinity of these Irish men. On the other hand, *Hunger* is not political as such: the precise context, although meticulously depicted, does not matter. These men are universal soldiers, fighters against a (neo)colonial power. Even though the film faithfully follows the events of the conflict and shows everything very realistically – or perhaps precisely for that reason – it raises the themes to a more universal level. The naked male body symbolizes everyman, man in general. Stripped of clothes, shorn of identity symbols, these men become universal soldiers fighting for their country, their beliefs, their freedom. Clothes are a marker of identity; the prisoners' nakedness erases their identities, turning them into everymen, universal soldiers. Viewed today, it also reminds viewers of the real-life news and images of such places as Abu Ghraib or Guantánamo. The guards are intransigent and inhuman in their own way, unmovable even, their orders coming from the (invisible) government. People get destroyed and trampled on on both sides in the name of states, borders, governments. The film underlines the brutalizing and dehumanizing effect of the prison situation on both guards and prisoners. The guards' treatment of the prisoners is depicted to the audience as shameful and appalling. Yet at the same time, the IRA is shown killing the guards brutally; one of them is killed in front of his mother in a nursing home. Violence and atrocities are thus shown as being in a kind of balance of terror. There are no victors or heroes here.

Conclusion

Both *Some Mother's Son* and *Hunger* portray the Republican protest and hunger strikes of the late 1970s and early 1980s as strongly gendered. As has become traditional in Troubles drama, there is a separation in these films between the public and male world of politics and violence and the private and female world of home and domesticity. George's film offers a fresh cinematic perspective on the Troubles in Northern Ireland by depicting the conflict from women's point of view. The gender roles in the film, however, are fairly conventional. The two mothers are hurled into the public sphere of politics and violence through their sons. Though ostensibly a new configuration, the film does not ultimately broaden or alter traditional gender roles. The two main protagonists are first and foremost mothers; while both of them get involved in the political struggle, nothing good comes out of it. The fundamentally apolitical mother Kathleen makes her decision to save her son on the basis of emotions and humanism; Annie, on the other hand, who is influenced by ideology and politics, consequently loses her son. While Kathleen can return to her domestic role with all her children alive, Annie, a kind of Mother Ireland figure, has now lost two sons to the struggle and is left grieving in the masculine world of politics. The film signals that women should occupy the domestic space of home and not get too involved in politics.

McQueen's film focuses on the world of men, one of (universal) violence and masculinity. The male body takes centre stage in *Hunger,* compelling spectators to have a full-on sensory experience. The young men in these films operate in the domain of the public and political; ultimately they carry the political battle to the extreme, the terrain of their body, fighting on the last frontier. The negotiation and construction of masculinity is played out in the spectacle of the male body. Significantly, men are given more variety and space in their gender role than women. The hunger strike might be seen as a feminine, passive means of starving and harming oneself, and in fact it was women who first used it for political purposes in Ireland; but it is depicted in the films as broadening the men's role. Rather than portraying women as symbolic of the nation, *Some Mother's Son* and *Hunger* cast men as embodying the nation and its contested border. The political battle is then fought on the site of their body. Change is also encouraged: the violent activities of men are not endorsed but condemned.

Some Mother's Son and *Hunger* – made, interestingly, by Irish and Black British filmmakers – can be read as postcolonial films. They depict a conflict which one side, the IRA, saw as a nationalist war against colonialism. *Some Mother's Son* was made during the Peace Process, at a time when the conflict was still alive. *Hunger* came out a decade after the Good Friday Agreement and was made in the very different post-9/11 world. *Hunger* is more universal in its storytelling, and is as much about current world events as it is about Northern Ireland in the early 1980s. It has much less in common with other Troubles films than the more conventional *Some Mother's Son*. The 'blanket' and 'dirty' protests and the hunger strikes are represented as postcolonial, 'feminine' methods of standing up against powerful masculinist state or foreign forces. Violence, whether active or passive, directed against others or oneself, is shown to corrupt, brutalize and dehumanize. The message in both these films is that masculinity needs to be constructed on a different basis and borders drawn in something other than blood.

References

Barton, R. (1999), 'Feisty Colleens and Faithful Sons: Gender in Irish Cinema', *Cineaste*, 24: 2–3, pp. 40–45.

———— (2004), *Irish National Cinema*, London and New York: Routledge.

Bell, J. B. (1993), *The Irish Troubles: A Generation of Violence, 1967-1992*, New York: St. Martin's Press.

Byrne, T. (1997), *Power in the Eye: An Introduction to Contemporary Irish Film*, Lanham, Md. & London: The Scarecrow Press.

Carlsten, J. (2007), 'Mourning and solidarity: The commemorative models of *Some Mother's Son* and *H3*', in B. McIlroy (ed.), *Genre and Cinema: Ireland and Transnationalism*, New York and London: Routledge, pp. 233–44.

Coogan, T. P. (2002), *On the Blanket: The Inside Story of the IRA Prisoners' "Dirty" Protest*, New York: Palgrave MacMillan.

Crowdus, G. (2009), 'The Human Body as Political Weapon: An Interview with Steve McQueen', *Cineaste*, 34: 2, pp. 22–25.

Crowdus, G. & Leary, O. (1997), 'The "Troubles" He's Seen in Northern Ireland: An Interview with Terry George', *Cineaste*, 23: 1, pp. 24–29.

Cullingford, E. B. (1997), 'Gender, Sexuality and Englishness in Modern Irish Drama and Film', in A. Bradley and M. G. Valiulis (eds), *Gender and Sexuality in Modern Ireland*, University of Massachusetts Press, pp. 159–86.

Davis, R. and Maloney T. (2009), 'Tran Anh Hung's Body Poetry', in S. Fouz-Hernández (ed.), *Mysterious Skin: Male Bodies in Contemporary Cinema*, London and New York: I. B. Tauris, pp. 111–25.

Edwards, T. (2008), 'Spectacular Pain: Masculinity, Masochism and Men in the Movies', in V. Burr and J. Hearn (eds), *Sex, Violence and the Body: The Erotics of Wounding*, Houndmills, Basingstoke, Hampshire: Palgrave Macmillan, pp. 157–76.

Enloe, C. (1989), *Bananas, Beaches and Bases: Making Feminist Sense of International Politics*, London: Pandora.

Farley, F. (2001), 'In the Name of the Family: Masculinity and Fatherhood in Contemporary Northern Irish Films', *Irish Studies Review*, 9: 2, pp. 203–13.

Flynn, P. (2000), 'Some Mother's Son: Post-Colonial, Post-National... Post-Historical?', *Bright Lights Film Journal*, 29, http://www.brightlightsfilm.com/29/somemothersson.php. Accessed 2 March 2011.

George, T. (1996), 'Some Mother's Son', *The Irish Times*, Letters to the Editor, 1 October 1996, p. 15.

George, T. and Sheridan J. (1996), *Some Mother's Son: The Screenplay*, New York: Grove Press.

Hill, J. (1997), 'Some Mother's Son', *Cineaste*, 23: 1, pp. 44–45.

—— (2006), *Cinema and Northern Ireland: Film, Culture, Politics,* London: BFI Publishing.

Holohan, C. (2010), *Cinema on the Periphery: Contemporary Irish and Spanish Cinema,* Dublin and Portland, OR: Irish Academic Press.

Hunt, L. (1993), 'What Are Big Boys Made of? *Spartacus, El Cid* and the Male Epic', in P. Kirkham and J. Thumim (eds), *You Tarzan: Masculinity, Movies and Men,* London: Lawrence & Wishart, pp. 65–83.

Kandiyoti, D. (1991), 'Identity and Its Discontents: Women and the Nation', *Millennium – Journal of International Studies,* 20: 3, pp. 429–43.

Kiberd, D. (1996), *Inventing Ireland: The Literature of the Modern Nation,* London: Vintage.

Kirkham, P. and Thumim, J. (1993), 'You Tarzan', in P. Kirkham and J. Thumim (eds), *You Tarzan: Masculinity, Movies and Men,* London: Lawrence and Wishart, pp. 11–26.

Lehman, P. (1993), *Running Scared: Masculinity and the Representation of the Male Body,* Philadelphia: Temple University Press.

—— (2001), 'Crying over the Melodramatic Penis: Melodrama and Male Nudity in Films of the 90s', in P. Lehman (ed.), *Masculinity: Bodies, Movies, Culture,* New York: Routledge, pp. 25–41.

Linehan, H. (1996), '"There's no such thing as an unbiased film"', *The Irish Times,* 13 September, p. 11.

Maher, K. (2008), 'Steve McQueen's Hunger: featuring one of cinema's greatest ever scenes', *The Times,* 9 October 2008, http://entertainment.timesonline.co.uk/tol/arts_and_entertainment/film/london_film_festival/article4908509.ece. Accessed 3 April 2011.

McClintock, A. (1997), '"No Longer in a Future Heaven": Gender, Race, and Nationalism', in A. McClintock, A. Mufti and E. Shohat (eds), *Dangerous Liaisons: Gender, Nation, & Postcolonial Perspectives,* Minneapolis: University of Minnesota Press, pp. 89–112.

McIlroy, B. (1993), 'The Repression of Communities: Visual Representations of Northern Ireland during the Thatcher Years', in L. Friedman (ed.), *British Cinema and Thatcherism: Fires Were Started,* London: UCL Press, pp. 92–108.

—— (2001), *Shooting to Kill: Filmmaking and the "Troubles" in Northern Ireland,* (revised and updated first Canadian edition), Richmond B. C.: Steveston Press.

McKittrick, D. and McVea, D. (2000), *Making Sense of the Troubles,* Belfast: The Blackstaff Press.

McLoone, M. (1999), 'Reimagining the Nation: Themes and Issues in Irish Cinema', *Cineaste,* 24: 2–3, pp. 28–34.

—— (2000), *Irish Film: The Emergence of a Contemporary Cinema,* London: British Film Institute.

Meaney, G. (1998), 'Landscapes of Desire: Women and Ireland on Film', *Women: A Cultural Review,* 9: 3, pp. 237–51.

Nash, C. (1994), 'Remapping the Body/Land: New Geographies of Identity, Gender, and Landscape in Ireland', in A. Blunt and G. Rose (eds), *Writing Women and Space: Colonial and Postcolonial Geographies,* New York and London: The Guildford Press, pp. 227–50.

Parpart, L. (2001), 'The Nation and the Nude: Colonial Masculinity and the Spectacle of the Male Body in Recent Canadian Cinema(s)', in P. Lehman (ed.), *Masculinity: Bodies, Movies, Culture,* New York: Routledge, pp. 167–92.

Pettitt, L. (2000), *Screening Ireland: Film and Television Representation,* Manchester and New York: Manchester University Press.

Pine, E. (2011), *The Politics of Irish Memory: Performing Remembrance in Contemporary Irish Culture*. Houndmills, Basingstoke, Hampshire: Palgrave Macmillan.

Sharp, J. P. (1996), 'Gendering Nationhood: A feminist engagement with national identity', in N. Duncan (ed.), *Bodyspace: Destabilizing Geographies of Gender and Sexuality*, London and New York: Routledge, pp. 97–108.

Tasker, Y. (1993), 'Dumb Movies for Dumb People: Masculinity, the Body and the Voice in Contemporary Action Cinema', in S. Cohan and I. R. Hark (eds), *Screening the Male: Exploring Masculinities in Hollywood Cinema*, London and New York: Routledge, pp. 230–44.

White, A. (1996), 'Those Riverdance Feet', *The Irish Times*, 25 September, p. 14.

Willemen, P. (1981), 'Anthony Mann: Looking at the Male', *Framework*, 15–17, p. 16.

Yeats, W. B. (1926), *Plays in Prose and Verse*, London: Macmillan and Co.

Notes

1   Examples of writing on the representation of gender in Irish film are Barton, R. (1999), 'Feisty Colleens and Faithful Sons: Gender in Irish Cinema', *Cineaste*, 24: 2–3, pp. 40–45; Cullingford, E. (2001), *Ireland's Others: Ethnicity and Gender in Irish Literature and Popular Culture*, Cork: Cork University Press in association with Field Day; Edge, S. (1995), '"Women are Trouble, Did You Know that Fergus?": Neil Jordan's *The Crying Game*', *Feminist Review*, 50, pp. 173–86; Edge, S. (1998), 'Representing gender and national identity', in D. Miller (ed.), *Rethinking Northern Ireland*, Longman, pp. 211–27; Farley, F. (2001), 'In the Name of the Family: Masculinity and Fatherhood in Contemporary Northern Irish Films', *Irish Studies Review*, 9: 2, pp. 203–13; Gibbons, L. (1996), *Transformations in Irish Culture*, (Critical Conditions, Field Day Essays), Cork: Cork University Press in association with Field Day; Gibbons, L. (1997), 'Engendering the State: Narrative, Allegory, and *Michael Collins*', *Eire-Ireland*, 31: 3–4, pp. 261–69; Morgan, E. (1998), 'Ireland's Lost Action Hero: *Michael Collins*, a Secret History of Irish Masculinity', *New Hibernia Review*, 2: 1, pp. 26–62; Negra, D. (2009), 'Irishness, Anger and Masculinity in Recent Film and Television', in R. Barton (ed.), *Screening Irish-America: Representing Irish-America in Film and Television*, Dublin and Portland, OR: Irish Academic Press.

2   Tim Pat Coogan (2002: 94) writes that it was the guards that initiated the dirty protest by returning the blanket men's piss pots half full or even overturning them on the floor. The inmates then started throwing their slops out the window and later daubing them on the wall. (See also Bell 1993: 548–49).

3   Edwards (2008: 161) admits that '[t]his is of course a broad definition that opens up many questions concerning intention and interpretation.'

Chapter 12

Heartlands and Borderlands: *El Dorado* and the Post-Franco Spanish Cinema as a Bridgehead between Europe and Latin America

Petteri Halin
University of Turku

Commemorative events, such as the bicentennial anniversaries of the French Revolution in 1989 or that of the birth of the United States of America in 1976, are often devised to generate a sense of participation for individuals and to stimulate economic benefits for event-organizing communities. In order to create something worth celebrating, these commemorative events are more often than not crafted to fill irritating gaps in the historical record or to gloss over dull ambiguities and complexities; if needed, they rely on historical amnesia or distorted interpretations of the past. In the 1989 French celebrations, for example, liberty, equality and brotherhood were hailed as national virtues and bloodshed was represented as the crime of only a few. As a result, these commemorative pasts often appear as offensively romanticized 'Disneyland' stories, as interpretations of spectacle and nostalgia (e.g. Linenthal 1994: 986–91). However, as the past has demonstrated, history does not provide celebratory events alone.

If commemorations of past events reveal the applauded and heralded principles on which nations, societies and communities rest and strengthen their bonds, and if commemorating the past can create pride and confidence in the future and provide a more tolerant understanding of the present, is it possible or even appropriate to celebrate failure, destruction and disaster? Is it appropriate to commemorate, for example, the beginning of a great war? The year 1992 marked the five-hundredth anniversary of Christopher Columbus's voyage of 1492, the Columbian quincentennial. Prior to the quincentennial, there was no shortage of academic commentary on the significance of this historical milestone. For many academic historians (for instance Paolo Emilio Taviani 1991 and Felipe Fernández-Armesto 1991), it represented a landmark in human history, as the anniversary of the voyage that set drastic changes in motion. For many other historians (such as Kirkpatrick Sale 1990 and Hans Koning 1991), the year marked, among other calamities, the beginning of Native American depopulation and destruction and the exploitation of the western Hemisphere (for a summary of this critical approach, see Ramirez 1992: 56–62; Simon 1993: 73–88). Outside academia the debate was even more heated, on both sides.

With the approach of the Columbian quincentennial, official jubilee organizations were established in several countries, the most important of such bodies being those in Spain, Italy and the United States. Many of these state-orchestrated preparations were fuelled by social, political and economic forces (Fields 1988: 1–14). In Spain the Columbian quincentennial project was marked by a series of spectacular events, including the Barcelona Olympic

Games and the Seville World Fair. These monumental undertakings secured international visibility for Spain, placing the country in the international spotlight. One of the main Spanish contributions came in the form of the feature film and historical spectacle *El Dorado* (Carlos Saura, 1988), which was an early start in the series of grand international commemorative events. Why this early start? And why was this particular event chosen to celebrate the Spanish experience in the Americas? In this chapter I explore the Spanish *Quinto Centenario* commemoration agenda and its manifestation in *El Dorado*, as well as in other celebratory events, within the broader framework of the international campaign waged by Spain over many years to improve the country's image. I examine, for instance, the relationship between *El Dorado*, the post-Franco Spanish rebranding project and Spain's commitment in Latin America. I demonstrate that, while it was a sensitive subject, *El Dorado* was an integral element in the range of worldwide Spanish commemoration practices, tailored to celebrate the five-hundredth anniversary of Christopher Columbus's maiden voyage to the western Hemisphere and to reconnect Spain back to the Latin Americas.

The past as a commodity

With the Columbian quincentennial, politicized commentaries and biographies with clear-cut ideological agendas proliferated. Relying on early critical accounts of Spanish atrocities in the Americas, Native Americans in particular saw the Columbus-worshipping and commemorative jubilee preparations as an insult (Ramirez 1992: 56–62). At the core of the term *la leyenda negra*, the Black Legend (Juderías 1914), is the stereotype of the cruel, rapacious, self-serving Spaniard. In this narrative, Spaniards were characterized as inherently barbaric, corrupt and intolerant, in love with cruelty and bloodshed. The essence of this Black Legend held that the black-hearted Spanish conquistadors, disregarding human lives, treated the native American population with unspeakable cruelty, decimating their numbers in warfare and harsh slavery, and thus despoiling the true earthly Eden of the Indies. These early demonizing attempts relied on the work by Bartolomé de las Casas, *Brevísima relación de la destrucción de las Indias* (1552). Especially the de Bry engravings from the late sixteenth century established the Black Legend as part of the contemporary European imagination. While present-day scholars regard the Black Legend mainly as politically motivated propaganda, designed to impugn Spain's right to her colonies and to incite animosity against Spanish rule, it has remained alive (e.g. Powell 1971). In this heated quincentennial climate, the official Spanish celebrations were a provocative but more or less obligatory undertaking for Spain.

In comparison to other quincentennial commemorative national programmes, the Spanish *Quinto Centenario* project was the first to be established, the most expensive, and in terms of its accomplishments the most productive and successful (Summerhill and Williams 2000: 127). *The Comisión Quinto Centenario del Descubrimiento de América* was created already on 10 April 1981, by a statute which defined the functions and responsibilities of the Commission as well as its funding. After a preliminary period of programme preview and preparation, the President of the Institute of Iberoamerican Cooperation was named as the Commission's president. This choice for the head of the organization emphasized the fact that the undertaking was intended to consolidate Spanish and Latin American relations. This stress on Latin America in the *Quinto Centenario* programme was carried out through existing bodies.[1] Relying on direct government funding and on co-operation with already existing organizations and institutions, the Spanish celebratory commitments were remarkably state-driven undertakings. It is clear that social, political and economic background forces fuelled the Spanish *Quinto centenario* programmes and gave them their flavour (Summerhill and Williams 2000, 127, 138; *Crónica de la Comisión y Nacional Agenda* 1984: 6–7).

The quincentennial serves here as a textbook example of the flexible use of the past: how the problematic and even difficult past can be remodelled and put to service. After Francisco Franco's death in 1975, Spain started an international image-improvement campaign to emphasize the democratic transition and introduce an updated, tolerant, European Spain. In the course of this campaign, which has continued for many years, the year 1992 offered a grand opportunity to place Spain at centre stage and to introduce the new, democratic Spain worldwide (CQCDA 1992: 8–9, 171–75). To whitewash the current portrayal of Spain in the international arena, and to show the long democratic voyage undertaken by the new Spain since the end of the intolerance and international isolation of the Franco regime, Spain gave itself an enormous coming-out party, and in 1992 the world was invited to participate. Spain enjoyed the international spotlight for a number of important spectacles: the World Fair in Seville, the Summer Olympics in Barcelona and Madrid's designation as a European cultural capital. Many of these quincentennial commemorations relied on a heavy historical sugar-coating. According to these public displays, fifteenth-century Spain was introduced with bright colours, the Moorish and Jewish expulsion after the Reconquista was barely mentioned and no one apparently conquered or invaded the Americas. In these commemorative narratives, previously celebrated conquistadors like Pizarro were not invited to participate. In fact, negotiating with history, Spain used its worldwide centre-stage anniversary to get rid of the negative attributes usually attached to its sixteenth-century history.

The Spanish European-centred commemorative displays and installations were designed to leave a lasting legacy. The Seville World Fair project, for example, was intended to improve the Andalusian political, infrastructural, administrative and economic image. La Junta de Andalucía, in addition to government funding, budgeted 3440 million pesetas for its 1992 regional celebrations (CQCDA 1992: 45–51). Leaving a lasting infrastructure legacy, this official high-profile Andalusian flagship programme brought urban reform to Seville. Improvements in the economic infrastructure focused in particular on transportation. Railways that had previously split the city apart were rerouted to an impressive, newly designed station. Infrastructural improvements included a *tren de alta velocidad* (high-speed) train connection between Madrid and Seville, improved airport facilities and an upgraded motorway network. Within the city of Seville itself, resources were directed to upgrading and developing tourist accommodation and to the restoration of local Andalusian cultural patrimony. According to the exposition project Cartuja '93, after the closing of the exposition the site was to be transformed into a centre for high technology (*Cartuja 93: un espacio abierto al futuro*). Although the actual expo theme, *La Era de los Descubrimentos*, referred to the events of 1492, the main Spanish expo section guideline seemed to focus on portraying Spain to the world as a contemporary and high-tech country, picking up on the idea of a particular national genius and mission in the world.

El Dorado – failure celebrated on extraordinary level

It is important to note that the Spanish Ministry of Culture funded all major international film productions about Columbus's voyages. In the triumphalist *Christopher Columbus: The Discovery* (John Glenn, 1992), Columbus was represented as a saintly Renaissance Rambo, adventurous and human, tolerant and brilliant. This version, directed by John Glenn (who has also directed James Bond films) projected the mythologized and folklore-legend version of the first voyage to the western hemisphere. *1492: Conquest of Paradise* (1992), directed by Ridley Scott, with Gerard Depardieu playing the lead character, provided a more complex and multi-layered story about the Genoese explorer and his legacy. In contrast to the Glenn production, in the Scott epic Columbus was portrayed as a man with vision, an arch-democrat and Renaissance genius, the brightest star of individualism, who – against his own will – carried old world tyranny and intolerance aboard his ships, bringing about the destruction of an earthly paradise. The Glenn film was partly funded by the *Quinto Centenario* fund; Ridley Scott's historical epic received an investment of 200 million pesetas from the Spanish Ministry of Culture (*Production Notes: Christopher Columbus: The Discovery; Production Notes: 1492: Conquest of Paradise*; Fisher 1992: 26–32; Jordan and Morgan-Tamosunas 1998: 31; Stam 1993: 66–72). Vilifying the aristocratic Spanish conquistadors, both of these Hollywood-engineered feature films hinted at the occurrence, from the beginning, of atrocities against Native Americans. In these films, however, the demonized Spaniard was more the exception than the rule; such men were portrayed as fallen individuals. Most of the ordinary colonists and settlers were portrayed with positive attributes.

Christopher Columbus: The Discovery and *1492: Conquest of Paradise* are textbook examples of the enormous magnitude of historical interpretation in the form of spectacle film. They demonstrated that resurrecting the past is not an easy enterprise, but a process that relies on firm economic commitment, a precise timetable from pre-production to post-production and beyond and advance marketing and distribution. A historical spectacle is an expensive undertaking, demanding large recreated constructions and settings, authenticity-creating props and large numbers of extras. Because of the high cost associated with spectacle-scale historical projects, historical spectacles are a rarity not only in Spanish but in European cinema as a whole. In order to challenge the hegemonic Hollywood-geared spectacle industry and share the potential financial risk, the European film industry has adopted an international co-production format (Kinder 1993: 412–15). In terms of Spanish filmmaking and the European film industry in general, the *El Dorado* project itself was a high-risk project – due not only to the choice of topic but also to its exceptionally large budget. Carlos Saura (born 1932), often praised as Spain's foremost living auteur, was chosen to take command as director and lend his prestige to the project. Saura's contribution to the Spanish *Quinto Centenario* program, *El Dorado* (*A peso d'oro*), was a chronologically structured spectacle-scale historical feature about early Spanish colonization in South America.

The Spanish commemoration programme was designed to stimulate, to entertain and to make a profit. *El Dorado* was a good example of American-flavoured auteurist European historical spectacle – *espectáculo más cine de autor* (Hopewell 1989: 419). High expectations were attached to it. At the time, with its budget of 1050 million pesetas (approximately $10 million), it was the most expensive Spanish film production ever. Although the epic was a joint, multinational Spanish-French-Italian venture, co-produced by Canal+, Chrysalide Film, Compañía Iberoamericana de TV, France 3 Cinéma, Iberoamericana Films Producción, Radiotelevisione Italiana, SACIS, Televisión Española (TVE) and Union Générale Cinématographique (UGC), it can be described as a product of modern Spanish cinema because of the emphasized Spanish ideological and financial commitment to the project. There were high expectations attached to the Saura undertaking: exotic locations, a huge cast and detailed period accuracy. The production team included for example some sixty local specialists, including carpenters, craftsmen and painters, and involved over six hundred local extras. Carlos Saura wanted to create as accurate a historical narrative of the topic as possible. In order to create the illusion of authenticity and of the true challenge of the natural environment, *El Dorado* was shot in the tropical rainforests of Costa Rica (*Production notes: El Dorado* 1988; Jordan and Morgan-Tamosunas 1998: 28–31; Paskin 1989: 298). The production was completed according to schedule and was released for national and international circulation.

Colonization rewritten and reconstructed

The Carlos Saura historical narrative centres on a time that has a very bad historical reputation: the times in which *la leyenda negra* was forged, crafted and placed in wider European circulation. While the American-engineered movie productions focused on the historical figure of Christopher Columbus, his triumphs and his failures, the Spanish epic adopted a somewhat more complex and challenging approach. The factual basis of *El Dorado* is beyond dispute. After the initial encounter between two diverse worlds, the Spanish conquistadors and adventurers, settlers and colonizers started to explore and invade the Americas in the early sixteenth century. There were numerous expeditions, but only a handful of them form part of our basic knowledge: Cortés plundered the already decaying

Aztec Empire and Pizarro was able to conquer the mighty Inca Empire with a mere handful of Spanish conquistadors. Historical records demonstrate, however, that only a few Spaniards made a career by the sword, with many of them facing oblivion. *El Dorado* is about the somewhat less familiar Spanish conquistadors involved in the sixteenth-century quest for the fabulous lost city of gold. The movie is not about knights armoured in shining steel breastplates, a glamorous, swashbuckling tale of chivalry and glory, heroism, conquest and courage, but about bloodshed and misery, human failure and breakdown in the face of devastating nature and the gradual deterioration of the human mind. One is tempted to ask: was the story of the failed Spanish expedition suitable and appropriate for celebration or commemoration? Or was the narrative selected to re-bridge colonial ties through the grammar of the Spanish Latin-American legacy, *la Hispanidad*?

In the sixteenth century, expectations among the conquistadors were high; stories were circulating about a city of gold and a fountain of youth. After the fall of the Inca Empire, the Spanish launched several expeditions to find the fabulous city of gold, with unfortunate and non-rewarding results. Carlos Saura's historical epic is in fact basically the story of the expedition of Pedro de Ursua, which took place between 1559 and 1561. The Saura production was inspired by Ramón Sender's novel *La aventura equinoccial de Lope de Aguirre* (1968) and was a loose remake of Werner Herzog's highly applauded *Aguirre, Der Zorn Gottes/Aguirre: The Wrath of God* (1972). Herzog portrayed his anti-hero as a true megalomaniac and blood-thirsty madman, who craved power from the beginning, but who was ultimately defeated by the untameable wilderness. Dissatisfied with Herzog's inaccuracies, Saura crafted his script as a faithful narrative about the actual historical expedition. The *El Dorado* script also included chronicled events from the previous Spanish expedition, recorded by the eyewitness account of Dominican friar Gaspar de Carvajal (c. 1500–1584) in his work *Relación del nuevo descubrimiento del famoso río Grande que descubrió por muy gran ventura el capitán Francisco de Orellana*, published in 1895 (*Production notes: El Dorado* 1988). Although relying on primary sources and involving some rewriting of history, the broad outline of Saura's screenplay is nevertheless reasonably accurate in its representation of early Spanish attempts to take command over uncharted and hostile territories in South America.

In search of El Dorado – doomed expedition of fools and tyrants

The *El Dorado* story structure is in with line with the Columbian literature that challenges the heroic portrayal of the early European stages in the Americas. The feature stresses that the Spanish conquistadors had high expectations, which did not correspond to the rude reality. The feature film starts with a dream-like prologue, an opening episode that presumably presents the legend of the city of gold as historical truth – at least to sixteenth-century Spaniards, who had witnessed the fall of the mighty Inca civilization. The actual story opens in 1560, in the heart of the Amazon jungle. The expedition to find the fabulous lost city of gold is about to start. The opening scene is absurd and foreboding: the Spanish soldiers are dressed in their shining armour, and aristocrats of noble birth are wearing their best costumes. From the beginning the stress is on the absence of reality among the aristocratic Spaniards: they are not dressed to face the hostile jungle, but to take part in a feast or a parade. Only the common craftsmen and settlers accompanying the expedition are dressed to meet the challenge of the jungle. After the expedition is finally launched, with great expectations, a small advance party is sent out to meet with friendly natives and to find food and resources for the main expedition's marching army. Soon a native village is found destroyed, its people massacred. Later the armada of the main expedition finds their search-party comrades slaughtered in combat. The story is basically one of fools in pursuit of a legend.

In contrast to laudatory Franco-era stories of European courage and bravery in early sixteenth century America, *El Dorado* provides a different and fresh conquistador adventure. This is underlined by the deteriorating atmosphere among the Spanish. As the expedition advances into the physically alien and never-ending jungle, the hostile territory starts to take a heavier toll, and the members of the expedition start to lose faith in their mission. Fatalism translates into violence; as high hopes become an obsession, the quixotic and Machiavellian journey turns into a battle for survival. Enthusiasm is replaced by bloodshed, apathy and distrust. In unknown and hostile territory, rumours start to circulate; the Spaniards turn against each other and start to fight for power and for the half-caste femme-fatale figure Doña Inés. In this frustrated and violent atmosphere, betrayal and treason become common. In the face of overwhelming odds, the Basque-born nobleman Lope de Aguirre (played by the Italian-born actor Omero Antonutti) is among the first to suggest the futility of advancing into the ever thickening jungle, to encounter certain destruction. After the assassination of the expedition leader Pedro de Ursua (played by the French actor Lambert

Figure 12.1: The opening scene introduces the El Dorado legend in a dream-like format.

Figure 12.2: The Spanish conquistadors are ready to launch the search for the golden city.

Wilson), while others hail the Spanish king, de Aguirre shouts 'viva la libertad!' Later de Aguirre declares himself a traitor because they have challenged the King's representative. Although de Aguirre serves the new governor well, he is humiliated and displaced as the new field-marshal. The new, despotic and cruel administration relies on terror and bloodshed. Violence among the power-hungry conquistadors holds centre stage.

El Dorado underlines the Machiavellian character of the conquistador presence in the Americas, in which the most dangerous enemy is found on one's own side. This theme is constant in the narrative. Although he is set aside, de Aguirre becomes the true leader of the expedition. After the failed assassination attempt Lope de Aguirre starts to plot a coup d'état, in order to secure his life and create something fundamentally new, a utopian world that will challenge existing power structures. In his speeches, Lope de Aguirre declares that they have to claim independence from King Philip II of Spain and establish the Kingdom of Peru, ruled by one of the highest nobles as King, with the rest serving as his aristocracy. Lope de Aguirre finally orchestrates the death of the new leader, and even the church representative faces violent death by de Aguirre's sword. After his main antagonists are slaughtered and only a few nobles left alive, de Aguirre finally claims power. In his declaration of independence ceremony he is confused and uneasy, unfamiliar with occupying centre stage. In the final scenes, Lope de Aguirre, king of the unconquered jungle, is sick, feverishly hallucinating about killing her own beloved daughter. He wakes up horrified in his daughter's arms. The dream, however, proves prophetic. As the voyage continues down the river, the closing narrator chronicles what is about to happen: 'the troops loyal to the King defeated and killed Lope de Aguirre, finding his daughter's lifeless body, stabbed by her own father. Lope de Aguirre was beheaded and quartered, his head was exhibited in a cage and shown to all so that his perverted memory would not sink into oblivion.'

Figure 12.3: After noble Spanish blood is shed, it becomes easier to rely on the sword to stage a new coup d'état.

Lope de Aguirre – villain or voice of reason?

The dream factory of the Franco era had promoted a *mitología franquista*, crafted to legitimize the existing power structure and to pay tribute to the authoritarian social order. With historical narratives relying on remembrance and forgetting, on emphasis and ignoring, Francoism celebrated in particular the remote past, the golden colonial era, during which myths and legends were crafted by heroes through blood and honour. Cortés and Pizarro were applauded, while less fortunate conquistador adventures and their weaker leaders were ignored (Jordan and Morgan-Tamosunas 1998: 17; Paskin 1989: 298). In this line of thinking, flavoured by nationalist mythology and history-writing, for instance the historical museum of Spanish American history, the Museo de América, became the true stronghold of a one-sidedly straightforward glorification of the conquest of the Americas. Within the museum walls, playing fast and loose with the evidence, the boundaries between documentary and fiction were intentionally and unintentionally blurred (Cabello 1993: 11–20). The Franco regime also simplified and remodelled the Iberian cultural climate: the foregrounded Castilian culture was heralded over other regional cultural identities, with Spain constructed as an ethnically homogenous country (*Descubre el Quinto Centenario: Guia de la Programacion* 1992: 126–30). Manipulating the Iberian heritage, Franco's nationalism promoted a single national identity by repressing Spain's cultural diversity and glorified Spanish accomplishments in the Americas. As a result, the regime's view of Spanish tradition and culture was somewhat artificial and arbitrary: a stereotypical image, corresponding only partly to the reality of the Spanish nation. Saura's *El Dorado* is in fact in stark contrast with this Franco-era culture factory vision of Spanishness.

In comparison to mitología franquista conquistador stories, *El Dorado* is not a traditional story of the conquest of the American Indian population in the name of God, glory and gold.

The main characters of *El Dorado*, in line with classic conquistador adventure narratives, are nobles and high-ranking soldiers. There are two main protagonists who are shown in detail. The governor and leader of the expedition, Pedro de Ursua, is portrayed from the very beginning as a weak leader, incapable of commanding his soldiers or earning their respect. He is ready to take unnecessary risks and sacrifice his men. After he falls ill, this portrayal is underlined even more forcefully. Saura's other protagonist, Lope de Aguirre, in stark contrast to Herzog's narrative and those of earlier chroniclers, is actually quite different from the figure suggested by the historical record. Chroniclers, for example, describe the conquistador Lope de Aguirre as a disreputable avenger figure, a petty low-ranking nobleman who turned criminal, earning his nickname El Loco (Jay 1999; Jos 1927). Although Saura identifies de Aguirre as 'the most terrible of all those Spaniards who reached America 500 years ago' (*Production notes: El Dorado* 1988: 10), *El Dorado* portrays de Aguirre as the rare voice of reason as well as a loving and protective father – he is the main antagonist to de Ursua. In fact, in contrast to other vicious and arrogant noble Spaniards, de Aguirre lives in harmony with people of lower rank, has his soldiers' unquestionable admiration and treats the natives in the same way that he treats Spaniards. During most of the film Lope de Aguirre is a cynical bystander, a pragmatic soldier and – ironically – the voice of reason. From the beginning, by stereotyping nobles as weak and vulnerable leaders, *El Dorado* vilifies the tyrannical leadership.

Rebranding Spain – the European quincentennial centre-stage

When Franco's designated successor, Prince Juan Carlos de Borbon, became King of Spain following Franco's death in November 1975, there was little indication that he would serve as the key instrument in the democratization of Spain. Although the process was not without its difficulties, the transition to democracy was signalled for example by the establishment of fundamental freedoms, by a respect for and development of human rights, and by a thorough institutional modernization and regional devolution. Reimagining and reconstructing Spain as a multi-ethnic nation, and discrediting the Franco-regime notion of national unity and homogeneity, Spanish nationalism was downplayed in favour of internationalism and regionalism. The new constitution made possible the establishment of autonomous regional governments, with the requisite powers and resources to salvage their respective cultures and to make their languages co-official with Castilian in their own regions (Gilmour 1985: 133–48; Payne 1991: 479–91). These rapid national changes in domestic politics were followed by successes in the international arena. Where Franco's dictatorship had touted Spain's difference from the rest of Europe, Spain's new democracy hankered for acceptance by Europe and the democratic world more widely. With the improvements achieved at home, the king and his government were eager to represent Spain as a devoted member of the European family – democratic and tolerant, multicultural and scientific: a nation remarkably different from Franco's Spain. The programme of Europeanization highlighted in European

Community membership was seen as an opportunity to deal with historical backwardness, to portray Spain as a profoundly European country, and to improve its opportunities in the European common market (Viñas 1999: 245–68).

The 1992 programme provided an international identity campaign, which was promoted worldwide. The Spanish government considered the year 1992 to be a spectacular year for Spain, and the official commission adopted a programme that involved gargantuan expenditure. Where previously Spanish strength was seen in unity, now diversity was perceived as an asset. As a result of the new Europe-friendly agenda, one of the main Spanish objectives was to shake off the long-lived totalitarian legacy of the Franco era, with its intolerance and jingoistic nationalism. The 1992 celebrations offered an opportunity to promote a new Spain, one which was tolerant, democratic and contemporary in every sense – economically and scientifically, culturally and historically – and to challenge the stereotypical, traditional Spain, as represented by bullfighting, paella and the tourist attractions of the sunny south. The program stressed unity in diversity, without mentioning for example the expulsion of religious minorities in the late fifteenth century. In reality, the programme underlined the Spanish democratic path from 1975 onwards, with a focus on burnishing the image of Spain as a profoundly European country. Through this programme, the Spanish *Quinto Centenario* Commission promoted unity in regional diversity. The image-improving campaign was carried out through international installations on a spectacular scale, the vehicles of the new, European-centred Spanish brand construction. As already noted, the campaign included for example the Barcelona Olympic Games and the Seville World Fair. According to the *Quinto Centenario* programme, and as demonstrated in international events, Spain was one of the world's most advanced and prosperous nations (CQCDA 1992: 25, passim; *Descubre el Quinto Centenario. Guia de la Programacion* 1992: 14–23).

The Spanish quincentennial commission conceived a number of projects as part of a sweeping project of cultural unity that involved defining Spanish identity in terms of diversity. In these portrayals, Spain was introduced in bright colours. The 1992 Barcelona Olympics, for example, were a golden opportunity to promote Spain as a contemporary nation and to introduce the Catalan heritage (ORGOB 1992: 85; Malaret i Garcia 1993, passim). The Olympic Games broadcasts, for example, applauded Spanish diversity and increased Spanish territorial fragmentation, with a heavy emphasis on Catalan culture. Political and cultural objectives were manifested in the spectacles of the opening and closing ceremonies, which were aired worldwide. The Olympics underlined the great difference between Catalonia and other parts of Spain. In addition, the great achievements of the country both in the past and today were hailed, while the era preceding 1975 was ignored. In the end the Olympics served the host city well, exerting a significant influence on architecture and urban beautification. As a result of the Olympics undertaking, the region ended up with improvements in its technological base, communication network, sport facilities, hotel capacity and transportation facilities. In retrospect, Barcelona officials estimated that the city had built fifty years' worth of infrastructure in eight years (*1992 España y el Mundo* 1991: 14–17). All in all, these identity campaigns, carried out as part of various quincentennial events, projected the image of a unanimous society. The Spanish installations were well in line with the official agenda, but only selectively with the recent Columbian literature. In the official quincentennial displays, no one conquered the Americas or waged a Reconquista of the Iberian Peninsula.

European quincentennial displays focused on tolerance. At first glance, *El Dorado* seems to be part of the growing Western concern with the horrors of victimization of Native Americans: the tradition that celebrates the native populations and demonizes the invading European forces. In Saura's film, the conquistadors fight each other in the untamed wilderness. When we take a closer look, however, it becomes clear that the feature makes only minor reference to the apologetic perspective of present-day political correctness. The Native members of the expedition, for instance, are executed as rebels in a fast-forwarding scene, but this theme is not further explored. In fact, the Native American voice is muted in the narrative; they do not have status as voice characters and their cultures are not introduced at all. In fact, the story challenges the stereotypical *la leyenda negra* approach, which stresses the Native American lack of power in the face of the invading Spanish army. In contrast to the Black Legend thesis, the Native people and the wilderness over-power the Spanish. In *El Dorado*, the frustrated Pedro de Ursua asks: 'Where is El Dorado?' In answer, the Native Indian waves his hand vaguely, indicating that El Dorado is somewhere ahead, further in the jungle. This sequence underlines the point that it is the Spanish conquistadors who have lost their power in the face of an unknown territory, and that it is the Native Americans who are actually in control, capable of leading the mission into oblivion. Providing only a sweeping and rather sugar-coated perspective, *El Dorado* provided little new insight into the multiple and complex issues arising from the quincentenary debate that vilified the Spanish invaders. This approach, silencing negative stories about Spanish atrocities by ignoring them, enjoyed popularity in the *Quinto Centenario* programme. Rather than foregrounding the Native American tragedy, *El Dorado* openly celebrates the Spanish presence in Latin America.

La Hispanidad, economy and the Latin American Spain

While the international academic community noted that the relations between Europeans and Native Americans were multifaceted, the Spanish *Quinto Centenario* programme chose a rather one-sided perspective, setting the Native American issue partly aside and stressing the Hispanic heritage of Latin America. This approach was not new in Spanish contemporary foreign and cultural policy; Spain has always stressed this shared history, ethnicity and culture between Spain and Latin America, under the title of 'Hispanic heritage' (*Descubre el Quinto Centenario – Inventario de Programas* 1992: 19–20). Together with the European and Western dimension, Latin America soon became another key area in democratic Spain's foreign affairs policy, especially from the early 1980s onwards. After this new launch of a shared Hispanic experience, Spain engaged in an aggressive economic programme to enter

Latin American markets (Baklanoff 1996: 105–27). This Latin American commitment was carried out especially through the *Quinto Centenario* programme. While the first *Quinto Centenario* agenda stressed Spain as the European heartland, the second agenda was somewhat schizophrenic in that regard, indicating that Spain differed greatly from the other European nations of colonizers and neo-colonizers. According to this line of thought, 1992 provided a unique opportunity to unite and mobilize the Hispanic peoples around the noble ideas of modernity and democracy. The quincentennial commemoration programme had a stark contemporary subtext: it was the Spanish presence in Latin America that was highlighted.

Saura's story ends with a haunting and thought-provoking dichotomy. In his first speech as new emperor of the conquered land, de Aguirre declares:

> Henceforth I shall rule you! I shall be your Prince of Liberty! Prince of terra firma, Peru and Chile! Soldiers, we'll not rest before Peru is Ours! [...] In my Kingdom, there shall be no slaves. As we are all born the same way, let us be equals. Now, blacks, Indians, half-castes will be my friends, as the Spaniards are.

The speech refers to democracy and equality, based on a concept of constitutional monarchy that would be born only centuries later. It hinted that fundamental rights, although occasionally set aside, were ultimately deeply rooted in the Spanish culture. The speech also glorifies the theme of unity in diversity (in fact one of the main guidelines of post-Franco Spain). Lope de Aguirre is portrayed by Saura as the protagonist and harbinger of modern democracy and equality; in chronicles and historical narratives, on the other hand, he is demonized as a murderous rebel, who actually dared to challenge the Spanish King. Is the traditional story of de Aguirre as homicidal rebel truthful? Or is that demonized portrayal merely the product of official Spanish history-making, celebrating the Spanish monarchy? In contrast to the Franco regime's version of early Spanish experience in the Americas, *El Dorado* provided something fundamentally fresh: a challenging perspective on the conquistador era of the sixteenth century, demonizing the megalomaniac Spanish tyrannical leaders – an approach that had been impossible in the *mitología franquista*.

In *El Dorado* the stress is on the early Spanish experience that created present-day Latin America: the common settlers were here to rebuild a better world and to repopulate the Americas, even to introduce noble ideas of liberty, tolerance and equality. This approach enjoyed popularity in the agenda of Spanish Latin America, manifesting itself in economy-centred quincentennial programs. With the help of the planned *Quinto Centenario* undertaking, Spain wished to remove the term *la leyenda negra* from the contemporary lexicon and grammar of Latin American history, and to promote Spain's good intentions and generosity in its former Latin American colonies. Spain's 1992 undertaking was tailored to modernize the country's relations with Latin America. In the effort to reconnect and rebridge, Spain used the upgraded concept of *la Hispanidad* as its main tool. The Spanish programme for the European – Latin American relationship stressed political and economic

Figure 12.4: After claiming power as Prince of Peru and Chile, Lope de Aguirre stresses that in his realm all people are equal.

equality between the two continents. The *Comisión Quinto Centenario del Descubrimiento de América* sponsored international congresses, meetings and seminars. The Latin American arm of the quincentennial agenda, *el Plan Especial de Cooperación Quinto Centenario* stressed the importance of greater cooperation among a community of Iberoamerican peoples in the fields of economics and politics, culture, science and technology. *Quinto Centenario* promoters explicitly set out to demonstrate and display the modern European Spain that serves as a bridge between Europe and Latin America (*1992 España y el mundo* 1991: 20–23). Given that the quincentennial programme and its heavy governmental funding started before the Spanish economy began to improve, the programme played an exceptionally high role in Spanish foreign policy. In reality, however, the programme was engineered to burnish and whitewash the image of Spain at the international level.

The *Quinto Centenario* programme noted that although the Latin American countries faced economic difficulties, in the domain of democracy and civil liberties they had progressed rapidly; it further noted that, especially with Spain's protection and help, economic difficulties could also be solved (CQCDA 1992: 61–62). The programmes were drafted, at least in their rhetoric, to reduce the gap between a technology-driven Europe and Latin America as an exporter of raw materials. In order to underline its generosity and support for Iberoamericanism, Spain for example pledged twenty billion dollars in support of economic, scientific and cultural assistance to Latin American countries that participated in the Spanish *Quinto Centenario* programme. The major high-priority programmes of the *Plan Especial de Cooperacion Quinto Centenario* stressed the importance of progress in the fields of science and technology.[2] In addition, the Spanish government endowed the Inter-American Development Bank with $500 million for infrastructure projects. The final attempt was to create a united Iberoamerican market that would play a more prominent role in world affairs – an idea that had been strongly endorsed already under Franco (*500 Años,*

500 Programas 1985; CQCDA 1992: 62; Ottone 1997: 27–48). Spain's economic investment made the country's presence in the Western Hemisphere visible.

El Dorado – *Quinto Centenario* celebration of *la Hispanidad*

The *Quinto Centenario* stress was on a Latin American population sharing a Hispanic gene pool. This took the form of a Hispanic brotherhood that existed on the western and eastern shores of the Atlantic. The commemorative palette had a clear educational side, aimed at improving the image of Spain in Latin America. According to the *Quinto Centenario* programme, most of the Spaniards who arrived in the New World were not Pizarros or Cortéses but devoted fathers and hard-working peasants and artisans, anything but the stereotypical conquistadors, lean and blood-thirsty in appearance, in morion helmets and armour. Through programmes such as *Hispasat, Con Iberoamérica de pueblo a pueblo, Taller de actividades sobre Iberoamérica, Universidad 92', Cooperacion educative con Iberoamerica* and *Aventura 92'*, Spain tried to improve geographic, social, cultural, artistic and historic knowledge of Spain in Latin America. In order to emphasize the Hispanic roots of Latin America, the Spanish Commission gave priority to the protection and conservation of the historical and artistic heritage in Latin America, thus emphasizing the historical and present-day Spanish presence in Latin America. From 1983 onward, the programme worked together with the Institute of Iberoamerican Cooperation, the Department of Cultural Relations of the Ministry of Foreign Affairs and the General Directorate of Fine Arts and Archives to carry out a programme of restoration of civil-engineering, military and religious works, of urban centre renewal and of archaeological research. Through this programme, budgeted at some 193 million pesetas, restoration programmes were carried out in twelve Iberoamerican countries (*500 Años, 500 Programas* 1985: 44–53; *Patrimonio Común Histórico-artístico: Programa de Restauraciones y rehabilitaciones* 1992; *Programa de revitalización de centros históricos de Iberoamérica* 1991). The concept of cultural equality underlying these programmes had to do with the assumption of a shared Hispanic heritage, not with the indigenous cultures that were encountered.

Like the other Spanish Latin American quincentennial projects, Saura's film underlined the Hispanic heritage of contemporary Latin America. *El Dorado* was part of the Spanish quincentennial brand-making, introducing the highly heterogeneous nature of Spain. The true heroes of the feature were the common, low-ranking Spaniards, who colonized and remodelled Latin America, who witnessed Spanish conquistadors fighting for power. It underlined the early presence of the Spanish culture in the Western Hemisphere and celebrated *la Hispanidad*. In accordance with the *Quinto Centenario* programme, and challenging the stereotypical idea of the conquistador as simplistic brutal killer, *El Dorado* introduces a somewhat heterogeneous Spanish population. The common settlers and colonists are distanced from the bloodshed. They are merely bystanders and witnesses to the terrible brutality of the few. According to the film, conquistadors and adventurers, settlers and colonists represented different parts of Spain, different cultural nuances, even sexual minorities (homosexual relationships between some of the nobles are hinted at, but not elaborated). Introducing conquistadors and settlers who tried to craft and remodel the Spanish America in their homeland image, *El Dorado* was part of the Spanish attempt to reconnect with the Latin American nations of Hispanic heritage. In *El Dorado*, the conquistadors have nostalgic and warm dreams about Spain. When they have time to settle down, they describe Spain with positive attributes. *El Dorado* stressed the Spanish roots of Latin America. By introducing the heterogeneous backgrounds of Spanish conquistador and settlers, *El Dorado* was also in line with the agenda of the new democratic Spain, that of unity in diversity.

Conclusion

Competing agendas revise, distort and lay claim to history and memory. Post-colonial guilt and environmental concerns ensured that the Columbian legacy was heavily debated prior to the quincentennial year. Academic debates, however, seldom enter into public perception, which means that in official commemoration installations the past more often than not remains simplified. How did the Spanish quincentennial programme correlate with history? By selective remembering and forgetting – by rewriting history – it became possible to create and promote positive official *Quinto Centenario* images, from which all negative attributes had been swept away. In order to present a new, updated, democratic and international Spain, the new government embarked upon a massive, two-stage campaign of image improvement. The first stage stressed the democratic, scientific and cultural European Spain; the second emphasized Spain as an important bridge between Europe and Latin America. The first agenda was constructed to get rid of the flavour of a European borderland, the second to demonstrate the role of Spain as the heartland of the Hispanic world. The European-based spectacular installations foregrounded the place of Spanishness at the core of a border-less 'Europeanity'.

The major quincentennial displays were designed to serve Spain's European image, while the Latin American commitment was carried out with lower visibility, in the form of programmes of cultural exchange along with economic ones. *El Dorado*, with its openly Spanish point of view, was one of the cultural *Quinto Centenario* programmes that stressed Latin America's Spanish roots. Although seen as an opportunity to convey and promote a view of Spain as a democratic and technologically sophisticated European nation and as a major player in the international policy arena, the foremost object in the quincentennial celebrations remained presenting Spain as a member of the Iberoamerican peoples. Spain's Latin American commitment stressed Hispanic culture, and in muting the Native American voice downplayed the Native legacy. Although technology and science played a major role in the quincentennial plan, the Spanish programme stressed the importance of culture as a force for unity. Thus the Spanish heroes of the quincentennial year were not the Genoese-born Christopher Columbus or the swashbuckling conquistadors but the ordinary Spaniards, who came to the New World to start afresh: they were the true Spanish American 'Adams' and 'Eves' – the bystanders who were presented in *El Dorado* as silent participants.

References

1992 España y el mundo (1991), Madrid: Ministerio del Portavoz del Gobierno.

500 Años, 500 Programas (1985), Quinto Centenario del Descubrimiento de America. Madrid: Sociedad Estatal para la ejecución de Programas del Quinto Centenario.

Baklanoff, E. N. (1996), 'Spain's Economic Strategy toward the Nations of its Historical Community: "The Reconquest" of Latin America', *Journal of Interamerican Studies and World Affairs*, 38: 1, pp. 105–27.

Cabello, P. (1993), 'El Museo de America', *Anales 1: Museo de América 1993*, Madrid: Ministerio de Cultura.

Cartuja 93: un espacio abierto al future (1992), Sociedad Estatal para la Exposicion, Universal Sevilla 92, S.A.

'Crónica de la Comisión y Nacional Agenda: America '92' (1984), *Mayo 1984*: 1.

Descubre el Quinto Centenario. Guia de la Programacion (1992), Madrid: Sociedad Estatal para la ejecución de Programas del Quinto Centenario.

Descubre el Quinto Centenario – Inventario de Programas (1992), Madrid: Sociedad Estatal Quinto Centenario.

Fernández-Armesto, F. (1991), *Columbus*, New York: Oxford University Press.

Fields, R. C. (1988), *A Jubilee in the Making*, International Columbian Quincentenary Alliance.

Fisher, B. (1992), '1492: Conquest of Paradise: Epic Film Recounts Legendary Epoch', *American Cinematographer*, LXXIII: 10, pp. 26–32.

Gilmour, D. (1985), *The Transformation of Spain: From Franco to Constitutional Monarchy*, London: Quartet Books.

Hopewell, J. (1989), *El cine español despútes de Franco*, Madrid: Ediciones El Arquero.

Jay, F. (1999), *Sin, Crimes, and Retribution in Early Latin America: A Translation and Critique of Sources – Lope de Aguirre, Francisco de Carvajal, Juan Rodríguez Freyle*, Lewiston and N.Y.: E. Mellen Press.

Jordan, B. and Morgan-Tamosunas, R. (1998), *Contemporary Spanish Cinema*, Manchester: Manchester University Press.

Jos, E. (1927), *La expedición de Ursúa al Dorado, la rebelión de Lope de Aguirre y el itinerario de los "Marañones," según los documentos del Archivo de Indias y varios documentos inéditos*, Huesca: Imprenta V. Campo.

Juderías, J. (1914), *La leyenda negra y la verdad histórica: contribución al estudio del concepto de España en Europa, de las causas de este concepto y de la tolerancia política y religiosa en los países civilizados*, Madrid: Tip. de la Revista de Archivos.

Kinder, M. (1993), *Blood Cinema. The Reconstruction of National Identity in Spain*, Berkeley: University of California Press.

Koning, H. (1991), *Columbus: His Enterprise: Exploding the Myth*, New York: Monthly Review Press.

La Conmemoracion Del Quinto Centenario Del Descubrimiento de America: Balance y Realization (1992), Madrid: Quinto Centenario. (referred as CQCDA).

Linenthal, E. (1994), 'Committing History in Public', *The Journal of American History*, 91: 3, pp. 986–91.

Malaret i Garcia. E. (1993), *Público y privado en la organización de los Juegos Olimpicos de Barcelona 1992*, Madrid: Civitas.

Official Report of the Games of the XXV Olympiad Barcelona 1992: Volume I: The Challenge: From the Idea to Nomination 1992. Roma Cuyas (ed.), Barcelona: COOB'92, S.A. (referred as ORGOB).

Ottone, E. (1997), 'Desarrollo y Cultura: una vision critica de la modernidad en América Latina y el Caribe', in *La economía de la cultura iberoamericana: III Seminario sobre Politicas Culturales Iberoamericanas, Madrid, 11 al 15 de diciembre de 1995*. Secretaria de Estado de Cultura de Española de Cooperación Internacional Casa de América de Madrid, Organización de Estados Iberoamericanos para la Educación, la Ciencia y la Cultura (OIE), Fundación CEDEAL 1997, pp. 27–48.

Paskin, S. (1989), 'El Dorado' *Monthly Film Bulletin* LVI: 669, pp. 298–99.

Patrimonio Común Histórico-artístico: Programa de Restauraciones y rehabilitaciones (1992), Madrid: Secretaria de Estado para la Cooperación Internacional y para Iberoamérica: Quinto Centenario.

Payne, S. G. (1991), 'Nationalism, Regionalism and Micronationalism in Spain', *Journal of Contemporary History*, 26:4/4, pp. 479–91.

Powell, P. W. (1971), *Tree Of Hate: Propaganda and Prejudices Affecting United States Relations With The Hispanic World*, New York: Basic Books.

Production Notes: *1492: Conquest of Paradise* (1992), Gaumont, Légende Enterprises, France 3 Cinéma, Due West & Cyrkfilms.

Production Notes: *Christopher Columbus: The Discovery* (1992), Warner Bros Pictures.

Production Notes: *El Dorado* (1988), Madrid: Iberoamericana distribucion.

Programa de revitalización de centros históricos de Iberoamérica (1991), Madrid: Sociedad Estatal de Ejecución de Programas Conmemorativos del V Centenario del Descubrimiento de América.

Ramirez, O. (1992), '1992 – The Year of Indigenous Peoples', *Social Justice* 19: 2, Columbus on Trial, pp. 56–62.

Sale, K. (1990), *The Conquest of Paradise. Christopher Columbus and the Columbian Legacy*, New York: Knopf.

Simon, R. I. (1993), 'Forms of Insurgency in the Production of Popular Memories: The Columbus Quincentenary and the Pedagogy of Counter-Commemoration', *Cultural Studies*, 1: 2, pp. 73–88.

Stam, R. (1993), 'Rewriting 1492: Cinema and the Columbus Debate', *Cineaste* XIX: 4, p. 66.

Summerhill, S. J. and Williams J. A. (2000), *Sinking Columbus: Contested History, Cultural Politics, and Mythmaking during the Quincentenary*, Gainesville: University of Oklahoma Press.

Taviani, P. E. (1991), *Columbus: The Great Adventure. His Life, His Times, and His Voyages*, (trans. L. F. Farino and M. A. Beckwith), New York: Orion Books.

Viñas, A. (1999), 'Breaking the Shackles from the Past: Spanish Foreign Policy from Franco to Felipe González', in S. Balfour and P. Preston (eds), *Spain and the Great Powers in the Twentieth Century*, New York: Routledge, pp. 245–67.

Notes

1   Especially the Organización de estudios Iberoamericanos para la Educación, la Ciencia y la Cultura, the Comición Economica para America Latina; the Instituto para la Integracion de America Latina y el Caribe; the Asociación Latinoamericana de Integración; the Banco Iberoamericano de Desarrollo and UNESCO, as well as relatively new undertakings such as CYTED-D carried out the *Quinto Centenario* project objectives.

2   These high-priority programmes included, for example, *Ciencia y Technología para el Desarollo, Proyecto de Integración Ferroviara, Sistema de Interconexión Eléctricia de los Países de América Central* and *Programas de Cooperación en Artesanía, Minería Iberoamericana y Cooperación Municipal.*

Chapter 13

Subverted and Transgressed Borders: The Empire in British Comedy and Horror Films

Rami Mähkä
University of Turku

In the British horror film *Dead of Night* (Alberto Cavalcanti et al., 1945), a group of people are gathered in a country house, telling each other horrendous stories. A peculiar ghost story told by one of the characters is revealed, though actually only at its very end, to be a 'wind-up'. What might be labelled as a 'comic relief' directed at the characters is, at the same time, a reminder of connections between horror and comedy, two important British film genres. One such connection is laughter, which typically is a reaction to something comical, but can also stem from a feeling of anxiety or distress. Hence, it is perhaps not surprising that the two genres have not only been utilized together in horror genre parodies but also in 'camp horror comedies', as well as the 'splatter' genre of the 1970s and 1980s. However, the genres appear to share some other important similarities, too.

The idea for this chapter was born out of an increasing sense that as audiovisual genres, comedy and horror have many things in common. Its aim is to explore popular cartographies of the Empire in horror and comedy genres. The chapter explores similarities between comedy and horror using the concepts of the grotesque, transgression, subversion and the uncanny. The grotesque and transgression are key phenomena in both genres, and, for example, the distinction between comic and horrific grotesque can only be established through the genre of the film.[1] However, even then the meaning of the grotesque can be vague: films such as the two *Dr. Phibes* films (Robert Fuest, 1971 and 1972) contain comic tones, which I see as proof of the two genres' close relations. Hence, it is not enough to consider the *Dr. Phibes* films only from the perspective of parody. The article begins by exploring the concept of the uncanny, established by Sigmund Freud in his 1919 essay. While the uncanny has traditionally been associated with horror (ghosts, madness ...), it is a way of referring to something which is at once both strange and familiar (strangely familiar); I believe comedy offers similar moments of 'strange familiarity'.

Cinema was born at a high point of imperialism at the end of the nineteenth century, and as such, it began to participate in 'the imperial project' alongside more traditional arts such as literature. Cinema, however, with its means of representation and also mass consumption (one does not have to be literate to watch a film), transformed the ways in which the Empire was depicted and understood. As Ella Shohat and Robert Stam have argued, 'the cinematic experience mobilized a rewarding sense of national and imperial belonging, on the backs, as it were, of otherized peoples' (Shohat and Stam 2001: 368–69, passim.).[2] In the comedies and horrors discussed in this article, the stereotypical borders of East and West, the 'other' of the colonies and the European, are either confirmed or inverted. The basic dichotomies such as (pagan) East–(Christian) West, primitive–scientific, superstition–rationality, are often challenged by the ambivalent modes of comic and horrific.

The basic 'divides' of those dichotomies are present in the Hammer film *The Stranglers of Bombay* (Terence Fisher, 1959), a film sometimes classified as a horror film (most likely because of Hammer's prolific horror production), but it actually is more an adventure film about the British discovery and early fight against the Thuggee cult and the terror it unleashed on the population in early-twentieth-century India. It carries several stereotypical ideas of imperialistic fiction, most notably in the representations of the Indians, and as a whole can be seen as an 'apology' for imperialism. The film does contain criticism of the British (and especially the East India Company), most notably portraying many characters as arrogant towards the local population, an attitude also important in another (and quite similar) Hammer Empire action/adventure film *The Terror of the Tongs* (Anthony Bushell, 1961). It is thus fitting that *The Stranglers of Bombay*, produced only a decade after the independence of India, ends with a kind of testimony to the colonial rule in the shape of a quote from Major General Sir William Sleeman, an officer of the East India Company, who was responsible for the capture of thousands of murderous Thugs: 'If we have done nothing else for India, we have done this good thing.' The general's statement, even if it was given over one hundred years before this film was made, must have not sounded out of place in the 1950s. India was a colony for a long time after the implicitly critical words of Sleeman, but ending a 'horrendous' film about the British fighting and defeating an extremely violent 'pagan' cult gives the positive part of the quote an extra amount of credibility.

A concept which has been discussed in the context of genre is verisimilitude, which means the appearance of reality, plausibility. This relates to genre expectations – when we are watching a comedy, we both expect and accept its contents based on our experience and knowledge of the genre. This, in turn, has effects on the broader social and cultural verisimilitude in a given film. We accept (or do not accept) events and representations in a film based on our understanding of the world, but the influence of the genre verisimilitude should be taken into account. As Steve Neale has argued, many critics have considered horror and comedy to be inferior to more 'serious' genres because their genre verisimilitudes are less committed to 'realism' (Neale 2003: 161–63). The relationship of horror and comedy and realism is indeed complicated. It is important to emphasize that comedy always refers to non-comic reality, but as it is always self-referential, the ways in which it refers to, and makes sense of, non-comic realms can only be explained by studying the comic mechanisms applied in each particular context. This notion is actually quite close to the concept of metafiction (see, for example, Waugh 1984), which at the very extreme means that fiction has no actual relationship with reality: all that is contained within fiction is fiction. It is not my intention to make such an argument, but it is crucial not to forget the nature of comedy described above. The same is true for horror: one must read a horror story as a horror story which refers to 'reality' in alternative ways to non-horror works. Finally, genres such as comedy and horror are always potentially critical of their subject matter, and in each case, this criticality is essentially different from other forms of cultural criticism. In doing so, they tap into 'deep cultural strains and tensions' (Chibnall and Petley 2002: 2–3) by means not usually available for other genres.

Both comedy and horror also typically include, but also construct and de-construct, acts of transgression and subversion. For example, in comedy the Bakhtinian notion of the carnivalesque has been understood as a temporary inversion, and subversion, of society, which certainly appears true in its original context, the European carnival tradition. However, I believe this does not necessarily apply to modern comedy, such as Monty Python. This is because of the ever-present critical potential of comedy. Comedy has the ability, satire being the most obvious example, to criticize using means not available to non-comic genres. Further, in comparison, it may, and should, be asked how often, and on what terms, does a non-comical work have the ability to influence audiences' opinions and attitudes? The same question has to be asked in the case of horror fiction.

By using a number of film (and television) comedies and 'horrors' mainly from the 1960s to the early 1980s, my article attempts to map how these works articulated, de-constructed and re-constructed various borders of the British Empire. The films discussed here do not form any solid body of works. However, most of them were produced during the post-war decades by popular filmmakers. An era of British regular filmmaking which, according to John Hill, came to a virtual end in the 1970s after the solid output of *Carry On* films and Hammer horror (Hill also mentions the *Confessions* cycle) ceased (Hill 2001: 167). Although several of both the *Carry On* films and Hammer films are analysed in this chapter, my aim is not to form any complete overview of how the Empire was depicted, dealt with or even present in horror and comedy. Rather, as a cultural historian, I am interested in the various cultural interactions of the films and the Empire. This approach means one scene from one film can be just as meaningful as an out and out film either about or set in the Empire: works such as individual sketches from *Monty Python's Flying Circus* (1969–1974) both serve to parody the conventions of cinema whilst also working as interpretational 'keys' to many comic references to the Empire. However, this article focuses on films, as highlighted in its title.

Comedy and horror are highly self-referential genres. This means that their ways of dealing with the Empire refer both to the non-generic realms as well as to generic modes. It is the twofold nature of the genres, and the similarities between the two genres, that create opportunities to find new information on British popular culture's relationship with the Empire. It attempts to present some answers for how the loss of empire affected the British identities in the country's popular culture after the World War II, which, according to historian Wendy Webster (Webster 2005), remains a question much neglected. What kind of ideological and social borders do the films contain? In which ways are borders artificially created, or removed? The article's hypothesis is that in dealing with 'Imperial' subjects, comedy and horror participated in imagining and mapping the past and present of Britain in ways not possible for other genres. In so doing, they articulated, in their distinctive ways, important themes of the post-war era.

The uncanny, horror and comedy

There is an element in the film *Dead of Night* which requires attention and is one of the features that I see comedy and horror as sharing. The protagonist of the film (Walter Craig) reveals to a group of people – all of them strange to him – sharing ghostly stories together that he knows exactly what will happen next. He proves this by predicting each occurrence in the house. He explains that he has had a recurring nightmare of the same situation that he is now apparently living: he has learned enough from the nightmare to be able to locate the house. He has arrived to see how things will continue as each time he has had the nightmare he has woken up at the same moment of the dream. The characters of the film speculate how the man can know all this: they believe the situation to be real. Of course, a concept that one immediately considers is déjà vu, – a feeling that something present has been experienced before – might be an illusion, or a correct impression. Déjà vu is a term related to psychology, or psychoanalysis, and it is worth noting how it overlaps both horror and comedy genres.

When déjà vu has been addressed in comedy, one question appears relevant: just how 'comical' is the concept in itself? For example, in the film *Groundhog Day* (Harold Ramis, 1993), a man (Bill Murray) is forced to live the same day over and over again – and because the film carries both fantastic as well as comedic elements, we are bound to accept that this is actually what is happening. Similarly, in a *Monty Python's Flying Circus* sketch, the host of a television show on psychology ('*It's the Mind*') gets caught in a 'terrible feeling of déjà vu'. Like the *Groundhog Day*'s protagonist, the spectators are convinced that the host's experience is 'real'. This is accomplished by a central comedy vehicle: repetition. The sketch, not untypically for *the Flying Circus*, basically starts over and over again. The host is terrified, and runs away from the studio. At each attempt he gets a little further from the studio, only to find himself at the beginning of the events. The sketch's comic appeal stems from the repetition of the same filmic shots, but I do not think the content of the sketch is 'funny' in other ways. In fact, I find it nightmare-like, and certainly not unlike the déjà vu-style horror setting of *Dead of Night*.

Déjà vu is one concept within the uncanny, a feeling that something is 'strangely familiar'. Nicholas Royle writes of the uncanny that it is 'a crisis of the proper', which 'entails a critical disturbance of what is proper'. In his analysis, the uncanny can be applied to a great number of contexts, and it has often been used in association with horrific matters, ultimately with death (Royle 2003: 1–2). Importantly for my article, Royle sees that the uncanny contains a sense of repetition, or a return of something (such as in 'return of the repressed'[3]). This appears clear in the case of déjà vu (see Royle 2003: 172–86), but it is also related to the idea of a double, a feature common for both comedy and horror. The uncanny nature of the 'double', understood as being potentially both comedic and horrific, is somehow encapsulated in probably the best-known double role in the history of cinema, *The Great Dictator* (Charlie Chaplin, 1940), in which Charlie Chaplin plays both a Jewish barber and a dictator of an imaginary European state. It is clear that a potentially horrendous meaning in this case was that of the resemblance of this to Hitler, the Nazis and the fate of Jewish people in the 1930s and 1940s, rather than the nature of the uncanny described above. Another crucial feature of the uncanny, as Royle's analysis of the word's etymology reveals, is that it refers to archaic connotations of the supernatural. Finally, there is also 'a lurking presence of the comic' (Royle 2003: 10–11).

David B. Morris is, I believe, correct when he writes about a 'neglected link between comedy and pain', in which the common ground is the body (Morris 1991: 79–102). While Morris is discussing the matter from various important perspectives, for the purpose of this article, I would like to make a comment on the porous border between cinematic violence in comedy and in horror. As in the case of déjà vu, repetition appears to be one of the key elements which differentiates between realistic violence and comedy. One famous example of this is the scene in *Monty Python and the Holy Grail* (Terry Gilliam and Terry Jones, 1974) in which King Arthur (Graham Chapman) arrives at a bridge guarded by a knight in black armour (John Cleese). The comedic nature of the film has been obvious from the very beginning, and fittingly, the bridge arches over a very small ditch. The black knight informs the king that he will not allow anyone to use the bridge. As both are adamant, the two men realize there is no other option than fighting. Arthur manages to cut off the knight's arm, and puts away his sword, praising the bravery of the knight. Just as with the ditch, the scale of the injury is approached via the logic of comedy: the knight wants to carry on fighting. What results is an extremely bloody battle, during which Arthur successively removes limb after limb, leaving the knight a torso shouting insults at the king, who continues his journey. This is not realistic, but it is acceptable in the realm of comedy, because comedy is not dependant on reality. Dialogue aside, this scene is not unlike those in 'splatter' horror films (and parodies of them, the distinction is often very difficult to make) such as *Braindead* (Peter Jackson, 1992), which are built on depictions of graphic violence involving human bodies being mutilated. In more traditional horror films, the supernatural is used to explain the 'monster's' ability to sustain otherwise mortal traumas. For example, in *The Mummy* (Terence Fisher, 1959), the mummy (Christopher Lee) is shot several times to no effect. When the mummy finally *is* killed, it appears as if it is the result of extensive gunfire, but the protagonist (Peter Cushing) knows better: the mummy died from a broken heart.

A film which is an interesting case for this article, as it combines an apocalyptic horror setting with utterly dark comedy, is *The Bed Sitting Room* (Richard Lester, 1969). For a start, it is reasonable to ask what could be a more horrendous setting than a post-nuclear-war Earth (with forty million Britons dead)? The film does underline its comedy side in numerous ways, including silly opening credits. However, these tend to be undermined by the sheer madness of most of the characters and scenes. In addition, the film's notable preoccupation with the Empire (and World War II) is obvious, and this makes it an especially relevant film here. After London has been attacked and the nation's leaders all killed (the first target of the missiles is 10 Downing Street, which had been leased from the Chinese – the last detail being quite clearly an inversive reference to the former dominance of the Far East and to the ongoing

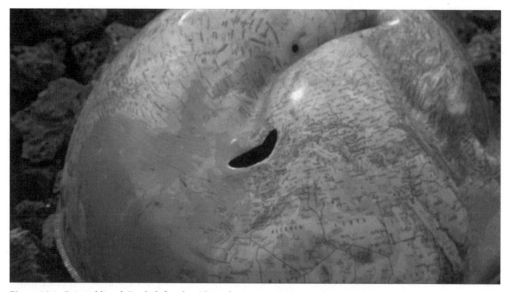

Figure 13.1: Britain blitzed, Earth deflated in *The Bed Sitting Room* (Richard Lester, 1969).

British control of Hong Kong), we hear of Japanese invasion forces reaching Singapore. Another example is the way in which the prime minister addresses the nation in his last speech, just prior to the missile strike: 'You know this great country of ours often sticks in the mud in the past, searches out and holds up to the light the mistakes of past times. We eat our hearts out with the canker of racialism and death east of Suez. But I am forced to ask, have we forgotten the bomb?' The prime minister's question highlights the film's clear relationship with Stanley Kubrick's *Dr. Strangelove* (1964), a dark satire about nuclear war, but the film appears to be even more about the national contexts Lester explored with a similarly cynical comedy style in his earlier films, most notably *How I Won the War* (1967). Even more than in those films, the absurdity and madness depicted in *The Bed Sitting Room* reach beyond the borders of comedy. In doing so, any laughter it might provoke is likely to be that of anxiety, rather than amusement.

Another example of how difficult it is sometimes to make a distinction between horror and comedy is that one of the key critics of British horror film, David Pirie, comments in the new edition of his classic *A Heritage of Horror* (1973) that his original 1970s evaluation of *The Abominable Dr. Phibes* as 'probably the worst horror film made in England since 1945' was incorrect. In 2009, Pirie prefers to call *Dr. Phibes* Comedy-Horror, writing that they were comedies of revenge, with too much emphasis on comedy to be proper horror. He does state that horror films can contain laughter or wit, but it is important that a film takes itself seriously enough to be horror (Pirie 2009: 165–66). I believe it depends on the context whether works such as the two *Dr. Phibes* films are considered more horror than comedy, but also that giving a film a final label is usually unnecessary. This is especially so because, as this article argues, the distinction is sometimes very difficult to make. This is, for example, particularly true in the case of *The Bed Sitting Room*. It is a dark comedy in which the comedic elements do not evoke laughter, except that of the nervous kind.

Transgressing cultural borders

One example of British horror's engagement with the Empire is the 'cycle' of *Mummy* films by Hammer, between 1959 and 1971 (*The Mummy*, Fisher, 1959; *The Curse of the Mummy's Tomb*, Michael Carreras, 1964; *The Mummy's Shroud*, John Gilling, 1967; *Blood from the Mummy's Tomb*, Seth Holt, 1971). The films have the same basic story: a group of archaeologists discover a mummy's tomb, and enter it regardless of the locals' warnings of a curse. The mummy is revived from death (basically through what might be understood as witchcraft), and it then seeks to kill everyone who disturbed the tomb. The rational, scientific thinking of the Westerners encounters the 'pagan' cult of the undead, but the setting is more complicated than that, as the British are also clearly cultural imperialists who appear to believe that the glorious ancient past of Egypt belongs more to them than to the locals.[4] The Westerners' capability to both understand and deal with the local culture is questioned: their transgression is to dismiss the 'superstition' of the local culture. In terms of geographical and mental borders, there is no use running away from Egypt to Britain, as one of the characters in *The Mummy's Shroud* says. Whatever issues the colonialists have raised in the colonies will follow them to Britain. This is one example of how horror addresses an important political and social matter, through a supernatural being.[5] The mummy is an allegory of the effects of imperialism, alluding to responsibilities – whatever they may be – falling on the former colonial power. The verisimilitude of horror explains the symbolic threat.

In contrast, the satirical comedy *Water* (Dick Clement, 1985) addresses the same thing in a more outspoken manner. The British foreign secretary (Richard Pearson) gives his subordinate a free hand to deal with the remote British colony of Cascara. In the worst scenario, the Caribbean island is threatening to turn into a new Falkland-like situation, so anything which avoids spending a lot of money on the problem is acceptable, especially as long as the islanders will not end up as bus drivers (i.e. as immigrants) in Britain. A similar statement by a character of such importance in a non-comedy film would give the production a much more political flavour. Here, it is made in the realm of comedy: the verisimilitude of comedy explains the racist-like attitude of the politician.

Transgression is a term which is not easily defined. The starting point is to consider it in its broad meaning, and as such, it is a concept very much connected to both comedy and horror. Typically in horror, a person or several persons commit a transgression, which often carries not only social or ethical problems, but at least implicitly ideas that are in conflict with Christian/Western beliefs. One of the most famous examples of this is Mary Shelley's *Frankenstein* (1818), a story used for countless horror films. Victor Frankenstein's transgression is, to put it simplistically, 'playing God'. In comedy, transgression is often connected to the body, just as in Bakhtin's study of the carnival (Bakhtin 1984; Stam 1989), but on a more general level, the comedic transgression appears to be very similar to that in the horror genre: the breaking of what is 'officially' considered as proper. In their study of transgression, Peter Stallybrass and Allon White (1986: 17–18, passim.) understand the term, using Barbara Babcock's 'symbolic inversion' as the complementing concept, as something that inverts, contradicts or otherwise presents an alternative to what is culturally accepted as the norm. While there is a clear separation between transgression and the uncanny, it is useful to note the similarity: if the uncanny is the crisis of the proper, then so in another way is transgression.

The film *The Legend of the 7 Golden Vampires* (Roy Ward Baker, 1974) has Dracula take the body of a Chinese priest of the occult. The priest has travelled from China to ask for the infamous count's help for the cult of the seven golden vampires, in gaining control of the province of Szechwan. Dracula is arrogant and dismissive, but in his lust for power, decides to exploit the situation by taking 'the form of your miserable carcass' and 'your vile image' – so the Transylvanian aristocrat becomes a kung-fu vampire. While the film is obviously a transparent attempt to tap into the kung-fu craze started by Bruce Lee (see, for example, McKay 2007: 267–69), it contains highly interesting themes from this article's perspective. First of all, there is the cartography, an element which is important for the Dracula tradition. In the original Bram Stoker novel and the films made based on it, Dracula is a Transylvanian count who travels to the UK and causes problems among the Victorians. In this film, the story has Dracula emigrate from Transylvania to China, where his arch enemy, Van Helsing (Peter Cushing), just happens to be lecturing (on vampires, of course). In other words, Dracula's menace is transferred from Britain to China, where the battle between good and evil will be fought. It is difficult to say whether this is just because of the novelty value: after all, two previous Dracula films (*Dracula A.D. 1972*, Alan Gibson, 1972, and *The Satanic Rites of Dracula*, Gibson, 1973) saw the count not just in the UK, but in the present day.

Despite merely just wanting to change the setting, the scene in *The Legend of the 7 Golden Vampires* in which Van Helsing is lecturing to Chinese historians contains an important juxtaposition, which can be seen as interfering with the local culture to more positive effect than the archaeologists in the *Mummy* films. His lecture, which argues that vampirism, with its best-known representative count Dracula, may actually originate from ancient China, is not well-received. One of the Chinese scholars says, 'These monsters may find sanctuary in the imagination of the peasants of Transylvania, but China has a sophistication that has flowered and bloomed over the course of more than 3000 years.'

Van Helsing's attempts to convince the Chinese scholars are unsuccessful. The film has the Chinese being modern and rational, in juxtaposition to what they see as European fairy tales and superstition. The setting is crucially different to that of the mummy films, in which the Westerners are forced to believe in the supernatural. If we interpret the setting from the perspective of the empire, through the character of Van Helsing the film is not only suggesting vampirism was born in China, but that the locals cannot solve the problem by themselves – a Westerner is needed to help them. In doing so, the film appears to be part of the story tradition described by Webster, that of a self-sacrificing missionary. Webster (2005: 3–4, passim.) notes how many of the post-war popular narratives concerning the diminishing Empire emphasized, both directly and indirectly, either the military power and conquest, or an idea of a 'civilizing mission' into which the protagonists throw themselves with dedication and a sense of high ideals. Most of the works discussed in this article collide with those narratives from multiple angles, depicting the events with a variety of stances.

Horror can be seen as a carnival of reality in the sense that the supernatural takes precedence over what is commonly accepted as reality: as Robert Stam has argued, in carnival all that is marginalized and excluded, such as madness or the scandalous, takes over (Stam 1989: 86). What is different in a 'horror carnival' when compared to Stam's formulation, is that there is no 'liberating sense of otherness' (ibid.). Instead, the central and the marginal, and the categories of 'one' and the 'other' become blurred. In this sense, horror is definitely subversive, and it is clear that characters such as Van Helsing can successfully fight vampires because he accepts their supernatural nature. The same can be said about those who manage to defeat the mummy: they are forced to believe that the 'scroll of life' has resurrected the mummy, and can also be used to kill it. When we combine this idea with the realization that running away from Egypt to Britain is just a temporary escape from the transgression committed, it seems clear that the filmmakers are addressing

Figure 13.2: Seeing is believing: the mummy is real. *The Mummy's Shroud* (John Gilling, 1967).

matters related to the Empire. What are they trying to say? It is clear more work needs to be done with understanding the highly self-referential and symbolic nature of horror fiction, but for the time being, it is obvious that whatever happened in the colonies will, in one form or another, follow the British to the Isles. Several of these films evoke 'geographical imagination', as Richard Phillips has written in the context of Empire adventure literature. The places of events and action become imaginary cultural spaces, in which it is possible to 'deconstruct and reconstruct, unmap and remap geographical and social worlds' (Phillips 1997: 12–13, 143–47, passim.). This is certainly happening in the horror and comedy films set in the colonies.

If in the horror films the menace arrives in the UK in the more or less symbolic shape of ancient Egyptian mummies, it seems that negotiating with the Chinese government is the reason for the downfall in *The Bed Sitting Room*. The British have let their guard down. Thus, they have underestimated the enemy. This conception is ridiculed in a later comedy set in late-1940s Malaysia, *Privates on Parade* (Michael Blakemore, 1982), in which an army major (John Cleese) explains in a bitterly humorous style how in World War II, the British trusted in the superiority of the fleet – and were taken by surprise when the Japanese invaded the British positions by land. The major's speech, then, comes across as a warning against believing traditional cultural stereotypes. This notion is present in many other films discussed in this article. Rather little is explicitly said about the (post-) colonial nations in comparison to the British. More often than not, this is executed through depictions of transgression and subversion. For example, in his analysis of *The Mummy* Peter Hutchings has argued that the countryside asylum in which archaeologist Stephen Banning (Felix Aylmer) is locked away, is very much of a symbol of England: at the same time a place of peace and tranquillity, and one of horrible secrets.[6] He knows the mummy is real (and the horror genre allows him to be right), and in England to kill him, but no one believes him (Hutchings 1993: 73–74). According to Wendy Webster, an idea of 'little England' was born in the early twentieth century. This concept was used in association with people who thought Britain should focus on domestic matters, and thus were thought to be anti-Empire. Later on, 'little England' was seen in relation to fears of national decline, and this feeling was strengthened by the growth of nationalism in colonies such as India and Ireland. Before the dismantling of the Empire, 'little England' was also used in the context of English home style settlements in colonies, giving the term a more ambivalent meaning: in the latter usage, the anti-imperialistic connotation was missing (Webster 2005: 130–35).

The concept of a British lifestyle in relation to the colonies is, not surprisingly, present in the films discussed here, and also from the point of view of 'little England'. For example, the scene in *The Meaning of Life*, in which the officers are busy attending to their daily routines (shaving, having tea, and so on) inside their tent while their troops are fighting the natives refers to keeping up the national way of life regardless of circumstances. There is a similar scene in *Carry On Up the Khyber* (Gerald Thomas, 1968), in which the governor and his guests are having supper regardless of their palace being bombarded by the Burpa army.

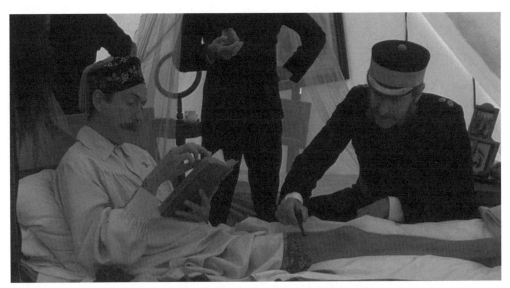

Figure 13.3: The officer class keeping a stiff upper lip in *The Meaning of Life* (Terry Jones, 1983).

The hosts claim that the explosions are merely a sound coming from drainage requiring maintenance. Meanwhile, the British troopers are trying desperately to keep the enemy from the gates. An idea of England as an asylum, out of contact with the outside world, is a pessimistic comment on the problematic situation in the Empire: another is the cynical conception of the upper classes pretending everything is in order while there is a bloody battle going on.

Subverting the Empire

When one particular empire is being discussed in the post-colonial era, the concept of an empire carries implications for several historical empires. For example, in Monty Python's comedy *Life of Brian* (Terry Jones, 1979), set in occupied Judea of the Roman Empire around the time of the birth of Christ, an anti-Roman resistance group is holding a meeting and planning their next strike against their oppressors.[7] The leader of the group (John Cleese) angrily states how the Romans came and took away everything from the local population, and concludes with a rhetorical question, 'and what have they ever given us in return?' One by one, the others start naming such things to the increasingly annoyed chairman: aqueducts, sanitation, roads, irrigation, medication, education, wine, public baths, and finally, 'they sure know how to keep order. Let's face it, they're the only ones who could in a place like this'. So while it is undeniable that an empire commands a political, social and in many respects a cultural hegemony – and sometimes, oppression – over its colonies, part of that hegemony is not unambiguously negative. I have always felt that that particular scene in *Life of Brian* is also a comment on the British Empire and her rule.[8] The implication seems clear to me, but at the same time, it is not unambiguous, either, just like the influence of an empire on its colonies. As Edward W. Said has acknowledged, during the era of imperialism, the Europeans brought technical changes – one might call some of them advances – to the colonies, and also education. The number of local people benefitting from these new developments was, of course, limited and thus they were not only positive in their consequences (Said 1994: 166). Depending upon the viewpoint, these changes can be seen as predominantly positive or negative. The stance taken in the scene of *Life of Brian* seems clear: they may have conquered us and our land, but so what? Writing about the John Huston film *The Man Who Would Be King* (1975), Chapman and Cull pose an important question in relation to post-Empire era fiction: while it is healthy to acknowledge the negative impact imperialism had on the conqueror, a full analysis of imperialism must also consider whether it was bad for the conquered (Chapman and Cull 2009: 165). The scene in *Life of Brian* seems to subvert that idea.

As noted above, by subversion I mean the carnivalesque 'world turned upside down', as formulated by Mikhail Bakhtin in his groundbreaking study of the carnival tradition (Bakhtin 1984). Bakhtin's study has practically become a multidisciplinary 'school' of its own. When the concept of empire is examined in terms of carnivalesque subversion, it is natural to see the situation as the homeland and its colonies. This is true also in the case of the horrors and comedies discussed here. Again, in the context of transgression – it is becoming increasingly obvious that the two concepts are heavily intertwined – basic assumptions about the British and the people of the colonies are challenged in the comedies and horrors set in the Empire. For example, Van Helsing's insistence that there are vampires, and this being dismissed by the Chinese scholars in *The Legend of the 7 Golden Vampires*, is one such occasion. Typically, the non-Westerners are 'superstitious', and the scientific rationality of the Westerners is compromised only by their religious convictions. Yet, even in this example there is a kind of 'imperialistic' idea that Westerners know better. The case of the mummy films is, however, different. The (cinematic) representatives of the local culture believe in the ancient myths, while the initially unbelieving Europeans are ultimately forced to believe in them. This actually poses a problem for the traditional concept of the carnival, for in that the key feature is the temporary nature of the carnival. Once the 'monster' has been destroyed, order has been restored – or has it? While it is true that in the traditional (Gothic) horror films typically only a handful of people will learn about the supernatural events, that handful is left with an experience that (surely?) has changed their worldview, at least to some extent. So, while in some of the old carnival traditions the 'false king' was killed, the fundamental problem would appear to have been more in the ethical problem of killing that person, rather than questioning the order and hierarchy of the society. The question of subversion's potential to change conceptions will be discussed further below.

Carry On Up the Khyber begins very much like a historical film: 'India 1895. Here the British rulers and their memsahibs enjoyed a life of luxury and ease matched only by that of the Indian rajahs'. This noble imagery of the ruling elite is undermined a moment later when the film's narrator is introducing the British governor Sir Sidney Ruff-Diamond (Sid James). The elephant he and his wife are riding breaks wind, to the displeasure of the couple. This kind of subversive bodily humour, so typical for *Carry On* films, is complemented in the film by the Indian aristocrat's (Kenneth Williams) title, 'the Khasi', which in British slang means a lavatory.

The film's central story is based on a transgression of tradition. A British soldier (Charles Hawtrey) is guarding a road post when two locals approach. According to the local legend, one 'Devil in a Skirt' (the nickname for the troopers of the 'Third Foot and Mouth Regiment') is enough to guard the border. After all, they are considered invincible. The reason for this is that they do not wear anything under their kilts. The (comedic) logic is that the Indians have feared the British because they have been given the impression that the Devils wear nothing under their kilts. Just as in a horror film, and above all one with supernatural elements, we, the spectators, are in need of an explanation. In a Dracula film, Van Helsing helpfully explains the vampire phenomenon to other characters, and these moments are directed as much (or more) to the film audiences. The Khasi explains the 'rationale' of the fear of the Devils to his puzzled daughter: 'Think how frightening it would be to have such a man (i.e. one not wearing underwear beneath the skirt) charging at you with his skirts flying in the air and flashing his great big bayonet at you!' However, the locals learn that many of the Devils actually do wear undergarments. The Khasi is certain that the revelation will cause such an uproar among the locals that they will drive the British out of India. In turns out that he might be on to something, as Private Widdle's transgression of unit traditions (he is the one who accidentally reveals the secret) causes a small panic among the British officers. At the end of the film, with the British garrison about to be overrun by the rebellious Burpas, the same logic is applied: the British troopers stand in line and reveal to the charging enemy that they are not wearing undergarments. The enemy flees in panic.

According to Chapman and Cull, as camp comedies, the *Carry On* films were largely about performing and playing with (especially sexual) identities, in which exaggeration and repetition – usually with twists – were key strategies, and how this creates a space for alternative ways of thinking and even being (Chapman and Cull 2009: 137).[9] It is easy to agree with this, but their argument that exaggeration and repetition lead to a subversion of the existing order is more problematic. It is certainly the case that in many of the *Carry On* films – for example the World War II film *Carry On England* (Thomas, 1976) – the concept was that of a carnival-style mayhem in which the 'lower ranks' were given a cinematic opportunity to ridicule and humiliate their superiors, but I do not think that in general the exaggerated or repeated performances or representations of identities lead to a subversion of existing order as such. I also believe this applies to 'imperial' *Carry On* films: sending up British and other stereotypes is not in itself subversive.

One film which is largely based on sending up the British class society, with explicit engagements with the Empire, *The Meaning of Life* (Terry Jones, 1983) is certainly about exaggerating identities (also sexual, as highlighted in the discussion between a Protestant couple on sexual practices), but as so often in Monty Python's comedy, the 'target' of the comedy is ambivalent and practically every social group gets its share of the ridicule. For example, in the scenes set in Africa, the class system is highlighted by having the officers let their subordinates fight the local warriors (depicted in a realistically violent fashion, again one of the trademarks of the Pythons), and basically die, while they themselves stay back in their tents, drinking tea while complaining about mosquito bites. This is contrasted by another bizarre scene, set in the trenches of the World War I. In the middle of a battle, a number of privates want to surprise their commanding officer by giving him a present (a big clock) and having managed to cook him a special meal, and they begin setting up the table. While the officer expresses his gratitude, he points out that they have to deal with the enemy first. His subordinates react by making it a class issue, telling him how much trouble they went through in arranging the surprise, but that officers are all alike, they just look down upon the common ranks.

Similarly, in *Up the Khyber*, when Ruff-Diamond hears the report about the incident, he appears nonchalant. The idea of a rebellion, possibly at the cost of thousands of lives, has no impression, nor does the grander catastrophe of Britain being forced out of India, but when his subordinate points out this would mean the Governor would lose his 'cushy job', Ruff-Diamond bursts into action. He concludes that the situation calls for a diplomatic bluff, 'The sort of thing that made our empire what it is. We are not called John Bull for nothing,' thus subverting the national symbol's name into empty talk. A Burpa, Bungit Din (Bernard Bresslaw), prior to discovering that the Devils are wearing undergarments, thinks that the legendary unit's invincibility only applies to fighting, and that bribery might be the only way to beat them. In other words, on some level the film refers to, or even subscribes to, the idea of imperial military invincibility, which actually is not surprising. While the *Carry On* films lampoon many British institutions, they do not question them as such, and often in the end support them. One example of this is *Carry On England* in which an army unit which has done everything to avoid learning military skills miraculously blows the Luftwaffe out of the sky. The story's conclusion is the binary opposite of the film's tagline 'The Luftwaffe has never had it so easy'.[10]

In films such as the *Carry Ons*, historical national efforts are trivialized and taken for granted at the same time.[11] In comparison, in *Water* Governor Baxter Thwaites (Michael Caine) casually plants 'pot' on the peripheral British colony island of Cascara in the Caribbean, with a population consisting mainly of descendents of shipwreck victims. Even the governor thinks the island should have been given independence 'years ago'. The island is a remnant from the past, kept out of habit than actual goals as it has no strategic or economic importance. Hurricanes and erupting volcanoes have wiped out the agricultural imports, and the island receives no financial support from home. Thwaites states, 'It would seem in the eyes of the British government that Cascara is the dot above the "i" in the word "shit"'.

He adds, 'My job is a somewhat outdated institution', a line that might well reflect the stance of the makers of this comedy in regards to colonialism: on the prospect of a Falklands-like conflict over the island (Cuba may be interested in it) the aforementioned foreign secretary comments, 'Maggie would love that'. In the film, whatever purpose colonialism has served in the past, to hold on to its last remnants is ridiculous.

As Robert Stam (1989: 85–87) has argued, subversive (carnivalesque) situations carry a sense of borders transgressed. By this, he means the meeting of 'decentralizing energies' (those of the carnival) and 'a hegemonic project of centralization' (officialdom). Interestingly, it appears that in many films discussed here, the first-mentioned stems in one way or another from within the very officialdom which it seeks to undermine. The subversive forces are not, as is usually the case, from 'lower ranks', but from the representatives of the centralized order. The transgressions and subversions very much originate from institutional levels such as scientists and high-ranking government officials. In contrast, the people of the colonies are shown to (temporarily) subvert the hierarchy, as in the case of Bungit Din, who in the scene described above, manages to outwit the British guard by referring to the stereotypes: 'I'm just a simple, ignorant Burpa'; the scene comments on the kind of imagery that saw local cultures as 'primitive, childlike, savage, irrational, and sometimes effeminate" when set against the British culture' (Webster 2005: 3–4). However, as Chapman and Cull have demonstrated (2009: 144–148), the *Carry On* films do not only 'camp up' the notions and conceptions of 'the other' (i.e. people of the colonies) but also

Figure 13.4: A horribly un-comical moment in *Carry On Up The Khyber* (Gerald Thomas, 1968).

'the self' (i.e. the British). One particularly interesting notion they examine is that in the *Carry On* universe dealing with the Empire, the foreigners are violent. Despite the British receiving almost an equal amount of ridicule, they are at least not explicitly depicted as violent.

There is a striking scene in *Up the Khyber*, in which a group of Britons arrive at an outpost which has been raided. Atypically for the *Carry On* films, the camera pans the landscape to some funeral march style music, and carefully captures the bodies of the dead British soldiers (no enemy dead are seen), most having a spear or a sword through them. The dialogue is surprisingly morbid as well. The sergeant comments, 'Look at them! Lying around like a lot of unwanted cocktail snacks!' This moment is followed by an unenthusiastic 'comic relief' moment, in which one of the troopers is found alive (only to die soon). The dialogue parodies similar scenes in more serious films in having one of the arrived Britons honestly tell the truth to the dying soldier: the latter will not survive his wounds. The parodic nature of the dialogue is highlighted by the mortally wounded man, as he says he wished his mate had just lied. The entire scene escapes any simple analysis. One thing seems clear: the film in no way required such a scene. Often a drama plot in a similar setting motivates the final battle by showing earlier scenes of violence, but this is unexpected in a *Carry On*-style comedy. As stated at the beginning of this article, comedy first and foremost refers to itself (that is, comedy) and only then to a non-comedic reality. This means that this particular film would have made as much sense without any explicit – and non-comedic, for it is difficult to find even a comedic reference to the grim image – violence. This notion is highlighted by the final battle of the story. As a 'last ditch' strategy, the soldiers lift their skirts to the enemy, revealing they are no longer wearing any underwear. The enemy, the Khasi included, run away in panic. In other words, we do not see British troops kill locals, but only the other way around.

In comparison to the idea of a horror carnival, Noël Carroll's analysis regarding the horror genre's ideological meanings states that the key ideological idea is 'order'. He assumes that in the bulk of horror fiction, the idea of order in a society is reactionary. This does not mean that the authors were (at least uncritically) offering support for the dominant ideology of the society (Carroll 1990: 203–06). In this way, mainstream horror fiction is, in its reliance on transgression and subversion, as problematic as carnevalesque comedy: it may not change things by restoring the existing order, but it certainly has the potential to criticize and provoke new ideas on society and culture. It would appear that this applies mainly to representations of the 'dominant' culture, and the 'other' is observed as something alien and strange. In her analysis of *The Mummy*, Sue Harper notes how the ancient Egypt of the film is that of a spectacle, and 'no effort is made to reduce its strangeness' (Harper 1998: 113–14). In a less spectacular but nonetheless strange style, *Up the Khyber* contains a scene about a public rally in which the customs of another culture are lampooned. The Khasi gives an uplifting speech, to which the Burpas react by firing their rifles, with bullets flying uncomfortably close past the Khasi. When the Khasi points out to other leaders that he wishes they would not fire their rifles, it is revealed to be a sign of disapproval. In other words, an unwanted response is a positive reaction, and vice versa. The implication is that the British may have their 'quirks', as the Khasi angrily acknowledges: 'I spit on the British phlegm! Pardon me, a most impolite expression, but these people, sometimes they infuriate me! Ooh, they come out here with their starched uniforms and their stiff upper lips, and their dirty great flags hanging around. Think they own the place!' His subordinate, Bungit Din, dryly points out, 'they do'.

Conclusion

As I stated at the beginning of this article, there is still much work to be done in mapping the overlapping genres of comedy and horror. It is a subject that at first glance may seem irrelevant and incidental, but as the study progressed, I became convinced that it is, in fact, important. As cinematic genres, they are not only truly popular but also highly adaptable for commenting upon social and cultural phenomena. In the decades following the war and Britain's loss of first class world power status, the Empire stories, just as with the popular narratives about the war, became a subject of varying treatment, including those of the comedy and horror genres. What is important is these genres' ability to address the audiences in alternative ways to other genres. Comedy and horror are genres that above all refer to their own discourses, and the relation to reality is secondary. Both can ignore what is accepted as the reality, and anything can be explained by the genre.

In their study of transgression, Stallybrass and White write: 'The ranking of literary genres or authors in a hierarchy analogous to social classes is a particularly clear example of a much broader and more complex cultural process whereby the human body, psychic forms, geographical space and the social formation are all constructed within interrelating and dependent hierarchies of high and low' (Stallybrass and White 1986: 2). Horror and comedy are genres typically placed in the 'low' of the cultural hierarchies to which Stallybrass and White are referring. When analysing films such as Hammer horror or *Carry On* comedies, one must also always keep in mind the temporal distance to the works in question. For example, a horror film that now appears unintentionally comical, might or might not have been considered 'horrendous' by audiences on the day of its release. Of course, the question of reception (outside more or less professional criticism) remains an acute problem for research, and this article makes no exception. My assumption is that most horror works discussed in this article were meant as credible 'frighteners'. Likewise, the comedies discussed are considered here as 'serious' comical works, though it has to be emphasized that comedy always carries within itself a potential self-critical possibility. Similarly, as Pirie argues, horror is not always 'dead serious' about itself. The self-consciousness of the makers of these films offer further challenges for research.

We are sometimes bound to believe our knowledge and consciousness of genres is superior to former generations, and that is why it is important to remember comedy and horror are genres much older than cinema. Tastes and mentalities change. A comedy that now feels unintentionally non-comical has quite possibly received hysterical laughter from the audiences in its own day. In the words of Sinclair McKay: 'The three words *On the Buses* are by themselves sufficient to make many of a certain age get up and leave the room' (McKay 2007: 231). This does not, however, mean that *On the Buses* is not an important source for someone studying comedy, or 1970s British culture.

References

Auxier, R. E. (2006), 'A Very Naughty Boy: Getting Right with Brian', in G. L. Hardcastle and G. A. Reisch (eds), *Monty Python and Philosophy*, Chicago and La Salle IL: Open Court, pp. 65–81.

Bakhtin, M. (1984), *Rabelais and His World*, Bloomington: Indiana University Press.

Carroll, N. (1990), *The Philosophy of Horror, Or, Paradoxes of the Heart*, New York and London: Routledge.

Cavallaro, D. (2002), *The Gothic Vision: Three Centuries of Horror, Terror and Fear*, London: Continuum.

Chapman, J. and Cull, N. J. (2009), *Projecting Empire: Imperialism and Popular Culture*, London and New York: I. B. Tauris.

Chibnall, S. and Petley, J. (2002), 'The Return of the Repressed? British Horror's Heritage and Future', in S. Chibnall and J. Petley (eds), *British Horror Cinema*, London and New York: Routledge, pp. 1–9.

Conrich, I. (1999), 'Trashing London: The British Colossal Creature Film and Fantasies of Mass Destruction', in I. Q. Hunter (ed.), *British Science Fiction Cinema*, London and New York: Routledge, pp. 88–98.

Harper, S. (1998), 'The Scent of Distant Blood: Hammer Films and History', in T. Barta (ed.), *Screening the Past: Film and Representation of History*, Westport, CT: Praeger, pp. 109–25.

Hill, J. (2001), 'British Cinema as National Cinema', in G. Turner (ed.), *The Film Cultures Reader*, London and New York: Routledge, pp. 165–72.

Hunt, L. (2002), 'Necromancy in the UK: Witchcraft and the Occult in British Horror', in S. Chibnall and J. Petley (eds), *British Horror Cinema*, London and New York: Routledge, pp. 82–98.

Hutchings, P. (1993), *Hammer and Beyond: The British Horror Film*, Manchester and New York: Manchester University Press.

Mähkä, R. (2011), 'A Killer Joke? World War II in Post-War British Television and Film Comedy', in H. Salmi (ed.), *Historical Comedy on Screen: Subverting History with Humour*, Bristol and Chicago: Intellect, pp. 129–51.

McKay, S. (2007), *A Thing of Unspeakable Horror: The History of Horror Films*, London: Aurum.

Medhurst, A. (2007), *A National Joke: Popular Comedy and English Cultural Identities*, London and New York: Routledge.

Morris, D. B. (1991), *The Culture of Pain*, Berkeley: University of California Press.

Neale, S. (2003), 'Questions of Genre', in B. K. Grant (ed.), *The Film Genre Reader III*, Austin, TX: The University of Texas Press, pp. 160–84.

Phillips, R. (1997), *Mapping Men & Empire: A Geography of Adventure*, London: Routledge.

Pirie, D. (2009), *A New Heritage of Horror: The English Gothic Cinema*, London and New York: I. B. Tauris.

Reid, D. M. (2002), *Whose Pharaohs? Archaeology, Museums, and Egyptian National Identity from Napoleon to World War I*, Cairo: The American University in Cairo Press.

Royle, N. (2003), *The Uncanny*, Manchester and New York: Manchester University Press.

Said, E. W. (1994), *Culture and Imperialism*, New York: Knopf.

Shohat, E. and Stam, R. (2001), 'The Imperial Imaginary', in G. Turner (ed.), *The Film Cultures Reader*, London and New York: Routledge, pp. 366–78.

Stallybrass, P. and White, A. (1986), *The Politics and Poetics of Transgression*, Ithaca, NY: Cornell University Press.

Stam, R. (1989), *Subversive Pleasures: Bakhtin, Cultural Criticism, and Film*, Baltimore: Johns Hopkins University Press.

Waugh, P. (1984), *Metafiction: The Theory and Practice of Self-Conscious Fiction*, London and New York: Methuen.

Webster, W. (2005), *Englishness and Empire: 1939-1965*, Oxford: Oxford University Press.

Notes

1   On Bakhtin and grotesque in horror, see Cavallaro (2002: 191–95).

2   On the multifaceted relationship between imperialism and early cinema, see Shohat and Stam (2001).

3   See also Chibnall and Petley (2002).

4   See, for example, Reid (2002). According to Leon Hunt (2002: 86, passim.), some British horror films dealing with witchcraft and occult, but set in the United Kingdom, have colonialist implications in their relation to the occult themes. Hunt sees these films as a counter-tradition to the Hammer Gothics.

5   See also Carroll (1990:199–201); passim.

6   The post-apocalyptic Britain of *The Bed Sitting Room* is like one big asylum, with devastated people engaged in strange activities.

7   There are several competing resistance groups, who are confused about which group is called what. In comparison, in *Water*, the 'obligatory' militant anti-colonial movement appears at least initially to be more interested in getting their reggae songs played on the local radio than actually driving the colonialist British away.

8   For a similar conclusion, see Auxier (2006: 73–76).

9   On identities in *Carry On* films, see also Medhurst (2007: 128–43).

10 See Mähkä (2011) for a discussion on World War II in British television and film comedy.

11 It is interesting to note that in British science fiction films of the 1950s and 1960s the global importance of London (and thus, Britain) in the post-war situation is constantly emphasized. See Conrich (1999: 95–96).

Notes on Contributors

Kimmo Ahonen (MA) is a researcher in the Department of General History at the University of Turku. His principal research interest focuses on the cultural history of the Cold War in the 1950s. Ahonen has written several articles about science fiction films and anti-communism in 1950s American culture.

Marco Bohr is a photographer and researcher in visual culture. Born and raised in Germany, Bohr was awarded a Ph.D. from the University of Westminster and appointed as Lecturer in Visual Communication at Loughborough University. His blog on photography, cinema and visual culture can be found at www.visualcultureblog.com.

Ipek Celik is an Assistant Professor in Cultures, Civilizations and Ideas at Bilkent University (Turkey). Her research explores representation of minorities in contemporary European film and literature. Her most recent publications include 'I Wanted You to be Present: Guilt and History of Violence in Michael Haneke's *Hidden*,' in *Cinema Journal* (Fall 2010).

Jessica Gallagher is a Research Affiliate in the School of Languages and Comparative Cultural Studies at The University of Queensland, where she also received her Ph.D. Her research focuses on the representation of the Turkish diaspora in contemporary Turkish-German cinema with an emphasis on space, identity and intercultural relationships.

Jehanne-Marie Gavarini writes about cinema, art and visual culture. Recent publications include 'Rewind: The Will to Remember, the Will to Forget in Michael Haneke's Caché' in *Millenial Cinema: Memory in Global Film* (2012), and 'Intimate Passports: The Subversive Performances of Tanja Ostojić', *Aspasia* (Spring 2011). She is co-translator of *Tomboy* (2007), an autobiographical novel by Franco-Algerian writer Nina Bouraoui.

Petteri Halin defended his European University Institute dissertation *Columbus on Display: The US and Spanish Columbian Quincentennial Commemoration Practices as Continuation and Re-Interpretation of Columbian Heritage* in 2005. His present undertakings centre on European cinema and European history on celluloid screen.

Kari Kallioniemi is Docent of History of Popular Culture in Cultural History at the University of Turku. He is the author of *Put the Needle on the Record and Think of England: Notions of Englishness in the Post-War History of British Pop Music* (1998) and recent articles

"'Take Me Back to Dear Old Blighty": The Smiths and Notions of Englishness in the Post-War Debate on British Pop' (2010) and 'Peter Gabriel and the Question of Being Eccentric' in *Peter Gabriel, From Genesis to Growing Up* (2011). He has written extensively about the history of British and Finnish popular culture. His contemporary work deals with the eccentricity in British (pop)stardom.

Raita Merivirta (Phil. Lic.) is a Research Fellow in the Department of General History at the University of Turku, Finland, and the author of the book *The Gun and Irish Politics: Examining National History in Neil Jordan's* 'Michael Collins' (2009). She has just completed her Ph.D. thesis on representations of history in post-Emergency Indian English novels for La Trobe University, Melbourne. Her research interests include Irish cinema and history, Indian English literature and modern Indian history.

Jacqui Miller (Ph.D.) is Senior Lecturer in Visual Communication at Liverpool Hope University teaching a range of Film Studies courses. Her recent publications include 'The French New Wave and the New Hollywood: *Le Samourai* and its American Legacy' and 'An American in Europe: US Colonialism in *The Talented Mr Ripley* and *Ripley's Game*'.

Heta Mulari (MA) is a researcher at the Department of Cultural History at the University of Turku, Finland. She is writing her doctoral dissertation about the representations of girlhood in Swedish youth films during the 1990s and the 2000s. Her research interests include feminist historiography, youth and girlhood studies and film history.

Rami Mähkä (MA) is a researcher at the Department of Cultural History at the University of Turku. His research interests include film and television, and post-war popular culture. He is currently writing his doctoral thesis under the working title *Monty Python, History and Comedy*. The study is part of the research project *Cinematic Cartographies of European History, 1945–2000*.

Sanna Peden recently completed her doctorate at the Discipline of European Languages and Studies at the University of Western Australia on the links between the auteur and nation in Aki Kaurismäki's Finland trilogy. She is now working as a researcher with the Graduate School of Education at UWA.

Hannu Salmi is Professor of Cultural History at the University of Turku and Director of the International Institute for Popular Culture (IIPC). His research focuses on nineteenth-century cultural history, history of popular culture and media history. His publications include a study on the emergence of Finnish fiction film in 1907–1916 (2002), *Nineteenth-Century Europe: A Cultural History* (2008), and *Historical Comedy on Screen: Subverting History with Humour* (2011). He has also published in *Film and History*, *Screening the Past* and *History and Theory*.

Index